FOREIGN POLICIES
OF THE SOVIET UNION

Books by Richard F. Staar

Arms Control: Myth Versus Reality (editor)

Aspects of Modern Communism (editor)

Communist Regimes in Eastern Europe

East-Central Europe and the USSR (editor)

Foreign Policies of the Soviet Union

Future Information Revolution in the USSR (editor)

Long-Range Environmental Study of the Northern Tier of Eastern Europe in 1990–2000

Poland 1944–1962: Sovietization of a Captive People

Public Diplomacy: USA Versus USSR (editor)

Soviet Military Policies Since World War Two (coauthor)

United States-East European Relations in the 1990s (editor)

USSR Foreign Policies After Detente

Yearbook on International Communist Affairs (editor)

★

FOREIGN POLICIES
OF THE SOVIET
UNION

★★★

RICHARD F. STAAR

Hoover Institution Press   Stanford University

Stanford, California

Hoover Press Publication 402

Copyright 1991 by the Board of Trustees of the
Leland Stanford Junior University

Manufactured in the United States of America
91 90 89 88 87   9 8 7 6 5 4 3 2 1

Library of Congress Cataloging in Publication Data
Staar, Richard Felix, 1923–
   Foreign policies of the Soviet Union / Richard F. Staar.
        p.   cm.
   Includes bibliographical references and index.
   ISBN 0-8179-9102-6
   1. Soviet Union—Foreign relations—1985–   I. Title.
DK289.S73   1991   90-25073
327.47—dc20   CIP

FOR

JADWIGA

CONTENTS

PART I

FOUNDATIONS

=== *PART II* ===

INSTRUMENTALITIES

PART III

REGIONAL POLICIES

TABLES

FIGURES

PREFACE

This volume, which is organized into twelve chapters, opens with an analysis of the USSR world outlook and attempts to show how Soviet perceptions differ from those of the West. Next, the USSR's decision-making process in the new Presidential Council and the problem of succession are discussed; historically succession has almost always involved a protracted struggle for power. The third chapter deals with implementation of policies through the governmental Ministry of Foreign Affairs' bureaucracy.

The second part of the book (chapters 4 through 7) treats the instruments of Soviet foreign policy: propaganda, intelligence and active measures, military strategy, trade. All play significant roles in the orchestration of USSR moves throughout the world, although they may be applied in different combinations.

Finally, part 3 uses a geographic approach to cover the disintegrating Soviet colonial empire in East-Central Europe; relations between East and West in Europe, the Third World, East Asia; and finally USSR relations with the United States.

The author expresses deep appreciation to his three associates—Joyce Cerwin, Anne Garvey, and Margit Grigory—for their invaluable help throughout the laborious process of preparing the typescript for press. This book could not have been written without access to the unique library collections of the Hoover Institution on War, Revolution and Peace at

Stanford University. The staff has been outstanding in its dedication to the pursuit of esoteric and elusive data, especially Molly Molloy, Marjorie Rauen, and Linda Wheeler.

Drafts of individual chapters received comments from Mikhail S. Bernstam (Hoover Institution), John J. Karch (formerly of the United States Information Agency), Carl McMillan (Carleton University), R. Judson Mitchell (University of New Orleans), Teresa Rakowska-Harmstone (U.S. Naval Academy), Harriet Fast Scott (U.S. General Advisory Committee on Arms Control and Disarmament), Col. Wallace Spaulding (U.S. Army, ret.), and Susan Woodward (Brookings Institution). None of them is responsible for errors or interpretations. The undersigned wishes to thank also the John M. Olin Program on Soviet and East European Studies at the Hoover Institution for its generous support, which made the research for and writing of this volume possible.

Richard F. Staar

Stanford, California
Mid-December 1990

Note: Two previous editions, one revised, of *USSR Foreign Policies after Détente* were sold out. Completely revised and rewritten, the book has been given a new title.

INTRODUCTION

The foreign policies of the USSR are still guided by a dogma that remains messianic in nature. Although faces and terminology have changed since Mikhail S. Gorbachev came to power in March 1985, the purpose behind both domestic reforms and the "new political thinking" in world politics has been to restore communism's dwindling credibility rather than to destroy it. Although the phrase "universal human values" has replaced "class struggle" and moral superiority is now claimed in place of military or economic superiority, the linkage between the old and the new remains strong. This was reiterated by Gorbachev at the July 1990 communist party congress:

> Step by step we have been deepening our understanding of the goal and the methods of the revolutionary transformations [belonging to *perestroika*]. As a matter of fact, that—in Lenin's words—involves a reconsideration of the whole of our view of socialism. As a result, we have arrived at an understanding of *perestroika* as a new revolution and as a logical continuation of the cause, the beginning of which was laid by the Great October [1917 Revolution].[1]

According to traditional doctrine, the world revolutionary process has no precise timetable and may indeed experience temporary setbacks. Just as

Lenin before him, Gorbachev has had to strike a compromise with capitalism to rebuild a country whose present devastated economic conditions resemble very much those rising out of the 1917 Revolution. In the long run, however, many who sit in the Kremlin believe that their political and socioeconomic system will eventually prevail over that of the West. Gorbachev restated this conviction, when he wrote the following:

> Today, we are facing the complex task of reviving the prestige of Marxist thinking. There is no doubt that the October Revolution was not an accident but a great breakthrough to the future in world history. . . . *Perestroika* transfers the original principles, since in the past they were merely proclaimed for the most part. . . . A special role in the new social organism is played by the communist party, which is called upon to be the political vanguard of Soviet society.[2]

Soviet ideology has always envisioned the communist movement as essentially international in character. The small core of party-ruled states (subtracting those of East–Central Europe currently in transition toward democracy) includes two that are antagonistic and three others that are neutral toward the USSR. The world system is supported by communist organizations in about eighty other countries or administrative units. The so-called national liberation movements, restricted for the most part to Africa[3] and the Middle East, are still considered allies of the Soviet Union in the struggle against the "imperialist" camp headed by the United States. In addition, communism is seen as eventually spreading throughout Latin America from its beachhead in Cuba.

Immediate prospects for expansion were impeded, however, when the former politburocrats in Moscow proved incapable of making main decisions until the succession problem was finally resolved in March 1985. The deaths of Leonid I. Brezhnev, Iurii V. Andropov, and Konstantin U. Chernenko within a twenty-eight-month period finally brought Mikhail S. Gorbachev to the top leadership position.[4]

Under Gorbachev, creation of a stable international environment, détente throughout the world, prestige in foreign affairs to bolster the home front, and encouraging Western concern for the success of *perestroika* made it possible for the government to focus on renovating the economy. Only with the "new political thinking" in place, could the USSR maintain the respite (*peredyshka*) necessary to rescue, modernize, and reactivate the production process. The need to make widespread economic and structural adjustments had been evident for some time. This task was entrusted to Gorbachev,[5] who was presumed to be young and vigorous enough to implement the changes. At age fifty-four, he was a generation younger than his three predecessors and therefore could be expected to oversee important changes.

Because decisions will be arrived at collectively until Gorbachev strengthens his position or until another man emerges preeminent, the current period of weakness in the Kremlin may last for some time. In the meanwhile, basic foreign policy decisions will continue to be implemented by the functionaries in the Ministry of Foreign Affairs' bureaucracy. Even though Gorbachev made it clear in 1987 that he intended to play an active role in all external policy, now recognized as a presidential function, many officials still view world developments in terms of Marxism-Leninism. Such a doctrinal framework inevitably tends to slant information dispatched from abroad on the basis of which decisions must be made. Perhaps for this reason, Gorbachev reshuffled the foreign ministry during the first two years in power and again replaced a large number of Soviet ambassadors during 1990, especially those who had served in East–Central Europe.[6]

According to an interview with Karen N. Brutents, who is in charge of the Middle East and Latin America for the International Department of the CPSU central apparatus, in formal terms the communist party no longer has control over foreign policy. "We have withdrawn from all state functions, but this does not mean that we do not have views on foreign policy. The Central Committee still represents the party in all fields, including foreign policy."[7]

One area that has remained unchanged despite the "new political thinking" is propaganda directed at foreign audiences, which has been used by Soviet regimes continuously for three-quarters of a century. Specific campaigns are supervised by an office in the central party apparatus, which decides how to present different aspects of USSR external policy to various publics. Slogans appearing twice each year, in April and October, provide the general themes. International communist front organizations, like the World Peace Council, disseminate such propaganda to support Soviet foreign policy objectives. Their activities are supplemented by the printed word and by radio broadcasts via official[8] as well as clandestine transmitters.

Official press agencies and newspapers also provide cover for USSR intelligence officers, whose assignments involve espionage and implementation of so-called active measures, including the use of fronts, manipulation of foreign media, spreading of disinformation, planting of forgeries, and recruitment of "agents of influence" to promote the Kremlin's objectives and undermine those of any opponent. Estimates are that between one-fourth and one-third of all Soviet officials abroad work for the KGB (civilian) or GRU (military) intelligence services.[9] Evidence also suggests that the United Nations is heavily penetrated by such individuals.

The KGB and its predecessor organizations have all been involved in attempted coups and terrorism. After the end of World War II such operations were conducted, often successfully, in such diverse regions as Western and East–Central Europe, Africa, the Middle East, Asia, and Latin America. An international terrorist network had been clandestinely financed by the Soviet Union and other bloc countries. Schools for terrorists were located not only in the USSR, but also in Bulgaria, Czechoslovakia, East Germany, and Hungary. Reportedly all these countries offered safe havens to specific groups and individuals. At the direction of the KGB, regime intelligence services produced and supplied lethal materials such as the almost undetectable Semtex plastic explosive. With the 1990–1991 changes throughout East–Central Europe, the Soviets are losing this valuable support structure. The USSR role in such activities is inconsistent, of course, with the tenets of "new thinking." A meeting in southern California on 29 September 1989 of retired high-level CIA and KGB officers was part of an attempt by the KGB to change its image[10] and give the impression that there is no essential difference between the two organizations.

During the 1980s, Soviet bloc clandestine services propagated a flurry of forged documents in an attempt to split the North American Treaty Organization alliance. Racist letters (allegedly from the Ku Klux Klan) threatening athletes from more than twenty developing countries were sent by the KGB in an attempt to win support for the East's boycott of the 1984 Summer Olympics in Los Angeles. Such fake messages were designed to demonstrate that U.S. policies are incompatible with those of the Third World, to discredit Western intelligence agencies, and in general to undermine the noncommunist world's resolve to defend itself against Soviet encroachments.

Assassination as an instrument of government policy is not new for the USSR, as mentioned above. Two anticommunist Ukrainian leaders were murdered by the same Soviet intelligence officer during the late 1950s at Munich.[11] The assassin, who later defected to the West, had been personally decorated in Moscow for his actions by the head of the KGB. According to a June 1984 report of the Italian state prosecutor, the failed attempt on the life of Pope John Paul II had been paid for by the Bulgarian secret services. High-level defectors have revealed that the USSR assigned such "wet" (bloody) projects to other bloc intelligence organizations. Andropov himself (at the time, head of the KGB) might well have transmitted the orders to kill the pope to the Bulgarians.[12]

A war-fighting and war-survival posture has characterized Soviet nuclear military doctrine from its origins. Under these precepts, a series of preemptive strikes would be directed at maritime lines of communication, reconnaissance satellites, military installations, and at important economic sites in the continental United States. Although Warsaw Pact troops, even in their most submissive years, were probably never considered reliable by the USSR High Command, East-Central European loyalty is now nearly nonexistent. Nevertheless, deployment of superior strategic offensive forces in 1991 already gave Moscow the capability of destroying nine out of ten U.S. land-based intercontinental ballistic missiles in their prelaunch configuration. The concept of a defensive military doctrine has yet to be translated into USSR military maneuvers and training manuals.[13]

Foreign trade is also used for political purposes by the Soviet Union. Commercial sanctions have been applied in the past against such diverse countries as Cuba, Iceland, Yugoslavia, Australia, China, and Romania. (Yugoslavia and Romania are maverick states, albeit communist-ruled ones.) In general the USSR has been forced to support most of its client regimes in East-Central Europe, although it became less generous in 1990. Soviet exports to these former satellites fell by 10.2 percent from what they had been in 1989, creating a 6.4 billion ruble deficit for Moscow by midyear.[14]

Trade with the West, meanwhile, has included large purchases of grain, which worldwide totaled a record 44 million metric tons during the 1988–1989 crop year. Over the decade of the 1970s, the Soviet Union also had acquired more than $50 billion worth of high technology from the industrialized West. Together with its former dependencies in East–Central Europe, the USSR as of 1990 currently remains in debt to capitalist countries for more than three times that amount. Meanwhile, in country after country, the Soviets are asking for emergency loans with which to pay off their debts.[15]

It is in the Third World where the political use of trade can be seen most clearly. Such countries as Afghanistan, Angola, Cuba, Ethiopia, Nicaragua, Vietnam, and the former South Yemen lack the means to pay for imports from the USSR. Moscow has permitted this adverse balance to continue because of the militarily important geographic location of these states. In 1990, however, the official Soviet government newspaper published details on the extent of the debt, most of which will never be repaid. In this way, the "nuisance factor" may have become prohibitively expensive to a newly accountable and impoverished USSR administration whose annual budget deficit has grown to 340 billion rubles.[16] In certain instances, the Soviet Union also obtains critical raw materials, of which it may have a surplus, in order to deny them to the West and at the same time build up its own strategic reserve stockpiles. Now, ironically, like other Third World countries, natural resources are basically all that the USSR has to offer for hard currency.

The Kremlin pursues many different foreign policies, depending on the extent of its influence over another country and the latter's power. Even with respect to its former client states in East–Central Europe, approaches have varied. Romania, for example, belonged both to the Warsaw Treaty Organization and the Council for Mutual Economic Assistance (CMEA), yet twice during the past decade (1980 and 1984) the USSR foreign minister traveled to Bucharest and in effect bribed the government of that country to change a public posture that had differed from bloc policy.

Soviet troops stationed on the "sovereign" territories of East Germany, Czechoslovakia, Hungary, and Poland have represented a symbol of Kremlin authority. Reunification of East and West Germany, and the agreements with Czechoslovakia and Hungary to have all troops withdrawn[17] by mid-1991, will make it impossible to intervene in support of puppet regimes or replace recalcitrant ones. Indigenous troops from bloc countries would not have defended the Warsaw Pact against NATO, in any event, especially if Western forces had crossed the borders into East–Central Europe. Apart from these military aspects, the Soviet Union has dominated its client states economically by supplying them with indispensable raw materials and energy resources. At the November 1989 CMEA meeting in Moscow, all bloc governments agreed to concentrate on development of nuclear power and high technology through the year 2000. By playing the energy card, the Soviet Union managed to keep moribund CMEA in existence. Forced to balance accounts during 1991 in hard currency, East–Central Europe will be faced with a $16 billion areawide deficit vis-à-vis its former metropole.[18]

USSR relations with Western Europe always had as their main objective the decoupling of that area from the United States which meant, of course, the withdrawal of American troops. Nonetheless, earlier Soviet threats that Scandinavian members of NATO would "burn in the fires of nuclear war," that all of southern Italy might be converted into "a Pompeii," and that the Federal Republic of Germany could be "ascending a nuclear gallows" did not prevent acceptance of U.S. ground-launched cruise and Pershing II ballistic missiles (requested by the West European allies) to counterbalance earlier massive deployments of Soviet triple warhead SS-20 nuclear missile launchers. This NATO posture resulted in the December 1987 Intermediate-range Nuclear Forces (INF) Treaty, which led to destruction of all such weapons over the ensuing three-year period.

That plans made in Moscow vis-à-vis Western Europe are long-term and consistent becomes apparent when one compares the 1975 Final Act at Helsinki with the objectives listed in the 1967 Karlovy Vary communiqué signed by Soviet and East–Central European leaders after a summit meeting in Czechoslovakia. Almost all of these goals were attained. Concessions agreed on at Helsinki by the 1975 Conference on Security and Cooperation in Europe regarding the human rights area, in contrast, were ignored for many years by all communist regimes. Review conferences in Belgrade (1977–1978), Madrid (1980–1983), and Vienna (1986–1989) unfortunately ended without specific condemnation of this behavior. The next review opens in 1992 at Helsinki.[19]

If progress was slow in subverting Western Europe, the opposite proved true of the Third World, where the USSR made considerable inroads. "Revolutionary democracies" and other regimes that had chosen the "non-capitalist" path of development existed in twenty-eight countries, with Nicaragua representing one of the spectacular losses after free elections in early 1990. Other setbacks have occurred, however, as Marxist-Leninist economies proved unsuccessful almost everywhere that they were introduced. The blow to Soviet prestige became compounded when the non-aligned countries refused to recognize the USSR as a "special friend."

Throughout East Asia, nonetheless, the USSR has met with opposition from the Chinese communists, who consider that part of the world as their sphere of influence. The Sino-Soviet conflict continued from the official break starting in July 1960 until the mid-May 1989 summit in the People's Republic of China. Beijing seems to have lost influence to Moscow in Vietnam, Laos, Cambodia, although perhaps not in North Korea.

By concentrating on economic instead of political restructuring, and by emphasizing agriculture over industry—the reverse of Gorbachev's approach—the Chinese have had greater success in their own version of *perestroika*. They may become the world vanguard and the "true communists," as the Soviet Union continues to fade.

The People's Republic of China (PRC) had made three demands upon the USSR, as a first step toward improving relations:

1. Reduction of troops along their common border
2. An end to support by the USSR for the Vietnamese occupation of Cambodia
3. Soviet military withdrawal from Afghanistan

Moscow finally accommodated the PRC in all three of the above; this resulted not only in normalizing government-to-government relations[20] at the above-mentioned summit in Beijing but also in resumption of party-to-party contacts in October 1989.

Finally, relations with the United States seem to have been centered on arms control. Vitriolic speeches by earlier party leaders, the previous foreign minister, the former defense chief, and others suggested that the Kremlin had decided against any arms reduction agreements, perhaps regardless of who sat in the Oval Office. Although the Soviets came back to restructured intermediate-range nuclear arms control talks at Geneva in March 1985, it took another two years and nine months before an agreement could be reached.

The record to date suggests that past Soviet leaders had not been serious about reaching equitable agreements. To Moscow, negotiations served as little more than camouflage for what has proven to be the most massive military buildup in history. When the United States offered in 1946 to give up its atomic bomb stockpile and transfer all fissionable material to a veto-free United Nations body, the highest-ranking USSR official at the U.N. privately responded to the American presidential representative as follows: "The Soviet Union doesn't want equality. The Soviet Union wants complete freedom to pursue its own aims as it sees fit."[21] At that time, the Kremlin had no atomic weapons.

Despite outward shifts in rhetoric from the USSR, this attitude essentially remained unchanged until recently. Indeed, in certain respects, it had hardened. George Shultz, former U.S. secretary of state, described Soviet international misconduct as based on

1. A continuing quest for military superiority

2. An "unconstructive involvement" in the Third World

3. An unrelenting effort to impose an alien "model" on clients and allies

4. The practice of stretching treaties to the brink of violation and beyond[22]

The last charge has been documented to date in five successive reports to the U.S. Congress on USSR noncompliance with arms control agreements. A more detailed study, prepared by the nonpartisan General Advisory Committee on Arms Control and Disarmament, covered a full quarter-century. Submitted to Congress by the White House, it cited seventeen major violations by the USSR (in addition to the five revealed previously by the president) since the 1958 nuclear test moratorium. Even now, as if to flaunt their disregard for treaty obligations, the Soviets continue to encrypt signals from their own ICBM test launches to prevent U.S. monitoring of compliance with nuclear arms control agreements between the two countries.

Despite the foregoing, dialogue between the United States and the USSR continues. Talks on preventing accidental war, nuclear weapons proliferation, establishing the precise boundary between Alaska and Siberia, as well as implementation of exchange agreements were all concluded satisfactorily. President Reagan authorized a ten-year extension of the economic cooperation accord, which had expired in July 1984. He also agreed to negotiations on antisatellite (ASAT) weapons, proposed by the USSR to open at Vienna. The Kremlin refused to send a delegation, explaining its decision with an

Orwellian "inversion of truth" by claiming that the United States had made it impossible to hold the talks. However, several summit meetings did take place after Mikhail S. Gorbachev became the Soviet leader.[23]

Multilateral NATO–Warsaw Pact negotiations with United States and Soviet participation continued on Mutual and Balanced Force Reductions (MBFR) in Central Europe between the two military alliances for fifteen years and three months, superseded by the Conventional Armed Forces in Europe (CFE) talks in March 1989; at the United Nations-sponsored forty-member Committee on Disarmament (CD); and at the Conference on Confidence- and Security-Building Measures and Disarmament in Europe (CDE), with 35 governments represented, which ended with an agreement in Stockholm. Regardless of the conventional arms reduction treaty, signed in Paris at the 19–21 November 1990 CSCE meeting, events seem to have overtaken this process in the face of Soviet unilateral withdrawals from East–Central Europe.

At the end of 1990, the fate of the USSR remains uncertain. Should the union disintegrate, it will leave a harsh legacy: impoverished former client states and constituent republics, a potentially catastrophic power vacuum where political and ideological control have failed, an economic devastation that may take decades to reverse, and the world's largest arsenal of nuclear weapons distributed among traditionally antagonistic ethnic groups.[24] Will the policies of *perestroika* and "new political thinking" be strong enough to hold this future at bay? The resignation of Foreign Minister Shevardnadze on 20 December 1990 seemed to answer this question in the negative.

NOTES

1. Doklad M. S. Gorbacheva, "Idti dal'she putem perestroiki," *Pravda*, 3 July 1990, pp. 3–4. See, however, Academician V. Kudriavtsev, "Nuzhna li nam ideologiia?" *Pravda*, 26 October 1990, p. 3.

2. M. Gorbachev, "Sotsialisticheskaia ideia i revoliutsionnaia perestroika," *Pravda*, 26 November 1989, pp. 1 and 2.

3. Thomas H. Henriksen, "Africa," in Richard F. Staar, ed., *Yearbook on International Communist Affairs: Parties and Revolutionary Movements (1990)* (Stanford: Hoover Institution Press, 1990), pp. 1–3.

4. R. Judson Mitchell, *Getting to the Top in the USSR* (Stanford: Hoover Institution Press, 1990), pp. 135–48.

5. For testimony on how Andropov's recommendation that Gorbachev be appointed acting head of the politburo and secretariat was deleted from his letter to the Central Committee in December 1983, see Arkadii I. Vol'skii, "Smotret' otkrytymi glazami," *Nedelia*, no. 36 (3–9 September 1990): 6–7.

6. These changes are recorded in *Vestnik Ministerstva Inostrannykh Del SSSR*. See, for example, no. 18 (30 September 1990): 62–63.

7. Quoted by Flemming Rose, "The Soviet Union Holds a Sale," *Berlingske Tidende* (Copenhagen), 10 September 1990, magazine section, p. 1; *Foreign Broadcast Information Service-Western Europe*, 179-U, 14 September 1990, pp. 26–27.

8. See the speech by L. P. Kravchenko, director general of TASS, "Na plenume TsK KPSS," *Pravda*, 10 October 1990, p. 4.

9. The promotion of V. M. Mikhailov, chief of GRU, to general of the army suggests that his organization may be performing better than the KGB. See "Ukaz Prezidenta SSSR," *Krasnaia zvezda*, 25 October 1990, p. 1.

10. "U.S. [anti-] Terrorism Policy Revisited," *RAND Research Review*: 13, no. 3 (Fall 1989): 3–4; V. Romanov, "SSSR-SShA: Vmeste protiv terrorizma," *Krasnaia zvezda*, 20 October 1989, p. 3.

11. The documented KGB murder of Ukrainian nationalist leader Stepan Bandera (confession by the assassin) on 15 October 1959 in Munich is attributed by a Soviet source to West German intelligence. I. Tikhomirov, "Psevdomoisei," *Pravda*, 19 October 1990, p. 6.

12. The new president of Bulgaria, Zhelyu Zhelev, announced he will seek help from other intelligence services in probing the papal assassination plot. His own "highly hypothetical theory" is that any Bulgarian role "might have been directed from another country that wanted Bulgarians involved, such as the KGB." Quoted by A. D. Horne, "Pope Shooting Probe," *Washington Post*, 28 September 1990, p. A-18.

13. Secretary of Defense Richard Cheney was told by his counterpart, Marshal D. T. Iazov, that the Soviet military budget would be cut by 5 percent in 1991. David Remnick, "Cheney Sees New Era," *Washington Post*, 20 October 1990, p. A-19; Andy Pasztor, "Soviet Military," *Wall Street Journal*, 19 October 1990, p. B7B. V. Petrovskii, "Voennyi biudzhet v svete glasnosti," *Pravitel'stvennyi vestnik*, no. 45 (November 1990): 9.

14. John Tedstrom, "Economic Slide Continues," *Report on the USSR* 2, no. 37 (14 September 1990): 9–12.

15. Soviet trading companies requested Japan for $1 billion with which to pay outstanding debts of $520 million. *The Times* (London), 4 October 1990; cited by Radio Free Europe/Radio Liberty *Daily Report*, no. 190 (5 October 1990): 6.

16. "Unikal'nyi dokument," *Izvestiia*, 1 March 1990, p. 3, for the debt; Boris El'tsin address to the 11 September 1990 RSFSR Supreme Soviet session, for the all-union budget deficit.

17. Defense Minister Iazov, replying to a question at the CPSU congress, stated that the USSR would leave behind military structures valued at 4 billion rubles in East-Central Europe. "Otvety chlenov Politbiuro," *Izvestiia TsK KPSS*, no. 8 (August 1990): 125.

18. Andrei Sharyi, "SEV: poiski novogo oblika," *Pravda*, 12 May 1990, p. 6, gives this estimated total in dollars.

19. Iurii Deriabin, "Khel'sinkskii ekspress," *Novoe vremia*, no. 35 (24 August 1990): 10–11.
20. See interview with the new Soviet ambassador to the People's Republic of China, N. N. Solov'ev, in *Sel'skaia zhizn*, 23 September 1990, p. 3.
21. Arkady A. Sobolev to Bernard Baruch, quoted by Flora Lewis in "Unthinking Doomsday," *New York Times*, 4 April 1983, p. A-19.
22. U.S. Department of State, "U.S.-Soviet Relations in the Context of U.S. Foreign Policy," *Current Policy*, no. 492 (15 June 1983): 2.
23. See the interview with Gorbachev's close adviser, E. M. Primakov, "SSSR i SShA v novom mire," *Literaturnaia gazeta*, no. 40 (3 October 1990): 14.
24. Alexander Rahr and R. Alex Bryan, "Concern over Security of Soviet Nuclear Arms," *Report on the USSR* 2, no. 41 (12 October 1990): 6–7; Gabriel Schoenfeld, "How Safe Are Moscow's Nukes?" *Washington Post*, 21 October 1990, p. C-2.

★ PART I ★

FOUNDATIONS

1

SOVIET WORLD OUTLOOK

It has been suggested that USSR behavior in the world arena has changed radically, based on the "new political thinking." Should one accept at face value official foreign policy statements that emanate from Moscow, or are they intended merely to create the illusion that Soviet global objectives have changed? USSR leaders are facing economic and social disaster in the early 1990s. Could it be that they will do anything to survive, applying the Leninist traditions of a New Economic Policy and the *peredyshka* (respite) of seventy years ago?

One place to find the answers to such questions is in the system of beliefs on the basis of which all Soviet leaders have operated since a small group of communists seized power in 1917. Working within the framework of this ideology, the current successors to the original Bolsheviks have a world outlook that differs radically from the one held by Western policy-makers. From this perspective, it can be argued that their weltanschauung remains fundamentally unaltered, despite indications of a major restructuring of USSR policies in many areas of the world. "The purge of dogma is only starting. And the success of this venture is not guaranteed by any means."[1]

Soviet foreign policy will soon be based on the fourth (1992) Communist Party of the Soviet Union (CPSU) program since 1917, the others having been adopted in 1919, 1961, and 1986. It will most probably remain applicable well beyond the year 2000. Objectives are stated, under the Orientation of International Policy section, by the programmatic statement of the twenty-eighth CPSU congress in the following terms:[2]

1. Demilitarization of international relations
2. Global and regional security structures
3. Freedom of sociopolitical choice, sovereignty, and independence
4. Normalization of Soviet-U.S. relations, overcoming the split in Europe, consolidation of relations with the People's Republic of China, collaboration with the Non-aligned Movement, and cooperation with developing countries

These four goals of the USSR remain essentially unchanged from the 1986 CPSU program.[3] The importance of ideology was reemphasized in the Soviet Union by the decision that V. A. Medvedev, a member of the Politburo and a Central Committee secretary, become chairman of a new twenty-five-member CPSU commission on ideology. His appointment in mid-1990 as a member of the new Presidential Council suggests that he no longer holds the earlier position.[4] The individual who appears to be the chief ideologist is Aleksandr N. Iakovlev, long the closest confidant of Gorbachev and also a member of the new Presidential Council.

Until the latter part of the 1980s the ideological framework within which the foreign policies of the USSR operated had as its point of departure the belief that the industrialized countries of the West were in the third stage of a general crisis. By positing this periodization of modern history, the Soviets projected an optimistic image of world developments in which the areas under capitalist control were constantly shrinking whereas those under "progressive" rule in the communist and less-developed states were expanding and being strengthened (see table 1.1).

Boris N. Ponomarev, during the time he was candidate CPSU Politburo member and International Department head, summarized the earlier, more optimistic belief about Marxist-Leninist territorial advances made during the decade of the 1970s when he spoke of "the unification of Vietnam, the consolidation of people's power in Laos, the liquidation of the Pol Pot regime in Kampuchea [Cambodia]." Adding that "Ethiopia, Angola and Mozambique" had "secured liberation," he said that all of the countries had carried out "major social transformations" and represented "advance posts of socialist orientation"—language generally restricted to so-called revolutionary democracies or governments well on their way to communism. Ponomarev then stated that "South Yemen is playing an important role" in this field and mentioned Nicaragua, Afghanistan, Iran, and Zimbabwe

TABLE 1.1
SOCIOPOLITICAL WORLD MAP, 1950 AND 1989

	POPULATION (PERCENTAGE)		TERRITORY (PERCENTAGE)		INDUSTRIAL PRODUCTION (PERCENTAGE)	
	1950	1989	1950	1989	1950	1989*
Major developed capitalist countries	22.4	11.9	24.9	8.1	73.0	49.2
Communist-ruled states	35.0	31.8	25.8	26.2	ca. 20.0	40.4
Less-developed countries	42.6	52.4	49.3	62.3	7.0	7.4
Total	100.0	96.1	100.0	96.6	100.0	97.0

*None of the figures in this column has changed since 1978, which probably reflects the downturn in the economies of communist-ruled states.
SOURCES: M. M. Avsenev, chief ed., *Krizis kapitalizma* (Moscow: Mysl', 1980), p. 62; USSR, *Narodnoe khoziaistvo SSSR, 1989* (Moscow: Finansy i statistika, 1990), pp. 676, 684; the 1989 column is an estimate provided by Dr. Eugene Zaleski, Centre National de la Recherche Scientifique, Paris.

(formerly Rhodesia) as examples of "blows against imperialism" in the world revolutionary process.[5] A first deputy director of the International Department in the central CPSU apparatus conceded, five years later, that "the collapse of capitalism is not imminent . . . partly because the undeniable scientific and technological revolution has led to an enormous social realignment in the West."[6]

CPSU general secretary Mikhail S. Gorbachev, in his political report to the twenty-eighth party congress, stated that the CPSU is "following the creative approach to the theory and practice of socialism based on an analysis of twentieth-century experience, following Marx, Engels, and Lenin, as well as other revolutionary and progressive thinkers."[7] However, V. A. Medvedev, the above-mentioned ideology chief, admitted on the following day that "the ideological situation [has begun] to change rapidly for the worse," stating that "the Academy of Sciences has organized a theoretical seminar for developing a contemporary concept of socialism . . . and that a new concept of socialism will be activated in connection with the new program of the party."[8] Medvedev may have been optimistic in predicting that the "new thinking" will have been adopted and implemented by mid-

1992. Judging from the past, it could take ten years before any new ideology can be thoroughly formulated and accepted.

PERIODIZATION OF HISTORY

According to traditional Soviet ideology, stage one of the alleged crisis in world capitalism, guided by the "objective laws of social development," began with World War I and the 1917 revolution in Russia. The next phase commenced during World War II and included "the communist revolutions in a number of countries of Europe and Asia." The third, contemporary stage began during the mid-1960s. A deepening crisis in capitalism is a hallmark of the contemporary stage,[9] even though this condition may have temporarily abated. (One difference between the current period and the two preceding ones is the absence of a general war involving the major powers.)

Competition and conflict between the two worldwide socioeconomic systems are accompanied, in the Soviet view, by increasingly aggravated problems—monetary crises, rampant inflation, decline in production, price increases, and unemployment—within all developed Western countries and the United States in particular. Such domestic difficulties supposedly represent only one of four basic contradictions affecting the capitalist world. The others include the conflict between newly emergent nations and former colonial powers, competition among so-called imperialist countries (especially the United States, Japan, and the Economic Community in Western Europe), and, most important, the struggle between what the Soviets call *socialism* (that is, communism) and capitalism.

The current acknowledgment of poor economic conditions in the USSR should not be seen as a prelude to the surrender of ideological principles. Gorbachev told delegates to the twenty-eighth CPSU congress that he "would never have anything to do with restoration of capitalist practices."[10] Indeed, the objectives of *perestroika* and *demokratizatsiia* are to correct the "deformations" brought about through abuses of the socialist system, especially by Stalin and Brezhnev, so that Marxist-Leninist principles may be allowed to operate as originally intended. The precept concerning the "historical inevitability of replacing capitalism by communism" presumably remains in force, never having been explicitly revoked.

This last struggle, it is claimed, will be won by means of a policy based on the principle of "peaceful coexistence," which has been enunciated from time to time ever since the days of Lenin. For example, the Bolshevik government's Foreign Affairs Commissariat (ministry) reported to the All-Russian Central Executive Committee (council of ministers) as far back as 17 June 1920 that "our slogan was and remains one and the same, peaceful coexistence with other governments of whatever kind they may be." During the late 1980s this slogan was defined authoritatively as follows: "a specific form of class warfare in the international arena between capitalism and socialism."[11]

PEACEFUL COEXISTENCE AND THE BREZHNEV DOCTRINE

Contemporary decision makers in the USSR are resurrecting this seventy-year-old principle as one foundation of Soviet foreign policy, because they identify the alternative as nuclear war. Thus, the concept of peaceful coexistence provides a relatively safe framework within which to support "wars of national liberation" in the underdeveloped areas of the world, on the one hand, and so-called active measures (see chapter 5) within the capitalist states, on the other. In terms of propaganda, peaceful coexistence is also useful as a slogan for mobilizing domestic public opinion within noncommunist-ruled countries in support of USSR foreign policy. This is called *public diplomacy* and bypasses foreign governments in an effort to reach Western elites.

In this respect peaceful coexistence, according to the late Mikhail A. Suslov, the most prominent Soviet ideologist and a full member of the CPSU Politburo at the time of his death in 1982, "has nothing in common with class peace between exploiter and exploited, colonialist and victims of colonial oppression, or between oppressors and oppressed."[12] This means that the USSR by definition will be on the side of any movement that has at least an even chance of weakening and destroying governments not moving toward "socialism" in the Third World. When he served as foreign minister, Andrei A. Gromyko made this clear in the following words: "International détente does not in any way suggest artificial restraints on the objective processes of the historical development and struggle by oppressed people for their liberation."[13]

Previously, communist ideology affirmed the "inevitability of a world conflict" between capitalism and Soviet-style socialism, a formula that prevailed as dogma until February 1956, when it was revised at the twentieth CPSU congress. There, a new position emerged—that war was not inevitable[14]—a formula that has been repeated at the three postwar world conferences of communist parties (1957, 1960, 1969), as well as the last five CPSU congresses (1971, 1976, 1981, 1986, 1990). Members of the international communist movement, some friendly and some not so friendly toward Moscow, send delegates to such meetings. However, no foreign delegations were invited to the 1990 party congress. These gatherings are used as a podium for making policy statements.

As for the so-called Brezhnev Doctrine, when originally propounded one month *after* the USSR military occupation of Czechoslovakia, it limited the sovereignty of only those communist-ruled states within the USSR's reach. Every fraternal party inside the East-Central European bloc was said to be "responsible, not only to its own people, but to all the socialist [that is, communist-ruled] countries and the entire communist movement."[15] Moscow, thus, retroactively fulfilled its "international duty" by invading Czechoslovakia in August 1968 and allegedly preventing a "counterrevolution" from taking place. Approximately eighty thousand USSR troops—five divisions—have remained in that country since they entered it on a "temporary" basis, although a complete Soviet withdrawal is to take place during 1990 and through mid-1991.

Brezhnev, speaking to a group of high-ranking Czechoslovak party and government officials who had been arrested in Prague and flown to Moscow as prisoners during the 1968 invasion, said the following:

> We in the Kremlin came to the conclusion that we could not depend on you any longer. You do what you feel like in domestic politics, even things that displease us, and you are not open to positive suggestions. But your country lies on territory where the Soviet soldier trod in the Second World War. We bought that territory at the cost of enormous sacrifices, and we shall never leave it. The borders of that area are our borders as well. Because you do not listen to us, we feel threatened. In the name of the dead in World War Two, who laid down their lives for your freedom as well, we are therefore fully justified in sending our soldiers into your country, so that we may feel truly secure within our common borders. It is immaterial whether anyone is actually threatening us or not: it is a matter of principle, independent of external circumstances. And that is how it will be, from the Second World War until eternity.[16]

Thus, the Czechs and Slovaks were made to understand that the USSR's borders extended to the Elbe River and that Soviet leaders considered all lands conquered during World War Two as their own.

Not quite ten years later, a coup in Afghanistan brought a de facto communist regime to power. After twenty months of anarchy, USSR armed forces occupied Kabul at the end of December 1979 and installed a puppet ruler. His predecessor, Hafizullah Amin, and most members of the deposed cabinet were murdered in the process.[17] This could also be considered an application of the Brezhnev Doctrine in that the Soviet Union and Afghanistan are territorially contiguous. The subsequent annexation of the Wakhan land corridor gave the USSR a border with Pakistan, a development of geostrategic importance.

In Soviet eyes, apart from the claimed irreversibility of communist rule, this meant that: (1) the "socialist [communist] commonwealth of nations" considered itself powerful enough to determine the course of world events; (2) the world balance of forces already favored a "socialist" encirclement of capitalism; (3) economic development had been subordinated to ideology, coercion, and the threat of force; and (4) no single country or geographic region remained immune to communism.[18] Soviet writers did not hesitate to propound these conclusions in Russian-language publications, although they used the third point as a criticism of the pre-Gorbachev period.

During the first five years after the invasion of Afghanistan, successive leaders in the Kremlin conducted themselves as if they had the means to support the foregoing objectives. In his speech before the nineteenth CPSU national conference, however, M. S. Gorbachev talked about "mistaken decisions" by his predecessors, who allegedly made them "without comprehensive examination or analysis," and said that if this had continued, the USSR could have found itself "on the brink of a military confrontation" with the United States.[19] What the current Soviet leader claims to have achieved is a determined reshaping of foreign policy. Foreign Minister Eduard A. Shevardnadze admitted that the decision to invade Afghanistan in 1979 had been made "behind the back of the party and the people." An official USSR government statement called the decision to occupy Czechoslovakia in 1968 as "unfounded" and "erroneous."[20]

CORRELATION OF FORCES

Why a world war is no longer considered inevitable is found in a concept enunciated by the CPSU Central Committee in a formal resolution, adopted at a plenary session on 23 June 1980, as follows:

> Détente is the natural result of the correlation of forces in the world arena that has formed in recent decades. The military-strategic balance between the world of socialism and the world of capitalism is an achievement of principled historic significance. It is a factor which contains imperialism's aggressive aspirations and which meets the vital interests of all peoples. The hopes to shake this balance are futile.[21]

Those Kremlin leaders believed that the West had been forced to accept détente or peaceful coexistence because of a "correlation of forces" that was changing to the advantage of the USSR. One pair of Soviet writers explained this idea in terms of the relationship between (1) the military-strategic capabilities of the two "antagonistic" social systems and (2) their sociopolitical potentials.[22] The former issue is dealt with in subsequent chapters; only the sociopolitical potentials will be considered here.

According to the two authors, the USSR always had been opposed to the status quo for any country whose policy was not based on the "objective requirements of world social development," which corresponds to the concept of internationalism as originally formulated by Lenin. Although the Soviet Union, "as is well known," does not export revolution, it always will give assistance to the "struggle for social progress." Only in this light can one evaluate the "revolution as well as events concerning Afghanistan, problems of the Iranian revolution, the [USSR] attitude toward the revolution in Nicaragua, and elimination [by Vietnam] of the Pol Pot regime in Kampuchea [Cambodia]." The Soviet Union "has never made any secret of its interest in changing the correlation of forces within the world arena, so that it favors socialism [that is, communism] to the disadvantage of imperialism."[23]

A perceived superiority in political, economic, social, and, above all, military factors allowed the USSR to apply a double standard. From the Kremlin's point of view, a Western ideological offensive that threatened the "socialist" system, United States' support for "antiprogressive" movements anywhere in the world, and NATO attempts to revise East-Central European borders would violate détente.[24] The Soviets, however, accepted no such constraints, especially in areas that they considered off-limits to the West, as can be seen from their definition of proletarian internationalism as "the fundamental principle of USSR foreign policy [meaning] that this policy consistently upholds the basic interests of world socialism, of the forces of the international communist and workers' movements, as well as the national liberation movement."[25] The foregoing are the major components of the "world revolutionary process," as described by Soviet writers and spokesmen. A more detailed explanation follows.

WORLD REVOLUTIONARY PROCESS

Moscow, nevertheless, cannot control all fraternal communist movements. At the twenty-seventh CPSU congress in early 1986, Albania and China did not send representatives, which limited the number of ruling parties in attendance to thirteen. In contrast, the approximately sixty delegations that could be identified came from communist parties in noncommunist-ruled countries (two each from Sweden and India) or administrative units like West Berlin.[26] The national liberation movement was represented by thirty-three "revolutionary democratic" parties and clandestine groups. In addition, there were about twenty-three left-socialist and social democratic delegations as well as members of the Congress Party from India and the Center Party from Finland.

The diverse elements making up the "world revolutionary process" are linked together because of a mutual enemy: imperialism.[27] Components of this process include (1) the world communist movement, (2) the national liberation groups, and (3), implicitly, the left wing of socialist (in the Western sense of that term) parties.

World Communist Movement

Communist and workers' parties recognized by the CPSU operated in 108 countries or administrative units throughout the world during 1990, and their total claimed membership was about eighty-four million[28] (see table 1.2). This figure includes the Chinese, who claim well over half the global figure. The "world socialist system" comprises only twelve communist-ruled states. Two (Albania and China) are highly antagonistic or indifferent toward the Soviet Union as well as toward each other, although the latter

TABLE I.2

GROWTH OF THE WORLD COMMUNIST MOVEMENT, 1917–1990

Year	Number of Parties	Number of Members
1917	1	400,000
1928	46	1,700,000
1939	69	4,200,000
1946	78	20,000,000
1960	87	35,000,000
1969	88	50,000,000
1985	95	>80,000,000
1990	108	<84,000,000*

*The last figure for membership represents a decline of more than six million from the previous year, primarily because of developments in East–Central Europe.

SOURCES: V. V. Zagladin and G. A. Kiselev, comps., *Politicheskie partii: spravochnik* (Moscow: Politizdat, 1986), p. 10; Alexander Subbotin, ed., *First-Hand Information: Communists and Revolutionary Democrats of the World Presenting Their Parties* (Prague: Peace and Socialism International Publishers, 1988); Richard F. Staar, ed., *1990 Yearbook on International Communist Affairs* (Stanford: Hoover Institution Press, 1990), pp. xii–xxxi.

relationship is changing, and two ruling parties (those in North Korea and Yugoslavia) are more or less neutral toward the CPSU.

The "socialist commonwealth" through the end of 1990 still formally included ten full members of the Council for Mutual Economic Assistance (CMEA) plus Laos and Cambodia, with observer status only. Thus (except for Poland, Czechoslovakia, East Germany until 3 October 1990, and Hungary), the so-called commonwealth remains limited to the pro-Soviet core group of communist-ruled countries. Albania has not been a member of the USSR bloc de facto since 1961 and de jure since 1968, when it formally withdrew from both CMEA and the Warsaw Pact after the Soviet invasion of Czechoslovakia. Tiranë finally agreed on 30 July 1990 to resume diplomatic relations with Moscow. Yugoslavia maintains associate status within CMEA, although it is not considered a member of the "socialist commonwealth" (see table 1.3).

USSR leaders most likely expect that both Albania and Yugoslavia in the future can be influenced to rejoin the bloc. The Kremlin must also hope that a future Chinese leadership may forget previous anti-Soviet policies and draw closer to Moscow. Relations with North Korea remain ambiguous, although Kim Il Sung has visited the USSR and East-Central Europe in recent years.[29]

Alongside the world socialist system within the world communist movement stands, according to Soviet writers, "the revolutionary movement of the working class in capitalist countries." It consists of approximately eighty communist parties, generally one for each country or political entity (for example, Puerto Rico). Not all are pro-Moscow. Some had remained neutral in the former Sino-Soviet dispute, and others adopted a pro-Chinese stance.[30] The CPSU leaders probably consider this latter attitude of a transitory nature that can be modified over time. No serious attempts, however, have been made to organize an international meeting of communist parties. Gorbachev himself even spoke out against the endeavor.[31]

National Liberation Groups

When discussing organizations fighting for "national liberation," USSR ideologists have limited their comments largely to Africa and Asia, that is, to former colonies or semicolonies. The situation in Latin America differs because it has a relatively developed capitalist economy, a strong and experienced working class, a long history of revolutionary struggle, and communist parties in most of the countries throughout the region. Therefore, in Soviet terms, the "laws of natural evolution" could be allowed to determine the outcome here. Even in Latin America, however, implementation of these so-called laws has been hastened by Moscow. If a country's

TABLE I.3
WORLD SOCIALIST SYSTEM, 1989

Socialist Commonwealth of Nations
(Council for Mutual Economic Assistance Members)

Country	Year Joined
1. Bulgaria	1949
2. Cuba	1972
3. Czechoslovakia*	1949
4. East Germany	1950
5. Hungary*	1949
6. Cambodia	(observer)
7. Laos	(observer)
8. Mongolia	1962
9. Poland*	1949
10. Romania	1949
11. Soviet Union	1949
12. Vietnam	1978

Other Communist-ruled States

1. Albania	
2. China	
3. North Korea	
4. Yugoslavia	(associate member)

*Since 1989, these East–Central European governments have been reconstituted without communist participation.

SOURCE: Cambodia appears as one of the sixteen "socialist" countries in *New Times* (Moscow), 8 November 1987, p. 12; supplement. The first twelve countries sent delegations from ruling parties to a conference in East Berlin of secretaries in charge of ideology. *Pravda*, 23 September 1989, p. 5.

policies are anti-imperialist, USSR leaders consider it "progressive" and therefore to be helped along the path toward "socialism."

A good example of how Marxist-led insurgents were clandestinely assisted not only by the Soviet Union but also by other "fraternal" regimes can be documented in El Salvador. During June and July of 1980, the communist party leader in that country, Shafik Jorge Handal, traveled in his capacity as a representative of the Farabundo Martí National Liberation Front (FMNLF) to Cuba, Vietnam, Ethiopia, the USSR (twice), Bulgaria, Czechoslovakia, Hungary, and East Germany. All eight regimes supplied uniforms, weapons, and ammunition. According to captured documents, evaluated as genuine by U.S. intelligence agencies,[32] Handal met with a deputy head of the CPSU International Department, K. N. Brutents, and that body's Latin American sector chief, M. F. Kudachkin. Moscow also began providing military training for young communists from El Salvador who were studying in the USSR at that time. Two dozen Soviet-made SAM-7 antiaircraft weapons, destined for the FMNLF, were found on 24 November 1989 in the wreckage of a light plane that had taken off from Managua.[33]

Other documentation, discovered by U.S. troops on Grenada, indicates similar communist involvement on that Caribbean island. For the period 1983–1984, North Korea obligated itself to deliver without charge weapons and ammunition as well as six thousand military uniforms. These items were listed on a two-page addendum to a secret agreement. Cuba specified the exact numbers of its military personnel that were to be stationed in Grenada through the end of 1984. Secret agreements with the USSR included three-, seven-, and fourteen-page addenda itemizing weapons and ammunition to be delivered to the Marxist island regime.[34]

According to the Soviet world outlook, the most important grouping within the overall "national liberation movement" category comprises those countries with a "socialist orientation," most of which are controlled by a single so-called revolutionary democratic party. It has been possible to identify about twenty-eight of them from USSR sources, as indicated in table 1.4. Although theoretically developing toward communism, these states generally

1. Allow some private capital investment (foreign as well as domestic) to remain
2. Emphasize nationalism and religion in their ideologies as well as Marxism-Leninism to varying degrees
3. Consider a multiclass (as opposed to simply a proletarian) party to be the leading revolutionary force[35]

The "revolutionary democratic" movements, more highly developed with regard to ideology and pro-Soviet orientation, are called *vanguard parties* by the USSR. Fourteen of these have been noted during recent years in Afghanistan, Angola, Bahrain (nonruling and illegal), Benin, Chad, Congo/Brazzaville, Ethiopia, Grenada (nonruling), Mozambique, Nicaragua (nonruling), South Korea (nonruling), South Yemen (united with North), Suriname, and Zimbabwe.

The second grouping that Soviet ideologists identify as belonging to the "national liberation movement" consists of those still fighting to achieve power. Examples of such organizations include the African National Con-

TABLE I.4
Movements with a "Socialist" Orientation in Third World Countries

Country	Name of Movement
1. Afghanistan (1978)	People's Democratic Party of Afghanistan*
2. Algeria	National Liberation Front (FLN)
3. Angola (1976)	Movement for People's Liberation of Angola—Labor Party*
4. Bahrain	National Liberation Front*
5. Benin (1981?)	People's Revolutionary Party of Benin*
6. Burkina-Faso	National Council of the Revolution (CNR)
7. Burundi	Union for National Progress (UPRONA)
8. Cape Verde	African Party for Independence of Cape Verde (PAICV)
9. Chad	National Democratic Union*
10. Congo/Brazzaville (1981)	Congolese Workers' Party* (PCT)
11. Ethiopia (1978)	Workers' Party of Ethiopia*
12. Ghana	Provisional National Defense Council
13. Grenada	Maurice Bishop Patriotic Movement*
14. Guinea	Democratic Party of Guinea (PDG)†
15. Guinea/Bissau	African Party for Independence of Guinea (PAIGC)
16. Madagascar	Congress Party for Independence of Madagascar (AKFM)
17. Mali	Democratic Union of the Mali People (UDPM)
18. Mozambique (1977)	Mozambique Liberation Front (FRELIMO)*
19. Nicaragua (1980?)	Sandinista National Liberation Front (FSLN)
20. Sao Tome and Principe	Movement for the Liberation of Sao Tome and Principe
21. Seychelles	Seychelles People's Progressive Front
22. South Korea	National Democratic Front of South Korea*
23. South Yemen (1979)	Yemen Socialist Party*
24. Suriname	National Democratic Party*
25. Syria (1980)	Arab Socialist Resurrectionist (Ba'th) Party
26. Tanzania	Revolutionary Party of Tanzania (CCM)
27. Zambia	United National Independence Party
28. Zimbabwe	Zimbabwe African National Union-Patriotic Front*

*Called vanguard parties by Soviet writers.

†The PDG was dissolved after the April 1984 military coup.

SOURCES: The Soviet Union signed twenty-year friendship treaties with those countries where

gress (ANC), directed against the Republic of South Africa, and the South-West African People's Organization. The latter assumed control on 21 March 1990 over Namibia, formerly administered by the Republic of South Africa. Another "liberation movement," the Polisario, remains active in the western Sahara. Those operating in the Middle East include the People's Front for the Liberation of Oman and the Palestine Liberation Organization (PLO). The Association of Revolutionary Organizations of Guatemala and the FMNLF in El Salvador belong to this same category, as does or did the National Liberation Movement of the Caribbean Basin.[36] These organizations are aligned with the Soviets to varying degrees: at one extreme, the ANC, almost openly, had been dominated until August 1990 by the Moscow-line Communist Party of South Africa, whereas the PLO relationship with the USSR might best be described as a marriage of convenience.

In a survey of twentieth-century revolutions, one Soviet scholar has concluded that twenty-one of what he counted as fifty-eight upheavals resulted in war, meaning that thirty-seven had taken place peacefully. Two years earlier Brutents claimed that the Third World in 1986 could boast "57 communist and about 40 revolutionary-democratic parties," the latter having chosen the path toward "socialism."[37]

Left Wing of the Socialist Parties

In third place, within the broad context of the "world revolutionary process," after the world communist and national liberation movements, are the

the year is indicated in parentheses. A ruling party delegation from Benin spent May and June 1981 in Moscow, and a secret agreement could have been signed at this time (A. M. Prokhorov, chief ed., *Ezhegodnik bol'shoi sovetskoi entsiklopedii, 1981* [Moscow: Sovetskaia entsiklopediia, 1981], p. 212).

Seven of the vanguard parties are listed by A. P. Agofonov and V. F. Khalipov, *Sovremennaia epokha i mirovoi revolutsionnyi protsess* (Moscow: Vysshaia shkola, 1988), p. 158. Two additional ones, Chad and South Korea, appear in Alexander Subbotin, ed., *First-Hand Information: Communists and Revolutionary Democrats of the World Presenting Their Parties* (Prague: Peace and Socialism International, 1988), pp. 91–92 and 120–21. In the case of Nicaragua, an understanding about relations between the CPSU and FSLN was signed on 19 March 1980 in Moscow (*Archiv der Gegenwart, 1980 50*, no. 23/24 [4–18 May 1980]: 23533). Grenada and Nicaragua had been described, along with Cuba, as having "taken the road of building a new society in Latin America" (see Raul Valdez Vivo, "The Latin American Proletariat and Its Allies in the Anti-Imperialist Struggle," *World Marxist Review* 23, no. 8 [August 1980]: 33). This description ceased to apply in the case of Grenada after U.S. and Caribbean troops occupied the island during the seven weeks before 15 December 1983.

Mozambique announced that its ruling FRELIMO had been transformed into a Marxist-Leninist party, according to *Tempo* (Maputo), 8 May 1983. Hence, it became a "vanguard" party. In Nicaragua, the Sandinistas lost the election and surrendered power when Violeta Barrios de Chamorro was sworn in as president on 25 April 1990. See *Facts on File*, 27 April 1990, p. 297. Ghana and Mali have been cited in Soviet literature as countries that reverted to nonrevolutionary democratic status. The two Yemens merged on 22 May 1990. See "Two Yemens Merge," *Facts on File*, 25 May 1990, p. 381.

left-wing socialists from parties of various political coloration.[38] Moscow attempts to co-opt socialist trade unions and youth groups as well as individuals to become members of international communist front organizations, which, in turn, can enlist them to serve Soviet foreign policy interests. In addition, over the past several years, communists have cooperated organizationally and individually with moderate socialist parties such as those in Finland, France, and Portugal and with the semisocialist ones in India, Sri Lanka, and Bangladesh. At least fifteen socialist groupings of various stripes have members on the World Peace Council presidential committee,[39] the best-known Soviet-controlled international communist front organization.

Perhaps the most important vehicle through which the Kremlin hopes to influence moderate West European socialists, especially those in the Federal Republic of Germany, the United Kingdom, and the Scandinavian countries, has been the Socialist International (SI), which includes eighty-nine political parties and more than twenty million members worldwide. Only a few days after the Soviet invasion of Afghanistan, the current SI president (West German Willy Brandt) wrote in a report that there was a need for "continuing the process of détente."[40] The following month, Brandt and his colleague the late Olof Palme of Sweden convinced the SI meeting in Vienna not to mention Afghanistan but rather to concentrate on promoting arms control. This conference led to the idea of an SI disarmament commission, headed by Palme.

On the basis of Palme's visits to Moscow and Washington, D.C., it would seem that the SI may have become an unwitting, indirect instrument of Soviet foreign policy. One USSR objective had been to discourage West European governments from implementing the NATO council's decision to commence deployment in December 1983 of U.S.-made Pershing II and ground-launched cruise missiles. Interviews with moderate socialist leaders throughout northern Europe indicated a definite move toward Moscow's position on this arms control issue. Several of these individuals, who are no longer in power, called for abandoning the original modernization schedule even if the U.S.-USSR arms control negotiations in Geneva should fail. The Soviet Union broke off the intermediate-range and the strategic weapons reduction talks before the above NATO deployments commenced, as discussed in chapter 12.

The communist attempt to penetrate the SI can also be seen in the minutes from a secret meeting during 6–7 January 1983 at Managua, where the Sandinistas hosted representatives of El Salvador guerrillas, the Radical Party from Chile, the People's National Party of Jamaica, the New Jewel Movement on Grenada, and the Communist Party of Cuba.[41] Participants in the meeting agreed that "progressives" already controlled the SI Committee on Latin America and the Caribbean. The most important enemies were identified as socialists in Italy and Portugal as well as the Social Democrats. U.S.A. Scandinavian and Dutch socialists were counted among the best of friends. Not mentioned were the ruling (until 1989) Greek socialists (PA-SOK), whose first congress in May 1984 had been attended by representatives from the Sandinistas, the PLO, the Fatherland Front in Bulgaria, and the CPSU.[42] The SI's centenary (eighteenth) congress in June 1989 brought together delegations from seventy-seven social democratic parties.

It is possible that only left-wing socialists (which include certain members of moderate parties) are consciously in tune with the "world revolutionary process," manifested by their active participation in international communist front organizations. Less reliable but even more useful to the USSR on occasion are people like Brandt, the late Palme, Andreas Papandreou, and even the late Mrs. Indira Gandhi because of their international influence and imputed moderate orientation. Such individuals do not appear Soviet-controlled and most probably reached their positions—at times relatively pro-USSR—independently and hence became all the more credible. Even if certain SI decisions were made as a result of action taken by these "agents of influence,"[43] it is debatable whether that body as a whole could be included in the "world revolutionary process."

FUTURE PROSPECTS

The fundamental Soviet world outlook had been reemphasized in a series of articles by Boris N. Ponomarev.[44] Short-term victories for the world revolutionary movement were envisaged during the early 1980s throughout Latin America, which was portrayed as a "continent in upheaval." Medium-range expectations referred to what Ponomarev called the "zone of developed capitalism." An acute sociopolitical crisis in the United States allegedly would become even more aggravated. Unfortunately, according to Ponomarev, local communist parties in this zone (which includes Western Europe) remained unprepared for revolutionary contingencies and faced problems of coordination with the USSR as well as with their "socialist" counterparts. Although Ponomarev's articles did not represent anything new in terms of ideology, they were reformulated in the next CPSU program.[45]

It was the late Nikita S. Khrushchev, however, who coined the term *revolutionary democracy* to justify Moscow's support for Third World leaders of lower-middle-class origin from within the armed forces or the intelligentsia. Moscow endorsed Gamal Nasser in Egypt and Houari Boumedienne in Algeria, even though their "socialism" did not correspond to the Soviet model. In fact the USSR considers petit bourgeois elements to represent budding revolutionary forces in the less-developed countries, and it appears to be correct in this assessment.

The problem of dealing with the Third World had been complicated by intense Sino-Soviet rivalry.[46] Among the twenty-seven independent Asian states, only six (China, Cambodia, Laos, Mongolia, North Korea, Vietnam) are ruled by *recognized* communist parties. To date there are none in this category in Africa, where political movements completely subservient to Moscow remain weak. However, the USSR has been working on a long-range program of academic training for youth from less-developed countries at its People's Friendship University, named after the late Patrice Lumumba, a pro-Soviet leader from the Congo. It had been giving priority to providing students from "revolutionary democracies" with political training in the Soviet Union as well as in several former East-Central European client states.

A total of 34,305 young people were enrolled during 1989 for academic, technical, and military training in similar colleges and universities.[47] China temporarily lost in this competition when, during the ten-year-long Great Cultural Revolution, all foreign students (other than those being trained in guerrilla warfare or sabotage) were forced to leave the country on two weeks' notice. Concurrently, their Chinese professors were sent to work on collective farms.

Yet, if Soviet relations with the People's Republic of China could currently be described as competitive regarding influence throughout the world communist movement, those vis-à-vis the West were fundamentally hostile. Peaceful coexistence in the 1970s remained a one-way street that did not slow down Moscow's attempts to mobilize world public opinion against the United States. Diplomacy and "active measures" continued to be viewed by the Soviets as two sides of the same coin. During the period of so-called détente the USSR persisted in a crash buildup of its armed forces, with the aim of intimidating Western Europe and decoupling it from the United States. The men who made, and continue to make, the basic decisions for the Soviet Union and the process itself are dealt with in the next chapter.

NOTES

1. Evgenii Bazhanov, "Chto nam pomozhet?" *Novoe vremia*, no. 28 (6 July 1990): 31.
2. "K gumannomu, demokraticheskomu sotsializmu," *Pravda*, 15 July 1990, pp. 1 and 3, at p. 3. A resolution of the twenty-eighth congress appeared establishing a commission to prepare a new CPSU program for adoption by a national

conference or congress before the middle of 1992. See *Pravda*, 14 July 1990, p. 2, which lists members of the commission, chaired by Gorbachev.

3. *Programma KPSS* (Moscow: Politizdat, 1988), pp. 60–74.

4. "O komissiakh Tsentral'nogo Komiteta KPSS," *Pravda*, 29 November 1988, pp. 1–2, lists ideology commission members and gives their other positions. Medvedev's new appointment was announced in *Izvestiia*, 18 July 1990, p. 1, together with a brief biographical sketch and photograph.

5. Address delivered in the Palace of Congresses on the anniversary of Lenin's birth entitled, "Velikaia zhiznennaia sila Leninizma," *Pravda*, 22 April 1980, p. 2.

6. V. V. Zagladin, "On the Theory of World Politics," *Political Affairs* (Moscow) 64, no. 10 (October 1985): 38–39.

7. M. S. Gorbachev, "Politicheskii otchet TsK KPSS XXVIII s"ezda KPSS i zadachi partii," *Pravda*, 3 July 1990, pp. 2–4, at p. 4.

8. V. A. Medvedev, "Otvety chlenov Politbiuro, Sekretarei TsK KPSS," *Pravda*, 4 July 1990, p. 2.

9. V. P. Agafonov and V. F. Khalipov, *Sovremennaia epokha i mirovoi revoliutsionnyi protsess* (Moscow: Vysshaia shkola, 1988), p. 15. See also V. V. Zagladin, "Obshchestvennyi progress v sovremennom mire: nekotorye metodologicheskie aspekty problemy," in G. G. Vodolazo, chief ed., *Problemy mirovogo revoliutsionnogo protsessa* (Moscow: Mysl', 1989), pp. 82–102.

10. "Vystuplenie M. S. Gorbacheva," *Pravda*, 11 July 1990, p. 2.

11. E. A. Anufriev, chief ed., *Nauchnyi kommunizm* (Moscow: Politizdat, 1988), pp. 56–65. See also V. G. Afanas'ev et al., eds., *Kratkii slovar' po nauchnomu kommunizmu* (Moscow: Politizdat, 1989), pp. 206–8, which discusses the reasons behind Lenin's policy, almost a mirror image of what Gorbachev is doing.

12. M. A. Suslov, "Kommunisticheskoe dvizhenie v avangarde bor'by za mir, sotsial'noe i natsional'noe osvobozhdenie," *Kommunist*, no. 11 (July 1975): 7; see also his article entitled "Istoricheskaia pravota idei i dela Lenina," *Kommunist*, no. 4 (March 1980): 11–29.

13. A. A. Gromyko, ed., *Istoriia diplomatii* (Moscow: Politizdat, 1979)5: 725. The same official wrote "Leninskaia vneshniaia politika v sovremennom mire" for *Kommunist*, no. 1 (January 1981): 13–27, in a similar vein.

14. Kommunisticheskaia Partiia Sovetskogo Soiuza, *XX s"ezd, 14–15 fevralia 1956 goda: Stenograficheskii otchet* (Moscow: Politizdat, 1956)1: 37–38.

15. Sergei Kovalev, "Suverenitet i internatsional'nye obiazannosti sotsialisticheskikh stran," *Pravda*, 26 September 1968, p. 4.

16. Zdenek Mlynar, *Nightfrost in Prague: The End of Humane Socialism* (New York: Karz Publishers, 1980), p. 240. The Czech author, educated in law at Moscow State University, reports that he himself heard this statement. See also his recent book, *Can Gorbachev Change the Soviet Union?* (Boulder, Colo.: Westview Press, 1990).

17. Anthony Arnold, *Afghanistan's Two-Party Communism* (Stanford: Hoover Institution Press, 1983), pp. 97–98. See also Gr. Baklanov, "Kak ubivali Kh. Amina," *Argumenty i fakty*, no. 44 (November 1990): 2.

18. R. Judson Mitchell, "A New Brezhnev Doctrine," *World Politics* 30, no. 3 (April 1978): 389–90.

19. "Doklad general'nogo sekretaria Gorbacheva M. S.," *Pravda*, 29 June 1988, p. 3. The complete transcript of this national conference was published as KPSS, *XIX vsesoiuznaia konferentsiia Kommunisticheskoi Partii Sovetskogo Soiuza*, 2 vols. (Moscow, Politizdat, 1988).

20. Shevardnadze speech before the USSR Supreme Soviet in the *New York Times*, 25 October 1989, p. A-6; statement on Czechoslovakia in the *New York Times*, 5 December 1989, p. A-7.

21. "O mezhdunarodnom polozhenii i vneshnei politike Sovetskogo Soiuza," *Pravda*, 24 June 1980, p. 2. See also N. V. Ogarkov, chief ed., "Sootnoshenie sil i sredstv," *Voennyi entsiklopedicheskii slovar'* (Moscow: Voenizdat, 1983), p. 691.

22. Iurii Zhilin and Andrei Ermonskii, "Eshche raz po povodu sootnosheniia mirovykh sil," *Novoe vremia*, no. 46 (14 November 1980): 18.

23. Ibid., p. 20.

24. R. Judson Mitchell, *Ideology of a Superpower: Contemporary Soviet Doctrine on International Relations* (Stanford: Hoover Institution Press, 1982), especially pp. 54–70.

25. A. A. Gromyko, "Leninskaia vneshniaia politika v sovremennom mire," *Kommunist*, no. 1 (January 1981): 14. See also F. Konstantinov, "V bor'be za budushchee: s ideologicheskogo fronta," *Pravda*, 18 November 1983, p. 3, on the worldwide struggle against capitalism.

26. Some of the communist party delegations remained unidentified, probably because they operated on an illegal basis. Between 24 February and 7 March 1986, *Pravda* listed most of the delegation heads. By contrast, no foreign communists were invited to the twenty-eighth CPSU congress in July 1990.

27. V. V. Zagladin, ed., *Mezhdunarodnoe kommunisticheskoe dvizhenie* (Moscow: Politizdat, 1984), pp. 12–16.

28. Richard F. Staar, "Register of Communist Parties," *1990 Yearbook on International Communist Affairs* (Stanford: Hoover Institution Press, 1990), pp. xii-xxxi (henceforth cited as *YICA*).

29. M. S. Kapitsa and G. F. Kim, eds., *SSSR i Koreia* (Moscow: Nauka, 1988), pp. 295–324. See also the interview with a former North Korean ambassador to the USSR who states that Stalin personally approved Kim Il Sung's plan to invade South Korea. A. Makhov, "Stalin odobril prikaz Kim Ir Sena," *Moskovskie novosti*, no. 27 (8 July 1990): 12.

30. Australia, Costa Rica, Finland, Great Britain, India, Jamaica, New Zealand, the Philippines, Senegal, Spain, and Sweden each have two Soviet-recognized communist parties. See Richard F. Staar, "Checklist of Communist Parties," *Problems of Communism* 39, no. 2 (March–April 1990): 75–84, at p. 75.

31. Sylwester Szafarz, "Światowy ruch komunistyczny," *Trybuna ludu* (Warsaw), 24 February 1984, p. 6, claimed the total number of communist parties in favor of a world conference to be sixty but gave no source. Gorbachev admitted that holding such a conference would be inappropriate, according to Giulietto

Chiese, "Cervetti racconta il suo incontro con Mikhail Gorbaciov," *L'Unita* (Milan), 22 May 1985, p. 4.

32. U.S. Department of State, *Communist Interference in El Salvador*, Special report no. 80 (23 February 1981); with documents reproduced in an appendix. See also John Norton Moore, "The Secret War in Central America and the Future of World Order," *American Journal of International Law* 80, no. 1 (January 1986): especially pp. 80–103.

33. "What Did Gorbachev Know?" *Wall Street Journal*, 28 November 1989, p. A-14.

34. U.S. Information Agency, *Documents Pertaining to Relations between Grenada, the USSR, and Cuba* (December 1983), in three packets. The agreements with the USSR are dated 27 October 1980, 9 February 1981, and 27 July 1982, in both Russian and English. See also U.S. Department of State, *Lessons of Grenada*, publ. no. 9457 (Washington, D.C.: GPO, February 1986).

35. V. V. Zagladin, chief ed., *Revoliutsionnyi protsess* (Moscow: Mysl', 1985), pp. 167–81.

36. Represented at the Eighth Congress of the Guadeloupe Communist Party, as reported by TASS in *Pravda*, 1 May 1984, p. 4.

37. B. I. Koval', "Mirovoi revoliutsionnyi protsess na poroge XXI v.," in A. A. Galkin, ed., *Rabochii klass v mirovom revoliutsionnom protsesse* (Moscow: Nauka, 1988), pp. 12–13; K. N. Brutents, "Osvobodivshiesia strany i antiimperialisticheskaia bor'ba," *Pravda*, 10 January 1986, p. 3.

38. V. V. Zagladin et al., *Mezhdunarodnoe rabochee dvizhenie* (Moscow: Politizdat, 1984), pp. 72–106.

39. World Peace Council, *List of Members, 1983–1986* (Helsinki: Information Center of the WPC, 1986), pp. 12–31. See the essay by Wallace Spaulding, "Soviet-line Fronts," *Problems of Communism* 38, no. 1 (January–February 1989): 69–75.

40. Brandt Commission report, *North-South: A Programme for Survival*, 12 February 1980, reproduced in *Keesing's Contemporary Archive*, 12 September 1980, p. 30457.

41. *Wall Street Journal*, 2 December 1983, p. 28; *Il Giornale Nuovo* (Milan), 11 December 1983. Only the groups from Chile, Jamaica, and Grenada belonged to the Socialist International.

42. Socialist Prime Minister Andreas Papandreou of Greece stated publicly that "the world is now convinced the [Korean] jumbo jet was on a spy mission for the CIA and that it really did violate Soviet airspace for intelligence gathering purposes," without citing any evidence. See *International Herald Tribune* (Hong Kong), 6–7 October 1984.

43. See the SI publication *Common Security: A Programme for Disarmament* (London: Pan Books, 1982). The Seventeenth Socialist International Congress, held in Lima, Peru, called for settlement of problems in Central America, Namibia, and the Middle East but did not mention Afghanistan or Cambodia (Moscow radio, 24 June 1986; *Foreign Broadcast Information Service (FBIS)-Soviet Union*, 25 June 1986, p. CC-1). See also Mezhdunarodnyi otdel TsK

KPSS, "Sotsialisticheskii Internatsional segodnia," *Izvestiia TsK KPSS*, no. 7 (July 1990): 142–46.

44. B. N. Ponomarev, "Socialism's Role in the Present Day World," *World Marxist Review* 18, no. 1 (January 1975): 4–19; "Real'nyi sotsializm i ego mezhdunarodnoe znachenie," *Kommunist*, no. 2 (January 1979): 17–36; "Neodolimost' osvoboditel'nogo dvizhenia," *Kommunist*, no. 1 (January 1980): 11–27; "Uchenie Marksa-rukovodstvo k deistviiu," *Pravda*, 31 March 1983, pp. 1–2.

45. *Programma KPSS* (1988).

46. B. N. Slavinskii, *Vneshniaia politika SSSR na Dal'nem Vostoke* (Moscow: Mezhdunarodnye otnosheniia, 1988), pp. 233–53.

47. Central Intelligence Agency, *Handbook of Economic Statistics 1990*, CPAS-90–10001 (Washington, D.C.: Directorate of Intelligence, September 1990), table 164, p. 198. Over half these foreign students in the USSR came from Asia, Africa, and Latin America. Forty percent were from "fraternal socialist countries." For the ideological content of what foreign students are taught, see E. A. Anufriev, *Nauchnyi kommunizm: Uchebnoe posobie* (Moscow: Politizdat, 1988).

2

THE DECISION-MAKING PROCESS

The locus of power in the Soviet foreign policy decision-making process had been centered in the Communist Party of the Soviet Union (CPSU) and specifically its Political Bureau, or Politburo, rather than the government. A congressional study that appeared one year before N. S. Khrushchev's ouster concluded that he had applied a "balance of interests" principle whenever the Politburo convened to discuss policy alternatives.[1] This had most likely been the general pattern of Soviet decision making in external affairs as well. That is, fundamental decisions concerning the five-year economic plan and the annual budget, both of which involve basic resource allocations and thus represent important foreign policy constraints, probably had been dealt with by a plenary session of full members and candidates for membership in the Political Bureau.

The new Politburo, elected on 14 July 1990, has doubled in size, from twelve to twenty-four members, the majority being CPSU leaders from the fifteen republics (see table 2.1). Just one individual remains from the previous body, namely, General Secretary M. S. Gorbachev. Only a few newcomers have had any experience in foreign affairs. The CPSU statute specifies that the Political Bureau is elected "for [the purpose of] deciding political and organizational questions of the party between plenums of the Central Committee,"[2] which suggests that the government henceforth will be in charge of external relations.

TABLE 2.1

CPSU POLITICAL BUREAU AND SECRETARIAT, 1990

Name	Born	Elected to Politburo and/or Secretariat	Nationality	Responsibility (appointed/elected)
Politburo members				
Gorbachev, M. S.*	1931	1980	Russian	CPSU general secretary and Defense Council chairman (March 1985); USSR president (March 1990)
Ivashko, V. A.*	1932	1989	Ukrainian	Deputy general secretary; socioeconomic policy (1990)
Dzasokhov, A. S.	1934	1990	Ossetian	Chairman, Supreme Soviet International Affairs Committee (1990); secretary for ideology (1990)
Frolov, I. T.	1929	1989	Russian	Editor in chief, *Pravda* (1989)
Ianaev, G. I.	1937	1990	Russian	International policy
Prokof'ev, Iu. A.	1939	1990	Russian	First secretary, Moscow CPSU organization (1989)
Semenova, G. V.	1937	1990	Russian	Women and family; editor, *Krest'ianka* (1981)
Shenin, O. S.	1937	1990	Russian	Primary party organizations; ranks 3d
Stroev, E. S.	1937	1990	Russian	Agrarian policy
Party Leaders of the Republic (ex officio Politburo members)				
Burakevicius, M. M.	1927	1990	Lithuanian	First secretary, Lithuanian CP (1990)
Margiani, A. A.	1944	1990	Georgian	First secretary, Georgian CP (1990)
Gurenko, S. I.	1936	1990	Ukrainian	First secretary, Ukrainian CP (1990)
Karimov, I. A.	1938	1990	Uzbek	First secretary, Uzbek CP (1989)
Luchinskii, P. K.	1940	1990	Moldavian	First secretary, Moldavian CP (1989)
Makhkamov, K.	1932	1990	Tadzhik	First secretary, Tadzhik CP (1985)

TABLE 2.1 (*continued*)

Name	Born	Elected to Politburo and/or Secretariat	Nationality	Responsibility (appointed/elected)
Masaliev, A. M.	1933	1990	Kirghiz	First secretary, Kirghiz CP (1985)
Pogosian, S. K	1932	1990	Armenian	First secretary, Armenian CP (1990)
Mutalibov, A. N.	1938	1990	Azerbaijani	First secretary, Azerbaijani CP (1990)
Nazarbaev, N. A.	1940	1990	Kazakh	First secretary, Kazakh CP (1989)
Niiazov, S. A.	1940	1990	Turkmen	First secretary, Turkmen CP (1985)
Polozkov, I. K.	1935	1990	Russian	First secretary, RSFSR CP (1990)
Rubiks, A. P.	1935	1990	Latvian	First secretary, Latvian CP (1990)
Sillari, E. A.	1944	1990	Estonian	First secretary, Estonian CP (1990)
Malofeev, A. A.	1933	1990	Belorussian	First secretary, Belorussian CP (1990)
Secretaries				
Baklanov, O.D.	1932	1986	Ukrainian	Military policy (1988)
Dzasokhov, A. S.*	1934	1990	Ossetian	Ideology (1990)
Falin, V. M.	1926	1990	Russian	International policy (1990)
Gidaspov, B. V.	1933	1990	Russian	First secretary, Leningrad CPSU Committee (1989)

Name	Year	Nationality	Position
Girenko, A. N.	1936	Ukrainian	Nationalities (1989)
Ianaev, G. I.*	1937	Russian	International policy (1990)
Kuptsov, V. A.	1937	Russian	Sociopolitical organizations (1990)
Manaenkov, Iu. A.	1936	Russian	Liaison with RSFSR CP
Semenova, G. V.*	1937	Russian	Women and family (1990)
Shenin, O. S.*	1937	Russian	Primary party organizations affairs (1990)
Stroev, E. S.*	1937	Russian	Agriculture (1989)
Members of the Secretariat			
Aniskin, V. V.	1990	Russian	Chairman, Gor'ky kolkhoz in Moscow region
Gaivoronskii, V. A.	1990	Russian	Worker
Mel'nikov, I. I.	1990	Russian	Secretary, Moscow State University CPSU Committee
Teplenichev, A. I.	1990	Russian	Secretary, Novolipetsk Metallurgical Combine CPSU Committee
Turgunova, Gulchakra	1990	Azerbaijani (?)	Farm worker

*Senior secretary with seat on Politburo

SOURCES: Central Intelligence Agency, Directorate of Intelligence, *Directory of Soviet Officials: National Organizations*, series LDA 90-14379 (Washington, D.C.: GPO, September 1990), pp. 149–51. For interviews with individual Politburo and Secretariat members, see *Pravda*, 31 July 1990, pp. 1–2; 18 August 1990, p. 5; 20 August 1990, pp. 1 and 5; 22 August 1990, pp. 1–2; 31 August 1990, p. 2; 29 October 1990, p. 2; Dawn Mann, comp., *CPSU Politburo and Secretariat* (Munich: RFE/RL, October 1990), pp. 1–2.

It appears that the regular weekly Politburo meetings became fortnightly beginning in September 1988 and then monthly sessions in early 1990. They are restricted to CPSU affairs. Leonid I. Abalkin, a deputy prime minister, confirmed to Agence France Presse on 9 April 1990 that the former decision-making process in the Politburo had been dismantled, with Gorbachev assuming all executive power as head of the government.

At the twenty-eighth CPSU congress, Lev N. Zaikov revealed the existence of a secret Politburo "military-technical" special commission, which he chaired. Other members included A. N. Iakovlev and Eduard A. Shevardnadze as well as heads of the KGB, the Defense Ministry, and other key government agencies. Apart from work on arms control talks, Zaikov claimed that the commission's achievements involved ending the war in Afghanistan, easing international tensions, reducing troops unilaterally, and eliminating the USSR's image as an aggressor.[3]

Day-to-day operations of the CPSU Political Bureau will be conducted by the deputy general secretary, a new position. Elected at the twenty-eighth party congress, despite a better-known opposition candidate, the nondescript first secretary of the Ukraine party organization, Vladimir A. Ivashko, became second in command to Gorbachev on 11 July 1990. He had only served in the CPSU at the republic level over the past four years.[4]

THE PRESIDENTIAL COUNCIL

The new locus of authority resides in the Presidential Council (*Presidentskii Sovet*), with nineteen members including the USSR president as chairman. Ten individuals (names marked with asterisks on table 2.2) from the previous CPSU Political Bureau should have more influence on foreign policy than the others. Gorbachev—together with his closest adviser A. N. Iakovlev and Foreign Minister Shevardnadze—probably participate in all foreign policy decisions. The other key Presidential Council members are there because of the positions they fill (defense, Gosplan, interior, KGB, and prime ministership). Special commissions also may be established to work on important foreign policy problems, although little evidence of such arrangements has been found to date.

Not much information as yet exists on the functioning of the new Presidential Council and exactly how foreign policy decisions are made. However, each successive leader or "collective leadership" group will have a specific modus operandi. A group of council members—including Bakatin, Iazov, Kriuchkov, and Iarin, who has proclaimed that he will defend the interests of the USSR armed forces[5]—had been established under Iakovlev to deal with national security.

TABLE 2.2
PRESIDENTIAL COUNCIL, 1990

Name	Born	Election/ Appointment	Nationality	Responsibility
Gorbachev, M. A.*	1931	14.3.90	Russian	President of the USSR
Bakatin, V. V.†	1937	25.3.90	Russian	Minister of the Interior (public order)
Boldin, V. I.	1935	25.3.90	Russian	Chief, General Affairs Department, CPSU Central Committee
Gubenko, N. N.	1941	4.11.90	Russian(?)	Minister of Culture
Iakovlev, A. N.*	1923	24.3.90	Russian	Principal adviser (ideology and all security organs)
Iarin, V. A.	1940	24.3.90	Russian	Cochairman, United Workers' Front of Russia
Iazov, D. T.	1923	24.3.90	Russian	Defense minister and marshal of the Soviet Union
Kauls, A. E.	1938	24.3.90	Latvian	Chairman, Adazhi Agricultural Society (agriculture)
Kriuchkov, V. A.*	1924	24.3.90	Russian	Chairman, Committee for State Security (KGB)
Luk'ianov, A. I.*	1930	15.3.90	Russian	Chairman, USSR Supreme Soviet; ex officio member
Masliukov, Iu. D.*	1937	24.3.90	Russian	Chairman, State Planning Commission (Gosplan)
Medvedev, V. A.*	1929	17.7.90	Russian	Advisor (mass media and communications); former Politburo member
Osip'ian, Iu. A.	1931	25.3.90	Armenian	Vice-President, USSR Academy of Sciences (science and technology)
Primakov, E. M.*	1929	26.3.90	Russian	Adviser (parties, organizations, parliaments, mass media)
Rasputin, V. G.	1937	24.3.90	Russian	Secretary, USSR Writers' Union; noncommunist (ecology and culture)

TABLE 2.2 (*continued*)

Name	Born	Election/ Appointment	Nationality	Responsibility
Revenko, G. I.	1936	26.3.90	Ukrainian	Adviser (nationality questions)
Ryzhkov, N. I.*	1929	24.3.90	Russian	Prime Minister, ex officio member (overall economy)
Shatalin, S. S.	1934	24.3.90	Russian	Advisor (socioeconomic policy)
Shevardnadze, E. A.*	1928	24.3.90	Georgian	Minister of foreign affairs

*Member of CPSU Political Bureau *before* twenty-eighth party congress

†Replaced as interior minister by Boris K. Pugo, who will probably become a presidential council member. *New York Times*, 4 December 1990, A-10.

SOURCES: Central Intelligence Agency, Directorate of Intelligence, *Directory of Soviet Officials: National Organizations* series LDA 90-14379 (Washington, D.C.: GPO, September 1990), pp. 1–2; Elizabeth Teague, "The Presidential Council," *Report on the USSR* 2, no. 14 (6 April 1990): 1–3; Alexander Rahr, "From Politburo to Presidential Council," *Report on the USSR*, no. 22 (1 June 1990): 1–5; *Izvestiia*, 18 July 1990, p. 1, for Medvedev appointment; Alexander Rahr, *USSR Presidential Council* (Munich: RFE/RL, October 1990), pp. 1–3; TASS, 4 November 1990, for Gubenko.

Fifteen of the nineteen members on the Presidential Council are of Great Russian ethnic background. In this respect the new body resembles the old Politburo, which gave only token representation to the other nationalities. The most unexpected appointment was that of Valentin G. Rasputin, who is an adherent of the Russian Orthodox church, a proponent of spiritual and moral regeneration, and the only non-CPSU member on the council. The other conservative is Veniamin A. Iarin, a former metal worker from the Urals and a populist who heads the *Rossiia* club of parliamentary deputies.

According to Evgenii M. Primakov, in an interview on 22 June 1990 with the *Novosti* Press Agency (APN), the Presidential Council lacked a staff and had not yet found a building. Gorbachev discussed the first council session over Soviet television, which also broadcast his opening address. He said that a "controlled transfer to market relations" had been discussed, although state ownership of the means of production would dominate the economy. The audience was told that independent-minded individuals who enjoyed the confidence of the people had been selected (and can be removed) by Gorbachev and that their task is to make available a wide range of policy options for the president.

An article based on interviews with seven of the Presidential Council members as well as Gorbachev himself gave the average age as 58.4 years, which is close to that of the president. Only one (V. A. Iarin) lacks a higher education. Fifteen are Russians, with one each from Armenia, Georgia, Latvia, and the Ukraine. All are men. The Council included three groups: presidential functionaries (Boldin, Primakov, Revenko, Iakovlev, Medvedev); the premier and his ministers (Ryzhkov, Bakatin, Gubenko, Iazov, Kriuchkov, Masliukov, Shevardnadze); and the remainder (Kauls, Luk'ianov, Osip'ian, Rasputin, Shatalin, Iarin). The second and third groups took part in drafting documents for the president.[6]

All policy decisions depend to a large extent on the quality of information. In the case of the Presidential Council, reports are prepared by political, economic, and military government agencies with representatives stationed abroad as well as by certain commissions within the central apparatus of the CPSU Secretariat, whose function may be transferred to the Presidential Council in the future. In addition, a classified and unedited digest of the foreign press, called *White TASS* after the color of its cover, is reportedly distributed among council members. Research centers like the Institute on the World Economy and International Relations (IMEMO) or one of the think tanks dealing with regional affairs may periodically submit information on specialized problems.

Data from independent sources are mandatory because only on this basis can decisions be made with reference to the outside world. One should not compare the current situation to conditions under Stalin or even Brezhnev, when the reporting system generally yielded information conforming to the leader's distorted image of areas outside USSR borders. Apparently some improvement has occurred. Distortions cannot be avoided completely, however, because many of those reporting from foreign countries evaluate developments in terms of a world outlook they have absorbed since kindergarten.

At the nineteenth CPSU conference in June 1988, Gorbachev stated that the quality of information on international affairs must be substantially improved. The objective was not only a more realistic assessment but also a higher quality of analysis that would permit policymakers to look at a range of options. New research units thus were established, such as a "scientific coordination center" for arms control analysis at the USSR Ministry of Foreign Affairs.[7]

In the past there were at least three different channels in which a matter might find its way onto the agenda of the decisionmakers, a system that may be adopted by the current group. First, each Presidential Council member's personal staff might gain a hearing for a subordinate. Second, the heads of government agencies' executive staffs could represent another channel for approaching the council. Finally, certain unrepresented ministries, such as the one charged with responsibility for foreign trade, might be called on to brief the Presidential Council on issues involving their areas of expertise.

It is likely that proposals originating at lower echelons within the governmental apparatus would be coordinated laterally, before submission, through one of the three channels mentioned above. In most cases, the next stage would involve clearance by the executive staff of the Presidential Council. This new organization might consider a particular question independently only if it deals with a matter of little significance. A process of review and approval, including staff work and in certain instances modification of a proposal, certainly would occur before submission to the Presidential Council. On 17 December 1990, the Congress of People's Deputies took up Gorbachev's proposal on concentrating all executive powers under his control, which would involve amendments to the constitution.

THE CENTRAL PARTY APPARATUS

The executive staff of the national CPSU Secretariat in the past represented the main locus of power for both formulation of policy alternatives (though not decision making per se) and subsequent implementation. Until 30 September 1988 the central apparatus had twenty-two departments employing about one thousand persons in its various branches and sections. Each department's responsibilities were carefully defined. After September 1988, a reorganization established six commissions with only nine subordinate departments.[8] For the 9 October 1990 reorganization into a larger number of units, see figure 2.1.

For example, the Administration of Affairs Department supervised administrative operations of the entire central apparatus. The Military Policy Commission had performed the same function for twelve ministries—defense industry, aviation, shipbuilding, electronics, radio industry, communications equipment, chemical industry, electrical equipment, petrochemical industry, general machine building, machine building, and medium machine building (a cover name for nuclear weapons production)—all of which work on requirements for the armed forces. The Main Political Directorate of the Armed Forces, a Central Committee department, exercised political control over the military until it reverted to the Defense Ministry. The General Department was responsible for all staff work and the Politburo's agenda. Administrative Organs, absorbed by the new Security Council under the president, approved important appointments in the armed forces and the KGB through the *nomenklatura* system, which may include up to 750,000 positions in the CPSU and the government. The system is under heavy criticism.[9] The Cadres Abroad section, now under the expanded International Policy Commission, decided on travel by key personnel to foreign countries.

CPSU relations with other political parties and movements were handled by the old International Department, with subsections for nonruling communist parties and noncommunist movements as well as liaison with the bloc for those communist parties in power. Either subsection may have had representatives in a Soviet embassy, depending on the status of indigenous communists.

Until the end of September 1988, the International Department[10] exercised decisive influence on Soviet foreign policy. Since then it has been headed by V. M. Falin and subordinated to the new International Policy Commission, although the International Department still controlled the monthly journal *World Marxist Review* until it closed down after the June 1990 issue. Several deputy chiefs' responsibilities were allocated to them by geographic area or function (for example, arms control or international communist front organizations). More than fifty others had been identified in the Soviet press as section heads, their deputies, and other high-ranking officials. That number, of course, has been reduced substantially.

The central apparatus at the end of 1989 reportedly had the following functions:

FIGURE 2.1
THE 1990 CENTRAL PARTY MACHINE

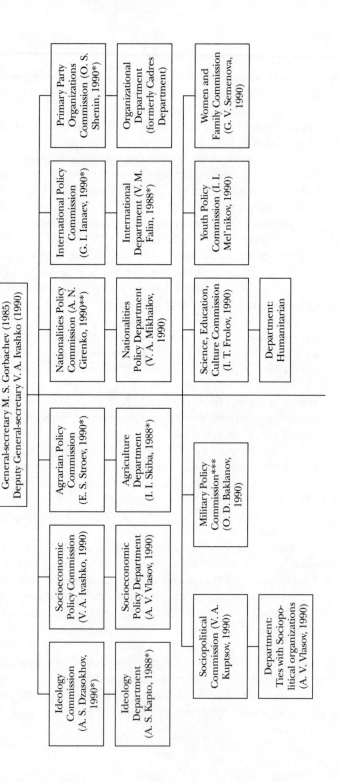

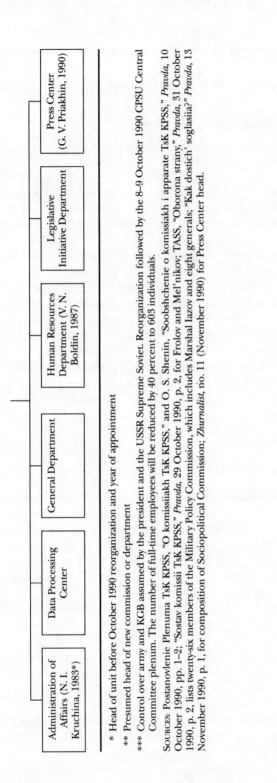

| Administration of Affairs (N. I. Kruchina, 1983*) | Data Processing Center | General Department | Human Resources Department (V. N. Boldina, 1987) | Legislative Initiative Department | Press Center (G. V. Priakhin, 1990) |

* Head of unit before October 1990 reorganization and year of appointment

** Presumed head of new commission or department

*** Control over army and KGB assumed by the president and the USSR Supreme Soviet. Reorganization followed by the 8–9 October 1990 CPSU Central Committee plenum. The number of full-time employees will be reduced by 40 percent to 603 individuals.

Sources: Postanovlenie Plenuma TsK KPSS, "O komissiiakh TsK KPSS," and O. S. Shenin, "Soobshchenie o komissiiakh i apparate TsK KPSS," *Pravda*, 10 October 1990, pp. 1–2; "Sostav komissii TsK KPSS," *Pravda*, 29 October 1990, p. 2, for Frolov and Mel'nikov; TASS, "Oborona strany," *Pravda*, 31 October 1990, p. 2, lists twenty-six members of the Military Policy Commission, which includes Marshal Iazov and eight generals; "Kak dostich' soglasiia?" *Pravda*, 13 November 1990, p. 1, for composition of Sociopolitical Commission; *Zhurnalist*, no. 11 (November 1990) for Press Center head.

1. Preparation of proposals for elective CPSU organs
2. Ideological work
3. Participation in administrative management[11]

Little information is available on how the Secretariat actually operated. Each national secretary involved with foreign affairs, however, must have exercised considerable power in his own right by virtue of having been in a position to deny access to the Politburo. The full Secretariat reportedly held only 97 meetings—fewer than the 187 by the Politburo—during 1986–1990.[12]

By resolution of a CPSU Central Committee plenum on 28 November 1988, authority over the central party apparatus (that is, all departments) was transferred from the Secretariat to six newly established commissions, each headed by a national secretary. This helped delineate clear responsibilities and strengthened Gorbachev's position by diffusing power among many subordinates. The six commissions had a total membership of only 138 CPSU officials. They were to meet at least once every three months,[13] although announcements in *Pravda* since that time suggest that this schedule had not been followed. The work of these commissions has been restricted to communist party affairs since the establishment of the Presidential Council in March 1990.

RESEARCH INSTITUTES AND ADVISERS

In addition to handling the general information flow for reports and drawing up the Presidential Council's agenda, the new executive staff most probably reviews position papers submitted by various government agencies and specialized research institutes before they are transmitted to the council. Among the best known of the "think tanks" are IMEMO, the Institute of the USA and Canada (ISKAN), and the corresponding regional institutes for Africa, the Far East, Latin America, and Western Europe.[14]

Founded in 1956, IMEMO had been headed from its inception by CPSU Central Committee member N. N. Inozemtsev, who died in 1983. He was succeeded by A. N. Iakovlev, current adviser to Gorbachev on the Presidential Council, who held the position for about a year. The third director was E. M. Primakov, elected candidate Politburo member (on 20 September 1989) and chosen in July 1990 for the Presidential Council. He was succeeded by a former deputy director, V. A. Martynov. This institute, with more than one thousand research and support personnel, may still be the leading center for the study of international affairs, although it overlaps with the regional ones mentioned above. An apparent duplication of effort takes place with regard to the so-called national liberation movements throughout Africa, Latin America, and Asia. Apart from the Russian-language journal, *Mirovaia ekonomika i mezhdunarodnye otnoshenia (World Economics and International Relations)*, IMEMO provided urgently needed ad hoc reports and *sitans* (situation analyses) for the previous Politburo.

Since its establishment in November 1967, ISKAN, with more than three hundred specialists, has been directed by G. A. Arbatov, a full Central Committee member.[15] In his memoirs, a former U.S. secretary of state gives the following assessment of this man:

> Arbatov was a faithful expounder of the Kremlin line, whom I had met at various international conferences on arms control when I was still a professor. He knew much about America and was skillful in adjusting his arguments to the prevailing fashions. He was especially subtle in playing to the inexhaustible masochism of American intellectuals who took it as an article of faith that every difficulty in U.S.-Soviet relations had to be caused by American stupidity or intransigence. He was endlessly ingenious in demonstrating how American rebuffs were frustrating the peaceful, sensitive leaders in the Kremlin, who were being driven reluctantly by our inflexibility into conflicts that offended their inherently gentle natures.[16]

Galina Orionova, who worked for ten years at Arbatov's research center and subsequently defected at Heathrow Airport in London, flatly states that ISKAN had no impact on Soviet foreign policy during the late 1970s and early 1980s. She claims it was being used to influence the United States by means of disinformation. A KGB general, R. G. Bogdanov, served as Ideology Department head and one of the three deputy directors for the institute at that time, according to Orionova.[17] Domestic developments and foreign relations of the United States are covered in the institute's monthly magazine, *SShA: Ekonomika, politika, ideologiia (USA: Economics, Politics, Ideology)*.

The Africa Institute, which was organized in 1959, was first headed by a former IMEMO director, V. G. Solodovnikov. He was succeeded in December 1976 by A. A. Gromyko (son of the then foreign minister), who previously served as a section chief at ISKAN. Apart from Soviet relations with Africa, the almost five hundred members of this research center study the so-called noncapitalist path of development, various economic and sociopolitical problems, the phenomenon of "neocolonialism," and the effects of Chinese influence in the Third World.

The Far East Institute publishes *Problemy dal'nego vostoka (Problems of the Far East)*. It has a staff of more than three hundred and, beginning with its establishment in 1961, was directed by M. I. Sladkovskii, who was succeeded in July 1985 by M. L. Titarenko. Most research efforts are concentrated on the People's Republic of China. The institute works closely with IMEMO, particularly regarding Japan. Information about Far Eastern studies is difficult to obtain, perhaps because of the sensitivity regarding Sino-Soviet relations in general.[18]

The Africa and Far East institutes jointly publish two magazines, *Narody Azii i Afriki (Peoples of Asia and Africa)* and *Azia i Afrika segodnia (Asia and Africa Today)*, in Russian, English, and French. The Oriental Studies Institute, headed by M. S. Kapitsa, concentrates on most of Asia and the Middle East.

The Latin America Institute, founded in 1961, has been led by V. V. Vol'skii since March 1966 and publishes a bimonthly journal in Russian called *Latinskaia Amerika (Latin America)*. Research sections deal with economics, sociopolitical problems, foreign policy and international relations, culture, and the Cuban regime as a model for other countries in the Western Hemisphere. The institute has expanded its staff to more than 350, in line with growing contacts between that part of the world and the USSR.

A relatively new Institute for (West) European Studies is headed by V. V. Zhurkin, formerly the deputy director of ISKAN. Established in May 1988, it is subordinate to the Problems of World Economics and International Relations Department in the USSR Academy of Science. Research work focuses on foreign policy formation in Western Europe.

These research institutes provide analyses of current foreign policy issues and engage in projects that may appear as journal articles or books. IMEMO reportedly receives assignments from both the CPSU Central Committee and the USSR Ministry of Foreign Affairs. Such institutes also serve as talent banks, with temporary assignments for their personnel at Soviet diplomatic installations abroad.[19]

In addition to the above, Gorbachev relies on foreign affairs advisers who most probably contribute to policy-making decisions. (See table 2.3.) They are not CPSU bureaucrats and hence would be expected to offer relatively unbiased opinions. These advisers have included Abel G. Aganbegian, Evgenii M. Primakov, and Tat'iana I. Zaslavskaia for economic problems; Anatolii S. Cherniaev as the principal assistant for superpower relations; Ivan T. Frolov, the aide for ideological questions; Georgii K. Shakhnazarov, for relations with the communist-ruled states of the world; and others.[20]

SHORT- AND LONG-RANGE PLANS

Although the central party apparatus submitted proposals to the old Politburo, there is no specific evidence that it ever functioned as a long-range

TABLE 2.3
PROBABLE FOREIGN POLICY-MAKING TEAMS, 1990

Diplomacy and Trade	Military and Intelligence	World Communism and Propaganda
Gorbachev, M. S.	Gorbachev, M. S.	Gorbachev, M. S.
Iakovlev, A. N.	Kriuchkov, V. A.	Medvedev, V. A.
Shevardnadze, E. A.	Iazov, D. T.	Primakov, E. M.
Adviser	*Adviser*	*Adviser*
Masliukov, Iu. D.	Baklanov, O. D.	Falin, V. M.

Position/Responsibility:

1. Gorbachev	CPSU general secretary; chairman, Defense Council; chief of state
2. Iakovlev	Ideology and security organs
3. Shevardnadze	Foreign minister
4. Masliukov	Chairman, Gosplan
5. Kriuchkov	Chairman, KGB
6. Iazov	Defense minister
7. Baklanov	Secretary for CPSU military policy
8. Medvedev	Member, Presidential Council
9. Primakov	Mass media
10. Falin	Secretary for international affairs

SOURCES: Central Intelligence Agency, Directorate of Intelligence, *Directory of Soviet Officials: National Organizations,* series LDA 90-14379 (Washington, D.C.: GPO, September 1990); and current press identifications.

planning staff in foreign affairs but may have done such work on an ad hoc basis. If a project involved several areas of responsibility, a small group of secretaries would form a subcommittee, which might study reports and policy papers, arriving at a consensus as a basis for recommendations. The expertise and personality of each subcommittee participant would certainly have influenced the proposed course of action.

Individual commissions and through them departments in the central party apparatus received, processed, and analyzed data on which foreign policy staff studies were based. These commissions maintained contact with Soviet diplomatic and military installations abroad, which sent communications directly to them or through an intermediary like the Chief Intelligence Directorate (GRU) of the Defense Ministry. In the past some of this information came via East-Central European military attachés and other bloc intelligence officers (for example, Cubans) stationed abroad or even from members of nonruling foreign communist parties loyal to Moscow.

For current Soviet foreign policy to remain both consistent and coordinated, the new Security Council will most likely submit two types of plans: (1) a strategic one, setting forth the basic objectives for different geographic areas of the world to be implemented within a relatively long-range time frame, and (2) an operational one for individual countries, which would delineate specific goals to fulfill overall objectives.

These plans, especially the short-range operational type, will probably be reviewed by the Ministry of Foreign Affairs or even originate there, for this is the governmental agency that implements foreign policy decisions. Along with the career diplomats, there are representatives of other government departments stationed at Soviet missions abroad. The several USSR intelligence services work independently of one another, probably even on a competitive basis.[21] Organizations whose operatives report directly to their own headquarters in Moscow, bypassing the ambassador, include the secret police (KGB) as well as military intelligence (GRU) and the Ministry of Foreign Economic Relations.

The Foreign Economic Relations ministry is the official vehicle through which foreign aid and military assistance are channeled to recipient countries and to so-called national liberation movements abroad. In addition, this agency has commercial personnel as part of the Soviet embassy. Yet another organization involved in this field is the Council for Mutual Economic Assistance, particularly in less-developed countries where East-Central European regimes in the past had provided foreign aid in coordination with the Soviet Union (see chapter 8).

The foregoing, although sensible in theory, did not work in practice. V. V. Zagladin, first deputy chief of the CPSU International Department at the time, revealed that major errors in foreign policy had been committed because of "conceptual inconsistency" and a concentration on polemics as well as propaganda. V. I. Dashichev, an historian at the Institute for Economics of the World Socialist System, stated to an American journalist that for many years Soviet foreign policy lacked any "thought-out, sensible, and scientifically grounded actions."[22]

THE SUCCESSION PROBLEM

The CPSU ended its twenty-sixth congress on 3 March 1981 with unanimous reelection of all Politburo members and candidates as well as all Central Committee secretaries. In the unlikely event that these same individuals had remained in their positions until the next congress met in 1986, their average age would have been seventy-five, almost double that of the 1919 leadership. Many changes have occurred since Leonid I. Brezhnev's death in November 1982 and his replacement by Iurii V. Andropov, who died fifteen months later, in February 1984. The latter's successor, Konstantin U. Chernenko, lasted a little more than a year. The current leader, Mikhail S. Gorbachev, was formally confirmed as general secretary by the CPSU Central Committee on 11 March 1985.

Before that date and for some time thereafter, the Politburo core group was composed almost entirely of individuals who had reached the supreme decision-making level after Stalin's terror machine had cleared the way for their advancement. During the great purge[23] of the mid-1930s, they vigorously denounced their superiors from their relatively safe third- and fourth-echelon positions. Most of them had not completed even a secondary education, having been selected for technical or political training with only an elementary school background. Many, thus, were semieducated, with their outlooks constrained by ideological blinders and their advancement dependent on ruthless cunning.

Certain analysts in the West expressed the hope that after Stalin's death the new generation of Soviet leaders might be different. Those who were in a position to succeed the gerontocracy, however, had been recruited into the party machine from among local Komsomol (Communist Youth Union) secretaries and thus were totally devoted to the system. They could not have reached positions close to the top without absolute dedication to their superiors. This new generation remained narrow-minded and cynical in its opposition to foreign governments, even communist-ruled ones, that were not under USSR influence. This mentality can be summed up by Lenin's slogan, *kto kogo*? or "who (will eliminate) whom?"

One great weakness of the Soviet system was that there had been no means for any constitutional transfer of power or for removal of overaged leaders except by conspiracy. In the past, heirs apparent fell victim to intrigue by rivals or became impatient to assume the mantle. The most recent example was Brezhnev himself who came to power after a successful plot in October 1964 against his benefactor, N. S. Khrushchev.[24]

Before Brezhnev's death, it seemed that the favorite to succeed him as party leader would be Chernenko, who had been promoted to secretary of the Central Committee and to candidate and then full Politburo member within two years. Such a rapid rise was unusual. A protégé of the general secretary, Chernenko was the youngest politburocrat to possess all prerequisites for the top position: ethnic Russian background, experience in the party apparatus, some knowledge of both foreign as well as economic affairs, and membership in the Brezhnev faction.[25] These qualifications did not ensure immediate success, however.

On 29 December 1988, the Kremlin issued an order to remove the names of Brezhnev and Chernenko from all towns, factories, farms, streets, ships, and the like. *Sic transit gloria mundi.* (On 8 July 1989, however, this writer saw a Soviet cruise ship named the *Leonid Brezhnev* at the port of Leningrad.) In December 1989, Brezhnev, who died in 1982, was stripped of the Order of Victory "because he did not deserve it." The transfer of power before 1985 has been described by an insider as "a system where people arrive in the country's leadership . . . by means of backstage deals, or worse, conspiracies and bloody purges." This Soviet writer went on to state that none of the leaders, not even Lenin, had trained a successor. "So a reform of the entire tradition of political leadership is needed."[26]

THE ANDROPOV INTERLUDE

Although much of what follows is based on informed speculation, the final stage in the struggle for power to succeed Brezhnev probably commenced in January 1982 after chief ideologist M. A. Suslov died. At that time the KGB arrested, for possession of stolen diamonds, a certain Boris Buriatia, who happened to be a friend of Brezhnev's daughter, Galina L. Churbanova. Such a development, that is, the arrest of an individual close to the general secretary's immediate family, indicated that the party/state chief may no longer have been in full control. Brezhnev reportedly suffered heart spasms during both February and March. The following month, Andropov delivered the address commemorating Lenin's birthday; by May, Andropov had succeeded the late Suslov as secretary in charge of ideology, the position that heir apparent Chernenko should have received.[27]

Next came the KGB disinformation campaign directed toward Western journalists that portrayed Andropov as an educated and cultured individual who spoke English and had an affinity for jazz. Supposedly, he voted in the Politburo against both the invasion of Afghanistan and the imposition of martial law throughout Poland. Scientists and intellectuals, he allegedly believed, should have access to scholarly publications from the West. The "liberal" Andropov, if he assumed power, would promote Jews to high positions in the Soviet Union. None of these "leaks" could be corroborated, and none of them corresponded to the man's actual background.[28]

In fact, Andropov began his career by assisting in the deportation of thousands of inhabitants from the Karelo-Finnish Republic—that part of Finland occupied by the Red Army—to forced labor camps in the Gulag Archipelago during 1940–1941. As ambassador to Budapest in 1956, he personally promised safe-conduct to Premier Imre Nagy and other Hungarian cabinet members. Instead, they were arrested and then executed after two years in prison. Under the fifteen-year chairmanship of Andropov, the KGB introduced the use of psychiatric hospitals to suppress dissidents.[29] This career pattern should have led observers to conclude that the new Soviet leader would be a ruthless individual and much more dangerous to deal with than his predecessor.

Andropov became chairman of the Supreme Soviet presidium (chief of state) on 16 June 1983, which gave him the third key post in the USSR. He had been identified previously as occupying the Defense Council chairmanship. Thus, in a little more than six months, Andropov attained what it had taken Brezhnev thirteen years to accomplish. At the end of 1983 it was anticipated that the new leader would appear either at the Central Committee plenum or the meeting of the USSR Supreme Soviet during the last week of December, although he had not been seen since 18 August. Suffering from a protracted illness, he attended neither. Nonetheless, other Central Committee plenary sessions promoted several Andropov supporters.

Despite the statements and speeches read in Andropov's name, the decision-making process seemed to have become moribund. Nobody appeared to know whether the leader would return to his office in the Kremlin; hence, the situation resembled a stalemate. Moreover, even on the expanded thirteen-member Politburo, the lineup did not overwhelmingly favor the ailing general secretary.

On the one hand, because of this delicate balance of power, Andropov had to move cautiously and slowly in consolidating his power position. On the other hand, many low-ranking leaders (seventy-five or older) were retired from Central Committee membership, Secretariat departments, government ministries, lower-ranking CPSU organizations (including 20 percent of the regional first secretaries), and even embassies in an attempt to break up the fossilization of the apparatus. This process reflected the tension between the Andropov and Chernenko factions, with the latter supporting the status quo.

ASCENDANCY OF CHERNENKO

Andropov, already ten years older[30] than either Brezhnev or Khrushchev when they acceded to power, died on 9 February 1984. Chernenko, elected four days later as the new CPSU general secretary, was of the same generation as his predecessor. In choosing him, the Politburo probably considered seniority and experience in the central party apparatus,[31] as well as the difficulties that might have resulted if a new leader had been selected from among the younger politburocrats, any one of whom might have been tempted to retire the septuagenarians.

Chernenko's appointment as funeral commission chairman signaled that he would be Andropov's successor, and there seems to have been no other serious contender. The old guard dominated the scene, with Chernenko (then seventy-two), Andrei A. Gromyko (seventy-four), and Dmitrii F. Ustinov (seventy-five) as the main speakers at the funeral. Nikolai A. Tikhonov (seventy-eight) proposed only one candidate for general secretary, and the motion was unanimously endorsed by the Politburo. Two months later the Supreme Soviet, also without a single dissenting vote, elected Chernenko chairman of its presidium, or titular USSR president. This time, Gorbachev (fifty-three) made the nominating speech.[32]

Gorbachev apparently ranked third, after Chernenko and Tikhonov, in the official hierarchy, a status confirmed by his place (third from last) among the speakers during the February-March 1984 election campaign for the Supreme Soviet. These and other signs seemed to indicate Gorbachev's emergence as the unofficial second secretary or deputy to Chernenko.[33] Whether he would remain the heir apparent, and for how long, could not have been predicted. In the past, individuals in such a position had often been eliminated from the race.

Among the twelve full Politburo members, only three others besides Gorbachev were at that time under sixty-five: G. A. Aliev (sixty-one), G. V. Romanov (sixty-one), and V. I. Vorotnikov (fifty-seven). Aliev was an Azerbaijani and had served as KGB chief in his native republic, both of which should have disqualified him from becoming the next general secretary. Vorotnikov would seem to have had a better chance, for he had foreign affairs experience as ambassador to Cuba (1979–1982). Interestingly, he was not retired from the Politburo until 20 September 1989.

In the past the leader had been a Central Committee secretary in addition to holding Politburo membership. Only two contenders were in this category: Gorbachev and Romanov.[34] Romanov apparently had a good record as CPSU first secretary for Leningrad province before he moved to Moscow. His family name, however—the same as that of the last tsarist dynasty—conjured up images of the ancien régime that were unwelcome to the communists.

Neither should one have discounted the two candidate Politburo members who were also national secretaries: B. N. Ponomarev (seventy-nine) and V. I. Dolgikh (sixty). Ponomarev would seem to have been eliminated from consideration because of age. Dolgikh had been in charge of the heavy industry department (1976–1984) in the central party apparatus and later supervised that important area of the economy. In addition, he gave the anniversary address[35] commemorating Lenin's birthday in 1984, which suggested possible future promotion to full Politburo status. Note that in 1981, Chernenko delivered this speech as Brezhnev's protégé and heir apparent.

GORBACHEV AT THE TOP

This time, however, the heir apparent did emerge as general secretary. Of peasant stock, Mikhail S. Gorbachev was born in the Stavropol region on a collective farm, where his father served as chairman. Because of young Gorbachev's work at a local machine-tractor station and his activities in the Communist Youth Union (Komsomol), he was selected to study law at Moscow State University. As secretary of the Komsomol organization in the law school, Gorbachev reportedly assisted the KGB in developing cases against other students.[36]

The new CPSU leader, who was elected unopposed and unanimously as general secretary on 11 March 1985, never practiced law, becoming instead a full-time apparatus worker. The late KGB chief Andropov promoted Gorbachev and saw to his protégé's advancement. A. A. Gromyko, who nominated Gorbachev, said, "this man has a nice smile but iron teeth." The new CPSU leader removed his only serious rival, Romanov, on 1 July and began co-opting supporters into the Politburo. The Central Committee chosen by the twenty-seventh CPSU congress confirmed Gorbachev in his position almost exactly one year after the initial election, and he was reelected on 14 July 1990 following the twenty-eighth congress. General Secretary Gorbachev seized the opportunity to direct foreign policy and see that it would be executed.

To establish control over the external affairs establishment, Gorbachev elevated veteran Foreign Minister A. A. Gromyko in 1985 to titular chief of state (USSR Supreme Soviet presidium chairman), replacing him with E. A. Shevardnadze, who had no previous experience in foreign policy. The new general secretary next began to strengthen the decision-making process in the International Department (ID) of the CPSU central apparatus.

A. F. Dobrynin became ID head in 1986, with control over diplomatic appointments and supervision of the Department for Cadres Abroad, which trained foreign service officers. He was given two first deputies, V. V. Zagladin, for CPSU relations with both developed as well as developing countries, and G. M. Kornienko (transferred from first deputy minister of foreign affairs) for arms control. Dobrynin was placed in charge of super-power relations, evidenced by Lt. Gen. V. P. Starodubov joining the ID staff from the U.S.-Soviet Standing Consultative Commission in Geneva.[37]

In 1987 Gorbachev transferred his personal aide, V. I. Boldin, to head the General Department, which not only functioned as central chancery but also controlled CPSU security and communications. Registering and verifying all classified documents, it was known as the Special Section (*osobyi otdel*) under Stalin. Thus, within two years, the Foreign Affairs Ministry had lost all its decision-making powers and retained only the implementation functions. As a French newspaper editorialized, "One is left with the uncomfortable feeling—which underlines the distance that still separates the USSR from democratic systems—that everything, or almost everything, depends on the personality of a single man."[38] The next chapter discusses how and why the USSR Ministry of Foreign Affairs has regained lost authority.

NOTES

1. U.S. Congress, Senate, Committee on Government Operations, Subcommittee on National Security Staffing and Operations, *Study on Staffing Procedures and Problems in the Soviet Union*, 88th Cong., 1st Sess., 1963, p. 24.

2. Chapter 3, article 28, "Vysshie i tsentral'nye organy KPSS," *Pravda*, 18 July 1990, p. 2.

3. L. N. Zaikov, "Otchety chlenov Politbiuro," *Pravda*, 4 July 1990, p. 3.

4. "Vladimir Antonovich Ivashko," *Pravda*, 13 July 1990, p. 1. For a listing of all Politburo and Secretariat members since 1919, see "Sostav rukovodiashchikh organov tsentral'nogo komiteta partii (1919–1990 gg.)," *Izvestiia TsK KPSS*, no. 7 (July 1990): 69–82.

5. V. Urban, "Rabochii v Prezidentskom sovete," *Krasnaia zvezda*, 27 March 1990, p. 1; Central Television, 27 March 1990, cited by Alexander Rahr in *Report on the USSR*, 1 June 1990, note 21 on p. 2.

6. Egor Iakovlev, "Prezidentskii sovet," *Moskovskie novosti*, no. 33 (19 August 1990): 8–9. One of the original members, Chingiz Aitmanov, told the Associated Press that he would resign to become USSR ambassador to Luxembourg. Radio Free Europe/Radio Liberty, *Daily Report*, no. 203 (24 October 1990): 3.

7. E. A. Shevardnadze, "Vneshniaia politika i diplomatiia," *Pravda*, 26 July 1988, p. 4, elaborated on Gorbachev's comments. See also O. G. Peresypkin, "Nauki na sluzhbu politike," *Pravda*, 24 June 1988, p. 5, for the new research center; the author of that article became director of the Diplomatic Academy in 1986.

8. Listed with incumbent chiefs and subordinate administrators in Central Intelligence Agency, *Directory of Soviet Officials: National Organizations*, series LDA 90–14379 (Washington, D.C.: GPO, September 1990), pp. 151–56.

9. On this key personnel appointment system, see Michael Voslensky, *Nomenklatura: The Soviet Ruling Class* (Garden City, N.Y.: Doubleday, 1984), especially pp. 356–85. See also "Nomenklatura kadrov," in I. A. Shvets, ed., *Slovar' po partiinomu stroitel'stvu* (Moscow: Politizdat, 1987), pp. 156–57. The system will become decentralized and CPSU secretaries elected rather than appointed

on the basis of recommendations by the old Cadre Policy Commission according to "Zasedanie komissii TsK KPSS," *Pravda*, 15 October 1989, p. 2.

10. Robert W. Kitrinos, "International Department of the CPSU," *Problems of Communism* 33, no. 5 (September-October 1984): 47–75; Wallace Spaulding, "Shifts in CPSU ID," *Problems of Communism* 35, no. 4 (July-August 1986): 80–86; U.S. Department of State, *The International Department of the CC CPSU under Dobrynin* (Washington, D.C.: Foreign Service Institute, September 1989), pp. 179.

11. V. Zhuravlev and M. Kodin, "Apparat—dlia politiki," *Pravda*, 28 October 1989, p. 2.

12. "Politburo TsK KPSS" and "Sekretariat TsK KPSS," in *Izvestiia TsK KPSS*, no. 9 (September 1990): 19 and 21, respectively.

13. "O komissiakh tsentral'nogo komiteta KPSS," *Pravda*, 29 November 1988, pp. 1–2. See also Theodore W. Karasik, *The CPSU Central Committee: Members, Commissions, and Departments* (Sherman Oaks, Calif.: September 1990).

14. Richard S. Soll, Arthur Zuehlke, Jr., and Richard B. Foster, *The Role of Social Science Research Institutes in Formulation and Execution of Soviet Foreign Policy* (Arlington, Va.: SRI Strategic Center, n.d.), pp. 18–31. This same source lists on pp. 58 and 59 about a dozen relatives of high-ranking CPSU officials who work at these institutes, which suggests widespread nepotism.

See also Igor S. Glagolev, *Post-Andropov Kremlin Strategy* (Washington, D.C.: Association for Cooperation with Democratic Countries, 1984), pp. 21–26, on his work at IMEMO. Yury Polsky, *Soviet Research Institutes and the Formulation of Foreign Policy: IMEMO* (Falls Church, Va.: Delphic Associates, 1987), pp. 38–39, provides more recent information.

15. V. A. Fedorovich, "Institut SShA i Kanady Akademii Nauk SSSR," *SShA: Ekonomika, politika, ideologiia*, no. 5 (May 1974): 12–16; Central Intelligence Agency, *Biographic Report: USSR Institute of the United States of America and Canada*, series CR 76–10864 (Washington, D.C.: GPO, April 1976), pp. 3–4. Arbatov became a member of the CPSU Commission on International Policies, according to "O Komissiakh Tsentral'nogo Komiteta," *Pravda*, 29 November 1988, p. 2.

16. Henry Kissinger, *White House Years* (Boston: Little, Brown, 1979), p. 112. For KGB connections within Arbatov's institute, see Glagolev, *Post-Andropov*, pp. 79–80. Polsky, *Soviet Research Institutes*, pp. 59–61, discusses joint publications between IMEMO and ISKAN.

17. Barbara L. Dash, *A Defector Reports: The Institute of the USA and Canada* (Falls Church, Va.: Delphic Associates, May 1982). This volume includes a 198-page appendix of biographical sketches. See also Central Intelligence Agency, *Foreign Studies Institutes of the USSR Academy of Sciences*, LDA 88–13522 (Washington, D.C.: GPO, July 1988), for the seven main research centers.

18. Soll et al., *Role of Social Science Research Institutes*, pp. 27–30. Numbers of institute staffs are from Daniel C. Matuszewski, "Soviet International Relations Research," *Foreign Area Research in the National Interest: American and Soviet Perspectives* (New York: International Research and Exchanges Board), *IREX*

Occasional Papers 1, no. 8 (1982): 33–44. Dr. Matuszewski states that seventy-four hundred specialists work at twelve key Moscow institutes.

19. Polsky, *Soviet Research Institutes*, pp. 100–102. For a listing of key institute personnel and brief descriptions, see Central Intelligence Agency, *Directory of Soviet Officials* (September 1990), pp. 192–96.

20. Alexander Rahr, "Gorbachev's Personal Staff," *Radio Liberty Report*, no. 216/88 (30 May 1988); *Directory of Soviet Officials* (September 1990), pp. 146, 149, 151, 158, 179, 181.

21. Ladislav Bittman, *The KGB and Soviet Disinformation* (Washington, D.C.: Pergamon-Brassey's, 1985), pp. 18–19.

22. Moscow radio, 30 July 1988; *Foreign Broadcast Information Service-Soviet Union* 88–147 (1 August 1988): 59, for Zagladin. Dashichev is quoted by Michael Parks in the *Los Angeles Times*, 30 August 1988, p. 10.

23. Robert Conquest, *The Great Terror: A Reassessment* (New York: Oxford University Press, 1990), pp. 484–89.

24. The KGB, not ideologist Mikhail A. Suslov or Brezhnev, orchestrated this plot according to Fedor Burlatskii, "Brezhnev i krushenie ottepeli," *Literaturnaia gazeta*, 14 September 1988, pp. 13–14. See also Roy Medvedev, "Advantages of Mediocrity," *Moscow News*, no. 37 (1988): 8–9, for a political profile of Brezhnev.

25. R. Judson Mitchell, "The Soviet Succession," *Orbis* 23, no. 1 (Spring 1979): 25. See also Joseph G. Whelan, "Soviet Successions from Lenin to Brezhnev: The Troubled Search for Legitimacy," *Congressional Research Service*, report no. 82–152S (20 September 1982), mimeographed.

26. Burlatskii, "Brezhnev i krushenie ottepeli." See also Michael Dobbs in the *Washington Post*, 30 December 1988, pp. 1 and 27, and AP despatch in the *International Herald Tribune* (Paris), 29 September 1989, p. 4.

27. Andrew Nagorski, "The Making of Andropov," *Harper's*, February 1983, pp. 23–26. See also Amy W. Knight, "Andropov: Myths and Realities," *Survey* 28, no. 1 (Spring 1984): 22–44.

28. Official biography in *Sovetskaia voennaia entsiklopediia* (Moscow: Voenizdat, 1976), p. 193. See also the study by Arnold Beichman and Mikhail S. Bernstam, *Andropov: New Challenge to the West* (New York: Stein & Day, 1983).

29. Charles Krauthammer, "The Andropov Factor," *New Republic*, 13 June 1983, pp. 19–21.

30. Ages at accession to power of the last three leaders increased over the years as follows: Lenin (forty-seven), Stalin (forty-four), Khrushchev (fifty-eight), Brezhnev (fifty-seven), Andropov (sixty-eight), and Chernenko (seventy-two). See also Myron Rush, "Succeeding Brezhnev," *Problems of Communism* 32, no. 1 (January-February 1983): 2–17.

31. On the unimpressive background of Chernenko, see *Strategic Survey, 1983–1984* (London: International Institute for Strategic Studies, 1984), pp. 50–51. He completed primary school at age twelve and much later served three years with the border guards, after which he attended the Higher School for Party Organizers.

32. See "Ob izbranii Prezidiuma Verkhovnogo Soveta SSSR," for election of Chernenko, and "Trud i znaniia, partii, rodine," for Gorbachev's speech in *Pravda*, 12 April 1984, pp. 1–2.

33. V. G. Afanas'ev, then editor of *Pravda*, during an interview with *Dagens Nyheter*, 15 March 1984, in Stockholm, made a flat statement to this effect.

34. R. Judson Mitchell, *Getting to the Top in the USSR: Cyclical Patterns in the Leadership Succession Process* (Stanford: Hoover Institution Press, 1990), pp. 131–34.

35. "Uchenie i delo Lenina Doklad tovarishcha V. I. Dolgikh," *Pravda*, 21 April 1984, pp. 1–2.

36. Andrew A. Michta, *An Emigré Reports: Fridrikh Neznansky on Mikhail Gorbachev: 1950–1958* (Falls Church, Va.: Delphic Associates, October 1985), p. 55. See also R. Judson Mitchell and Teresa Gee, "The Soviet Succession Crisis," *Orbis* 29, no. 2 (Summer 1985): 293–317.

37. Alexander Rahr, "Turnover in the Central Party Apparatus," *Radio Liberty Research* 256/87 (9 July 1987): 6.

38. Gorbachev has been described by a former Moscow law school classmate, Zdeněk Mlynář, as a "true believer in Marxism." See Jackson Diehl, "A Portrait of Gorbachev as a Young Reformer," *Washington Post*, 7 November 1987, pp. A-1 and A-19.

   Time magazine named Gorbachev its Man of the Year for 1989, a symbol of hope for a new Soviet Union. This same award had been won by Stalin twice (1939 and 1942), Khrushchev once (1957), and shared by Andropov with U.S. President Ronald Reagan (1983).

3

IMPLEMENTATION OF FOREIGN POLICY

As discussed in the preceding chapter, policy decisions in matters of great importance are made by M. S. Gorbachev, who received advice from his Presidential Council, on which the foreign minister served. Implementation of external policies is effected primarily through the Ministry of Foreign Affairs, while administration of military aid and civilian-type foreign assistance in general falls within the purview of the Defense and Foreign Economic Relations ministries. The daily functions of the Foreign Affairs Ministry, according to a standard textbook used at the USSR Diplomatic Academy, included

> the study of international conditions, external and domestic policies of foreign governments, international organizations and movements; [provision of] timely information to the Central Committee and Soviet leadership on international events deserving their attention; submission of suitable recommendations on necessary action in the interest of strengthening peace, cooperation between governments, and in the struggle against the aggressive activities of imperialistic forces.[1]

Ever since Gorbachev's address to the Congress of People's Deputies on 30 May 1989, the Foreign Affairs Ministry has been submitting major treaties to the USSR Supreme Soviet. It is the responsibility of A. I. Luk'ianov, as chairman of this legislature, to oversee discussion and approval of such agreements. He also had the right to attend meetings of the Presidential Council. The international affairs (joint) committee of the Supreme Soviet is chaired by A. S. Dzasokhov, one of Gorbachev's foreign policy advisers and a member of the CPSU Politburo.[2] The new system of legislative committees seems patterned after Western institutions.

However, in a volume designed for specialists as well as the educated public, a Soviet diplomat emphasizes the current ideological focus. In the last chapter, entitled "The New Thinking and Diplomacy," he states that

> Diplomacy is one of the more sensitive, and simultaneously possesses high-level characteristics, among instruments for implementing policies of the new thinking. For this reason, the process of *perestroika* must become part of the mind-set and outlook of diplomats in the spirit of new thinking . . . otherwise, a diplomat is not a diplomat.[3]

Many governments throughout the world systematically publish archival materials on foreign policy. The first annual volume of such documents released by the USSR, however, did not appear until December 1983. Covering the year 1966, it was entitled, *For Peace and the Security of Nations*. In 1989, two volumes for 1971 appeared. Annotated documentary compilations on the 1943 Moscow conference of foreign ministers as well as the first volume on Soviet-U.S. relations during World War II had been published earlier. Compilations of documents came out during 1988 entitled *Toward the New Political Thinking in International Relations* and *USSR in the Struggle for Security and Cooperation in Europe*.[4]

In the middle of 1987, a magazine called *Vestnik Ministerstva Inostrannykh Del SSSR* began appearing every two weeks. A monthly journal, *Mezhdunarodnaia zhizn'* (*International Affairs*), has been published since August 1954. In addition the late foreign affairs minister, A. A. Gromyko, and former Ambassador P. A. Abrasimov published their memoirs.[5] Although these do not contain any startling new information, there is the possibility of revelations in the future if "openness" continues. For the time being, one must rely on popular periodicals like *Moskovskie novosti*, *Argumenty i fakty*, and *Ogonëk* for eyewitness accounts of events in the Soviet Union.

ORGANIZATION

The USSR Ministry of Foreign Affairs, like other Soviet government agencies, includes an inner policy group known as the Collegium, made up, as of late 1990, of the minister (E. A. Shevardnadze) and the two first deputy ministers (A. G. Kovalev and I. A. Rogachev). In addition, there were nine deputies, a chief of the general secretariat, and fourteen other members for a total of twenty-seven persons on the Collegium.[6] This duumvirate of two first deputy ministers has established a different administrative structure at the apex of the foreign ministry, which for more than twenty years included only one individual with this rank. The existence of these two equal positions could be explained by a new appreciation for the complexities of managing rapidly changing foreign affairs.

Kovalev (born 1923), a more experienced party member than Rogachev, is responsible for the Conference on Security and Cooperation in Europe (CSCE) process, evaluation and planning, as well as United Nations' affairs. Rogachev (born 1932) had already served as a deputy foreign minister during four years preceding his 1990 promotion.[7]

Each of the nine regular deputy ministers is responsible for a specific region of the world or certain functional aspects of foreign affairs (see table 3.1). The remaining Collegium members also may hold posts as administration or department chiefs in the ministry. Some of these units are organized along functional lines (cadres, arms control, international organizations); twelve of the units pertain to geographic regions; and six departments do not seem to fit into either category. As the standard Soviet textbook on the diplomatic service explains the structure,[8]

> An important branch of the central apparatus, from the point of view of day-to-day operational diplomatic guidance, is the executive diplomatic division. The nature of activities engaged in by these divisions is determined by their territorial and functional characteristics. Territorial departments handle questions of foreign relations with specific groups of states. These groups of countries are divided by region.
>
> Functional divisions in the central apparatus are divided into such sections as consular, protocol, treaty-legal, press, international organizations and international economic organizations, cultural, planning of foreign policy tasks, general international problems.

Because "Europe de facto has become one," there is no longer any structural distinction made between the East and West European departments.[9] A separate administration, designated "embassy affairs," exists for servicing the foreign diplomatic corps in the USSR. The Moscow State Institute of International Relations and the Diplomatic Academy also are operated by the ministry. The latter began publishing an annual *Diplomaticheskii vestnik* (*Diplomatic Herald*) in 1983, which includes foreign policy documents and a chronicle of activities. It is edited by O. G. Peresypkin.

Reports from Moscow in late summer of 1986 indicated that several new functional departments were being established in the Ministry of

TABLE 3.1
USSR MINISTRY OF FOREIGN AFFAIRS COLLEGIUM, 1990

Members	Date of Appointment or Identification	Responsibilities
Minister		
Shevardnadze, E. A.	2 July 1985 (resigned 20 Dec. 1990)	Overall direction of foreign policy (member of Presidential Council)
First deputy ministers		
Kovalev, A. G.	21 May 1986	General foreign affairs
Rogachev, I. A.	id. Apr. 1990	Asian affairs (deputy minister, 1986–90)
Deputy ministers		
Belonogov, A. M.	22 May 1990	International organizations (permanent representative to U.N., 1986–90)
Chaplin, B. N.	21 May 1986	Protocol and consular affairs
Karpov, V. P.	2 Nov. 1988	Arms control and disarmament
Komplektov, V. G.	16 Dec. 1982	Latin America; Intl. economic affairs
Kvitsinskii, Iu. A.	id. 12 Apr. 1990	Soviet representative at 2 + 4 talks
Nikiforov, V. M.	8 Dec. 1985	Cadres; member, International Policy Commission (appointed Nov. 1988)
Obminskii, E. E.	id. 13 Dec. 1989	International Monetary Fund, World Bank, General Agreement on Tariffs and Trade
Obukhov, A. A.	22 May 1990	USA and Canada (deputy chief of administration, 1986–90)
Petrovskii, V. F.	31 May 1986	U.N. and related issues
General Secretariat		
Ivanov, I. S.	id. 15 Dec. 1989	Chief

TABLE 3.1 (*continued*)

Members	Date of Appointment or Identification	Responsibilities
Other Collegium members		
Bondarenko, A. P.	id. Oct. 1971	Chief, 3d European Department
Chernyshev, V. I.	id. Feb. 1988	Chief, State Protocol
Churkin, V. I.	id. Nov. 1990	Chief, Information Administration
Gorinovich. G. N.	id. Feb. 1988	Chief, Socialist Countries of Europe
Otunbaeva, R. I.	id. Feb. 1990	President, Commission to UNESCO
Peresypkin, O. G.	id. Feb. 1988	Rector, Diplomatic Academy
Piadyshev, B. D.	id. Jan. 1988	Editor, *Mezhdunarodnaia zhizn'*
Poliakov, V. P.	id. Sept. 1984	Chief, Near East and North Africa Administration
Stepanov, A. I.	id. June 1990	Rector, Moscow State Institute of International Relations
Shustov, V. V.	id. Aug. 1987	Director, Research Coordination Center
Suslov, V. P.	id. Nov. 1973	Ambassador-at-Large
Tarasenko, S. P.	id. Feb. 1988	Chief, Evaluation and Planning
Iakovlev, Iu. A.	id. Feb. 1989	Chief, African Countries
Kozyrev, A. V.	id. Nov. 1990	Minister of Foreign Affairs, RSFSR

Foreign Affairs. They dealt with problems of arms control and disarmament then under V. P. Karpov; international economic relations, at first headed by E. E. Obminskii; humanitarian and cultural relations, with Iu. B. Kashlev as chief; and a consolidation of press and information units into an administration for information, directed by G. I. Gerasimov. The same source reported that a realignment of geographic areas had resulted in new departments for the Near East and North Africa, the Pacific and Southeast Asia, socialist (communist-ruled) countries of Europe, and socialist countries of Asia.[10] Australia and New Zealand were moved from their previous place in the second European department to one for Pacific countries, and Canada is now part of the new USA-Canada department. The old groupings had remained unchanged since tsarist times.

This reorganization was followed, beginning in 1986 and 1987, by the replacement of many senior diplomats. Also introduced was the principle of limited duration for tours of duty. "Once an ambassador has been at the same post for 4 or 5 years, he loses the edge of his perceptiveness. The optimum period of service in one and the same post is three years as a maximum."[11]

The term *Collegium* implies collective administration, and advice for the minister indeed may emanate from this body. It is more probable, however, that the Collegium coordinates decisions regarding allocation of specific tasks on the basis of overall policy guidelines. This organizational unit would almost certainly be expected to check on the implementation of directives and undertake periodic reviews to evaluate the success of Soviet foreign policy endeavors. Guidelines and goals pertaining to the "new thinking" were announced toward the end of 1988, after a meeting of the Collegium.[12]

Goals adopted by the Collegium included attainment of "a comprehensive system of international peace and security; creation of decent, truly human, material and spiritual living conditions for all nations" as well as "international efforts . . . to save the world . . . the loftiest class notion of socialism. If socialism fulfills this mission, it will truly have carried out a world revolution."[13]

Foreign minister for a record twenty-eight years, Andrei A. Gromyko's career stood in sharp contrast to that of other such bureaucrats. His immediate predecessors, V. M. Molotov and D. I. Shepilov, involved themselves with intraparty politics; Gromyko refrained from doing so until late in life, which may have been the reason for his long tenure. A graduate of the Economics Institute, he entered the foreign service in 1939 when opportunities for rapid advancement existed after the massive purges. From the ministry's USA department in Moscow, Gromyko came to Washington as embassy counselor and was promoted to ambassador when he was only thirty-four. His subsequent positions included permanent U.N. representative, ambassador to Britain and, in 1957, foreign minister. Gromyko became titular chief of state in July 1985 to make way for Eduard A. Shevardnadze, a man without diplomatic experience. Gromyko retired at seventy-nine, when Gorbachev succeeded him as chairman of the USSR Supreme Soviet presidium on 1 October 1988 as part of a coup in the Politburo.

Foreign Minister Shevardnadze (born 1928) joined the CPSU at the age of twenty in the Republic of Georgia. Becoming a professional party apparatus worker, he served from 1965 to 1972 as minister of internal affairs and a police lieutenant general in his native republic. During the next thirteen years, he headed the CPSU of Georgia and reportedly cleaned up some of the corruption. Shevardnadze's unexpected transfer to national government in 1985 suggested at first that party leader Gorbachev intended to act as his own foreign minister. However, Shevardnadze has proven to be a loyal supporter of *perestroika* and has overseen major restructuring of the ministry and of the foreign policy process. He has lectured his subordinates on the "new thinking" and "today's realities," criticizing them for "considerable shortcomings" and "insufficient consistency" in their work; he has also spoken about technological literacy and understanding as a means to help decision-making in foreign policy: "The state's foreign policy activities today demand the constant saturation of diplomacy with new learning. . . . We have fallen well behind in our thinking. I would say by 50 years."[14]

TRAINING AND ACTIVITIES

As mentioned, the Foreign Affairs Ministry operates the Moscow State Institute of International Relations (MGIMO), founded in 1944, and the Diplomatic Academy for those who have made the foreign service their profession. Preparation at MGIMO lasts six years and includes a rigorous curriculum: foreign languages, history, culture, economics in the geographic area of specialization, a heavy emphasis on Marxism-Leninism (likened to a university education in politics),[15] and CPSU history, in addition to from six to eight hours a week of military training. The emphasis on military training equaled, if not exceeded, that allocated to the study of economics or CPSU history. According to a former Soviet diplomat, the regional orientation of the program tended to encourage a rigid approach rather than develop the analytic abilities of students. MGIMO reportedly still operates "very far from the level" required, although since mid-1990 career foreign service officer A. I. Stepanov has been its rector.[16] (See table 3.2.)

In the early 1960s, N. S. Khrushchev infused the diplomatic service with professional CPSU personnel. Brezhnev, his successor, is said to have taken such nepotism to extremes: Soviet ambassadors came from senior levels in the party apparatus or were friends or relatives of important officials. This trend also had a "detrimental effect on selection of students by MGIMO."[17]

During May–June 1986, a board was convened to consider shortcomings in "training and retraining" of diplomatic personnel at both specialized institutions. A decision by the CPSU Secretariat mandated genuinely competitive admission of secondary school graduates, a restructuring of the educational process, and a more flexible system geared to diplomatic requirements. A report by Shevardnadze recognized that it would take considerable time before "stagnant and conservative forces that had formed over the decades" could be broken.

Approximately 20 percent of all MGIMO graduates are assigned to the Foreign Ministry and later go abroad; about 30 percent of each class is sent to other government agencies for work as interpreters or consultants; and the remainder receives assignments in the mass media, the Committee on State Security (KGB), or MGIMO itself for research and teaching. The Diplomatic Academy (called a school until the 1970s and headed since 1988 by O. G. Peresypkin) apparently constitutes an in-service training center for personnel at advanced career levels; short-term specialized training of managers also takes place. "Graduation from the special courses should in time become obligatory stages in the career of every diplomat."[18]

Once attached to a geographic desk in Moscow, the young Soviet foreign service officer assists in filtering, consolidating, and synthesizing reports from field missions. In general, embassies abroad are responsible for monitoring all USSR citizens in the specific country to which they are accredited. They also prepare a comprehensive annual report or country study that analyzes political, economic, and cultural developments. Policy recommendations are added by the ambassador. Although each chief of mission is legally appointed via the Presidium of the Supreme Soviet as a representative of the USSR government, in the past he had to be cleared first by a unit within the central apparatus of the CPSU, which was responsible for cadres abroad.

Until the late 1980s, most ambassadors to other communist-ruled states were either former high-ranking party or government officials, which was understandable in that they dealt with their counterparts and matters where such a background would represent a definite advantage. The chiefs of mission accredited to "fraternal" countries seem to have had little chance in general for long-term tenure in their respective embassies. Of the ambassadors in East–Central Europe (excluding Albania, which had no Soviet representatives between December 1961 and August 1990), all were changed at least twice during the 1980s. Among the newly appointed chiefs of mission in that region, only the one in Czechoslovakia, B. D. Pankin, has a journalism rather than career diplomatic background. The USSR Ministry of Foreign Affairs announced in early 1990 that ties with East–Central European governments henceforth would be conducted through regular diplomatic rather than CPSU channels.[19]

In the past some of these individuals rotated between government and CPSU positions, as did the late Iu. V. Andropov, who had been ambassador to Hungary during the 1956 revolution. The reverse occurred when N. N. Rodionov became a deputy foreign minister after first being CPSU secretary for the Cheliabinsk region. He next served as ambassador to Yugoslavia. There were also instances where a subordinate ranked higher in the party hierarchy than the mission chief himself. Conversely, one ambassador, M. G. Pervukhin, formally at least, held a more important position in the party than even the foreign minister. Pervukhin, a former deputy prime minister and still at that time candidate member of the CPSU Politburo, was demoted to chief of mission in East Berlin (1958–1962) after the June 1957 Central Committee plenum, which resulted in defeat of the opposition to Khrushchev. Gromyko, the foreign minister at the time, received Politburo status only in 1973, not having gone through the probationary status of a candidate member.

In 1990, the USSR maintained regular diplomatic relations with approximately 141 foreign countries.[20] The People's Democratic Republic of Vietnam has had an ambassador in Moscow since 1969, although a Soviet envoy was not posted to Hanoi until five years later. The USSR quickly (May 1979) opened an embassy in the newly established People's Republic of Kampuchea (Cambodia). Relations exist, but no exchange of diplomats has taken place with either Guatemala or South Africa. Diplomatic ties were broken off and then resumed with Spain (1939–77), Japan (1945–56), Brazil (1947–61), Colombia (1948–68), Cuba (1952–60), Venezuela (1952–70), Iraq (1955–58), Albania (1961–90), Zaire (1963–67), Israel (1967–to date), the Ivory Coast (1969–86), Chile (1973–90), the Central African Republic (1980–88), Grenada (1983 to date), and Liberia (1985–86). Consular relations with South Africa were discontinued in 1956. Diplomatic relations with the Vatican were restored during May and June 1990 with the exchange of ambassadors, having been broken in 1923. The same happened with Saudi Arabia on 18 September 1990, after a break since 1938, and with Bahrein ten days later. The Republic of (South) Korea and the USSR agreed to formal recognition on 30 September 1990, as did Honduras, two weeks after Saudi Arabia had agreed to the same.

Soviet ambassador to the United States A. F. Dobrynin served in Washington, D.C., from 1961 to 1986, or almost a quarter century. He was reportedly on a first-name basis with a former U.S. secretary of state and

TABLE 3.2
USSR MINISTRY OF FOREIGN AFFAIRS, OFFICES, 1990

Administrations	Chief Officer	Date Identified
Socialist countries of Europe	Gorinovich, G. N.	Oct. 1986
First European Department	Afanas'evskii, N. N.	Oct. 1986
Second European Department	Uspenskii, N. N.	Sep. 1986
Third European Department	Bondarenko, A. P.	Sep. 1971
U.S.A. and Canada	Mamedov, G. E.	mid-1990
Latin American countries	Nikolaenko, V. D.	1990
Middle East countries	Alekseev, Iu. K.	June 1985
Near East and North Africa	Poliakov, V. P.	Oct. 1983
Socialist countries of Asia	Kireev, G. V.	June 1988
Countries of southern Asia	Bostorin, O. V.	Feb. 1989
Pacific Ocean and Southeast Asia	Panov, A. N.	Aug. 1990
African countries	Iukalov, Iu. A.	Feb. 1989
Personnel and educational institutions	Driukov, A. M.	July 1990
Arms control and disarmament	Karpov, V. P.	June 1986
Evaluation and planning	Tarasenko, S. P.	Dec. 1989
Embassy liaison	Vasev, V. M.	Feb. 1989
International economic relations	Maiorskii, B. G.	June 1990
International humanitarian cooperation and human rights	Reshetov, Iu. A.	May 1989
Cultural relations	Glukhov, A. I.	Mar. 1989
USSR Commission to UNESCO	Otunbaeva, R. I.	Feb. 1990
Information	Churkin, V. I.	Nov. 1990
Consular	Zelenov, V. M.	mid-1990
Historical-diplomatic	Kovalev, F. N.	Nov. 1986
International law	Iakovlev, I. I.	Mar. 1990
International scientific-technical cooperation	Maiorskii, B. G.	Nov. 1988
General international problems	Bogomolov, S. A.	1978
State protocol		
Interpreters and support for international organizations	Zaitsev, E. D. (acting)	1990
Communications	Kalinin, A. I.	Feb. 1990
Affairs administration	Matveev, L. I.	1987
Construction and maintenance of USSR embassies and private residences abroad	Tulinov, O. M.	Feb. 1990
Servicing the diplomatic corps	Kerestedzhiants, L. V.	Sep. 1989

TABLE 3.2 *(continued)*

Departments	Department Head	Date Identified
Foreign Exchange-Finance	Chulkov, Iu. A.	June 1989
Security and Cooperation in Europe (CSCE)	Deriabin, Iu. S.	May 1987
Supreme Soviet Relations & Interparliamentary Cooperation	Oleandrov, V. L.	July 1989
Union Republics	Kupliakov, Iu. V.	Nov. 1989
Questions of Non-aligned Countries	Sinitsyn, S. Ia.	Nov. 1986
Research Coordination Center	Shustov, V. V.	Aug. 1987
Information Processing & Labor Efficiency Organization	Zharov, Iu. F.	Feb. 1990

SOURCES: *Izvestiia*, 15 April 1990, p. 5; FBIS-SOV-90-074 (17 April 1990): 9–10; *Vestnik MID SSSR* 61, no. 3 (15 February 1990): 34–37; Central Intelligence Agency, Directorate of Intelligence, *Directory of Soviet Officials*, series LDA 90-14379 (September 1990), pp. 27–40.

could reach the president of the United States "just about whenever" he wanted. He accompanied Henry Kissinger to Moscow in April 1972 in preparation for the following month's summit meeting. The U.S. Department of State always waived restrictions on Dobrynin's travel if he expressed a desire to visit off-limit areas, allegedly because of the value to be gained from his "very accurate reporting and assessing of U.S. positions."[21]

In the wake of Dobrynin's transfer to Moscow, where he became one of the CPSU national secretaries and later foreign policy adviser to Gorbachev, an unusual successor in the person of Iu. V. Dubinin was named on 20 May 1986. Having been only two months at the United Nations, Dubinin had a background in West European assignments. A career foreign service officer, the man was neither a member nor a candidate for membership on the CPSU Central Committee, having been elected in March 1986 to the Central Audit Commission, which handles party finances. Dubinin spoke no English and relied on an interpreter,[22] which was also the case with the then career diplomat and U.S. ambassador to Moscow, Arthur A. Hartman, who spoke no Russian and had never served in the USSR.

As of 1990 the Soviet chief of mission in Washington, D.C., is A. A. Bessmertnykh, who had served previously at the same USSR embassy; on 21 October 1988 he reached the highest professional level in the career foreign service when he became one of three first deputy foreign ministers. Born in 1933, Bessmertnykh qualifies among the top specialists on the United States and speaks English fluently.[23]

In addition to regular foreign service officers and staff personnel, a

Soviet embassy also includes representatives from the defense establishment, the Foreign Economic Relations Ministry, the Committee on State Security, and at times the International Department of the CPSU central apparatus,[24] all of which have their own channels of communication back to Moscow. The size of the foreign mission often reflects a combination of interests that bears on the specific foreign country rather than on the requirements of purely diplomatic functions. For example, the Soviet embassy in Mexico City is staffed with several hundred personnel plus about as many spouses, each of whom fills a position: secretary, bookkeeper, telex operator, cook, janitor. No foreign nationals are employed in any USSR diplomatic mission. The particular installation in Mexico is probably one of the key USSR espionage and "active measures" facilities in the noncommunist world. Indeed, an East-Central European source states that in the Soviet mind, "a diplomat who doesn't work for the intelligence service is considered only half a diplomat."[25]

Important consulates general function as miniembassies in the USSR foreign service. Thus the consul general in San Francisco, Valentin M. Kamenev, ranks second only to Ambassador Bessmertnykh in Washington. Kamenev reports first to the Department for the USA and Canada, under G. E. Mamedov since 1990, and second to the consular administration under V. M. Zelenov in Moscow. The consulate general, in addition to Kamenev, had sixteen men (no women) listed as consul or vice-consul in San Francisco.[26]

In contrast with its policy of hiring only its own citizens to staff its missions abroad, the USSR has established a special department in Moscow to provide foreign diplomats with Soviet personnel. The Administration for Servicing the Diplomatic Corps (UpDK), under L. V. Kerestedzhiants since September 1989, functions as a liaison between all noncommunist representatives living in the USSR and the various governmental and official business establishments that cater to their domestic and personal needs. This service is portrayed by the Soviet government as relieving foreign diplomats from the mundane and often frustrating problems of dealing with the local population. It remains, however, another useful means of information gathering and provides a setting for controlled observation of foreign diplomats on a day-to-day basis.

Overall control and guidance for the Ministry of Foreign Affairs in the past emanated from the CPSU Commission on International Policies under A. N. Iakovlev, who was both a full member of the Politburo as well as one of the national secretaries. Having directed the Institute of World Economics and International Relations (IMEMO) from 1983 to 1985, he continued to utilize its expertise. As ambassador in Ottawa from 1973 to 1983, Iakovlev presumably also made contacts with the Institute for the USA and Canada.

On 24 March 1990, he became one of sixteen charter members of the Presidential Council, which provided policy options to Gorbachev.[27]

OTHER AGENCIES

The Ministry of Defense maintains an armed forces attaché office at all major posts abroad and junior military representatives in the smaller ones. These personnel are trained at the Military Diplomatic Academy. Information obtained through espionage is reported directly to the Main Intelligence Directorate (GRU). In addition, large numbers of military technicians and instructors are at times stationed abroad. In 1972, for example, after relations with the USSR had cooled, Egypt expelled as many as twenty thousand Soviet advisers. An estimated 2,300 of these advisers still remained during 1990 in Syria,[28] which contracted for about $19 billion in military equipment from the USSR through the year 1989. Delivery of weapons to foreign countries involves the Defense Ministry, which recommends types and quantities that it considers surplus.

In the area of trade, S. A. Sitarian, the chairman of the State Foreign Economic Commission, sits on the Council of Ministers. His agency supervises grants, the construction of enterprises, training of specialists in foreign countries, and technical cooperation abroad. A policy to expand commercial relations with another country, for example, would be implemented through this commission. In the case of a trade agreement, the Foreign Economic Relations Ministry assumes responsibility for implementation. However, for other economic or technical assistance matters, the commission is the pertinent agency. When established in January 1987, it had been restricted to dealings with communist-ruled states, but now covers "all countries to which the Soviet Union . . . renders economic aid." During 1989 seven favored ones received a total of $15.5 billion in military and economic assistance.[29]

The Ministry of Foreign Economic Relations maintains a bureaucracy that negotiates agreements with other countries and also prepares a commodity export/import plan. The actual exchanges, of course, are conducted by legal monopolies (called associations), of which there are about ninety-five, that deal in specific commodities. They have such descriptive names as *Eksportkhleb* (grain exports), *Eksportles* (forestry products), *Promeksport* (industrial commodities), and *Stankoimport* (heavy machine tool imports).[30] The USSR has used commercial agreements as instruments of foreign policy in such areas as the large-scale purchases of rice from Burma, cocoa from Ghana, cotton from Egypt, sugar from Cuba, and even wine from Algeria. In each of the above instances, the magnitude of imports was far greater

TABLE 3.3
SOME REPORTING UNITS ON FOREIGN AFFAIRS, 1990

Council of Ministers	CPSU Central Apparatus
Ministry of Foreign Affairs E. A. Shevardnadze[a]	International Commission G. I. Ianaev[b]
Committee on State Security V. A. Kriuchkov[a]	General Department V. I. Boldin[c]
Ministry of Defense D. T. Iazov[b]	Main Political Directorate of the Soviet Army and Navy N. I. Shliaga[c]

[a]Member, Presidential Council.
[b]Member, Political Bureau.
[c]Member, Central Committee.
SOURCE: Central Intelligence Agency, Directorate of Intelligence, *Directory of Soviet Officials: National Organizations*, series LDA 90-14379 (September 1990), pp. 3–12; current identifications from the press.

than Soviet requirements, if any. Dependence is thus established on purchases by and subsidies from the USSR. (See table 7.1 for debts owed to the USSR.)

Intelligence officers from the Committee for State Security (KGB) serve under diplomatic cover at all embassy and consular installations as well as international organizations overseas. A former Soviet ambassador estimated that half of the personnel assigned to the United Nations in New York works on espionage assignments.[31] Although such assignments are clandestine in nature, high-ranking defectors have provided details of these operations. The KGB station chief may and usually does occupy a low foreign service rank, for example, that of an embassy second secretary. He reports directly to his headquarters in Moscow, bypassing the ambassador, who is usually not informed of undercover operations and thus is in a good position to issue a denial if these are discovered.

ACTIVITIES WITHIN THE UNITED NATIONS

USSR influence at the United Nations has increased as that of the United States has declined. Until the end of the 1980s, Soviet policies benefited from a multiplier effect, given the automatic support of the former East–Central European client states as well as many so-called nonaligned Third

World governments. This pattern can be documented by the voting records in both the General Assembly and the Security Council during 1983 through 1986 as well as in U.N. media.[32]

In general, the USSR utilized the United Nations as a forum in which to repeat over and over again what George Orwell in his book *1984* called "inversions of truth." In this spirit the chief Soviet delegate charged the United States with the crime his own government had committed in shooting down an unarmed South Korean commercial airliner on 1 September 1983 off the coast of Siberia, killing all 269 civilians on board. To what degree such "double think" impressed the U.N. diplomats remains unknown.

What is apparent, however, is that the USSR skillfully courted the 97 nonaligned countries (out of a total of 158) at the United Nations. One study found that during 1985, Third World representatives in the General Assembly voted most of the time with the Soviet Union and less than one-fourth of the time with the United States.[33] Since the 1989 nonaligned meeting in Belgrade, however, the designation of the USSR as "special friend" has been dropped and a more conciliatory approach to the West adopted by this group.

Moscow maintains more than a hundred diplomats at the U.N. in New York, far more than any other member delegation. Fully 474 Soviet citizens are employed by the United Nations as international civil servants for the U.N. Secretariat, and their political neutrality has been questioned. Supposedly impartial and loyal to the U.N., they live in a housing compound at Riverdale owned by the USSR government, which provides buses to transport its citizens to and from work. Most, if not all, are members of the CPSU and attend party meetings at the Soviet mission to the United Nations on East Sixty-seventh Street. Article 100 of the U.N. Charter specifically states that no staff member "shall seek or receive instruction from any government," and yet these so-called international civil servants from the USSR at the United Nations are deeply involved with their own country's diplomatic work. Although it contributed just over 10 percent to the U.N. budget, the Soviet Union held 15 percent of the senior international secretariat posts.[34]

The USSR and its former East–Central European surrogates did act responsibly when they refused in mid-October 1987 to support the reelection of the incumbent United Nations Educational, Scientific, and Cultural Organization (UNESCO) director who had corrupted that organization. He withdrew his name, despite a large African constituency, and the Soviets were given credit in Paris newspapers for saving UNESCO from financial disaster. The United States had earlier withdrawn from the organization in protest. By 1988, however, the USSR was advocating a revitalization of UNESCO as a humanitarian duty.

Emphasizing the role of the United Nations in establishing "new thinking" precepts concerning international relations, Gorbachev has written that "this organization, the U.N., is the most appropriate forum for seeking a balance of the interests of states which is essential for the stability of the world."[35] A Soviet deputy foreign minister further developed this theme in an address at an international conference in Moscow on the "Future Role of the United Nations in an Interdependent World." The meeting attracted about seventy political, social, and scientific personalities from thirty countries.[36]

NEGOTIATIONS

Traditionally, diplomacy involves negotiation. Here, fortunately, there exist considerable data on USSR attitudes and practices. Lt. Gen. Edward L. Rowny, the Joint Chiefs of Staff representative to the Strategic Arms Limitation Treaty (SALT) delegation and the first ambassador to the Strategic Arms Reduction Treaty (START) talks, argues that U.S. foreign service officers have failed to recognize the fundamental differences between U.S. and Soviet approaches to bargaining. In negotiating with USSR diplomats, U.S. representatives have assumed that Moscow shares the same goals as Washington does and that the two countries are basically similar in their approaches. The United States, according to former Ambassador Rowny, tends to conduct negotiations as a means of problem solving; the Soviet Union, in contrast, traditionally has looked on such talks as competition, viewing them as just another aspect of the ongoing struggle against the imperialists.[37] This attitude held true until the dismal state of the USSR economy made a reduction in military spending imperative. The 1987 intermediate-range nuclear forces (INF) treaty also demonstrated Soviet ability to compromise when necessary.

A recent article in the CPSU daily newspaper notes that the traditional Soviet approach to negotiations, based on the simplistic win-lose principle, cannot be productive and that earlier ideas about the impossibility of conflict in a socialist society and there being no reason for a socialist government to compromise with a class enemy are out of date. The author of the article notes that MGIMO is studying negotiations in its "problems laboratory" and that social institutions and foreign expertise are needed to develop mechanisms to cope with conflicts.[38]

Harvard University historian Richard Pipes has observed that Soviet leaders generally have no use for compromise and are "predisposed toward exclusive possession," which stems from their perspective of the class struggle. In his view, the USSR adopts a negotiating position that "always represents the actual expectations of the Soviet government, weighted down with additional unrealistic demands to be given up in exchange for the other side's concessions."[39] Indeed, many examples of giving up something of little consequence to suggest a concession have recurred during the several decades of arms control talks that have been conducted off and on since the end of World War II. Successive U.S. negotiators have learned and relearned that the USSR always prefers to win rather than to compromise; the military status of a united Germany belonging to NATO as of 1990 may illustrate a Soviet change in attitude.

Max Kampelman, who served both in the Carter and Reagan adminis-trations at the Madrid follow-on meetings to the Conference on Security and Cooperation in Europe (CSCE), recounted his subsequent experience as chief of the U.S. delegation to the nuclear and space arms reduction talks with the USSR as follows: "Political negotiations resemble a battlefield, one that is frequently surrounded by an atmosphere of intimidation designed to persuade the rest of us that the alternatives are either an agreement on their terms or atomic cataclysm."[40]

However, decisions can be made rapidly by the Soviet leadership when the need exists. A draft four-power agreement on the status of West Berlin came soon after President Nixon's announcement that he would visit mainland China. Other negotiations may continue for years without success, like the Mutual and Balanced Force Reduction (MBFR) talks, which started in October 1973 and ended without agreement in March 1989 at Vienna between twelve NATO and seven Warsaw Pact countries (see chapter 9).

Even if the Soviets perceive negotiations as a form of struggle, however, agreements with an adversary are not impossible.[41] In addition to Soviet concessions for a treaty banning intermediate-range nuclear forces, the USSR has been willing to accept a superiority in NATO conventional forces as the Warsaw Pact seems to be falling apart. Only the future will tell whether the USSR will be as flexible in the strategic arms reduction talks as in the new conventional armed forces in Europe negotiations, which opened in March 1989, superseding the MBFR talks, encompassing all forces on that continent between the Urals and the Atlantic, and resulting in the 19 November 1990 treaty.[42]

OBJECTIVES

Pipes notes that Soviet foreign policy tends to concentrate on implementing one major objective at any given time. During the period from 1946 to 1953, the primary goal appeared to be elimination of United States' influence from Western Europe. At the invitation of Britain and France, then USSR foreign minister V. M. Molotov arrived in Paris with a staff of almost a hundred aides to discuss a U.S.-sponsored postwar recovery program. He left six days later, on 2 July 1947, after having denounced the Marshall Plan as an instrument of American "imperialism." The Soviet Union prevented Albania, Bulgaria, Czechoslovakia, Finland, Hungary, Poland, Romania, and Yugoslavia from participating in what turned out to be the first step toward the Common Market and European Community.

Unable to sabotage Western Europe's recovery, Moscow next concentrated on the Third World. The new thrust began during the mid-1950s and might have succeeded more rapidly had there been no opposition from communist-ruled China. This global Soviet flanking movement involved so-called peaceful coexistence, together with nuclear saber rattling, in an attempt to intimidate the United States. Beginning in the early 1960s, a new and complete redirection of the USSR's focus extended over the next two decades: détente in Western Europe and confrontation with China, the latter strategy stressing containment as well as isolation. In the view of Pipes, the above three primary thrusts during the recent past should be distinguished from diversionary activities that may receive considerable publicity but remain nonessential.[43] The "common European house," despite assurances that the U.S. has a role in it, may represent the latest variation in attempting to exclude U.S. influence from Western Europe.

In important matters, the operational code of Soviet negotiators is clear: use a compromise to buy time for the purpose of returning to the original position. According to former Deputy Foreign Minister V. S. Semenov, even Lenin himself combined "firmness with flexibility in international politics, resolute defense of vital interests and diplomatic maneuvering, including compromise when the new is not yet strong enough to overthrow the old." This need, in times of weakness, for a *peredyshka* (respite) may lead to "certain agreements with the imperialist countries in the interests of socialism."[44] Prophetic words, especially for the decade of the 1990s.

PAST ROLE OF THE COMMUNIST PARTY OF THE SOVIET UNION

The relation between ideology and policy expertise still remains an active issue. The above-cited Semenov commented on the connection between party supervision and the day-to-day conduct of foreign affairs by arguing that, although resolutions at CPSU congresses and Central Committee plenary meetings approved general parameters laid down at that time by the Politburo, these directives could not solve specific problems. He suggested that the latter had become so complex as to require experts who can understand these issues down to minute details. Examples given included the general field of disarmament, the German question, Middle East problems, and policy vis-à-vis the United States. The requisite knowledge for policy recommendations can be acquired only after many years of work and practical experience. *Glasnost'* is an essential element to ensure that experts are indeed telling the truth when they testify before USSR Supreme Soviet committees.

According to the former director of the Moscow State Institute of International Relations, all successful diplomatic activity is based on a Marxist-Leninist evaluation of the world situation, understanding the laws of social development in combination with concrete knowledge of particular countries as well as understanding their historical and national characteristics.[45] Another senior Soviet official has asserted that the Central Committee had provided day-to-day direction for measures to be implemented by the Ministry of Foreign Affairs. The latter reportedly at that time was staffed with "politically mature" individuals whose work is claimed to have been efficient, accurate, and precise. A model USSR diplomat had the following qualities: a high level of political awareness, Marxist-Leninist training, a sense of duty, communist party maturity, and diplomatic expertise. However, on more important questions, it was not permissible for a foreign service officer to say anything that had even the least real meaning.[46] This is corroborated by a former high-ranking Soviet official in the arms control field who wrote about the Directorate for Planning Foreign Policy Measures (UPVM) at the Ministry of Foreign Affairs. This group prepared only analyses, documents, and predictions for 1971–1975 (short term) and 1971–1980 (long term). The directorate then never actually planned the foreign policy of the USSR.[47]

Perhaps as a result of *glasnost'* and "new thinking," high-ranking party officials have begun admitting that the USSR "lacked a realistic view of the world." V. V. Zagladin, at the time (1988) first deputy chief of the International Department in the central party apparatus, stated that the CPSU had also "renounced its monopoly of truth in foreign policy" and that there must be a "transition from confrontation to non-confrontational cooperation."[48]

The twenty-first CPSU conference at the Foreign Affairs Ministry heard Shevardnadze claim that the USSR maintained stable relations with essentially all governments throughout the world. He stated that

> Soviet foreign policy has accomplished its main mission—creation of conditions most conducive to internal transformations in the country. The situation today is such that external circumstances are nowhere an impediment to our *perestroika* . . . . Yes, the threat of war has been moved back.

The "cold war" is becoming a thing of the past . . . . The new political thinking is in action.[49]

Although Soviet diplomats may be permitted to speak on substantive matters in the future, they will certainly continue to assist in foreign propaganda, which is the subject of the next chapter.

NOTES

1. V. A. Zorin, *Osnovy diplomaticheskoi sluzhby*, 2d rev. ed. (Moscow: Mezhdunarodnye otnosheniia, 1977), pp. 106–7.
2. Central Intelligence Agency (CIA), Directorate of Intelligence, *Directory of Soviet Officials*, LDA 90–14379 (Washington, D.C.: GPO, September 1990), pp. 130–31, 149–50.
3. A. G. Kovalev, *Azbuka diplomatii*, 5th rev. ed. (Moscow: Mezhdunarodnye otnosheniia, 1988), p. 270.
4. A. A. Gromyko, chief ed., *Za mir i bezopasnost' narodov*, 1971, vol. 1 (Moscow: Politizdat, 1989); Gromyko, ed., *Moskovskaia konferentsiia, 19–30.X.1943* (Moscow: Politizdat, 1984); Gromyko, ed., *Sovetsko-amerikanskie otnosheniia, 1941–1945*, vol. 1 (Moscow: Politizdat, 1984); V. L. Israelian, *Diplomatiia v gody voiny: 1941–1945* (Moscow: Mezhdunarodnye otnosheniia, 1985); L. F. Il'ichev, ed., *SSSR v bor'be za bezopasnost' i sotrudnichestvo v Europe, 1964–1987* (Moscow: Mezhdunarodnye otnosheniia, 1988).
5. A. A. Gromyko, *Pamiatnoe*, 2 vols. (Moscow: Politizdat, 1988–1989); P. A. Abrasimov, *Na diplomaticheskom postu* (Moscow: Mezhdunarodnye otnosheniia, 1987).
6. "Sovetskaia diplomaticheskaia sluzhba," *Vestnik MID SSSR*, no. 3 (15 February 1990): 33–37; CIA, *Directory of Soviet Officials*, pp. 140–41.
7. CIA, *Directory of Soviet Officials*, p. 25.
8. Zorin, *Osnovy sluzhby*, pp. 107–8.
9. M. Iusin, "Novye sovetskie posly," *Izvestiia*, 14 April 1990, p. 5.
10. Philip Taubman, "Soviet Diplomacy Given a New Look," *New York Times*, 10 August 1986, p. A-1.
11. Valentin Nikiforov, "On Personnel Policies," *International Affairs* (Moscow), October 1988, p. 56; quotation from M. Iusin, "Novye sovetskie posly."
12. See *Argumenty i fakty*, no. 12 (19–25 March 1988): 6, on the activities and composition of the Collegium. "V kollegii MID SSSR," *Vestnik MID*, no. 23 (15 December 1988): 15–16, and "V ministerstve v kollegii MID SSSR," *Vestnik MID*, no. 16 (1 September 1989): 43–44, discussed other Collegium meetings.
13. "Closing Speech by Shevardnadze," *International Affairs*, no. 10 (October 1988): 59 and 61.
14. Moscow radio, 23 November 1988; *Foreign Broadcast Information Service (FBIS)-Soviet Union*, 88–227 (25 November 1988): 64–65. Quotation is from

first meeting of MID's Scientific Council, broadcast on the *Vremia* television program and translated in *FBIS-Soviet Union*, 89–226 (27 November 1989): 86.

15. "O perestroike raboty s diplomaticheskimi kadrami v MID SSSR," *Vestnik MID*, no. 2 (31 January 1990): 26.

16. Vladimir Sakharov and Umberto Tosi, *High Treason* (New York: G. P. Putnam's Sons, 1980), pp. 81–144, provides firsthand experience with the MGIMO curriculum. See also "Doklad E. A. Shevardnadze, 3 maia 1987 g.," *Vestnik MID*, no. 1 (5 August 1987): 17–22, for the critique, and *Vestnik MID*, no. 12 (30 June 1990): 79, for biography of Stepanov.

17. Galina Erofeeva, "An Ambassador Is a Professional," *Moscow News*, no. 32 (13–20 August 1989): 6.

18. Nikiforov, "On Personnel Policies," p. 57.

19. G. Charodeev, "Ponedel'nichnyi brifing u ministra," *Izvestiia*, 27 February 1990, p. 4. For Pankin's biography, see *Vestnik MID*, no. 12 (30 June 1990): 78.

   Note however that high-ranking members of the miniscule pro-Moscow branch of the Communist Party of Lithuania, were receiving diplomatic assignments in Mozambique, the Ivory Coast, Sierra Leone, Mongolia, and so forth. S. Iur'ev, "V redaktsiiu postupilo voprosa," *Argumenty i fakty*, no. 30 (28 July–3 August 1990): 8.

20. "Diplomatic Relations of the USSR," *Vestnik: Magazine for Politics, Business, Science, and Culture*, May 1990, p. 78.

21. Anthony Austin, "Amb. Dobrynin, Long Esteemed as Bridge to Kremlin," *New York Times*, 4 June 1979, p. A-6; Bernard Gwertzman, "Inside Soviet Embassy with Dean of Diplomats," *New York Times*, 14 January 1984, p. 8; and Madeleine G. Kalb, "The Dobrynin Factor," *New York Times Magazine*, 13 May 1984, pp. 25–92 passim.

22. Elaine Sciolino, "Tale of Two Yuris," *New York Times*, 27 November 1989, p. A-10; Larisa Vyshinskaia, "Iurii Dubinin: Zhizn' diplomata zagadochnaia," *Sobesednik*, no. 30 (July 1990): 10.

23. "Bessmertnykh, Aleksandr Aleksandrovich," *Vestnik MID*, no. 11 (15 June 1990): 42, gives his biography.

24. U.S. Department of State, *The International Department of the CC CPSU under Dobrynin* (Washington, D.C.: Foreign Service Institute, 1989), especially pp. 5–42.

25. Vladimir Kostov, a defector and former member of the Bulgarian Communist Party, as quoted by Daniel Southerland, "The World of Espionage," *Christian Science Monitor*, 22 September 1980, p. 6. See also Z. A. Kruszewski, "Mexico City as a Venue of Front Activities," *Soviet Controlled Front Organizations in Crisis* (Washington, D.C.: U.S. Department of State, 1991).

26. U.S. Department of State, *Foreign Consular Offices in the United States* (Washington, D.C.: GPO, September 1990), p. 70.

27. Bill Keller, "Moscow's Other Mastermind," *New York Times Magazine*, 19

February 1989, pp. 31–43; Alexander Rahr, "From Politburo to Presidential Council, " *Report on the USSR* 2, no. 22 (1 June 1990): 1–5.

28. CIA, *Handbook of Economic Statistics, 1990*, CPAS 90–10001 (Washington, D.C.: September 1990), table 163, p. 197.

29. Zorin, *Osnovy sluzhby*, p. 125. The seven are Afghanistan, Angola, Cambodia, Cuba, Ethiopia, Nicaragua, and Vietnam, according to CIA figures in Michael R. Gordon, "U.S. Offers Moscow a Few Ideas," *New York Times*, 7 December 1989, p. A-22. CIA, *Handbook of Economic Statistics, 1990*, CPAS 90–10001 (Washington, D.C.: September 1990), tables 154, 157, 158 on pp. 181, 184, 185.

30. Zorin, *Osnovy sluzhby*. A new decree on Soviet trade missions abroad appeared in *Vedomosti Verkhovnogo Soveta SSSR*, no. 14 (1989): item 95.

31. Arkady N. Shevchenko, *Breaking with Moscow* (New York: Knopf, 1985), pp. 240–41.

32. U.S. Department of State, *Report to Congress on Voting Practices in the United Nations* (Washington, D.C.: GPO, 1984). See also U.S. General Accounting Office, *United Nations: Analysis of Selected Media Products* (Washington, D.C.: GPO, April 1986).

33. Richard L. Jackson, *The Non-Aligned, the U.N., and the Superpowers* (New York: Praeger, 1983), pp. 285–97, gives earlier data; see Elaine Sciolino, "Report Shows U.S. Outvoted in U.N.," *New York Times*, 4 July 1986, p. A-4, for percentages cited.

34. Richard Bernstein, "Russian Ex-U.N. Employee Says Soviet Violates Charter," *New York Times*, 17 July 1984, p. A-6. Note, however, that three Soviet employees at the United Nations in Geneva told the USSR government that they would no longer take orders or hand over part of their salary. *Radio Free Europe/Radio Liberty Daily Report*, no. 68 (5 April 1990): 7–8.

35. M. S. Gorbachev, *Perestroika i novoe myshlenie* (Moscow: Politizdat, 1988), p. 142. See also "Diplomatiia v kontekste razvivaiushchegosia novogo myshleniia," *Vestnik MID*, no. 16 (1 September 1989): 44–47.

36. V. F. Petrovskii, "Diplomatiia, nauka, obshchestvennost'," *Vestnik MID*, no. 18 (1 October 1988): 29–32.

37. Edward L. Rowny, "Negotiating with the Soviets," *Washington Quarterly* 3, no. 1 (Winter 1980): 60. See also his "The Soviets Are Still Russians," *Survey* 25, no. 2 (Spring 1980): 1–9.

38. M. Lebedeva, "Eto ne tak prosto—umet' vesti peregovory," *Pravda*, 4 May 1990, p. 5. See also V. L. Israelian, *Diplomaty litsom k litsu* (Moscow: Mezhdunarodnye otnosheniia, 1990), especially chapter 7, pp. 284–343, on negotiations.

39. Richard Pipes, *U.S.-Soviet Relations in the Era of Détente* (Boulder, Colo.: Westview Press, 1981), p. 370. See also Richard F. Staar, "Soviet Deception at MBFR: A Case Study," in Brian D. Dailey and Patrick J. Parker, eds., *Soviet Strategic Deception* (Lexington, Mass.: D. C. Heath, 1987), pp. 261–72.

40. Interview published by New York University in *NYU Law*, Summer 1988, p. 3.

41. Leon Sloss and M. Scott Davis, "The Soviet Union: The Pursuit of Power and

Influence through Negotiation," in Hans Binnendijk, ed., *National Negotiating Styles* (Washington, D.C.: Foreign Service Institute, 1987), p. 21. See also Raymond F. Smith, *Negotiating with the Russians* (Bloomington: Indiana University Press, 1989), pp. 118–25.

42. Richard F. Staar, "Military Balance between the Atlantic and the Urals," *Mediterranean Quarterly*, Fall 1989, inaugural issue, pp. 36–46.

43. Pipes, *U.S.-Soviet Relations*, pp. 41–42.

44. V. S. Semenov, "Leninskii stil' sovetskoi diplomatii," *Mezhdunarodnaia zhizn'* 16, no. 4 (1969): 3–11.

See also Gorbachev's speech to Ministry of Foreign Affairs employees (which uses the same formulations) in "Vremia perestroiki: vystuplenie M. S. Gorbacheva v MID SSSR 23 Maia 1986 g.," *Vestnik MID*, no. 1 (5 August 1987): 4–6.

45. N. I. Lebedev, chief ed., *Nauchnye osnovy sovetskoi vneshnei politiki* (Moscow: Mezhdunarodnye otnosheniia, 1982), pp. 10–27. A speech by Shevardnadze at the Foreign Affairs Ministry makes some of the same points in "Doklad E. A. Shevardnadze na soveshchanii v MID SSSR—3 Maia 1987 g.," *Vestnik MID*, no. 1 (5 August 1987): 17–22.

46. Zorin, *Osnovy sluzhby*, pp. 122–24.

47. Glagolev, *Post-Andropov Strategy*, pp. 72–75.

48. V. V. Zagladin, "Kursom razuma i gumanizma: obsuzhdaem tezisy TsK KPSS," *Pravda*, 13 June 1988, p. 6. See also the harsh criticism of Soviet foreign policy by Alexei Iziumov and Andrei Kortunov, "Diplomacy and Morals in Perestroika," *Moscow News*, no. 32 (13–20 August 1989): 6. The coauthors both worked at the USA and Canada Institute.

49. Eduard Shevardnadze, "Konsolidatsiia KPSS v usloviakh mnogopartiinosti," *Literaturnaia gazeta*, 18 April 1990, pp. 1 and 9.

★ PART II ★

INSTRUMENTALITIES

4
SOVIET FOREIGN PROPAGANDA

The magnitude of Moscow's effort to influence target audiences abroad can be seen from the size of Soviet expenditures for propaganda and related covert action, which the Central Intelligence Agency conservatively estimated a decade ago at between $3.5 to $4 billion per year (see table 4.1). If one included the propaganda efforts routinely directed at resident foreigners and visitors inside the Soviet Union, the total would increase substantially. Foreign Minister Shevardnadze stated that it had cost 700 billion rubles during the 1970s and 1980s to support "ideological confrontation," not including the military build-up.[1] Indeed, Western intelligence officials generally agree that the USSR probably devotes many times what the noncommunist world spends, in both human and financial resources, for propaganda and so-called active measures. Not only the dissemination of views favorable to the USSR, but also the use of accusation and derogatory terminology, harassment, censorship, radio jamming, forgeries, and general disinformation over the years became institutionalized as tools of the Soviet party-state.[2]

According to a former director of European and Soviet affairs on the U.S. National Security Council staff, the main objectives of Soviet foreign propaganda include eroding the belief that Moscow pursues adversarial goals and projecting an order that blurs East-West distinctions. Talk to outsiders of *glasnost'* and *perestroika* is intended to invalidate the rationale

TABLE 4.1

SOVIET EXPENDITURES FOR PROPAGANDA

Budget Item	Cost (in millions)
CPSU International Department	$ 100
TASS	550
Novosti (APN)	500
Pravda	250
Izvestiia	200
New Times and other periodicals	200
Moscow radio foreign service	700
Press sections in Soviet embassies	50
Clandestine radio stations	100
Communist international front organizations	63
Subsidies to foreign communist parties	50
KGB's Service "A"	50
Covert action operations by KGB foreign residencies	100
Support to national liberation fronts	200
Special campaigns (anti-NATO modernization)	200
Lobbying activities in the United States	5
Total	$3,318

NOTES: The estimate of more than $3 billion per year in Soviet expenditures for propaganda and covert action can be broken down as above if one counts only proportional costs for foreign as distinct from domestic propaganda and if other activities of the KGB are not considered. The indirect cost, borne by foreign communist organizations, is not included.

The annual Soviet budget for radio and television a few years ago totaled two billion rubles, according to the chairman of *Gosteleradio*, who revealed this over Moscow central television on 18 September 1987. Cited by Viktor Yasmann, *Radio Liberty Research* (Munich), RL 398/87 (8 October 1987): 1.

SOURCES: U.S. Congress, House, Permanent Select Committee on Intelligence, Subcommittee on Oversight, *Hearings on Soviet Covert Action: The Forgery Offensive*, 96th Cong., 2d sess. (Washington, D.C.: GPO, 1980), p. 60; see Kathryn Johnson, "How Foreign Powers Play for Status in Washington," *U.S. News & World Report*, 17 June 1985, p. 39, on the $5,469,000 officially reported by lobbyists for the USSR during 1984.

for the Western policy of deterrence. Finally, the basic propaganda themes focus on proving that American and West European interests differ, that more spending on defense is irrational, and that integration of the European Community (EC) with the Council for Mutual Economic Assistance (CMEA) has become an economic necessity for both sides.[3]

Soviet foreign propaganda uses four major techniques of persuasion: falsehood, omission, distortion, and suggestion. TASS statements about the shooting down of Korean Air Lines flight 007 exemplify the "big lie."

Omission was demonstrated by the USSR government responding to U.S. charges of seven arms control violations by making almost the same accusations against the United States without any evidence. Distortion and contradictory claims are seen in the explanation of détente in one way to leaders of client regimes and in another way to U.S. elites. The last technique presents data so that the target audience draws invalid conclusions. Finally, the crudest technique is name calling, with a label being substituted for absent proof.[4]

CENTRAL COMMITTEE APPARATUS

The CPSU Politburo supervises agitprop (agitation and propaganda) operations through several commissions and departments of the Central Committee. A distinction should be made between the two terms. *Propaganda* presents many ideas, primarily through the printed word; *agitation* uses a single, widely known "fact" and disseminates it via the spoken word in face-to-face contact, which today includes television.

Two Central Committee commissions each supervise one department in the overall propaganda effort. Most directly involved is the Ideology Commission, which apparently met periodically under its first chairman, Vadim A. Medvedev; this unit in turn exerted general supervision over the Ideology Department, headed by Aleksandr S. Kapto. The duties of his department can be seen from the designations of its six subdepartments: propaganda, basic scientific research, mass media, foreign political information and international ties, problems in training and education of young people, culture and the arts.[5] Medvedev, currently a member of the Presidential Council, had been the successive chief of two Central Committee departments: Science and Educational Institutions as well as Liaison with Communist and Workers' Parties of Socialist Countries. Kapto, a full member of the CPSU Central Committee until mid-July 1990, also had some experience with bloc relations, having served as ambassador to Cuba. Before that, he was ideological secretary for the Communist Party of the Ukraine.

The other Central Committee commission/department complex involved with the foreign propaganda effort, although apparently in a supporting role, is the one devoted to international affairs. The International Policy Commission, headed first by Aleksandr N. Iakovlev, supervised the International Department (ID) under Valentin M. Falin, who was responsible for the CPSU's relations with communist and other leftist political parties, directed the international front organizations (see below), and supervised the CPSU apparatus in Soviet diplomatic missions abroad (assuming that the ID had absorbed the former Cadres Abroad Department), with all three categories serving as propaganda vehicles. The ID also provided foreign policy expertise for other elements of the party and government apparatus.

The shared background of Iakovlev and Falin (a full Central Committee member since April 1989 who was reelected in July 1990) in the field of propaganda makes it likely that they still exert some influence over that area beyond what their respective present positions would dictate. Iakovlev headed the old CPSU propaganda department and wrote books on the cold war, American "falsifiers" in war and peace, U.S. imperialism, and Pax Americana. Falin[6] came to his current position as Central Committee secretary for international ties from the chairmanship of the *Novosti* press agency; he had earlier been first deputy chief of the now-defunct International Information Department. In addition, both had served as ambassadors, Iakovlev to Canada and Falin to the Federal Republic of Germany.

Twice a year, before May Day and the anniversary of the Bolshevik Revolution in November, official slogans appear in print[7] that are action directives for a coordinated domestic and international propaganda effort. A careful reading of them provides clues to the general line. For example, the seventeenth slogan of the October 1990 series proclaimed, "People of the world! Let us unite our efforts to resolve common problems of humanity and global problems!"—a reference to Gorbachev's new foreign policy that goes beyond the "common European house." Slogans are prepared by the mass media and propaganda subdepartment, since 1989 under N. I. Efimov, who also supervised the Soviet press, publishing houses, radio and television, and possibly also the information sections at USSR embassies.

The purpose of external propaganda is to present Soviet foreign policy as being dedicated to peace and to characterize the USSR as having established the only just society on earth. Essentially, three methods, depicted as colors, are used to achieve these goals:

1. "White" or noncamouflaged and overt psychological warfare conducted openly by government and other official organs (Moscow radio, TASS [Telegraphic Agency of the Soviet Union], *Moscow News*, and other newspapers), directed by the propaganda subdepartment

2. "Gray," emanating from so-called independent organizations and groups (Radio Peace and Progress, international communist front organizations, Soviet friendship societies), where the USSR role is in part concealed, albeit orchestrated by the International Department

3. "Black, a particularly insidious form of ideological diversion,

closely combined with terrorist and covert activities,"[8] allegedly originating from within target countries (clandestine radio stations broadcasting from the USSR, forgeries, disinformation) where the Soviet hand is concealed because this aspect originates with the KGB, although disinformation may require Ideology Department approval

FRONT ORGANIZATIONS

International communist front organizations play a key role in projecting a positive image of the USSR and an unflattering one of the West in general and of the United States in particular. These fronts are especially useful because they are less likely to fall under suspicion of operating as tools of Moscow or of local communist parties. Officially, fronts pretend not to adhere to the tenets of Marxism-Leninism, although in practice they are virtually controlled by the Soviet Union. The most important groups are listed in table 4.2.

Sectors within the International Department direct the fronts and provide for their ultimate coordination. All activities are supervised by the World Peace Council, on which most of the other organizations are represented, through joint meetings held once or twice a year. Iulii F. Kharlamov (for the World Peace Council) and Georgii V. Shumeiko (for the Afro-Asian People's Solidarity Organization and World Federation of Trade Unions) are two International Department sector chiefs known to have been in charge of front activities. Although the groups have national affiliates in many countries, it is the USSR affiliate through which they are directly controlled. Usually this is accomplished by a full-time Soviet secretary sitting in the international headquarters.[9]

Some of the units listed in table 4.3 are official subdivisions of the front indicated (e.g., International Bureau for Tourism and Youth Exchange); some have organizational slots on the World Peace Council (e.g., the Esperantist Movement for World Peace); others have the same leader as the parent front (e.g., International Liaison Forum of Peace Forces) or overlapping membership and similar policies (e.g., International Physicians for the Prevention of Nuclear War).

Front organizations form a vital link in the Soviet worldwide propaganda network, and the USSR provides them with an estimated subsidy of more than $100 million per year. They gather local support based on a broad range of political appeals. Not infrequently they have enlisted the sympathies of apolitical Western scholars and scientists who, in their pacifist zeal, become unwitting instruments of Soviet foreign propagandists. There

TABLE 4.2

INTERNATIONAL COMMUNIST FRONT ORGANIZATIONS, 1990

	Year Founded	Claimed Membership	Headquarters	Number of Affiliates	Number of Countries	Soviet Support
Afro-Asian People's Solidarity Organization (AAPSO)	1957	no data	Cairo	87	—	$1,260,000
Christian Peace Conference (CPC)	1958	no data	Prague	—	ca. 80	210,000
International Association of Democratic Lawyers (IADL)	1946	25,000	Brussels	—	ca. 80	100,000
International Federation of Resistance Movements (IFRM)	1951	5,000,000	Vienna	78	27	125,000
International Institute for Peace (IIP)	1957	no data	Vienna	no data	no data	260,000

International Organization of Journalists (IOJ)	1946	ca. 250,000	Prague	—	120 plus	515,000
International Union of Students (IUS)	1946	40,000,000	Prague	117	110	905,000
Women's International Democratic Federation (WIDF)	1945	200,000,000	East Berlin	142	124	390,000
World Federation of Democratic Youth (WFDY)	1945	150,000,000	Budapest	270	123	1,575,000
World Federation of Scientific Workers (WFSW)	1946	1,000,000	London	ca. 46	70 plus	1,575,000
World Federation of Trade Unions (WFTU)	1945	ca. 214,000,000	Prague	92	81	8,575,000
World Peace Council (WPC)	1950	no data	Helsinki	—	145 plus	49,380,000
Total						$63,445,000

SOURCES: U.S. Congress, House, Permanent Select Committee on Intelligence, Subcommittee on Oversight, *Hearings on Soviet Covert Action: The Forgery Offensive*, 96th Cong., 2d sess. (Washington, D.C.: GPO, 1980), pp. 79–80, which also gives a breakdown of Soviet financial support (staff, salaries, administration, travel, publications, conferences, and in-house meetings); Wallace Spaulding, "International Communist Organizations," in Richard F. Staar, ed., *Yearbook on International Communist Affairs 1990* (Stanford: Hoover Institution Press, 1990), p. 501.

TABLE 4.3
ORGANIZATIONS CLOSELY CONNECTED WITH FRONTS

Name of Organization	Fronts*
African Workers' University, Conakry	WFTU
Afro-Asian/Latin American Peoples' Solidarity Organization	AAPSO
All-Africa Students' Union	IUS
All-Africa Women's Organization	WIDF
Arab Peoples' Congress	WPC
Asian Buddhists' Conference for Peace	CPC
Berlin Conference of Catholic Christians	CPC
Center for Professional Education of Journalists	IOJ
Conference of Non-Governmental Organizations in Consultative Status with ECOSOC	WPC
Continuing Liaison Council of the World Congress of Peace Forces	WPC
Esperantist Movement for World Peace	WPC
Federation of Latin American Journalists	IOJ
Fritz Heckert Trade Union College, Bernau	WFTU
Georgi Dimitrov Trade Union School, Sofia	WFTU
International Association of Lawyers Against Nuclear Arms	IADL
International Association for Social Tourism and Leisure of Workers	WFTU
International Bureau of Tourism and Exchanges of Youth	WFDY
International Campaign Committee for a Just Peace in the Middle East	WPC
International Children's Assembly	WFDY
International Club of Agricultural Journalists	IOJ
International Club of Science and Technology	IOJ
International Commission of Children's and Adolescents' Movements	WFDY
International Commission of Enquiry into the Crimes of the Military Junta in Chile	WPC
International Commission of Enquiry into the Crimes of the Racist Regimes in Southern Africa	AAPSO
International Commission of Enquiry into Israeli Treatment of Arab People in Occupied Territories	WPC
International Commission for the Investigation of American War Crimes in Vietnam	IADL
International Committee against Apartheid, Racism, and Colonialism in Southern Africa	WPC
International Committee for European Security and Cooperation	WPC
International Committee for Solidarity with Cyprus	WPC
International Committee for Solidarity with the Arab People and their Central Cause—Palestine	WPC
International Committee for Solidarity with the Palestinian People	WPC
International Committee for the Cooperation of Journalists	IOJ

International Committee for the U.N. Debate on Women	WIDF
International Committee of Lawyers for Democracy and Human Rights in South Korea	IADL
International Confederation of Arab Trade Unions	WFTU
International Defense and Aid Fund for Southern Africa	AAPSO
International Fund for Survival and Development of Humanity	WPC ?
International Journalists for Peace	IOJ
International Liaison Forum of Peace Forces	WPC
International Physicians for Prevention of Nuclear War	WPC
International School of Journalism and Agency Techniques, Prague	IOJ
International School of Solidarity for Journalists, Havana	IOJ
International Student Research Center	IUS
International Trade Union College, Moscow	WFTU
International Trade Union Committee for Peace and Disarmament ("Dublin Committee")	WFTU, WPC
International Trade Union Committee for Solidarity with the People and Workers of Africa	WFTU
International Trade Union Committee for Solidarity with the People and Workers of Chile	WFTU
International Trade Union Committee for Solidarity with the People and Workers of Korea	WFTU
International Trade Union Committee for Solidarity with the People and Workers of Palestine	WFTU
International Voluntary Service for Friendship and Solidarity of Youth	WFDY
Interpress Graphic Club	IOJ
Interpress Motoring Club	IOJ
Journalists' School of Solidarity, Bucharest	IOJ
Journalists' School of Solidarity, Sofia	IOJ
Latin American Federation of Journalists	IOJ
Latin American Information Center, Lima	IOJ
Latin Confederation of Associations of University Professionals	WFTU
Organization of African Trade Union Unity	WFTU
Organization of Solidarity of the Peoples of Africa, Asia and Latin America	AAPSO
Permanent Congress of Trade Union Unity of Latin American Workers	WFTU
Retired Generals and Admirals for Peace	WPC
School of Solidarity of the GDR Journalists' Union, East Berlin	IOJ
Vienna Dialogue on Disarmament and Detente	WPC
Women for a Productive Summit	WIDF ?

*See table 4.2 for spelled-out versions of acronyms.

SOURCE: Richard F. Staar, ed., *Yearbook on International Communist Affairs* (Stanford: Hoover Institution Press), published annually in June, passim.; World Peace Council, *List of Members* (Helsinki: WPC Information Centre, 1987), pp. 164–69; WPC, *Session of the World Peace Council: Athens, Greece, 6–11 February 1990, Documents* (Helsinki: WPC, February 1990), pp. 40–47, 92–95.

also exist many "friendship societies" that perform tasks similar to those of fronts on a bilateral country-to-country basis, linking groups in Western countries to various entities of countries that remain aligned with Moscow.

In general, the purpose of front organizations, as one witness described it at U.S. congressional hearings on Soviet covert activity, is "to spread Soviet propaganda themes and create a false impression of public support for the foreign policies of the Soviet Union."[10] At times, Moscow employs the fronts directly to promote its ideology abroad. Members of such organizations, called "useful idiots" by Lenin, are introduced to the alleged virtues of the USSR way of life. The most important function of the fronts, however, is to drum up support in various noncommunist-ruled countries, including the United States, for policies whose effects would be favorable to Soviet foreign policy goals. A major objective under Gorbachev is to isolate the United States from its NATO allies by proposing the formation of a common European house comprising both West and East Europe, including the USSR, although in the long run excluding the United States.

Moscow formulates a wide range of ideologically based programs and campaigns that coincide subtly or not so subtly with similar goals. Characteristically, fronts adopt a line (for example, the campaign for disarmament, the various "peace offensives," the condemnation of the West for its alleged economic subjugation of the Third World) that effectively parallels USSR initiatives abroad. Usually front leaders will insist on actively collaborating with various nonfront groups that share ostensibly similar goals. At times the pro-Soviet groups will work actively as members of a much larger coalition of organizations, most of which are clearly noncommunist, steering the coalition when possible in directions most agreeable to Moscow.

Directives for the World Peace Council are sent by the CPSU International Department to WPC headquarters in Helsinki through the Soviet Peace Committee, headed by Genrikh A. Borovik (brother-in-law of KGB chief V. A. Kriuchkov). The latter provides financing from the Soviet Peace Fund, whose nominal chairman is international chess champion Anatolii E. Karpov. Other communist front organizations are similarly directed through such USSR bodies as the Committee of Youth Organizations, the Women's Committee, the Union of Journalists, the General Confederation of USSR Unions, and so on.

FRONT CONFERENCES

The most active front organizations are the World Peace Council (WPC), the World Federation of Trade Unions (WFTU), the World Federation of Democratic Youth (WFDY), and the International Union of Students (IUS).

An important WPC-staged event, the 1980 World Parliament of Peoples for Peace in Bulgaria, reportedly attracted 2,260 persons from 134 countries claiming to represent 330 political parties and 137 international organizations. A 1983 World Assembly for Peace and Life Against Nuclear War supposedly did even better in Czechoslovakia, with 2,645 delegates from 140 countries, according to the organizers. Both meetings issued standard USSR appeals for peace. In 1986, the WPC was the de facto sponsor of a world congress devoted to the International Year of Peace in Denmark (2,468 delegates). By early 1990, however, the USSR had cut back its financial subsidies to the WPC, which precipitated reductions in secretariat staff and a decline in morale. The WPC's fortieth anniversary meeting convened during 6–11 February 1990 at Athens, where Evangelos Makheras was elected president.[11]

The other front organizations have tended to take their lead from the WPC. Sometimes there is a show of independence by administrative organs or members. Interestingly enough, the WFTU secretariat condemned the Soviet occupation of Czechoslovakia when it met during August 1968 (by coincidence in Prague) at the height of the invasion.[12] The organization held its ninth world congress ten years later in the same city. Almost a thousand persons from 126 countries were said to have attended representing three hundred organizations, most of them from the Soviet bloc and the Third World. At this conference, the communist-controlled General Confederation of Labor (CGIL) in Italy announced it would leave the WFTU. A spokesman for the corresponding organization (CGT) in France also made public a decision that no individual from his country would be a candidate for the post of WFTU secretary general and hinted that the CGT might emulate the CGIL.[13] The tenth world congress was held in Havana during February 1982, at which the WFTU called for a new international economic order, trade union rights and democratic freedoms (only in the West, of course), security and disarmament in Europe, solidarity with Arabs and peoples of southern Africa, and support for "progressive" movements in Latin America. A similar appeal emanated from the eleventh congress during 16–22 September 1986 at East Berlin. The twelfth congress met from 12 to 20 November 1990 in Moscow.[14]

The WFDY and IUS, meanwhile, cooperate in holding world youth festivals, the largest single event sponsored by any front organization. The most successful was the eleventh, held at Havana, Cuba, where attendance reportedly totaled about 18,500 delegates from 145 countries.[15] WFDY and IUS meetings echo the same kind of declarations as the WPC, that is, calls for "peace, disarmament, and détente" as well as an end to "imperialist oppression." However, the twelfth World Youth Festival, 27 July–3 August 1985 at Moscow, claimed twenty-two thousand delegates, and as many as sixty speakers—some of whom criticized the Soviet Union for its military occupation of Afghanistan. The thirteenth youth festival was held during 1– 8 July 1989 at Pyongyang, North Korea.

The main assignment of all fronts is to convince well-intentioned but politically naive persons to support Soviet objectives; the fronts also served as a nongovernmental channel for free or low-cost trips to East-Central Europe or the USSR and as a means of recruiting potential communist party members. After their primary functions became widely known outside the Soviet bloc, supplementary techniques have had to be devised for influencing public opinion in the West. Nevertheless, the overall effectiveness of Soviet propaganda is perhaps reflected by the report that six U.S. congresssmen facilitated establishment of a World Peace Council chapter in Washington, D.C.[16]

SPECIALIZED PEACE MOVEMENTS

Numerous high-level conferences and international meetings also draw together scientists, artists, medical doctors, academicians, and former high-ranking civilian as well as military officials, ostensibly for open discussion of relevant topics, but in reality to serve as sounding boards for anti-American and pro-Soviet propaganda. Membership in them remains much smaller than that of front organizations.

One such example is the Pugwash movement of "scientists for peace, disarmament and security." Established by the late Canadian industrialist Cyrus Eaton, on the initiative of Albert Einstein and Bertrand Russell, its first meeting in 1957 drew only twenty-two participants. Since then, it has attracted hundreds of prominent individuals from seventy-five countries. The common denominator is the participants' concern for the future and for worldwide acceptance of the Pugwash manifesto's declaration that "science must only be used for the good of mankind and never for its destruction."[17] In recent years meetings have been held in Munich, Mexico City, Warsaw, Plovdiv, Venice, Bucharest, Geneva (nine workshops), Campinas (near São Paulo), Budapest, and Schwäbisch-Gmünd in the Federal Republic of Germany. The thirty-eighth meeting, with scientists from fifty-one countries, took place in the fall of 1988 at Tbilisi, USSR, and focused on the theme Farewell to Arms: Man's Survival Is the Watchword. A session on chemical weapons toward the end of January 1990 in Geneva discussed how to expedite a ban on and eliminate chemical weapons. Attendees included approximately seventy scientists and arms control experts from the Soviet Union, Western Europe, and the United States. The fortieth anniversary session was held in September near London.[18] The president of

Pugwash, Dorothy Hodgkin, has won both the Lenin and the Nobel peace prizes. The next meeting is scheduled for 1991 in the People's Republic of China.

Another series of conferences, which began in October 1960 and which are restricted to Soviet and American public figures or influential personalities, are the so-called Dartmouth meetings. The eleventh one was held at Jūrmalā, Latvia, where bilateral economic relations, the environment and conservation, disarmament, prospects for peace in the Middle East, and European problems were discussed. The Soviet delegation to Jūrmalā informed the U.S. participants about a six-point "peace program" first advanced at the twenty-fourth congress and then refined by the next two CPSU congresses.[19] Georgii A. Arbatov, director of the USA and Canada Institute, attended a Dartmouth conference held on the campus of Grinnell College in Iowa. U.S. Department of State instructions insisted that the visit not be used for propaganda purposes, although Arbatov gave interviews to the *Des Moines Register* and appeared on public television. He also took advantage of the supposedly private symposium to lecture in public before approximately a thousand people as well as to speak at a series of breakfast and luncheon meetings.[20] By contrast, Lt. Gen. Brent Scowcroft, USAF (ret.), as of 1990 the assistant to President George Bush for national security affairs, was not allowed to deliver a personal letter from President Reagan to Soviet leader Chernenko on the occasion of a Dartmouth conference held in 1984 at Moscow.

In connection with a conference during mid-February 1988 in Moscow, Soviet Peace Committee chairman Genrikh A. Borovik stated that he found "the Dartmouth process extremely useful." Three task forces were established to deal with arms control, regional conflicts, and Soviet-U.S. relations. They meet, according to Borovik, "behind closed doors, free from propaganda, in an open and sincere atmosphere."[21] The most recent Dartmouth conference took place between 21 and 28 July 1990 at Leningrad.

Another specialized group is the International Physicians for the Prevention of Nuclear War (IPPNW). This organization, formed in December 1980 when the USSR inaugurated its campaign to prevent NATO from deploying U.S. intermediate-range nuclear missiles in Western Europe, claims a membership of 145,000 medical doctors (some 30,000 of whom are Soviets) from forty-three countries. The ostensible purpose of the first conference, held in Virginia, was to increase public awareness of the consequences of a nuclear war. The Soviet delegation to the Amsterdam meeting in 1985 included Dr. Evgenii I. Chazov, later designated USSR health minister and a full CPSU Central Committee member (dropped in mid-July 1990), formerly the personal cardiologist for Soviet leaders as well as the man who signed a letter to *Izvestiia* denouncing Andrei Sakharov;

nuclear physicist and director of laser research, E. P. Velikhov; and the ubiquitous Arbatov. The presence of this last man, a key shaper of the USSR propaganda message, made it clear that Moscow uses this forum, as it has other international peace and disarmament conferences, to promote its image as a peacemaker and supporter of disarmament. Only one of the eleven Soviet speakers identified himself on the program as a medical doctor. Some two thousand delegates from sixty countries reportedly took part in the eighth congress, held from 4 to 6 June 1988 at Montreal. A Soviet deputy foreign minister, V. F. Petrovskii, gave a presentation on Strategic Thinking: The Policy of Deterrence, a strange subject for physicians.[22] The ninth international congress convened at Hiroshima in October 1989, with members from some seventy countries. This meeting focused on the theme Cease-Fire '89, a worldwide campaign to force the end of nuclear testing and a ban on nuclear weapons.

Another specialized group, Generals and Admirals for Peace and Disarmament, is composed of retired flag officers. The second Soviet-U.S. meeting, held at Moscow during the summer of 1988, reportedly had only twenty participants. Rear Adm. Gene R. La Rocque, USN (ret.), leader of the U.S. delegation, was received by A. F. Dobrynin, to whom he presented a commemorative medal from his Center for Defense Information to be given Gorbachev in recognition of the latter's "great contribution to the relaxation of international tension and the prevention of nuclear war." Progress Publishing House brought out the book *Thoughts about Security in a Nuclear Age: Generals for Peace Committee* (1989), which resulted from these talks. The third meeting, sponsored by La Rocque's center, convened during 3–4 May 1989 in the United States. Its theme, Preventing War through Mutual Respect and Cooperation,[23] suggests moral equivalence as the basis for this endeavor between the United States and the USSR.

RADIO BROADCASTS

Apart from the front organizations and the various specialized conferences at the elite level, the bulk of Soviet propaganda floods the world via the printed word and radio broadcasts. The major theme, whether the issue involves the Arab-Israeli dispute or the problems of southern Africa, is the "anti-imperialist struggle." Not only military alliances such as NATO but cooperative regional organizations like the European Community (EC) or the Association of Southeast Asian Nations (ASEAN) remained more or less under constant attack by USSR propagandists as threats to peace.

Propaganda policies are carried out through the State Committee for Television and Radio (*Gosteleradio*) Broadcasting. On 16 May 1989 Mikhail F. Nenashev replaced the retiring A. N. Aksionov as chairman. Nenashev (born 1929) has been involved in CPSU work since becoming a communist party member in 1952, including duties as deputy chief of the propaganda department (1975–78) and as chief editor of *Sovetskaia Rossiia* (1978–88). Most recently he served as chairman of the State Committee for Publishing, Printing, and the Book Trade. A professor with a doctorate in history, Nenashev was promoted as of April 1988 and reelected in mid-July 1990 to full CPSU Central Committee membership.[24]

As of 1 January 1990, Radio Moscow was devoting 2,179 hours per week to foreign radio broadcasts in eighty-four languages to more than one hundred countries, a decrease of 269 hours over the previous year. With repeats, the total came to 3,810 hours. Dissemination of propaganda is supplemented by radio services from other communist-ruled states (see table 4.4). Altogether, communist regimes broadcast 7,355 hours a week of original programs, or 10,590 hours weekly with repeats, a slight change

TABLE 4.4
COMMUNIST FOREIGN RADIO BROADCASTS, 1950–1989

Year	USSR[a] (hours/week)	East–Central Europe (hours/week)	China (hours/week)
1950	533	412	66
1960	1,015	1,072	687
1970	1,897	1,264	1,591
1980	2,097	2,210	1,374
1982	2,162	1,644[b]	1,423
1986	2,547[a]	2,064[b]	n.a.
1988	2,252	1,635[b]	1,510
1989	2,179	2,270[b]	1,518

[a]Includes foreign radio broadcasts from Alma Ata, Baku, Dushambe, Kiev, Magellanus (to Chile), Minsk, Peace and Progress (to Third World), Tashkent, Vilnius, and Erevan, in addition to Moscow

[b]Warsaw Pact members only

SOURCES: United States Information Agency (USIA), "Communist International Radio Broadcasting," *Research Memorandum* (Washington, D.C.), 7 December 1985, pp. 1–2; *Research Memorandum*, 17 December 1985 and 14 January 1986; "The War of Words," *U.S. News & World Report*, 7 October 1985, p. 37; BBC Monitoring Services, *Schedules* (London: 1986); USIA, *Research Memorandum*, 19 April 1989; USIA, "Communist International Radio Broadcasting Decreased in 1989," *Research Memorandum*, 25 May 1990, tables 1 and 15; Board for International Broadcasting, *1990 Annual Report* (Washington, D.C.: GPO, 1990), pp. 41–49.

from the previous year. The East-Central European members of the Warsaw Pact broadcast 2,270 hours a week: East Germany led with 485 hours, an increase of 37 hours a week over 1987; second, the USSR; and third, in total hours, was Bulgaria with 320. Radio East Berlin in 1988 augmented its programs to Europe by 57 percent, to 320 hours weekly. Kabul radio in Afghanistan, not included in the above overall figure, increased its transmissions from only 40 hours a week to 105 hours in 1987. This number remained unchanged in December 1989 and included 84 hours to Asia in Arabic, Baluchi/Pashto, English, French, German, Pashto/Dari, and Urdu. Broadcasts from Cuba totaled 352 hours a week at the end of 1989, with more than half of those directed at North, Central, and South America, the remainder at countries around the Mediterranean and in the Middle East, sub-Saharan Africa, Western Europe, and even East Asia. Moscow also transmitted 61 hours a week in English from Havana, which can be received on any automobile radio throughout the southern United States. It broadcasts on the 1040 AM band, which is registered to a U.S. station. Also, the Cuban shortwave transmitters relayed 95 hours a week of Moscow's broadcasts. Southeast Asia is the main target of Radio Hanoi, which had been on the air 187 hours a week in December 1989, a 5 percent decrease from a year earlier.[25]

Radio Peace and Progress (RPP), although it has used Moscow radio transmitters since its establishment in 1964, claims to be independent of the Soviet regime, thus allowing it to assume a more strident tone than the official broadcasts. Complaints from foreign governments about RPP have been rebuffed by the USSR on the grounds of the station's alleged independence, even though it remains under full Soviet government control and direction. RPP broadcasts 158 hours a week in fifteen languages and dialects. Its programs for the Western Hemisphere are highly inflammatory and anti-United States. For example, it quoted a guerrilla as stating that Cuba might intervene militarily in El Salvador. RPP also claimed that Iran and Iraq "now realize that imperialist U.S. circles are their common enemy." The USSR has reduced RPP's broadcasts to 61 hours in eleven languages as of December 1988, with the major change occurring over the preceding year. RPP's programs in Mandarin dropped from 49 hours weekly in 1986 to only 7 in 1988, targeted toward Southeast Asia for the overseas Chinese.[26]

In addition, clandestine stations are operated by communist party leaders exiled to the Soviet Union. Using transmitters located in the USSR and East–Central Europe, stations of this type were broadcasting a total of 209 hours a week at the end of 1989, a decrease of 25 percent over the previous year. Two are known to have been situated on Soviet territory: Radio Ba Yi (Eight One, for the 1 August 1927 establishment of the Chinese Red Army) first came on the air in early 1979 and directed its broadcasts at the armed forces of mainland China. The clandestine station National Voice of Iran transmitted from 1959 through 1986 in Farsi, Kurdish, and Azerbaijani from Baku, including inflammatory statements made before the seizure of the U.S. embassy at Teheran. On 7 November 1979, as the world learned about the American hostages, this station continued inciting Iranian mobs to violence. It has since been taken over by Radio Peace and Progress, maintaining the same frequencies and same announcers. In July 1984, Radio Iran Toilers began broadcasting in Farsi from Afghanistan; by the end of 1988 it was transmitting twenty-one hours a week. Another new station, Voice of the Communist Party of Iran, was first heard in August 1984 also broadcasting twenty-one hours in Farsi and one hour in Azeri during this same period. All three stations broadcast commentaries hostile to Khomeini. The local communist party's Voice of the Iraqi People, first monitored in 1982, broadcast seven hours in Arabic and one hour in Kurdish[27] during the last week of 1988.

Clandestine transmissions to Turkey have been heard over Bizim Radyo (Our Radio) since 1958 and over the Voice of the Turkish Communist Party from 1968 through November 1987 emanating from Magdeburg in East Germany. At the end of 1988 Our Radio could be heard forty-nine hours weekly from Romania, in addition to East German broadcasts, which were targeted at Turkey and Turkish nationals working abroad, especially those in West Germany. Our Radio went off the air in 1989, suggesting improved Soviet-Turkish relations. In the past, the Iberian Peninsula had been the target of so-called Radio Free Portugal (1962–1974) and Radio Independent Spain (1941–1975), the latter originating from Romania after World War II. Stations called *Deutscher Freiheitssender 904* and *Deutscher Soldatensender* were at one time directed against the Federal Republic of Germany from the German Democratic Republic. Other discontinued stations include Voice of Truth to Greece (1958–1975) and Voice of Italian Emigré Workers (1971–1978). Certain of these clandestine transmitters closed down after underground communist parties received legal status.[28]

USSR jamming of foreign radio transmissions commenced in 1948 against the British Broadcasting Corporation (BBC) and the Voice of America (VOA), subsequently including Radio Liberty (RL) and Radio Free Europe (RFE) in 1953 when these stations began broadcasting to the Soviet Union (RL) and Eastern Europe (RFE). Later transmissions by RFE to Czechoslovakia and Bulgaria were severely blocked, less so to Poland, and not at all to Romania and Hungary after 1963 and 1964.

On 20 August 1980, the Soviets resumed jamming VOA, BBC, and *Deutsche Welle* (Federal Republic of Germany) transmissions, which had been free from such interference during the preceding several years in accordance with the Final Act signed on 1 August 1975 at Helsinki.[29] This move undoubtedly was an effort by the Soviet government to keep news of the Solidarity movement in Poland from Soviet citizens. The USSR reportedly employed about five thousand people and used an estimated 2,000 to 2,500 transmitters, thus costing the Soviet Union and East-Central Europe approximately $1 billion annually to continue these jamming efforts, which openly violated the Helsinki agreement. Moscow stopped interfering with BBC Russian-language broadcasts in January 1987 and with VOA programs on 23 May 1987, except those in Polish, Dari, and Pashto. These transmitters were then used to intensify interference with RFE/RL broadcasts. In January 1988 the USSR halted jamming of Polish-language broadcasts and on 29 November of that year stopped interfering with all RL broadcasts and RFE's programs to the Baltic states. In December 1988, Czechoslovakia and Bulgaria stopped jamming RFE broadcasts.[30]

THE PRINTED WORD

Official USSR government news organizations, under the aegis of the CPSU Ideology Department, disseminate propaganda through print and radio. TASS has several hundred correspondents stationed in 125 foreign countries and transmits more than one thousand air hours daily to its foreign subscribers. The general directorship of TASS since December 1988 had been held by Leonid P. Kravchenko (b. 1938). He previously served as first deputy chairman of *Gosteleradio* and, before that, as editor of the trade union newspaper *Trud*. The news agency has about five thousand employees, yet lags behind world industry standards. In celebrating Press Day for 1989, a *Pravda* editorial, pointing to *glasnost'* and democracy, invoked "party-mindedness" and the responsibility of every journalist or editor to uphold Lenin's "strictly defined direction . . . the ideas of Marx and Engels."[31]

Another organization, *Novosti* Press Agency (APN), ostensibly unofficial but in fact controlled by the CPSU, produces translations and feature articles on a worldwide basis. The Soviets refer to it as a "social organization." Chairman of the board is Albert I. Vlasov, promoted in October 1988 from first deputy chief of the CPSU propaganda department. Before that, he served in the USSR embassy at Stockholm and earlier worked as a TASS correspondent. This man exploits the positive perceptions of the USSR in Western countries and thus propagates *perestroika* and *glasnost'* abroad.[32] APN claims connections with 120 foreign publishing houses as well as 140 international and national news agencies. It reportedly has entered into agreements with more than six thousand foreign periodicals and seventy television companies. Bureaus or correspondents operate in 115 foreign countries, and excerpts from the Soviet press are translated into fifty-six languages. The previous head of APN, Ivan I. Udaltsov, was a KGB officer who helped plan the 1968 invasion of Czechoslovakia. According to John Barron's study, "An entire division of *Novosti*, known as the Tenth Section, is staffed with KGB men." In fact, both news agencies are centers for subversion and espionage. "A sizable portion of the Soviet nationals posted abroad as staff members of TASS, Aeroflot, *Novosti*," Barron writes, "are KGB and GRU officers."[33]

APN provides material abroad for about fifty journals, ten newspapers, and more than a hundred press bulletins. The agency claims that forty-five hundred titles (for the most part, pamphlets) and thirty million copies of its publications are distributed each year. Titles are also published in noncommunist-ruled countries under a contract with the Soviet international distribution agency *Mezhdunarodnaia kniga* (International Book). Others are sold through normal channels at reduced prices. A recent gift from the USSR government of a thousand books in French, dealing with Marxism-Leninism for the national party school, arrived in Bamako, Mali. In mid-1990, APN was renamed *Novosti* Information Agency (IAN-*Informatsionnoe Agentstvo Novosti*),[34] which could mean that it has become an organ of President Gorbachev, who issued the decree.

In the less-developed countries, newspapers and journals are easier to circulate than books. Thus more than twenty-four Soviet periodicals and six newspapers are printed in forty-five foreign languages, including *Asia and Africa Today* (in two languages), *Culture and Life* (five), *New Times* (ten), *Soviet Literature* (ten), *Soviet Union* (twenty), and *Soviet Woman* (fourteen). A new weekly, *Ekho planety (Echo of the Globe)*, commenced publication in April 1988. It deals with life as reported from "fraternal socialist countries" and has a press run of 200,000 copies.

The theoretical and informational journal of communist and workers' parties for some thirty-two years had been the monthly *World Marxist Review*, with headquarters in Prague. It appeared in thirty-nine languages and sixty-nine national editions and was distributed throughout 145 countries. Each print run reportedly exceeded half a million copies. Aleksandr M. Subbotin, the editor in chief from December 1986, also held membership on the CPSU Central Audit Commission until July 1990, when he retired. A bimonthly *Information Bulletin*, in six languages, provided an additional and more frequent outlet for dissemination of speeches and articles by prominent figures in the world communist movement. Both of these publications were discontinued in mid-1990.[35]

The weekly *Moskovskie novosti (Moscow News)* has been in existence since 1930. English, French, Spanish, and Arabic translations circulate in 140 countries, and it claims a press run of one million copies per issue. This newspaper promotes the Soviet way of life, including articles on USSR economic "successes," communist peace initiatives, and international relations, some by Americans. The USSR publishes more than seventy-four million books in foreign languages (almost twelve million in Spanish alone) each year.[36]

A rather specialized operation is conducted by the Progress Publishing House in Moscow, where about 180 translators prepare the works of Lenin, sociopolitical literature, and documents from CPSU congresses in forty foreign languages for sale in roughly twice as many countries.[37] The All-Union Copyright Agency (VAAP) claims to have negotiated more than 1,750 contracts with publishing enterprises in noncommunist-ruled states, covering a total of 3,345 titles. In 1980, a ten-year agreement was signed between VAAP and Pergamon Press of London, which had already brought out Brezhnev's *Selected Speeches and Writings on Foreign Affairs*. In one article, the late CPSU leader explained that his purpose for this English-language edition was to "familiarize [readers] with our understanding of human rights and their realization in the Soviet Union." Pergamon Press also published a volume of Andropov's articles and speeches in English translation and did the same for Chernenko. It reportedly agreed to bring out a yearbook, entitled *Restructuring in the USSR*, in the main West European languages.[38]

At times, a country may become the target for propaganda saturation. This was the case in India, where 50 separate Soviet journals or bulletins appear, compared with a total of 111 for the remaining ninety-two foreign countries that have diplomatic representation at Delhi. Most USSR publications are distributed in the capital as well as in Bombay, Calcutta, and Madras. The journal *Soviet Land* (circulation 550,000 copies in India) holds annual essay competitions for the Nehru Award, with fifteen prizes including free trips to the USSR. Five other USSR periodicals are printed locally in English and sixteen additional languages. Among approximately 150 inexpensive Soviet technical books, some 40 to 50 have been adopted by various Indian colleges and universities as texts. USSR deputy foreign minister Petrovskii addressed a conference in New Delhi, where he drew a parallel between Jawaharlal Nehru's philosophy and Gorbachev's "new thinking."[39]

PROPAGANDA IN LESS-DEVELOPED COUNTRIES

Certain types of technical assistance are also provided to the Third World as a means of establishing influence over the mass media. Provisions for radio transmitters and printing presses, training of journalists (at special schools in Moscow and formerly at Bucharest, East Berlin, Prague, Sofia), as well as visits by Soviet specialists are written into cultural treaties. These agreements also cover film and radio material, exchanged as a normal part of the aid program. Such cultural cooperation agreements have been signed by the USSR with twenty-seven African states. Similar treaties have been entered into with Jordan, Lebanon, and Iraq. An agreement with the then People's Democratic Republic of (South) Yemen provided for construction of a 200-kilowatt shortwave radio transmitter at Aden to reach the entire Arab world. Algeria, Egypt, and Syria also have entered into telecommunications cooperation with the Soviet Union. Before the combined U.S.-Caribbean invasion, the USSR signed a contract with Grenada[40] to provide a ground communications station as part of the *Intersputnik* satellite system.

The best-publicized example of Soviet initiative in extending its influence throughout the Third World is the Peoples' Friendship University, founded at Moscow in 1960 and named after Patrice Lumumba, one of the Congolese leaders who had been supported by the USSR. A decade later it boasted 700 Africans, 650 Middle Easterners, 460 Southeast Asians, and 802 Latin Americans among its approximately 3,500 enrolled students. In 1971, diplomas were handed out to 80 Asians, some 140 Latin Americans, more than 140 Africans, and about 100 Soviet citizens. By 1985, total enrollment had reportedly reached 5,000 from 105 foreign countries.[41]

Those selected receive one or two years of preparatory instruction to fill gaps in their previous schooling and to teach them Russian. Departments include economics and law, history and philosophy, agriculture, medicine, science, and engineering. Students are given free dormitory space plus eighty to ninety rubles a month for food. Many graduates support Soviet foreign policy through international communist front organizations, the most important of which is probably the Afro-Asian Solidarity Organization, which maintains a strong pro-Soviet and anti-Western stance. Revolutionaries apprehended in Mexico[42] and insurgents among the radical leftists of Sri Lanka reportedly received part of their training in Moscow.

However, there have been several confrontations between Soviet authorities and those attending Lumumba University. A newspaper in Zambia reported that foreign students demonstrated in Red Square to protest and demand an investigation concerning the death of a colleague from Ghana. Africans were subsequently arrested for distributing pamphlets received at the Chinese embassy. Fifteen others from Kenya were expelled, allegedly for political reasons, but probably because they had resisted communist indoctrination. The twenty-five thousand Afghan youths sent to the USSR over the past several decades have had no choice in the matter.[43]

FUTURE ACTIVITIES

During the early 1990s, the USSR probably will continue to direct its propaganda to the less-developed countries of Africa, Asia, and Latin America. In the view of Kremlin decisionmakers, the fate of these recently independent states will decide whether or not communism can establish itself as the most important sociopolitical and economic form of organization over most of the globe. For this reason, the Soviet Union attempts to identify itself with all types of national liberation or separatist movements. Elites within the Third World are especially the target, because they decide the direction that local developments will take. In this connection, techniques and propaganda themes vary considerably.

Throughout Latin America the USSR makes a verbal show of condemning violent revolution and terrorist movements, although in practice the Soviets are disposed to support any activity undertaken by groups that profess anti-United States and anticapitalist beliefs. Moscow has made no secret of its friendly and mutually beneficial ties with the government of Cuba, attempting to promote that regime as a model for the region. Meanwhile, Soviet propaganda concentrates on the issue of the allegedly "oppressive" and "exploitative" policies pursued by U.S.-based multinational companies. Cuban communists are predominantly responsibile for disseminating propaganda in the Western Hemisphere. A nationality-adapted edition of the *World Marxist Review* (Cuban title, *Revista Internacional*), until mid-1990, and a Spanish edition of the Soviet journal *Latinskaia Amerika* were published for wide distribution throughout the area. Havana also controls a large network of periodicals, of which the weekly edition of the communist party newspaper *Granma* is the most prominent. It appears in Spanish, English, and French.

The USSR approach to Africa shows greater variation than does its approach to Latin America, because the Arab states throughout the northern Maghreb region of the continent seem more stable than the non-Arab ones south of the Sahara. The latter were long the targets of Soviet propaganda, which had previously been directed both against Portugal's control over its territories in Angola and Mozambique as well as against the white-dominated government of Rhodesia (now Zimbabwe). Currently, the target is the Republic of South Africa. There were 31,630 students from sub-Saharan Africa being educated during 1986 at Soviet and East-Central European universities.[44]

The Middle East also remains a fertile area for Soviet propaganda because the USSR has been successful in projecting its image as an ally in the struggle against Israel, the U.S. "puppet." The Soviets continue to indirectly discredit the United States, support the Palestine Liberation Organization (PLO) as the sole representative of the Palestinian people, and attack Israel's "expansionism" and "oppression" in Arab lands. Most students from this region who have been schooled in the Soviet Union and East-Central Europe have come from the two Yemens (now united), Lebanon, Iraq, and Syria; during 1986, there were 30,150 of them in academic programs.[45] The war between Iran and Iraq from 1980 to 1988 posed a slight complication for the USSR: Moscow remained officially neutral in reporting the military developments.

Throughout East Asia and the Pacific, Moscow's propaganda activities seek to exploit cultural relations, although contacts are necessarily limited. A maximum of about 410 students a year have been recruited from this region, mostly in Burma, Indonesia, and Laos, for education in the USSR or formerly in East-Central Europe, and this number is declining. In the Pacific basin, USSR propaganda opportunities tend to be limited to such things as a trade fair in Malaysia or visits by journalists from Moscow to the Philippines. Nevertheless, Soviet activity increased during 1987 through 1990.[46]

The need for technology to develop Siberia has spurred tourist travel and frequent exchanges of official delegations between Japan and the USSR. Thousands of students have graduated from the Russian-language program at the Japanese-Soviet Academy in Tokyo. Moscow's propaganda goals also have been effectively served by communist-supported campaigns against the Strategic Defense Initiative[47] and the security treaty with the United States. A new theme, prompted by U.S. efforts to persuade the Japanese to expand their defense effort, alleges that Washington wants Tokyo not only to increase its military potential for the fulfillment of certain tasks currently facing the U.S. armed forces in the Far East but also to provide economic support for pro-American countries throughout the region.

The USSR also is attempting to undermine the Association of Southeast Asian Nations (ASEAN), regularly conveying messages to the governments of Indonesia, Malaysia, Singapore, Thailand, the Philippines, and other states in the area urging them to adopt Soviet proposals for peace. The united stand by ASEAN members against Vietnam and their resistance to the Hanoi-installed puppet regime of Heng Samrin in Cambodia, however, represented attitudes that Moscow found difficult to combat until recently. (See chapter 11.)

Meanwhile, during the ten-year (1979–1989) abortive Soviet attempt to conquer Afghanistan, USSR propaganda alleged that mainland China and the United States were aiding "counterrevolutionaries" against the "legitimate" (that is, Moscow-installed) regime of Mohammed Najibullah and that Pakistan was being used by "the imperialists" as a "base for hostile operations."[48]

A special place in Soviet foreign propaganda activities is reserved for the People's Republic of China. Although both countries again exchanged ambassadors in 1970 after a four-year hiatus, this did not prevent them from attacking each other in the media as well as at the United Nations, where the Chinese supported Pakistan, while the USSR lined up on the side of India. Beijing has been accused in the past by Moscow of discriminating against minorities in Tibet, Xinjiang, and Inner Mongolia. Publication of a Chinese atlas in 1979, which laid claim to 600,000 square miles of territory within the Soviet Union, evoked an attack in the official government daily newspaper, *Izvestiia*. Over the past decade, these disputes have become muted as relations improved, culminating in Gorbachev's 15–18 May 1989 visit to Beijing. At that time, both sides agreed to normalize relations.[49]

Throughout Western Europe, Soviet propaganda themes have concentrated on peace and détente. Attacks against the Federal Republic of Germany, once a mainstay of the USSR propaganda message, have notably moderated. As in the case of Tokyo, Moscow anticipates substantial future gains in capital investment (loans) and technology transfer from Bonn. Consequently, closer economic and political integration of Western Europe is no longer presented as an obstacle to bilateral trade with individual East-Central European countries. The most sustained USSR propaganda campaign in postwar history, however, was directed during the early and mid-1980s against U.S. deployment of Pershing II and ground-launched cruise missiles in Europe, a move requested by NATO to counter the earlier Soviet emplacement of SS-20 intermediate-range launchers in the western part of the USSR. One of the latest themes, as mentioned already, is the "common European house." More recently, *Pravda* took the United States to task for the invasion of Panama as a "return to imperialist thinking."[50]

Freedom of the press in the West provides the East with a multitude of printed and spoken criticisms of public figures, organizations, society in general, and government policies that Soviet propagandists then play back in their own articles and speeches. Of great value to the USSR is the opportunity to place full-page advertisements and op-ed pieces in major U.S. newspapers,[51] paid for by the information department of the USSR embassy in Washington, D.C. One such ad appeared in the *New York Times*, where Gorbachev reprinted his statement on Nuclear Disarmament by the Year 2000, complete with a photograph of a younger version of himself, to satisfy "the demand on the part of Americans for the full text."[52]

Soviet attempts to apply pressure on the U.S. government by appealing directly to the U.S. public can also be found in letters and articles written by Soviet spokesmen that appear in such papers as the *New York Times*, the

Washington Post, and the *Houston Chronicle*. They contain information assumed to be factual by readers, although it may be distorted. Deputy Foreign Minister Viktor P. Karpov's article[53] states in boldface that "We'd like to sign a treaty within six months but NATO won't be ready." By implication, the West is inflexibly locked into patterns of old thinking. That such a treaty could not possibly be negotiated, drafted, approved, or signed by both sides in such a short time, even under the most favorable circumstances, remains unmentioned. Finally, the Soviets have also taken advantage of the journalistic focus on equal time in other media as well. In particular, the commentator for Moscow radio, Vladimir V. Pozner, has been favorably received in "dozens of appearances on ABC's "Nightline" and other "American programs."[54] Perhaps his greatest success came in a seven-minute "rebuttal" to President Reagan's speech on defense spending. ABC inadvertently suggested to the viewing public that Pozner's argument carried as much weight as that of the president of the United States.

Clearly, propaganda activities overlap with espionage and active measures, which are discussed in the next chapter. Intelligence gathering involves professionals who frequently use TASS or *Novosti* as a cover. This approach should not be confused with Western-style investigative reporting. The reports of such Soviet "journalists" go directly to KGB or GRU headquarters in Moscow, where the measure of their success is often the degree of damage they can do to the West in general and the United States in particular.

NOTES

1. U.S. Congress, House, Permanent Select Committee on Intelligence, Subcommittee on Oversight, *Hearings on Soviet Covert Action: The Forgery Offensive*, 96th Cong., 2d sess. (Washington, D.C.: GPO, 1980), p. 7; Charles Z. Wick, *Soviet Active Measures in the Era of Glasnost'* (Washington, D.C.: United States Information Agency, July 1988), pp. 1–6, prepared at the request of the Committee on Appropriations, U.S. House of Representatives; E. A. Shevardnadze, "Otchety chlenov Politbiuro," *Pravda*, 5 July 1990, p. 2.

2. Earlier studies of this subject include Frederick C. Barghoorn, *Soviet Foreign Propaganda* (Princeton, N.J.: Princeton University Press, 1964); Lyman B. Kirkpatrick, Jr., and Howland H. Sargeant, *Soviet Political Warfare Techniques* (New York: National Strategy Information Center, Inc., 1972), pp. 41–82; Paul Roth, *Sow-Inform: Nachrichtenwesen und Informationspolitik der Sowjetunion* (Düsseldorf: Droste Verlag, 1980), pp. 205–47, for the Brezhnev period; U.S. Department of State, *Soviet Influence Activities: A Report on Active Measures and Propaganda, 1987–1988*, Publication 9720 (Washington, D.C.: GPO, August 1989).

3. John Lenczowski, "Soviet Propaganda and Active Measures: 1988," *Disinfor-*

mation, no. 8 (Winter 1988): 10. See also N. V. Shishlin, chief ed., *Sovremennaia ideologicheskaia bor'ba: slovar'* (Moscow: Politizdat, 1988), especially the definition of propaganda on pp. 308–9.

4. Ted J. Smith III, *Moscow Meets Main Street* (Washington, D.C.: Media Institute, 1988), pp. 56–68.

5. A. S. Kapto, "Siloi primera, siloi ubezhdeniia," *Pravda*, 20 February 1989, p. 2.

6. Aleksandr Lavrin, comp., *Kto est' kto v perestroike* (Marburg, Germany: Blaue Hörner Verlag, 1990), p. 165.

7. Only seventeen slogans appeared in "Prizyvy Politburo TsK KPSS k 73-i godovshchine," *Pravda*, 24 October 1990, p. 1. The May Day slogans were published in "Prizyvy TsK KPSS k 1 Maia 1990 goda," in *Pravda*, 18 April 1990, p. 1, and numbered eighteen.

8. Petr N. Fedoseev, "Imperialisticheskaia agressia i psikhologicheskaia voina," *Pravda*, 10 September 1984, p. 6. This academician was writing about alleged Western propaganda directed against the USSR, although it is a mirror-image of what the Soviets themselves do. See Wick, *Soviet Active Measures*, p. 1, for these definitions and Shishlin, *Sovremennaia ideologicheskaia bor'ba*, p. 315, on psychological warfare.

9. Wallace Spaulding, "Front Trends in the 1980's which Should Continue into the 1990's," in U.S. Department of State, *The International Fronts in Crisis* (Washington, D.C.: GPO, 1991).

10. U.S. Congress, House, Permanent Select Committee on Intelligence, *Soviet Covert Action*, p. 80. See also Wallace Spaulding, "Soviet-Line Fronts in 1988," *Problems of Communism* 38, no. 1 (January–February 1989): 69–75; B. Stanishev, "Ot lozungov—k delam," *Argumenty i fakty*, no. 35 (1–7 September 1990): 4.

11. U.S. Department of State, "The World Peace Council," in *Foreign Affairs Note*, (Washington, D.C.: GPO, April 1986); Richard F. Staar, ed., *Yearbook on International Communist Affairs 1987* (Stanford: Hoover Institution Press, 1987), p. 405 (hereafter cited as *YICA*). V. Potapov, "Izmeneniia v rukovodstve VSM," *Pravda*, 15 February 1990, p. 1; E. Kaliadina, "Ves' mir v invaliutnykh rubliakh," *Komsomol'skaia pravda*, 29 May 1990, p. 5, claims that the WPC receives only $1.2 million per year from the Soviet Union.

12. Staar, *YICA 1969*, p. 953. See also Herbert Romerstein, "Reorganization and New Forms," in U.S. Department of State, *The International Soviet Fronts in Crisis* (Washington, D.C.: GPO, 1991).

13. *L'Unità* (Rome), 15 March 1978; *L'Humanité* (Paris), 13 April 1978. See also A. V. Shumeiko, *Vsemirnaia Federatsiia Profsoiuzov: 1945–1985* (Moscow: Profizdat, 1985); Free Trade Union Institute, *Continuity and Change: The World Federation of Trade Unions and International Labor Unity* (Washington, D.C.: AFL-CIO, 1988). Labor Minister Petr Miller of Czechoslovakia ordered WFTU to vacate its headquarters in Prague on 5 October 1990.

14. U.S. Department of State, "World Federation of Trade Unions: Soviet Foreign Policy Tool," in *Foreign Affairs Note*, (Washington, D.C.: GPO, August 1983).

See "Vstrecha M. S. Gorbacheva s predstaviteliami mezhdunarodnogo rabochego klassa," *Pravda*, 1 November 1986, pp. 1–2. Ladislav Bognar, "Riziko roztristenosti," *Pracé* (Prague), 3 March 1990, p. 3; *Pravda*, 15 December 1990, pp. 1 and 4, on WFTU congress.

15. *Juventud Rebelde* (Havana), 28 July–4 August 1978.

16. Herbert London in the *Detroit News*, 7 January 1988; reprinted by *Hudson Opinion* (February 1988), p. 1, in Indianapolis. See also E. Kaliadina, "Ves' mir v invaliutnykh rubliakh," *Komsomol'skaia pravda*, 29 May 1990, p. 5, for interviews with the Soviet representative at the WPC, Vladimir Orel, and especially the American WPC secretary, Robert Prince, who is highly critical of the organization.

17. The manifesto appears in the *Pugwash Conference on Science and World Affairs* (Geneva: Pugwash Council, 1984), pp. 10–12. For KGB control of the Soviet side, see I. G. Glagolev, *Post-Andropov Strategy*, pp. 53–57.

18. For these meetings, see Martin M. Kaplan, ed., *Proceedings of the Thirty-second Pugwash Conference on Science and World Affairs* (Geneva: Pugwash Council, 1984); *Pugwash Newsletter* 22, no. 2 (October 1984): 29–39, on Bjerkliden. Moscow radio, 9 July 1986, "Pugwash Conference Cited on Space-based Weapons," *Foreign Broadcast Information Service (FBIS)-Soviet Union* 85–132 (10 July 1985): AA-4 (Campinas); "Pugwash Meeting Urges Observance of SALT II," *FBIS-Soviet Union* 86–116 (17 June 1986): AA-15 (Geneva); and "Pugwash Meeting Ends in Prague," *FBIS-Soviet Union* 88–074 (18 April 1988): 56, respectively; "Itogi konferentsii," *Izvestiia*, 8 September 1988, p. 5; A. Liutin, "Mozgovoi shturm," *Pravda*, 24 September 1990, p. 4.

19. Iu. Zhukov, "SSSR-SShA: dostizhenie progressa-real'nogo," *Literaturnaia gazeta*, 20 July 1977, p. 10; A. M. Aleksandrov, ed., *Radi mira na zemle: Sovetskaia programma mira dlia 80-kh godov v deistvii* (Moscow: Politizdat, 1983), discusses the "peace plan." Interview with Aleksandr Kislov, deputy director of the Institute of World Economics and International Relations (IMEMO) over Moscow radio, 17 February 1988; *FBIS-Soviet Union*, 18 February 1988, p. 26.

20. Philip Geyelin, "Arbatov Off Limits," *Washington Post*, 1 May 1983, p. B-7. That same month thirty Soviet delegates appeared in Minneapolis at a conference on Creating the Conditions for Peace sponsored by the Institute for Policy Studies (IPS) in Washington, D.C. A list of U.S. participants appeared in the *Minneapolis Daily American*, 17 May 1983.

IPS later sponsored Arbatov at the World Affairs Council of Northern California. See the *San Francisco Chronicle*, 5 September 1985, p. 24, and "Za normalizatsiiu otnoshenii," *Izvestiia*, 11 September 1985, p. 4. On the IPS and its hidden agenda, see S. Steven Powell, *Covert Cadre: Inside the Institute for Policy Studies* (Ottawa, Ill.: Green Hill Publishers, 1987).

21. Moscow radio, 17 and 20 February 1988; "Dartmouth Meeting Held," *FBIS-Soviet Union* 88–032 (18 February 1988): 26, and "Dartmouth Meeting Ends," *FBIS-Soviet Union* 88–036 (24 February 1988): 15–16.

22. "Healing Our Planet: A Global Prescription," *IPPNW Programme*, 2–6 June

1988, pp. 23–24. See also Jack Rosenblatt, *Soviet Propaganda and the Physicians' Peace Movement* (Toronto: Mackenzie Institute for Study of Terrorism, Revolution and Propaganda, 1988), p. 36. "V. Shelkov, "Retsept vyzhivaniia," *Pravda*, 5 June 1988, p. 5; and "Viel zahl von Aktionen," *Neues Deutschland* (East Berlin), 21 April 1989, p. 2.

23. "Vstrecha v TsK KPSS," *Pravda*, 22 July 1988, p. 5; Michael Fumento, "The Center for Defense Misinformation," *The American Spectator*, April 1988, pp. 20–23; TASS, 10 May 1989, in "Military Experts Meeting on Disarmament," *FBIS-Soviet Union* 89–091 (12 May 1989): 21.

24. "Nenashev, M.F.," *Izvestiia*, 17 May 1989, p. 1; "Sostav TsK KPSS," *Pravda*, 15 July 1990, p. 4. He was succeeded by L. P. Kravchenko on 14 November 1990 and moved to chief of the USSR State Committee for the Press (Goskompechat').

25. United States Information Agency (USIA), "Communist International Radio Broadcasting Decreased in 1989," *Research Memorandum*, 25 May 1990, tables 1 and 15.

26. U.S. Department of State, "Moscow's Radio Peace and Progress," in *Foreign Affairs Note*, August 1982, p. 1. USIA, *Soviet Propaganda Trends*, no. 41 (27 October 1988): 6; BBC, *World Broadcasting Information*, no. 49, section B (2 December 1988): 32; USIA, "Western Europe in 1988," *Research Memorandum*, 27 March 1989; USIA, "Communist International Radio Broadcasting in 1989," *Research Memorandum*, 25 May 1990.

27. U.S. Congress, House, Permanent Select Committee on Intelligence, *Soviet Covert Action*, p. 79; USIA, "Communist International Radio Broadcasting," *Research Memorandum*, 17 December 1985, pp. 1–2; *Foreign Report*, no. 1948 (11 December 1986) about takeover by Radio Peace and Progress; USIA, "Near East, North Africa, and South Asia in 1988," *Research Memorandum*, 4 April 1989.

28. U.S. Department of State, "Communist Clandestine Broadcasting," in *Foreign Affairs Note*, December 1982, p. 3; Voice of the TCP (clandestine), 14 November 1987 in *FBIS*, 16 November 1987, p. 21; USIA, "Western Europe in 1988," *Research Memorandum*, 27 March 1989.

29. U.S. Board for International Broadcasting (BIB), *1986 Annual Report* (Washington, D.C.: GPO, 1986), pp. 24–30; *Los Angeles Times*, 1 March 1988, p. 5; BIB, *1989 Annual Report*, pp. 65–67.

30. Jamming transmitters in the USSR and Eastern Europe cost an estimated $250 million to construct. David Brand, "Soviets Continue Jamming," *Wall Street Journal*, 14 July 1983; USIA, "Jamming of Western Radio Broadcasts to the Soviet Union and Eastern Europe," *Research Report*, April 1983, p. 5; Thomas F. O'Boyle, "Change of Signals," *Wall Street Journal*, 25 March 1988, pp. 1 and 7; BIB, *1990 Annual Report*, p. 73.

31. Sh. P. Sanakoev, ed., *Voprosy sovetskoi vneshnepoliticheskoi propagandy* (Moscow: Mezhdunarodnye otnosheniia, 1980), pp. 203–4; John J. Karch, "News and Its Uses in the Communist World," in L. J. Martin and A. G. Chaudhary, eds., *Comparative Mass Media Systems* (New York: Longman, 1983), pp. 111–

31; S. A. Losev, "Dva podkhoda k informatsionnoi politike," *Mezhdunarodnaia zhizn'* 32, no. 12 (December 1985): 28–36; "General'nyi direktor TASS," *Izvestiia*, 29 December 1988, p. 2, about Kravchenko; *FBIS-Soviet Union* 89–053 (21 March 1989), on TASS employees; "Sil'naia i smelaia pressa," *Pravda*, 5 May 1989, p. 1, on Press Day. Kravchenko was succeeded in November 1990 by L. N. Spiridonov, deputy editor of *Pravda*.

32. Sanakoev, *Voprosy propagandy*, p. 207; see "Novosti" v epokhu glasnosti," *Izvestiia*, 31 October 1988, p. 4, for interview with Vlasov; and Paul Roth, *Glasnost und Medienpolitik unter Gorbatschow* (Bonn: Studiengesellschaft für Zeitprobleme, 1990), pp. 365.

33. John Barron, *KGB: The Secret Work of Soviet Secret Agents* (New York: Bantam Books, 1974), pp. 15 and 27.

34. One example is the late Leonid I. Brezhnev's *Istoricheskii rubezh na puti k kommunizmu* (Moscow: Politizdat, 1977). More than 1.5 million copies of this pamphlet were published in English, Arabic, Spanish, German, and French. The number of publications distributed during 1982 totaled seventy million copies, according to Colin Walters, "World's Bookshelves out of Kilter," *Insight*, 17 March 1986, p. 72. S. Taranov, "APN stanovitsia IAN," *Izvestiia*, 1 August 1990, p. 3, gives an interview with IAN chairman A. I. Vlasov on the change in name and the 100 million ruble annual budget.

35. *WMR* was also known as *Problems of Peace and Socialism*. See Wallace Spaulding, "World Marxist Review," in Staar, ed., *YICA 1984*, pp. 426–27; *YICA 1988*, pp. 381–82, for an update. "Ot redaktsii izdatel'stva," *Problemy mira i sotsializma*, no 6 (June 1990): inside cover.

36. Sanakoev, *Voprosy propagandy*, p. 191. See also S. I. Beglov. *Vneshnepoliticheskaia propaganda* 2d. rev. ed. (Moscow: Vysshaia shkola, 1984), pp. 283–89; and V. G. Panov, chief ed., *Ezhegodnik bol'shoi sovetskoi entsiklopedii* (Moscow: Sovetskaia entsiklopediia, 1987), p. 23.

37. A. M. Prokhorov, chief ed., *Bol'shaia sovetskaia entsiklopediia*, 3d ed. (Moscow: Sovetskaia entsiklopediia, 1975): 21, 29–30.

38. L. I. Brezhnev, "Sotsializm, demokratia i prava cheloveka," *Kommunist*, no. 2 (January 1981): 14. However, another U.S. company published two similar volumes by Gorbachev, according to "Priem M. S. Gorbacheva s Richardsona," *Pravda*, 5 April 1986, p. 1. See also S. Iezuitov, *Vremia* newscast over Moscow television, 25 February 1988; "U.K. Publishers to Develop Restructuring Yearbook," *FBIS-Soviet Union* 88–038 (26 February 1988): 33.

39. Moscow radio, 14 November 1988; "Petrovskii Greets Nuclear-Free World Conference," *FBIS-Soviet Union* 88–221 (16 November 1988): 7.

40. Timothy Ashby, "Grenada: Soviet Stepping Stone," *Proceedings of the U.S. Naval Institute* 109, no. 12 (December 1983): 34. See also V. Listov, "Uroki Grenady," *Pravda*, 25 October 1985, p. 5.

41. Alvin Z. Rubinstein, "Lumumba University: An Assessment," *Problems of Communism* 20, no. 6 (November–December 1971): 65–67; more than thirteen thousand graduates were working in 110 Third World countries, according to Moscow radio, 7 February 1985, in "Zimianin Attends Gala," *FBIS-Soviet*

Union 85–028 (11 February 1985): R-16; Edward B. Fiske, "Education Watch," *New York Times*, 16 June 1985, p. 22, sec. 4, for 1985 enrollment figures. See also Marc Fisher, "Political Offices," *Washington Post*, 20 October 1990, p. A-24, for transfer to Lumumba University of $67 million embezzled by East German communists.

42. Barron, *KGB*, pp. 317–25, provides a discussion of activities in Mexico by former students from Lumumba University.

43. U.S. Department of State, "Soviet Influence on Afghan Youth," *Special Report*, no. 139 (February 1986): 2.

44. U.S. Department of State, Bureau of Intelligence and Research, *Warsaw Pact Economic Aid Programs in Non-Communist LDCs, 1986*, Publication 9345, August 1988, table 7, p. 5.

45. Ibid.

46. Mikhail Nenashev, "Vsegda li vinovata propaganda," *Pravda*, 8 August 1990, pp. 3–4.

47. U.S. Arms Control and Disarmament Agency, *Soviet Campaign against SDI* (Washington, D.C.: GPO, August 1986), p. 15.

48. TASS dispatch from the United Nations entitled "Presech' genotsid," *Pravda*, 9 February 1986, p. 5.

49. Gorbachev's speech at Vladivostok called for better relations with the People's Republic of China (Moscow television, 28 July 1986; *FBIS-Soviet Union*, 29 July 1986, pp. R 14–15). A report on his visit to Beijing appeared in "Sovmestnoe sovetsko-kitaiskoe kommiunike," *Pravda*, 19 May 1989, p. 1.

50. Alexander R. Alexiev, *The Soviet Campaign against INF* (Santa Monica, Calif.: Rand, February 1985), N-2280-AF. Gennadii Zafesov, "Retsidiv imperskogo myshleniia," *Pravda*, 8 January 1990, pp. 1 and 5, on Panama.

51. See, for example, Gorbachev's report to the twenty-seventh CPSU congress in *Pravda*, 26 February 1986, pp. 2–10, excerpts from which appeared as full-page ads in the *Los Angeles Times* and other major U.S. newspapers. See also Alexander Malyshkin, "NATO Has to Move beyond the Cold War," *New York Times*, 11 August 1990, p. 16. This man is identified as a senior information officer, USSR embassy, Washington, D.C.

52. *New York Times*, 5 February 1986, p. A-13. The statement is clearly labeled advertisement.

53. Victor Karpov, "Moscow's View: The Bush Proposal on European Arms," *New York Times*, 12 June 1989, p. A-19.

54. Quotation from Philip Taubman, "Soviet Spokesman on American TV," *New York Times*, 30 December 1985, p. C-18. See also Alan Cooperman, "Kremlin Spin Doctor Pozner," *Los Angeles Times*, 10 June 1990, p. 3.

5

INTELLIGENCE, DISINFORMATION, AND ACTIVE MEASURES

The Soviet civilian intelligence organization, known today as the Committee for State Security (KGB), has had sixteen different chiefs since the 1917 revolution. Four were executed, and only three of the last seven can be classified as career secret police officials. The majority had been transferred from work in the CPSU apparatus, which indicates attempts to maintain tighter party supervision over activities that include a substantial domestic component. This chapter will discuss only the foreign operations of the USSR intelligence services.

The functions of the KGB were described by an open source as foreign intelligence; counterintelligence, the struggle against foreign espionage, terrorist acts, sabotage, and ideological subversion; protection of state borders; investigation and prevention of activities directed against the Soviet state and society; and, since 1989, defense of the USSR constitutional system. Gorbachev acquired direct authority over the KGB when he became USSR president after the 26 March 1989 national elections. In addition a new Supreme Soviet committee on defense and state security, headed since mid-June 1990 by Leonid V. Sharin, hears reports from the KGB chairman.[1]

After the execution in 1953 of Lavrentii P. Beria, the secret police chief and CPSU career functionary who had attempted to seize power on the death of Stalin, a professional intelligence officer, Gen. Ivan A. Serov, took over the organization. Serov had directed the mass deportation of Lithuanians, Latvians, and Estonians at the beginning of World War II and later of the Chechens, Kalmyks, Crimean Tatars, and other non-Russian nationalities. Party control over the secret police could not be firmly reestablished until 1958, when N. S. Khrushchev appointed former Komsomol leader Aleksandr N. Shelepin to head what then became known as the Committee on State Security, or KGB. (It had been placed under the Council of Ministers four years earlier.)

The KGB soon accelerated operations abroad, slightly curtailing domestic work. A meeting with its military counterpart, the GRU (by then under the direction of Serov who had been moved from the KGB), and foreign intelligence organizations from fourteen other communist-ruled countries resulted in an agreement to cooperate on the basis of "equality." The Chinese and Albanians broke this compact in 1960, and the KGB began to direct its operations against mainland China.[2]

Vladimir Y. Semichastnii, like Shelepin, a former Komsomol leader, took over the KGB in October 1961. One of his missions included penetrating the International Confederation of Free Trade Unions in Brussels. A year and a half later, the trial of a senior GRU colonel, Oleg V. Penkovskii, revealed that he had delivered approximately ten thousand negatives from photographs of classified documents to British and American intelligence services over an eighteen-month period.[3] Apparently, one motive for Penkovskii's activity was his hatred of the KGB and its personnel. In 1965 General Serov was expelled from the communist party for "violations of socialist legality" while serving as a deputy to Beria. This reflected on both the KGB and the GRU because Serov also served as head of the latter from 1958 to 1962. His dismissal may have occurred as a result of the Penkovskii case.[4]

Semichastnii was succeeded in May 1967 by Iurii V. Andropov, a career party apparatus worker without previous experience in intelligence activities. This appointment, owing to Andropov's status as candidate Politburo member at the time, indicated an upgrading of the KGB. (Andropov, together with Lenin and Gorbachev, for a long time was off-limits to Soviet media, but in September 1989 the monthly magazine Ogonëk published the first criticism of him, stating that Semichastnii, during an interview earlier that same year with Moscow News, had blamed Andropov for corruption and other shortcomings.) The following year, former KGB Maj. Gen. O. D. Kalugin, revealed that Andropov had reinforced the apparatus for moral terror and political surveillance. An unidentified KGB colonel corroborated these charges and also held Andropov responsible for decisions to invade Hungary (1956), Czechoslovakia (1968), and Afghanistan (1979) because of the intelligence supplied to the Politburo.[5]

After fifteen years as head of the KGB, Andropov moved into the position of a CPSU national secretary. His replacement, V. V. Fedorchuk, was transferred in May 1982 from the Ukraine, where he had directed KGB activities for that republic. Subsequently, as the new CPSU general secretary, Andropov transferred Fedorchuk to the Internal Affairs Ministry with the rank of army general. The first deputy KGB chief, V. M. Chebrikov, succeeded to the chairmanship on 17 December 1982, the seventh secret police head in three decades.

Unlike his predecessor, Chebrikov had not made a career of such work. He served with the Red Army during World War II, then completed engineering studies at Dnepropetrovsk, and next worked briefly for industry. Between 1951 and 1967, Chebrikov occupied full-time CPSU positions. Brezhnev called him to Moscow and placed him in charge of KGB personnel, and in April 1982 Chebrikov became first deputy chairman of the entire organization. Thus, Chebrikov and Andropov worked for the KGB during the same fifteen-year period. At the end of 1983, Chebrikov became a candidate member of the Politburo and was promoted to full Politburo membership on 6 March 1986, after the twenty-seventh party congress. During a reorganization of the CPSU central apparatus on 1 October 1988, he became a national secretary and chairman of a new Commission on Questions of Legal Policy, from which he was dismissed a year later.

During the 1988 shake-up a two-decade veteran secret police official, Col. Gen. Vladimir A. Kriuchkov (born 1924), succeeded to the KGB chairmanship from a deputy chairman position after having spent fourteen years as head of the First Chief Directorate, which deals with foreign espionage. He had worked for Andropov (1954–1967) both in the USSR embassy in Budapest and at the Department for Liaison with Socialist Countries in the CPSU central apparatus. Kriuchkov was elected a full member of the Politburo on 20 September 1989, without going through the probationary period. He received confirmation as KGB head in mid-July 1989 after televised hearings before the Supreme Soviet, and in April 1990 he became a member of the new Presidential Council.[6]

ORGANIZATION

The center of the USSR's worldwide intelligence and counterintelligence operations is the State Security Committee (*Komitet Gosudarstvennoi Bezopasnosti*), whose headquarters are at 22 Lubianka Street, off Dzerzhinskii Square[7] in Moscow as well as in the suburb of Iasenevo. It is estimated that the KGB employs approximately 1.4 million persons, half of them part-time informants, both inside and outside the Soviet Union. Theoretically a government agency, the KGB in fact is subordinate to the Presidential Council. Although the organization exercises day-to-day responsibility for its own operations, work plans and especially intricate operations must first be approved by a special committee in the president's office. However, the KGB is involved in policy making and governing, with its top officials on the Defense Council (see chapter 6), the CPSU Central Committee, and the Presidential Council.

The KGB is subdivided into chief directorates, directorates, services, and departments (see figure 5.1). The First Chief Directorate, which has responsibility for clandestine activities abroad, is staffed by about fifteen thousand officers. It maintains three subdirectorates, three special services, two special departments, eleven geographic departments, and several functional ones.[8] From 1959 through 1967 the active measures department, comprising forty to fifty employees, was headed by a Maj. Gen. Ivan I. Agaiants. In 1968, however, this unit was reorganized and elevated in rank. Now referred to as Service A, it coordinates and plans the dissemination of "false and provocative information," which is designed to deceive foreign governments or the public in countries outside the Soviet bloc under the designation *active measures*.[9]

One of three subdirectorates, Directorate S is responsibile for foreign intelligence, or "illegals," that is, agents who reside abroad under deep cover and have no apparent connection with the USSR. The scientific and technical subdirectorate (Directorate T) coordinates the theft of Western technology and military secrets. This subdirectorate determines the composition of Soviet delegations to international scientific conferences as well as those individuals sent abroad on exchange programs. USSR scientists who travel to foreign countries are considered important for intelligence-gathering purposes. Executive Action (Department VIII of Directorate S) involves terrorism, kidnapping, and assassination under the euphemism *mokrye dela*, or wet (bloody) business.[10] It reportedly was reorganized to emphasize sabotage of foreign communications, transport, and public utilities.

The Second Chief Directorate is responsible for internal security and surveillance of foreigners inside the USSR. About half the personnel is assigned to subvert diplomats stationed in Moscow and prevent them from privately contacting ordinary Soviet citizens. The other half concentrates on tourists, artists, scientists, businessmen, students, and journalists from foreign countries. The Fifth Chief Directorate concerned itself with internal dissidents and reinforcement of controls over the general populace, until it was replaced by an unnumbered unit for "protection of the Soviet constitutional system." The Chief Directorate for Border Guards controls the frontiers and is occupied more with keeping Soviet citizens within the USSR than with preventing others from entering the country. Its personnel is estimated to number at least 300,000 uniformed and armed men.[11]

The USSR Supreme Soviet (legislature) appointed fourteen joint committees on 7 June 1989 to oversee all operations of the government, including the KGB. A week earlier, Deputy Iurii P. Vlasov made a televised speech in which he revealed that his diplomat father had disappeared in 1953 after having been interrogated by the secret police, which he described as an "underground empire." Vlasov received a standing ovation, brief applause from Gorbachev, and "stony silence" from Kriuchkov.[12]

PROMINENT ESPIONAGE CASES

Among Soviet foreign intelligence success stories, some of which have been publicized inside the USSR, is that of former German communist Richard Sorge. During World War II, Sorge was able to obtain advance information from the Nazi embassy in Japan, where he ostensibly worked as a journalist, as to the exact date the *Wehrmacht* would invade the Soviet Union and to transmit this by radio to Moscow.[13] Stalin apparently did not believe the message. Arrested by Japanese counterintelligence, Sorge was executed before the end of the Second World War. Another important intelligence officer, Col. Rudolf I. Abel, operated from 1948 to 1957 in the United States.[14] Lt. Col. Evgenii V. Runge worked successfully against the Federal Republic of Germany and NATO for twelve years until 1967, when he defected to the West. The vast majority of Soviet intelligence officers, however, operate under diplomatic cover.

A request for political asylum in 1971 by Capt. Oleg Lialin, an operative in what was then Department V, precipitated the expulsion of 105 individuals—one-fifth of all personnel—from the Soviet embassy, its trade mission, the Aeroflot office, and *Narodnii Bank* in London. This defection also had repercussions for the worldwide USSR espionage network. A number of Soviet intelligence officers throughout the Western Hemisphere, Asia, Europe, and Africa received orders to return home because their cover might have been compromised by the defector.[15] In 1983 the French government declared forty-five Soviet diplomats and two journalists personae non grata from among the 185 expulsions recommended by its counterintelligence service, the *Direction de la Surveillance du Territoire* (DST). This represented the largest setback to USSR espionage since the comparable British action mentioned above. Two years later, the United Kingdom expelled twenty-five Soviet diplomats and officials as a result of a defection by the KGB station chief in London, a man named Oleg A. Gordievskii. In October 1986, the United States gave the Soviet embassy the names of eighty-five USSR intelligence officers who were then forced to leave the country.[16]

To cope with a defection, Moscow headquarters has developed various

FIGURE 5.1

COMMITTEE FOR STATE SECURITY OF THE USSR, 1990

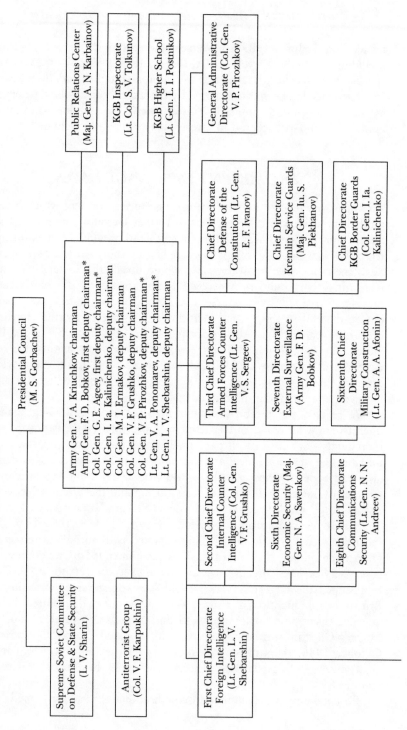

Information Directorate Processing of Secret Intelligence

Service A Disinformation and Active Measures

Directorate R Analysis of KGB Operations Abroad

Geographic and Functional Operational Departments

Directorate S Illegals (deep cover)

Directorate T Scientific and Technological Operations

Directorate K Counterintelligence Abroad

Department 8 Direct action and special operations

SOURCES: Central Intelligence Agency, Directorate of Intelligence, *Directory of Soviet Officials: National Organizations*, series LDA-90-14379, September 1990, pp. 465–74; *Izvestiia*, 27 October 1989, p. 3, for new unnumbered chief directorate; *Kommunist Tadzhikistana*, 21 October 1989; *Pravda*, 30 March 1990, p. 6; *Krasnaia zvezda*, 27 May 1990, p. 2; *Sovetskaia Rossiia*, 29 May 1990, p. 8; *Sobesednik*, no. 29 (July 1990): 4–5; *Pravda*, 26 August 1990, p. 2; *Pravda*, 16 September 1990, p. 2; *Argumenty i fakty*, 25–31 August 1990, p. 7; *Pravda*, 16 September 1990, p. 2, for chief of Eighth Directorate; *Soviet Ministrov SSSR*, spravochnik serii "Kto est' kto" (Moscow: Vneshtorgizdat, 1990), p. 98, for composition of the KGB leadership; *Krasnaia zvezda*, 6 March 1990; *Shchit i mech*, June 1990; *Vestnik granitsy*, no. 6 (1990): 48; *Ekonomika i zhizn*, no. 37 (1990): 15; *Komsomol'skaia pravda*, 23 August 1990; *Krasnaia zvezda*, 23 August 1990, 2 September 1990, and 21 September 1990; *Pravda*, 16 September 1990; *Krasnia zvezda*, 11 November 1990, p. 4.

* These individuals had been selected by and placed in these positions by KGB Chairman Iurii V. Andropov, beginning some 20 years ago. All signed the obituary of Lt. Gen. S. G. Bannikov, a former KGB deputy chairman, in Krasnaia zvezda, 30 December 1989, p. 6. KGB chairman Kriuchkov served with Andropov in Hungary (1950s) and came into the KGB with Andropov. Although Kriuchkov is noted for his long service as head of the First Chief Directorate (foreign intelligence), he has had prosecutorial training and experience, that is, internal security work. See also Valentin Korolov, former KGB counterintelligence officer, "Sekrety' sekretnykh sluzhb," *Ogonek*, no. 43 (October 1990): 28–31.

NOTE: Victor Yasmann, whose book Gorbachev and the KGB (Washington, D.C.: Pergamon-Brassey's) will appear in mid-1991, kindly provided some of the identifications and sources.

countermeasures to obscure the case and alert contacts to give them time to disappear. The KGB immediately draws up a damage assessment to neutralize possible repercussions. Files at headquarters in Moscow are scrutinized to establish which documents the defector had signed out and consequently might be compromised. Collective responsibility may dictate punitive measures against family, friends, colleagues, and those who had recommended the individual for employment.[17] In addition, officers serving abroad who knew the defector are recalled to Moscow because they would be assumed to have lost their cover. Many such operatives are destined to be used again, but only after a cooling-off period and in countries where they had not served before.

DIPLOMATS AS SPIES

At least one-fourth to one-third of all Soviet officials serving abroad work for the KGB or GRU. Among the approximately one thousand Soviet (and a smaller number of the three thousand East–Central European officials) U.N. employees, students, and others in the United States, at least the same fraction is estimated to be full-time intelligence officers or required to collect information on a part-time basis. During the past several years, the number of USSR diplomats expelled for espionage has varied (see table 5.1). Many cases go unreported so as not to "embarrass" the Soviet Union.

In the past some 492 Eastern bloc intelligence officers flagrantly abused

TABLE 5.1
EXPULSION OF SOVIET OFFICIALS, 1970–1988

	*1970–80**	*1982*	*1984*	*1986*	*1988*
Africa/Middle East	7	**	2	**	**
Asia/Pacific	108	7	1	**	**
Europe	163	23	16	12	4
Western Hemisphere	88	19	**	7	20
Total	366	49	19	19	24

*Figures are approximations.
**No publicly announced expulsions.
SOURCES: U.S. Department of State, "Expulsion of Soviet Officials, 1988," *Foreign Affairs Note,* November 1989, pp. 3–8 list names of those expelled. Actual numbers are higher because governments at times prefer not to publicize expulsions.

their U.N. Secretariat positions and ignored the formal pledge they signed to surrender all allegiance to their respective countries, as mentioned in the previous chapter. According to former high-ranking USSR diplomat Arkadii Shevchenko, who served as U.N. under secretary general, there is "very substantial penetration" by Soviet intelligence services at the United Nations, including a KGB officer who was a special assistant to former Secretary General Kurt Waldheim. Similar allegations have been made against Vladimir Kolesnikov, who was in that same aide position[18] from June 1985 until the end of 1986, when he was expelled by the United States government together with fifty-four other Soviet citizens who worked at the U.N. in New York. The same secret police affiliation reportedly applies to Geli Dneprovskii, chief of personnel since 1979, at U.N. headquarters in Geneva, where he assigned Soviet and East-Central European officials to key positions. Once filled, such jobs become a virtual preserve, with those vacated subsequently occupied by other Eastern bloc nationals.

Dneprovskii's office also gave him access to the confidential files on all U.N. employees in Switzerland, an asset for recruiting sympathizers. About 133 of the 429 Soviet citizens on the permanent staff of U.N. agencies in Geneva during the late 1980s were identified as KGB or GRU operatives. At the U.N. mission in New York, three members of the USSR delegation were arrested by the Federal Bureau of Investigation for espionage. Two received sentences of fifty years each in prison; the third man, protected by diplomatic immunity, was expelled from the United States. Those imprisoned were later exchanged for five Soviet dissidents jailed in the USSR, none of whom had worked for U.S. intelligence. Ilia Djirkelov, former press attaché at World Health Organization headquarters in Geneva (which has been called the nerve center of Soviet espionage for Western Europe), took files along when he defected to Britain. Moscow immediately recalled a large number of intelligence officers from the region, tending to confirm the importance of the documents Djirkelov had brought with him.[19]

The Federal Republic of Germany, however, has the largest concentration of Soviet and East-Central European intelligence officers. At least 407 individuals with diplomatic cover have been identified as KGB or GRU officers (about 30 were expelled in 1989), with another thirty thousand illegals working clandestinely.[20] France had approximately two hundred Soviet spies with diplomatic or other cover out of fourteen hundred persons in those categories. Some fifty-three espionage cases came before Paris courts between 1963 and 1971 involving East German, Czechoslovak, Polish, Romanian, Yugoslav, and USSR citizens.[21] Italy had an estimated 250 intelligence officers from the USSR and East-Central Europe, all carrying diplomatic passports. Clandestine services in its former bloc greatly enhanced USSR operational capabilities until 1990, when several of the newly elected noncommunist governments (in Poland, Czechoslovakia, Hungary, and East Germany) broke off cooperation with the KGB.

AGENTS OF INFLUENCE

A French journalist, Pierre Charles Pathé, was arrested in Paris on charges of disseminating Soviet propaganda. In the process of exchanging official government documents for money, he was caught together with his controller, Igor A. Kuznetsov, a second secretary in the USSR permanent delegation to UNESCO and son of the then KGB First Chief Directorate head, A. Sakharovskii. Pathé had worked eighteen years, publishing two newsletters and various articles under pseudonyms. One of the publications, *Synthesis*, was financed by the USSR and reached almost three-fourths of the deputies and half the senators in parliament as well as other opinion makers in France.[22]

More recently, a Greek newspaper, *Ethnos*, was established, reportedly with KGB financing. The publisher has been accused of serving as an agent of influence for the Soviet Union. This paper, which built up a circulation of 200,000 copies, the largest in Athens, described the USSR as the "world's first peace bloc," Solidarity leader Lech Wałęsa in Poland as an "agent of the CIA," and President Reagan and his assistants as "paranoid monsters." Correspondents for *Ethnos* in the United States and Britain have been identified as communists.[23] The foregoing is another example of promoting the objectives of the USSR without attribution.

One can see the long-range nature of Soviet intelligence operations in the cases of four British subjects, three of whom were recruited as students at Cambridge. All attained high government positions while working as ideologically committed spies. Harold A. R. Philby served as liaison between M.I. 6 (British foreign intelligence) and the CIA. In mid-1980 he fled the West and was decorated in Moscow for his "more than 40 years of difficult but honest work."[24] Two others, diplomats Donald MacLean and Guy Burgess, escaped to the USSR before Philby did. All three men hated the social system in England and willingly betrayed it. The fourth man, their recruiter, Anthony Blunt, was a respected art scholar and a member of M.I. 5 (British counterintelligence) during World War II. His knighthood was canceled after his involvement with the KGB became public knowledge. All these men are dead.[25]

Stanislav A. Levchenko, a former Soviet intelligence officer who defected to the United States, directed agent of influence operations over a four-year period while ostensibly a *Novoe vremia* (*New Times*) correspondent in Tokyo. He identified eight Japanese, among them three prominent politicians of the Socialist party, who knowingly or unwittingly helped the KGB. Arne Treholt, an official in the Norwegian Foreign Ministry, was convicted in 1985 for giving the Soviets copies of documents stolen from his own government and from NATO. He also used his position to influence other officials and his country's Labor party.[26] Dimitra Liani, a former Olympic Airways flight attendant, could have played an agent of influence role vis-à-vis then Prime Minister Andreas Papandreou in Greece. Liani, the wife of Dimitris Kapopoulos, an architect and secretary of the Marxist-Leninist (Maoist) Communist Party, and Papandreou subsequently divorced their respective spouses and were married in August 1989.

LOWER-LEVEL RECRUITMENT

Neither high-ranking diplomats nor clerks seem immune to KGB blandishments. Blackmail is a frequent technique of recruitment. Not long after arriving at the British embassy, John W. C. Vassall went to a party in Moscow given by a local Soviet employee. He became inebriated and was photographed engaging in a homosexual act. Threatened with exposure, Vassall began abstracting documents from the naval attaché's office for the KGB. Back in London, he continued his espionage work at the naval intelligence division and fleet section of the Defense Ministry. Vassall was arrested after eight years of spying.[27]

Americans, especially those with problems or grudges, represent KGB targets, with money as bait. U.S. Army enlisted man Robert Glenn Thompson, after he had been demoted and denied a transfer, was recruited by a Soviet intelligence officer in West Berlin and used to recommend other potential recruits. Sergeant Jack Dunlop, known to like women and fast cars, was approached in Moscow and took money as a down payment for classified documents he later stole from National Security Agency headquarters in the United States. (He later committed suicide.) Lt. Col. William H. Whalen, while attached to the Joint Chiefs of Staff, received a monthly stipend from the Soviet embassy in Washington, D.C.[28]

A twenty-three-year-old CIA watch officer, William F. Kampiles, was arrested after he sold the KGB a stolen reconnaissance satellite manual. Many other classified documents found their way to Moscow through a teletype encoding machine operator at a private company, including messages to CIA headquarters and the National Security Agency.[29] David H. Barnett, a former CIA officer, received eighteen years in prison for selling secrets to the KGB. Over a three-and-a-half-year period he sold the names of U.S. intelligence officers and several foreign collaborators as well as the details of at least one high-priority operation. An attempt to infiltrate

United States counterintelligence was frustrated by the arrest and trial in mid-1986 of an FBI special agent and two refugees from the USSR who had been receiving instructions through the Soviet consulate general in San Francisco. Between 1981 and the end of 1988, some sixty Americans were arrested for espionage on behalf of the USSR, and more than twice that many Soviet-bloc "diplomats"[30] were expelled from the United States.

American citizens convicted of selling information to the Soviet Union over the past few years include Thomas Cavanagh, who worked on the B-2 Stealth bomber at Northrop Corporation; Ronald Pelton, a former National Security Agency employee who monitored USSR communications; Edward Lee Howard, who, after being dismissed from the CIA, escaped from the United States and revealed operations of the Moscow station to the KGB; John A. Walker, Jr., his brother, his son, and his friend Jerry A. Whitworth, all of whom sold U.S. Navy cryptographic data; U.S. Army warrant officer James W. Hall III, arrested in March 1989 for delivering classified information to Soviet agents in West Germany; and a former U.S. Army sergeant, Roderick James Ramsay, who was charged in June 1990 with the same activities.[31]

NATO, another important target, has informants within the organization itself as well as among its member-state delegations. Georges Paques, deputy NATO press secretary, worked for USSR intelligence from 1944 onward while serving in eleven different French ministries. NATO financial controller Nahit Imre, caught photographing secret documents for the Romanian secret service, was extradited to Turkey. A translator, Francis Roussilhe, was arrested with classified documents by Belgian police. When NATO moved its headquarters to a suburb of Brussels, the Soviets built a $25 million auto assembly plant nearby. The factory came equipped with radio antennae and monitoring devices to intercept NATO telephone communications.[32]

USSR intelligence operations against the People's Republic of China are much more difficult to implement. Although speculation exists that the late Lin Biao (officially reported killed in an airplane crash while fleeing to the Soviet Union) may have had clandestine links with Moscow,[33] most KGB and GRU espionage remains at a relatively low level. There is some border infiltration by Turkestani natives into Xinjiang and probably crossings into Inner Mongolia by agents from the Mongolian People's Republic. According to Hu Yaobang, at the time general secretary of the Chinese Communist Party, during one year some two hundred Soviet spies were arrested by security organs. The PRC Foreign Ministry in mid-1986 accused the USSR of having conducted at least thirty unauthorized surveillance flights over its territory.[34]

HIGH-TECHNOLOGY TRANSFER

Much of the following information came from a senior KGB officer, code name Farewell, who supplied French counterintelligence with some four thousand documents on USSR industrial espionage during the early 1980s. President François Mitterrand reportedly briefed his U.S. counterpart, Ronald W. Reagan, about the materials at the economic summit in July 1981. The documentation had a top secret classification, some of it annotated and signed by then KGB chief Iurii V. Andropov. Materials included a complete list of technologies to be stolen from the West. Based on this information, a total of forty-seven Soviet "diplomats" were expelled from France.[35]

One of the highest Soviet priorities is the transfer (by overt and covert means) of technology from the West, especially the United States. USSR intelligence services have established elaborate procedures to circumvent the embargo list maintained by NATO (plus Australia and Japan) through the Coordinating Committee for Multilateral Export Controls, or CoCom. "Virtually every Soviet military research project . . . benefits from [Western] technical documents and hardware,"[36] which are obtained legally and illegally.

An important covert acquisitions program is directed by the Military-Industrial Commission (*Voennopromyshlennaia Kommissiia*, or VPK), officially attached to the USSR Council of Ministers. The VPK uses intelligence channels to obtain "one-of-a-kind military and dual-use hardware, blueprints, product samples, and test equipment." One such attempt—four techno-bandits from the Netherlands trying to smuggle out of Miami a $1.5 million VAX 8800 computer, which had the capability to operate ballistic missiles and radar—was frustrated by U.S. Customs Service agents.[37]

A parallel program under the USSR Ministry of Foreign Economic Relations also relies on intelligence organizations to acquire dual-use manufacturing and test devices that are installed on production lines. Soviet weapons-producing industries seek microelectronics, computers, communications, machinery, robotics, diagnostic, and other export-controlled equipment to increase their output. Twelve key defense manufacturing ministries[38] provide the desiderata for specific collection requirements.

The principal collectors who attempt to fulfill the above requirements include the First Chief Directorate (foreign intelligence) of the KGB. About a thousand officers, all scientific experts, make up the technology component. Some three hundred to four hundred of them are abroad at any one time, using embassies, trade missions, and academic exchange programs as cover. The other principal collector is military intelligence, or GRU,[39] which has approximately three thousand officers outside the Soviet Union as military attachés, with Aeroflot, in the merchant marine, as well as under KGB-type cover. Until 1990, all East-Central European counterpart intelligence services shared everything they collected with the USSR.

COUPS, TERRORISM, AND NARCOTICS

The KGB does not restrict itself merely to information-gathering efforts, agent of influence operations, and the theft of high technology. Evidence of past Soviet support for coups and terrorist activities is abundant. USSR policy in this regard tends to function simultaneously at three levels: (1) overt endorsement of "national liberation movements" through the media; (2) covert encouragement and support by international communist front organizations; and (3) spreading of disinformation by condemning terrorist activity, while simultaneously financing and training its forces (see table 5.2). According to a former KGB chief of station in Washington, D.C., "the backbone of KGB activities remains as it was 10 and 20 years ago."[40]

When President Ahmed Sekou Touré of Guinea discovered that Soviet intelligence officers had been plotting with the local teachers' union to overthrow his regime, he expelled USSR ambassador Daniil S. Solod. Touré had become aware of such activities during his years in France as a member of the communist-dominated trade union organization, *Confederation Général du Travail*.

Less experienced was the late Kwame Nkrumah of Ghana. Thanks to a popular revolt that took place during his visit to mainland China, he never regained power. The new government discovered an East German state security officer named Jürgen Krüger directing an espionage school at Accra under a cover name, the National Scientific Research Laboratory. With access to all Ghanaian classified materials, Krüger had been routinely passing them on to Moscow. Documented evidence[41] suggests that the USSR may have been planning to use the country as a base for subversion throughout sub-Saharan Africa. The new government of Ghana expelled more than eleven hundred Soviet advisers in the aftermath of these discoveries.

An attempt to subvert a Latin American government came to light when authorities in Mexico City declared the USSR ambassador, along with four of his senior diplomats, personae non grata. In another attempt, a Mexican citizen named Fabricio Gomez Souza was recruited by Soviet intelligence and received a four-year scholarship, along with thirty other students from his country. They took courses at Lumumba Peoples' Friendship University in Moscow, then headed by KGB Maj. Gen. Pavel Erzin. Later, three separate contingents of Mexicans, about fifty in all, were trained in guerrilla warfare

TABLE 5.2

MAJOR TERRORIST AND REVOLUTIONARY GROUPS

Acronym	Name	Area of Operation (targets)	Ties and principal sources of aid
AD	Action Directe	France: NATO	RAF, LARF
ANO	Abu Nidal Organization	Germany: U.S. interests U.S., England, France, Israel, various Arab countries	Libya, Syria, others
CCC	Communist Combatant Cells	Belgium: anti-U.S., anti-NATO	AD, RAF
ELN	National Liberation Army	Colombia: U.S.; other foreign oil	Cuba
ETA/M	Basque Fatherland & Freedom/ Military	Spain: French targets; France	Libya, Lebanon, PIRA
FARC	Revolutionary Armed Forces of Colombia	Colombia: anti-US	Cuba
FLNC	Corsican National Liberation Front	France	AD
FMLN	Farabundo Martí National Liberation Forces	El Salvador: anti-U.S.	Cuba, others
FPMR	Manuel Rodriguez Patriotic Front	Chile: anti-U.S.	Cuba
GRAPO	1st of October Group of Anti-fascist Resistance	Spain: anti-U.S., prorevolution	AD, BR
Hizbullah	Party of God	Middle East, Europe	Iran
IRA	Irish Republican Army	United Kingdom	Libya, others
JRA	Japanese Red Army	Lebanon, Europe, anti-U.S.	Libya
LARF	Lebanese Armed Revolutionary Faction	Lebanon, Western Europe	Syria? AD, RB, RAF, others
M-19	Movement of April 19	Colombia	Cuba, Libya?

TABLE 5.2 (continued)

Acronym	Name	Area of Operation (targets)	Ties and principal sources of aid
PIRA	Provisional Irish Republican Army	United Kingdom	Libya, PLO, ETA/M
PKK	Kurdish Workers' Party	Syria, Iraq, Turkey, Germany	Syria? Iran?
PFLP-GC	Popular Front for Liberation of Palestine, General Command	Middle East, elsewhere	Syria, Lebanon, Hizbullah?
RAF	Red Army Faction	Germany: anti-NATO, anti-U.S.	AD, formerly CCC
RB	Red Brigades	Italy	PLO
SL	Sendero Luminoso (Shining Path)	Peru	?

Sources: U.S. Department of State, *Patterns of Global Terrorism, 1989*, publication 9743 (Washington, D.C.: GPO, April 1990), pp. 33–35, 37–49, 35–80; U.S. Department of Defense, *Terrorist Group Profiles* (Washington, D.C.: GPO, 1989), pp. 15–26, 35–47, 50–67, 82–96, 102–11, 118–20; John Newhouse, "Changing Targets, Annals of Intelligence," *New Yorker*, 10 July 1989, pp. 71–82.

by the North Koreans. These groups came together in Mexico to form the *Movimiento de Acción Revolucionaria*, which began preparing a terrorist campaign under KGB direction. However, all members of the movement were arrested before they could develop any popular support.[42]

Only a few months later, President Jaafar al-Numeiry was ousted briefly in the Sudan and thirty-eight of his supporters shot to death. The Soviet-inspired revolution collapsed after only three days. About twenty-seven hundred local communists were rounded up and their leaders executed. Advisers and technicians had arrived from the USSR in the Sudan several years before to help build port facilities and assist with counterinsurgency operations against the black guerrilla movement in the south. President al-Numeiry revealed that the communist coup had received support and direction from the Soviet and Bulgarian embassies and expelled the third-ranking USSR diplomat as well as the Bulgarian ambassador.[43]

The successful coup against and execution of President Salim Rabayyi' 'Ali in South Yemen received support and most probably direction from Moscow, for it was Soviet naval ships and Cuban-piloted aircraft that bombarded Aden. After that, some two thousand East Germans controlled security in the People's Democratic Republic of (South) Yemen, and it appeared to have become the first Arab state with a Marxist-Leninist orientation.[44] (See chapter 10 for the abortive January 1986 coup that apparently caught the USSR by surprise.)

In Afghanistan, Soviet armed forces entered Kabul, allegedly at the invitation of communist Prime Minister Hafizullah Amin at the end of December 1979, surrounded his headquarters, and killed him as well as all the members of his family and government. The assassinations were carried out by the KGB *spetsnaz* (special designation) units trained for such assignments, with the active participation of the First Chief Directorate's eighth and twentieth departments. After almost ten years the USSR withdrew its "limited contingent" of more than 115,000 troops, although it continued to support the puppet regime of Mohammed Najibullah. It is not inconceivable that the secret police (WAD) and government in Kabul, with KGB assistance, engineered the plane crash on 27 August 1988 that killed thirty persons including President Zia of Pakistan.[45]

A task force on international terrorism, chaired by then Vice-President George Bush, had the following report on such activities:

> The surge in the level of international terrorist activity worldwide in 1987 and 1988 resulted from a wave of high casualty bombings in Pakistan carried out by agents of the WAD [Afghan secret police]. *The WAD is Soviet trained and organized.* The terrorist campaign is designed to deter the Government of Pakistan from aiding resistance fighters in Afghanistan.[46]

On occasion, East–Central European rather than direct Soviet assistance had been supplied to terrorists like those in the outlawed Irish Republican Army. Acting on a tip, police in the Netherlands stopped a DC-6 aircraft arriving from Czechoslovakia under charter by a Belgian company. Although the cargo manifest indicated London as its destination, the flight plan included a refueling stop in Amsterdam and listed Ireland as the final destination. Searchers uncovered 116 wooden crates containing antitank rocket launchers, mortars, grenades, machine guns, rifles, and ammunition. Western intelligence agencies have reported connections among Japanese, Palestinian, Turkish, Basque, and other terrorist movements.[47]

President Vaclav Havel of Czechoslovakia revealed that the former communist regime in his country had sold Libya one thousand tons of Semtex, enough of this almost undetectable explosive to last the world's terrorists about 150 years. This material had been used for a number of bombs, including the one that destroyed the Pan-American aircraft and all 259 persons aboard over Lockerbie, Scotland, on 21 December 1988. The sale to Muammar el-Qaddafi was made by the communists in his country "for political reasons," according to Havel.[48]

The Soviets also encouraged the notorious terrorist ("Carlos") Il'ich Ramírez Sánchez. Raised by prominent Venezuelan communist parents, Carlos studied at Lumumba University in Moscow. According to West European intelligence, he was then recruited by the KGB and served as a link with international terrorist organizations. The Carlos group spent time in Hungary as a guest of that country's previous communist regime. In a letter dated 2 April 1980, Ramírez thanked party leader János Kádár for his hospitality, which included a full year of rest and relaxation as well as financial assistance and probably forged passports.[49]

Military training reportedly had been provided for such groups at camps throughout the Middle East and North Africa as well as in North Korea, Cuba, East–Central Europe, and the USSR. Soviets, Cubans, East Germans, and North Koreans served as instructors. Major coordinating agencies for this network of terrorist schools included the GRU and the DGI (*Dirección General de Intelligencia*, Cuban intelligence), which operated under Soviet direction. On the issue of training, one Western specialist wrote the following:[50]

> The Palestine Resistance has been wholly armed by the Soviet Union since 1968. At least one in every ten of its guerrilla fighters and officers has been trained inside the Soviet Union or its East European satellites (not to mention North Korea, where some twenty-five hundred guerrillas were trained in the early days). The others were either trained in Cuba or had the

benefit of expert Cuban instruction in *fedayeen* camps from Algeria and Libya to Syria, Lebanon, and South Yemen.

According to defectors from the Soviet Union, more than one thousand Palestinians alone have gone through Soviet bloc training camps. The USSR military academy near Simferopol in the Crimea graduated terrorists from such groups as Al Fatah, Popular Front for the Liberation of Palestine, and the Palestine Liberation Front. The official representative of the Palestine Liberation Organization (PLO) at the United Nations confirmed that Palestinians received arms, money, and training from the Soviet Union. Libyan defectors in Western Europe cited the existence of nearly twenty terrorist camps in Libya under Cuban and East German control. Extensive military and guerrilla courses were taught at schools in Bulgaria, Czechoslovakia, East Germany, Hungary, and the USSR itself.[51] (Those in most East-Central European countries had probably been closed down by the end of 1990.)

However, an interview with an unidentified member of the East German state security (*Stasi*) ministry revealed that "training facilities . . . were opened precisely for this purpose—to train the fighters of the PLO security service in East Germany for reconnaissance and counterintelligence. . . . It was a program involving the division of labor with the KGB. . . . East Germany was primarily responsible for [South] Yemen . . . Mozambique . . . Ethiopia . . . fighters from Nicaragua.

Military training of 550 PLO members was discontinued at the officers' academy on Ruegen Island after this interview.[52]

Qaddafi in Libya uses surrogates to attack United States and Western targets. One of these (until Manuel Noriega's ouster on 20 December 1989) was Panama, which served as a base in the Western Hemisphere, with Cuba as the transportation hub. A Japanese Red Army member, Yu Kikumura, was arrested in November 1988 at a stop on the New Jersey turnpike transporting explosives he had smuggled into the United States through Canada. At the end of the previous year, the El Rukns gang leaders in Chicago, who had been convicted of planning terrorist attacks, claimed that Qaddafi had promised them $2.5 million for bombings and assassinations in the United States.[53]

DISINFORMATION AND MURDER

The above activities are supplemented by other intelligence-related operations called *active measures*, which, according to a U.S. Department of State report, include "a broad range of deceptive techniques—such as use of front groups, media manipulations, disinformation, forgeries, and agents of influence—to promote Soviet foreign policy goals and to undermine the position of USSR opponents."[54] Several of these have been dealt with earlier in this chapter and in the previous one. Long-term goals of Soviet active measures include

1. Influencing world public opinion against any foreign military, economic, and political programs perceived to threaten USSR objectives

2. Demonstrating that the United States is still "aggressive," "colonialist," and "imperialist"

3. Splitting the NATO alliance and discrediting governments that cooperate with it

4. Demonstrating that U.S. policies are incompatible with those of the Third World

5. Discrediting and weakening Western intelligence efforts, especially the CIA

6. Undermining the West's political resolve in protecting its interests against Soviet encroachments[55]

During the 1980s, many forgeries promoting the above objectives surfaced throughout the world. Examples of such falsified messages included the following: a bogus memo from the deputy secretary of state to the U.S. ambassador in Greece suggesting U.S. support for a military coup to preserve NATO bases; a letter to King Juan Carlos of Spain, purportedly from President Reagan, naming royal advisers who were against that country's entry into the Western alliance; and a forged memo from the U.S. Department of State about CIA contacts with the former communist president of Afghanistan, Hafizullah Amin. Other examples involved a fake speech by the U.S. ambassador to the United Nations on U.S. policy toward India; a forged West German government document accusing the United States of plotting to overthrow the regime in Ghana; another forgery from the U.S. embassy in Nigeria ordering the assassination of that country's leading presidential candidate; a bogus AFL-CIO letter and a falsified National Security Council memorandum proving United States' responsibility for the troubles in Poland; a forged note to the defense minister of Austria from the U.S. ambassador; and a secret document allegedly showing that President Reagan had authorized the deployment of forty-eight nuclear weapons on Iceland in case of war. Disinformation reportedly costs the USSR some $4 billion a year.[56]

In an address before the American Bar Association, then U.S. attorney general William French Smith disclosed that the KGB had mailed racist letters (allegedly from the Ku Klux Klan) before the 1984 Summer Olympics to more than twenty African and Asian countries anonymously threatening their athletes. None stayed away from the Los Angeles games. The envelopes were postmarked in northern Virginia or Prince George's County, Maryland, both easily accessible to Soviet intelligence officers from the USSR embassy in Washington, D.C. Linguistic and forensic analysis proved beyond doubt that the letters had been manufactured and mailed by the KGB.

These active measures continue despite Gorbachev's statement at the December 1987 summit meeting in Washington, D.C., wherein he promised U.S. Information Agency director Charles Z. Wick that there would be "no more lying, no more disinformation." Since that time, Soviet government media have made the following false allegations:[57]

- The FBI assassinated Martin Luther King, Jr. (*Literaturnaia gazeta*, 20 January 1988).
- U.S. citizens purchase live babies in Latin America to obtain their organs for transplants (*Sovetskaia kultura*, 25 October 1988). This particular item of disinformation was picked up and published in some fifty countries throughout the world.
- The 1978 massacre in Jonestown, Guyana, involved the U.S. government (*Novosti*, December 1988).
- The United States is manufacturing an "ethnic weapon" that kills only nonwhites (*Zaria vostoka*, 19 February 1989).
- The United States produced the AIDS virus in a military facility at Fort Detrick, Maryland (*Selskaia zhizn*, 3 March 1989; *Voennyi vestnik*, no. 11 [June 1989]).
- The CIA assassinated Prime Minister Olof Palme of Sweden, Prime Minister Indira Gandhi of India, and General Omar Torrijos of Panama and attempted to kill Pope John Paul II (*Pravda*, 18 August 1989).
- The CIA and an unnamed high-ranking Republican politician were behind the murder of Olof Palme (*Pravda*, 3 July, 25 July, and 2 August 1990).
- The assassination of President John F. Kennedy took place on direct orders of the CIA (*Pravda*, 8 August 1990).
- The CIA is planning to assassinate Saddam Hussein of Iraq (Moscow television news, 3 September 1990).
- A plan to create a union of the Baltic States, the Ukraine, and Belorussia was discussed by the CIA at a secret meeting (*Sovetskaia Rossiia*, 11 November 1990; *Izvestiia*, 20 November 1990).

In the Palme case, although Christer Pettersson was convicted of the murder in July 1989 (released on appeal three months later), the Swedish newspaper *Expressen* revealed that a Soviet diplomat/KGB officer did not show any surprise during a taped telephone conversation on the day (28 February 1986) of the murder.[58]

However, assassination of political opponents by the KGB, and more recently by a client secret service in East-Central Europe, has continued as state policy. Soviet intelligence officer Bogdan Stashinskii liquidated two anticommunist Ukrainian leaders in Munich: Lev Rebet and Stefan Bandera were both killed (at different times) with the same cyanide spray gun. The assassin, decorated personally by then KGB chief Aleksandr N. Shelepin, balked at a third assignment and surrendered to West German police. He received an eight-year prison sentence as an "accomplice" to murder.[59] Attacks on Bulgarian émigrés occurred in both London and Paris. Georgi Markov and Vladimir Kostov, former members of the communist party in Bulgaria, were victims of assassination attempts. Markov died from the effects of a ricin-filled metallic pellet fired from an umbrella; Kostov survived a similar attack in Paris. These attempts were carried out by the Bulgarian intelligence service, most probably with KGB permission, because the murder device had been produced in the Soviet Union.[60]

Strong circumstantial evidence indicates that the USSR ordered the assassination of Pope John Paul II because of his great influence on the Solidarity movement in Poland. A citizen of Turkey, Mehmet Ali Agca, who fired the shots and is now in an Italian prison, told reporters that he had been trained by the KGB in both Syria and Bulgaria. The plot presumably had the approval of KGB chief Iurii V. Andropov himself. Italian state prosecutor Dr. Antonio Albano, interviewed in Rome, expressed his belief in the Soviet-Bulgarian connection based on the twenty-five thousand pages of documentation in the case. Defectors from the Bulgarian state security service revealed that the KGB had decided to farm out political assassinations in the late 1970s and that four hundred Soviet intelligence officers helped devise clandestine programs and policies in Sofia.[61]

Thus, the Bulgarian connection in the plot to assassinate the pope is clear. Italian magistrate Dr. Ilario Martella devoted nineteen months to a careful investigation that included testimony by a former Bulgarian diplomat, Iordan Mantarov, who had informed French authorities in 1983 (the assassination attempt was 13 May 1981) about the details of the plan. Finally, the state prosecutor's seventy-eight-page report the following year explicitly contends that the plot originated with and was paid for by the "Bulgarian secret services." A total of three Bulgarians and five Turks were acquitted on 29 March 1986 "for lack of proof," although the Jesuit journal *La Civiltà Cattolica* subsequently concluded that the attack on the pope had resulted from an "international plot."[62]

The Bulgarian, Cuban, and Nicaraguan governments also helped smuggle shipments of narcotics to the United States, according to Francis M. Muller, Jr., head of the U.S. Drug Enforcement Administration. As much as 10 percent of the heroin that reached North American shores came through Bulgaria at that time. A deputy assistant secretary of state testified that Fidel Castro and former high-ranking Nicaraguan communist officials were involved with smuggling cocaine from Colombia into the United States.[63]

A 1990 U.S. government report asserts that Bulgaria has become an even more important transit point, with an estimated one ton of heroin moving across that country during 1989. Cuba also continued to offer its airspace and surrounding waters for narcotics smugglers from South America. Four senior Cuban officials are under indictment in the United States, although the Castro regime refuses to extradite them for trial.[64]

In the USSR the Chief Intelligence Directorate of the Soviet armed forces under Army Gen. Vladlen M. Mikhailov has organized about thirty thousand men and women into elite special designation units (*spetsnaz*), which are assigned to assassinate civilian and military leaders of NATO countries in time of war and engage in other acts of terror as well as sabotage. *Spetsnaz* located at Murmansk, for example, would attack targets in Norway.[65] Although assigned to military intelligence, these units are also a part of the regular armed forces, discussed in the next chapter.

NOTES

1. Nikolai V. Ogarkov, chief ed., "Komitet Gosudarstvennoi Bezopasnosti," *Sovetskaia voennaia entsiklopediia* (Moscow: Voenizdat, 1977), pp. 265–66. See Viktor Yasmann, "Supreme Soviet Committee to Oversee KGB," *Report on the USSR*, no. 26 (30 June 1989): 11–13.

2. John J. Dziak, *Chekisty: A History of the KGB* (Lexington, Mass.: D.C. Heath, 1988), pp. 145–65. See also Astrid von Borcke, *Unsichtbare Weltmacht KGB* (Stuttgart: Hänssler Verlag, 1989); Alexander A. Ushakov, *In the Gunsight of the KGB* (New York: Knopf, 1989); Herbert Romerstein and Stanislav Levchenko, *The KGB against the "Main Enemy"* (Lexington, Mass.: D. C. Heath, 1989).

3. Oleg V. Penkovskiy, *The Penkovskiy Papers* (Garden City, N.Y.: Doubleday, 1965); William Hood, *The Mole* (New York: W. W. Norton, 1982), pp. 284–87.

4. For more information on Serov, see Pierre de Villemarest, *G.R.U., le plus secret des services sovietiques, 1918–1988* (Paris: Editions Stock, 1988), pp. 258–71.

5. Mikhail Sokolov, "KGB: mif i strakh XX veka," *Sobesednik*, no. 29 (July 1990): 4, and "Lubianka: deistvuiushchie litsa i pokroviteli," *Sobesednik*, no. 36 (September 1990): 4, by the same interviewer.

6. Alexander G. Rahr, comp., *A Biographic Directory of 100 Leading Soviet Officials*, 4th ed. (Munich: Radio Liberty Research, January 1989), pp. 92–93,

for data on Kriuchkov. Major General Kalugin contends that the Presidential Council includes members who are dependent on the KGB. M. Sokolov, "KGB: mif i strakh," *Sobesednik*, no. 29 (July 1990): 4. See also interview with V. A. Kriuchkov, "V KGB o KGB," *Novoe vremia*, no. 32 (4 August 1989): 5–8.

7. Named after the first head of the secret police. See V. A. Mikhalkin, *Feliks Dzerzhinskii* (Moscow: Ekonomika, 1987); and Amy W. Knight, *The KGB* (Boston: Unwin Hyman, 1988). On 5 November 1990, the Moscow city council changed the name back to the original Lubianka Square.

8. John Barron, *KGB Today: The Hidden Hand* (New York: Reader's Digest Press, 1983), pp. 444–51. See also Herbert Romerstein, *The KGB Enters the 1990s* (Washington, D.C.: Center for Intelligence Studies, 1990), pp. 1–24.

9. U.S. Congress, House, Permanent Select Committee on Intelligence, Subcommittee on Oversight, *Hearings on Soviet Active Measures*, 97th Cong., 2d sess., 1982, p. 235. See also Ladislav Bittman, *The KGB and Disinformation* (Washington, D.C.: Pergamon-Brassey's, 1985), especially pp. 35–69, and the periodical *Disinformation*, no. 12 (Summer 1989): 1 and 12, on the use of Soviet émigrés by the KGB.

10. Lev Elin, "Delo Kalugina," *Novoe vremia*, no. 29 (13 July 1990): 27, cites Major General Kalugin on KGB potential that is "harmful to health and life."

11. Kriuchkov claims that the Fifth Chief Directorate was dissolved in 1989 and replaced by one charged "to protect constitutional rights," according to *New Times* (Moscow), 8–14 August 1989, p. 69; "Sovetskomu konstitutsionnomu stroiu-nadezhnuiu zashchitu," *Pravda*, 2 November 1989, p. 3, elaborates. N. Belov, "Pozvol'te ne soglasit'sia," *Argumenty i fakty*, no. 30 (28 July-3 August 1990): 7, for KGB border troops.

12. A former chief of counter intelligence charged that the KGB still remains a state within a state. See Maj. Gen. Oleg D. Kalugin, "KGB poka ne meniaet printsipov," *Komsomol'skaia pravda*, 20 June 1990, p. 2. See also former KGB officer Valentin Korolev, " 'Sekrety' sekretnykh sluzhb," *Ogonëk*, no. 43 (October 1990): 28–31.

13. An interview with the son of Sorge's assistant, Branko Vukelic, appeared in E. Fadeev, "Postaraius' byt' bodrym," *Pravda*, 1 September 1989, p. 5. The clandestine radio message from Tokyo warning that war was imminent reached Red Army military intelligence the day before Germany attacked and is reproduced as "Donesenie iz Tokio (21 Iuniia 1941)," *Izvestiia TsK KPSS*, no. 4 (April 1990): 222.

14. According to his tombstone, he was born William Henry Fisher in England, the son of Russian émigrés. "Tombstone Calls Abel British Born," *New York Times*, 27 August 1972, p. 8.

15. John Barron, *KGB: The Secret Work of Soviet Secret Agents* (New York: Bantam Books, 1974), pp. 413–15. For a defector who returned to Moscow, note the case of Vitalii S. Iurchenko, who was described as "100 percent traitor" by retired Major General Kalugin of the KGB (see note 12 above). Bill Keller "Ex-KGB Officer Asserts Spy Agency Is Unchanged," *New York Times*, 17 June 1990, p. 8.

16. Thierry Wolton, *Le KGB en France* (Paris: Bernard Grasset, 1986); "Britain Is Expelling 25," *Wall Street Journal*, 13 September 1985, p. 1; R. K. Bennett, "Expelled," *Reader's Digest*, January 1987, pp. 47–52. See also U.S. Department of State, "Expulsion of Soviet Officials," *Foreign Affairs Note*, November 1989, pp. 1–2. Christopher Andrew and Oleg Gordievsky, *The KGB* (London: Harper Collins).

17. Article 13–1 of the Soviet penal code bans revealing any official information to foreigners. It appeared in *Vedomosti Verkhovnogo Soveta SSSR*, no. 3 (18 January 1984): 91–93, later supplemented by Article 380, *Vedomosti Verkhovnogo Soveta SSSR*, no. 22 (1 July 1984).

18. Barron, *Hidden Hand*, p. 240. See also then FBI director William H. Webster in ABA Law and National Security, *Intelligence Report* 7, no. 12 (December 1985): 7, for numbers; U.S. Senate, Select Committee on Intelligence, *Soviet Presence in the U.N. Secretariat*, 99th Cong., 1st Sess. (Washington, D.C.: GPO, 1985); "Countering the KGB," *Wall Street Journal*, 3 October 1986, p. 28.

19. See *Facts on File*, 4 May 1979, p. 317; and "Spy Defection Reported Big Blow to Russia," *San Francisco Chronicle*, 5 May 1980, p. 16.

20. See report by M. B., *Sueddeutsche Zeitung*, 22 August 1990, p. 5, on increased Soviet espionage activities. About sixty East bloc spies were arrested during 1989 by the West German counterespionage service, according to *Innere Sicherheit* (Bonn), no. 3 (31 August 1990): 7. See also Bundesministerium des Inneren, "Spionageabwehr 1989," *Verfassungsschutzbericht 1989* (Bonn), August 1990, last 51 pages of mimeographed version. Only two hundred of an estimated four thousand East German spies had been arrested in West Germany, according to "Hohe MfS-Offiziere enttarnen Agenten gegen Straffreiheit," *Die Welt*, 11 September 1990, p. 1.

21. On agents in France, see "A Soviet Spy in Every French Port?" *Washington Post*, 13 April 1990, p. E-5. For the FRG, see *Der Spiegel*, 8 October 1990, pp. 25–28.

22. Wolton, *Le KGB en France*, pp. 221–28.

23. See Nikolaos A. Stavrou, ed., *Greece under Socialism* (New Rochelle, N.Y.: Aristide D. Karatzas, 1988), pp. 127, 130, 135, 139, and 156 on the *Ethnos* affair.

24. The Philby case is discussed by Robert J. Lamphere, *The FBI-KGB War* (New York: Random House, 1986), pp. 228–47. See also "Kim Filbi: Izvestnyi i neizvestnyi," *Mezhdunarodnaia zhizn'* (Moscow), no. 7 (1988): 110–19.

25. Blunt died three years after the public disclosure. MacLean's death in Moscow came two weeks earlier, according to the obituary, "D. D. Maklein," *Izvestiia*, 12 March 1983, p. 6.

26. U.S. House, Permanent Select Committee on Intelligence, *Soviet Active Measures*, pp. 138–69; John Barron, "The Spy Who Knew Too Much," *Reader's Digest*, June 1983, pp. 130, 207–14; Bittman, *KGB and Soviet Disinformation*, pp. 61–64; Romerstein and Levchenko, *KGB against the "Main Enemy,"* pp.

277–319; and "Agent of Influence," in *Disinformation*, no. 3 (Summer 1986): 10.

27. Jeffrey Richelson, *Sword and Shield* (Cambridge, Mass.: Ballinger, 1986), p. 85.

28. Lyman B. Kirkpatrick, Jr., "Soviet Espionage," in Kirkpatrick and Howland H. Sargeant, *Soviet Political Warfare Techniques* (New York: National Strategy Information Center, 1972), p. 28.

29. Robert Lindsey, *The Falcon and the Snowman* (New York: Simon & Schuster, 1979), relates the story of Christopher Boyce and John Lee, who worked together to steal materials from the TRW aerospace company and deliver them to the Soviet embassy in Mexico City.

30. This number includes the twenty-five spies at the United Nations and the fifty-five from Washington, D.C., and San Francisco expelled in October 1986. Frederick Kempe and John Walcott, "U.S.-Soviet Rift on Spying," *Wall Street Journal*, 23 October 1986, p. 7; *Insight*, 2 January 1989, p. 22, for total number of U.S. espionage cases; AP dispatch from Los Angeles, "F.B.I. Man Tried Again on Espionage Charges," *New York Times*, 23 August 1990, p. A-16.

31. U.S. Congress, Senate Select Committee on Intelligence, *Meeting the Espionage Challenge*, report 99–522 (Washington, D.C.: GPO, October 1986), pp. 121–31; Stephan Engelberg, "CIA Criticized," *New York Times*, 16 May 1988, p. A-11, on Edward Lee Howard; Stephan Engelberg, "Army Spy," *New York Times*, 11 March 1989, p. 9, on James W. Hall; Neil A. Lewis, "Ex-Sergeant Charged," *New York Times*, 9 June 1990, p. 5, for Roderick James Ramsay. See David Remnick, "CIA Defector Claims," *Washington Post*, 22 October 1990, pp. A-13 and A-20, for an interview in Moscow with Howard.

32. Barron, *Secret Work*, pp. 27–28 and 198; Kirkpatrick, *Warfare*, p. 30.

33. Yao, Ming-le, *The Conspiracy and Death of Lin Biao* (New York: Knopf, 1983), claims that Lin Biao had been assassinated by Mao's body guards and that it was Lin Biao's son, Lin Liguo, who died in the airplane crash.

34. Hu is quoted by Nayan Chanda in "A Threat from Peking," *Far Eastern Economic Review* (Hong Kong), 23 June 1983, p. 13. Beijing radio, 16 March 1982, in "Soviet Espionage Activities Said Increasing," *Foreign Broadcast Information Service (FBIS)-China*, 82–056, 23 March 1982, p. C-2, warned the Chinese population that Soviet espionage had expanded. See *Insight*, 28 July 1986, p. 39, for the PRC protest.

35. Henri Regnard, "L'URSS et l'information scientifique, technologique et technique," *Défense Nationale*, December 1983, pp. 107–21; Philip Hanson, "Soviet Industrial Espionage: Some New Information," *RIIA Discussion Papers* (London: Royal Institute of International Affairs, 1987); Jean Guisnel in *Liberation* (Paris), 16 February 1990, p. 1.

36. U.S. Department of Defense, *Soviet Acquisition of Militarily-Significant Technology: An Update* (Washington, D.C.: GPO, September 1985), p. 34. For a report from Switzerland, see "Soviet High-tech Spying," *Insight*, 27 November 1989, p. 34.

37. George Volsky, "Computer Suspect Called Part of Ring," *New York Times*, 24 December 1988, p. 6.
38. Richard F. Staar, "The High-Tech Transfer Offensive of the Soviet Union," *Strategic Review*, 17, no. 2 (Spring 1989): 32–39, lists the twelve ministries.
39. Carey Schofield ("Encounter with the Spy Master," *Daily Telegraph* [London], 17 April 1990, p. 17) interviewed Col. Gen. Vladlen M. Mikhailov, chief of the GRU.
40. Hesh Kestin, "Terror's Bottom Line," *Forbes*, 2 June 1986, pp. 38–40; former KGB Maj. Gen. Oleg D. Kalugin's interview with Bill Keller, *New York Times*, 17 June 1990, p. 18. See also his interview with Mikhail Sokolov, "KGB: mif i strakh XX veka," *Sobesednik*, no. 29 (July 1990): 4–5.
41. Ghana, Ministry of Information, *Nkrumah's Subversion in Africa: Documentary Evidence of Nkrumah's Interference in the Affairs of Other African States* (Accra-Tema: State Publishing Corporation, n.d.). It is conceivable, although not probable, that these East German activities were unknown to the KGB.
42. Barron, *Secret Work*, pp. 317–39.
43. Lewis H. Gann, "Sudan," in Richard F. Staar, ed., *Yearbook on International Communist Affairs 1972* (YICA) (Stanford: Hoover Institution Press, 1972), pp. 289–93.
44. John Duke Anthony, "People's Democratic Republic of Yemen," in *YICA 1984*, pp. 70–74; Robert W. Stookey, "Yemen" in Stookey, ed., *The Arabian Peninsula* (Stanford: Hoover Institution Press, 1984), pp. 96–107.
45. Anthony Arnold, *Afghanistan's Two-Party Communism* (Stanford: Hoover Institution Press, 1983), pp. 127–34; J. Bruce Amstutz, *Afghanistan: The First Five Years* (Washington, D.C.: National Defense University Press, 1986), pp. 283–322; "What Department 8 Does," *Foreign Report* (London), 6 November 1986, pp. 1–2; A. M. Rosenthal, "The Story Goes On," *New York Times*, 1 November 1988, p. A-31; Maj. William H. Burgess III, ed., *Inside Spetsnaz: Soviet Special Operations* (Novato, Calif.: Presidio Press, 1990).
46. Vice-President's Task Force on Combatting Terrorism, *Terrorist Group Profiles* (Washington, D.C.: GPO, January 1989), p. iii. Emphasis added.
47. The FBI has documented the KGB role supporting extreme terrorist factions in the United States, according to Eugene H. Methvin, "Terror Networks, U.S.A.," *Reader's Digest*, December 1984, p. 114. See also then FBI director William H. Webster, "Terrorism as a Crime," *FBI Law Enforcement Bulletin* 55, no. 5 (May 1986): 11–13; Vice-President's Task Force, *Terrorist Group Profiles*.
48. Reuters dispatch from London, "Communists Sold Libya Bomb Material, Havel Says," *Wall Street Journal*, 23 March 1990, p. A-12.
49. See the three-part series about "Carlos" in *Der Spiegel*, nos. 31–33 (1976); "Nem csak Carlos," *Népszabadság*, 29 June 1990, pp. 1 and 5.

See the letter by the Lumumba University rector, who claims that "Carlos" had been registered as a student for only fifteen months. V. F. Stanis, "Po povodu 'terrorista, kotoryi vernulsia s kholoda,' " *Komsomol'skaia pravda*, 31 August 1990, p. 2.
50. Claire Sterling, *The Terror Network* (New York: Holt, Rinehart & Winston,

1981), p. 292; Central Intelligence Agency, *Palestinian Organizations: A Reference Aid*, LDA 90–11155 (Washington, D.C.: Directorate of Intelligence, March 1990).

51. U.S. Congress, Senate, Foreign Relations and Judiciary Committees, *International Terrorism, Insurgency and Drug Trafficking* (Washington, D.C.: GPO, 1986), pp. 13, 15, 23, 30, 77, 95, 106–7, 167; U.S. Department of State, *Patterns of Global Terrorism: 1989* (Washington, D.C.: GPO, April 1990).

52. Manfred Schell and Werner Kalinka, "PLO at the *Stasi* College," *Die Welt* (Hamburg), 1 June 1990, p. 6; translated in *FBIS-Eastern Europe* 90–106 (1 June 1990): 23–24.

 East Berlin radio, 23 August 1990; "PLO Military Training," *FBIS-Eastern Europe* 90–165 (24 August 1990): 15, announced the end of this program.

53. "5 Are Convicted in Terror Scheme," *New York Times*, 25 November 1987, p. A-16, on the El Rukns gang; U.S. Department of State, "Libya's Qadhafi Continues Support for Terrorism," *Fact Sheet*, January 1989, p. 10.

 Qaddafi admitted to having sponsored terrorists in the past but claimed he no longer does so in an interview with *al Mussawar*. Associated Press dispatch from Cairo, "Qaddafi Says He Sponsored and Now Forsakes Terrorists," *New York Times*, 26 October 1989, p. A-8.

54. U.S. Department of State, "Soviet Use of Active Measures," *Current Policy*, no. 761 (18 September 1985). Some fifteen thousand individuals worked on these projects in Moscow, according to Richard H. Shultz and Roy Godson, *Dezinformatsia: Active Measures in Soviet Strategy* (McLean, Va.: Pergamon-Brassey's, 1984), pp. 155–57.

55. U.S. Congress, House, Permanent Select Committee on Intelligence, *Soviet Active Measures*, p. 33.

56. Shultz and Godson, *Dezinformatsia*, pp. 155–57; Stephen Engelberg, "If It's Too Bad to Be True, It Could Be Disinformation," *New York Times*, 18 November 1984, E-3; Stockholm radio, 5 December 1984, "Hermannson Rejects U.S. Nuclear Deployment Plan," *FBIS-Western Europe* 84–236 (6 December 1984): P-4, the following day; *Insight*, 1 December 1985, pp. 26–29; Gary Thatcher "Soviets Use Forged Documents to Deceive," *Christian Science Monitor*, 11 December 1986, pp. 1 and 5, for other forgeries.

57. U.S. Information Agency, "Soviet Active Measures in an Age of Glasnost," *Report to Congress* (Washington, D.C.: USIA Office of Research, March 1988), pp. 2–3 and 7, for Gorbachev's promise; U.S. Department of State, *Soviet Influence Activities* (Washington, D.C.: GPO, August 1989), updates the above report. See also interviews with Major General Kalugin in note 12 above and in *Sobesednik*, no. 29 (July 1990): 4, for testimony that disinformation continues.

58. *International Herald Tribune* (Paris), 29 September 1989, p. 1. See also Steven Prokesch, "Palme Conviction Upset," *New York Times*, 13 October 1989, p. A-3.

59. Karl Anders, *Mord auf Befehl* (Tübingen/Neckar: Schlichtenmayer, 1963). When asked about KGB murders, Major General Kalugin replied that he had no knowledge of any during the "past two or three years, although before that

there were." Leonid Zagal'skii and Oleg Moroz, "Tsenoi general'skikh lampa-
sov," *Sovetskaia molodezh'*, 18 July 1990, p. 1. See also former KGB officer
Mikhail Lyubimov, "Terror: The Last Act," *Moscow News*, no. 35 (9–16
September 1990): 15, who discussed these and other murders.
60. Georgi Markov, *The Truth That Killed* (London: Weidenfeld & Nicolson,
    1983). More than thirty people were liquidated in this manner by Lavrenty P.
    Beria, secret police chief and Stalin's accomplice, according to Andrei Sakharov,
    "A Truly Terrifying Human Being," *Time*, 14 May 1990, p. 46. See also "The
    Truth about Beria's Secret Laboratories," *Moscow News*, no. 39 (7–14 October
    1990), p. 6.
61. Paul B. Henze, *The Plot to Kill the Pope* (New York: Scribner's, 1983), pp.
    153–80; Claire Sterling, "Behind Agca's Gun," *New York Times*, 21 November
    1986, p. A-35.
62. Antonio Albano, *Report of State Prosecutor's Office* (Rome: Appeals Courts,
    28 March 1984), p. 76, of the English translation; E. J. Dionne, "Jesuit Journal
    Faults Verdict on Pope Attack," *New York Times*, 8 June 1986, p. 9, gives the
    acquittal and quotations from the Italian magazine.
63. *Castro and the Narcotics Connection: The Cuban Government's Use of Narcot-
    ics Trafficking to Finance and Promote Terrorism* (Washington, D.C.: Cuban
    American National Foundation, 1983); "The Communist Connection," *New
    York Times*, 13 September 1984, p. A-17.
64. U.S. Department of State, *International Narcotics Control Strategy Report*
    (Washington, D.C.: Bureau of International Narcotic Matters, March 1988),
    pp. 34–35; repeated in the same document of March 1990, pp. 24–25.
65. Former GRU Maj. Viktor Suvorov (pseud.), *Inside the Aquarium* (New York:
    MacMillan, 1986), pp. 31–40, discusses *spetsnaz*. See also Liv Hegna, "New
    Home Guard Anti-*Spetsnaz* Group," *Aftenposten* (Oslo), 1 October 1988, p.
    8; and Kirsten Amundsen, "*Spetsnaz* and Soviet Far North Strategy," *Armed
    Forces Journal International*, December 1989, pp. 69–80.

6

MILITARY STRATEGY

USSR attitudes toward military strategy differ fundamentally from those of Western leaders and experts. In the Soviet view, the objective is a "program of action for ensuring military-technical superiority over the armed forces of the probable enemies."[1] Principles are determined by the political leadership, that is, the Defense Council, which receives advice from the highest-ranking military officers. Mikhail S. Gorbachev, general secretary of the CPSU since March 1985 (reelected on 10 July 1990) and USSR president, also serves as chairman of the Defense Council, which is now attached to the presidential office. The Defense Council's main task is to implement supreme organizational, executive, and control functions on specific issues of the country's defense capability and security and to coordinate the activities of competent departments.[2]

Two U.S. authorities on the Soviet armed forces state that, although "doctrine is the military policy of the Party," the USSR defense establishment does have a voice in the matter: "The two sides of doctrine, the political and military-technical, permit the leadership great flexibility. The political side, which identifies imperialism or capitalism as the enemy, has remained relatively constant since Lenin's time."[3]

A country's strategic doctrine may be influenced by its geographic location and the characteristics of its people, as well as its economic resources, ideology, and foreign policy objectives. Taking all these elements into account, Soviet military strategists study the nature of future war, ways of preparing for different types of conflict, means of organizing the armed forces, and methods for conducting warfare. As expressed in mid-1987 by the current USSR defense minister, Marshal of the Soviet Union D. I. Iazov, "Our military doctrine constitutes a system of fundamental views on the prevention of war, military construction, preparation of one's country and its armed forces to repel aggression, and the methods of waging armed struggle in defense of socialism."[4]

At the twenty-seventh CPSU congress in early 1986, Gorbachev had stated that the Soviet Union "stands for . . . limiting the military potential to reasonable sufficiency" (*razumnaia dostatochnost'*). He also claimed that USSR military doctrine was "unequivocally defensive."[5] Both of these formulations were repeated in the May 1987 communiqué of the Warsaw Treaty Organization's political-consultative committee.

Yet when U.S. secretary of defense Frank C. Carlucci gave an address before the Voroshilov Military Academy at Moscow some thirteen months later, he stated that "what troubles us is when the USSR continues to develop forces far in excess to what it needs for purposes of its own defense, and especially when that newly added strength focuses on forces designed for massive offensive operations to seize and hold territory."[6]

The composition of the Defense Council during peacetime reportedly includes seven Presidential Council members (Gorbachev, Iakovlev, Kriuchkov, Ryzhkov, Shevardnadze, Pugo, Iazov). Apart from the defense minister, the high command was represented by only three other military officers: Generals of the Army M. A. Moiseev (chief of staff), P. G. Lushev (Warsaw Pact commander), and N. I. Shliaga (chief of the Main Political Administration).[7] The existence of the Defense Council, which is similar to the U.S. National Security Council, was revealed in early 1976, shortly before Brezhnev's promotion to the military rank of marshal became officially known. Gorbachev, by contrast, never served in the armed forces and does not hold any military rank.

The Defense Council is described in the 1977 constitution. Subordinate to this body is the Main Military Council, which includes the officers listed above as well as those who command the five individual services. Its mandate is to develop the armed forces on the basis of wartime experience, to coordinate national defense, and to expand the military potential of the country.[8]

During the July 1989 hearings before the USSR Supreme Soviet to confirm Iazov as defense minister, Gorbachev told the deputies that he was the one who had reactivated the Defense Council, which probably would become the locus for decisions on military policy. He had detached the KGB's border guards, Interior Ministry troops, and railroad units from the regular armed forces a few months earlier.[9] In effect, they remain under the KGB and the MVD (Ministry of Internal Affairs). The change appears to have been undertaken for cosmetic reasons, so that these formations are no longer technically part of the USSR armed forces, which thus overnight dropped by more than one million down to only 4.2 million men.

Western scholars disagree concerning USSR military doctrine. Some would accept at face value the following statement by a former Soviet chief of staff who, although retired, remains an adviser to President Gorbachev:

> The new political thinking and the defense doctrine are most inseparably connected. . . . The essence of this [new] policy can be defined by three characteristics. First, *demilitarization*, i.e., exclusion of force from foreign policy weaponry. . . . Second, *democratization*—creating a basis of equality in our relationship with any country, whether large or small. Third, *deideologization*, i.e., removal of ideological aspects from relations between countries.[10]

An unprecedented appearance before the defense policy panel at the House of Representatives' Committee on the Armed Services in Washington, D.C., by Andrei A. Kokoshin, deputy director of the USA and Canada Institute (discussed in chapter 4), only added to the confusion over Soviet military doctrine. This man claimed to have developed, together with Maj. Gen. V. V. Larionov, models for East-West relations that would proceed through the following stages: (1) offensive defense, (2) counteroffensive strategic defense, (3) operational counterattack, and finally (4) real "defensive defense."[11] Kokoshin admitted that these ideas had originated with unnamed but "sound" West German and Dutch analysts, although he contended that the same concepts had been discussed during the early 1920s in the general staff of the Red Army.

As if to emphasize these claimed changes, during 1988 Gorbachev promoted relatively unknown, reform-minded officers to defense minister (Iazov) and chief of staff (Moiseev). In addition, between 1985 and mid-1989, some thirty-seven top-level military commanders and fifteen of the seventeen Ministry of Defense Collegium members were changed. Those appointed were ten years younger than their predecessors and included every senior officer who had served in Afghanistan, despite the loss of that war.[12]

TYPES OF WARFARE

Military thinking in the USSR revolves around certain major themes. Soviet commentators divide world conflicts into several categories: general wars, national liberation or civil conflicts, low-intensity or geographically limited wars, and what Western strategists would call "police actions." A war is classified on the basis of its political nature, the class structure of the belligerent powers, the size of the military conflict, and the means used in the application of armed force.[13]

According to the Soviet world outlook, a conflict can be either just or unjust. USSR military doctrine claims to support only just wars and asserts that *any* conflict in which Moscow participates is just *by definition*. The same holds true for wars between "socialist" (that is, communist) and capitalist countries: they are always *just* on the communist side. The most just of all conflicts are those fought in defense of the Soviet Union. Moreover, USSR strategy emphasizes that retribution will be taken against all defeated countries and coalitions.

From the traditional Soviet point of view, there are four types of international class conflicts: wars between two diametrically opposed social systems (that is, capitalist and socialist), national liberation struggles, civil strife, and wars between capitalist states. By definition, armed conflict among communist-ruled countries can not occur and thus is never mentioned. The size of a military conflict may range from local to worldwide. Moscow assigns the highest priority to worldwide conflicts, although USSR strategy recognizes that a global war can escalate from a more limited one. Because of this danger, advance preparation remains the first priority.[14] In a world war, the Soviets would use their resources to destroy imperialism (that is, the Western democracies) as a system. The USSR has developed all its weapons, nuclear and nonnuclear, with such an eventuality in mind, even though "war as a means of attaining political objectives has become unacceptable," in the words of the USSR defense minister. However, the evolution of weapons follows advances in technology,[15] regardless of whether native or borrowed.

The USSR versus the United States

From the Soviet standpoint, the principal means to fight a global or world war would be strategic nuclear forces in general and intercontinental ballistic missiles (ICBMs) in particular, as these are capable of attaining objectives directly. USSR strategy, however, emphasizes that ultimate victory would require effective, wide-scale employment of all other branches of the armed forces: ground, air, navy, antiair and antimissile defense, as well as civil defense. Furthermore, large reserves for all categories are necessary to support frontline troops; hence, the national economy is structured for total mobilization. Indeed, even during peacetime, the Soviet economy appears to be almost, if not already, on a war footing, resulting in widespread shortages of consumer goods due to excessive expenditures on the military.

The permanent "wartime mobilization," with its absolute priority for defense, has absorbed a large part of the Soviet net material product over the years. Efforts to bring this under control have been hampered by reliable statistics on expenditures not being available, conversion of industries from military to civilian production proving slow and difficult, and spin-offs from high technology not as yet existing. All this is enveloped in traditional secrecy, so that even manpower resources remain largely unknown. When leaders of the Trilateral Commission were told by Gorbachev in January 1989 at the Kremlin that the defense budget would be reduced 14.2 percent by 1991, nobody seemed to know the absolute figure from which these cuts would be made. Four months later, the Soviet leader announced that military expenditures for 1989 would total 77.3 billion rubles rather than the 22.2 billion rubles his finance minister had reported earlier. Even these figures have been revised several times, with the foreign minister telling the twenty-eighth CPSU congress in July 1990 that defense still absorbed 25 percent of net material product[16] or about 250 billion rubles. The real amount may be much higher.

USSR strategists emphasize that it is imperative under conditions of general or world war to strike first, even though this contradicts their doctrinal claims. According to Soviet strategy, this option remains by far the best way to seize the strategic initiative,[17] with success resulting from the application of surprise and preemption. Principal land targets are located throughout the continental United States and Western Europe. Other military combat objectives include severing maritime lines of communication between the two areas separated by the Atlantic as well as others in the Pacific; damaging or destroying Western intelligence-gathering capabilities, which are not limited to satellites; and generally confronting the United States and its allies with a series of faits accomplis, whereby escalation of the war would be to Soviet advantage.

Peripheral theaters of military operations (*teatry voennykh deistvii*, TVDs) include western, southwestern, southern, far eastern, and northwestern TVDs. The Atlantic, Arctic, Indian, and Pacific oceans are also designated as individual TVDs. The USSR navy has had forward bases in Angola, Cuba, Ethiopia, Vietnam, and South Yemen.[18] Many of the world's choke points (the Panama Canal, the Suez Canal, the Mozambique channel, and the Cape of Good Hope) are within range of these Soviet or surrogate military installations.

Of special importance is the USSR's fortress on the Kola Peninsula. This area, bordering northern Scandinavia, maintains the highest concentration of "nuclear weapons found in any region of the world." It provides the

USSR with the only suitable ice-free water access to the Atlantic Ocean and sea-lanes of communication "over which more than 90 percent of reinforcements for NATO would have to pass from the United States to Western Europe in a long war."[19]

Warsaw Pact versus NATO

Soviet strategy for an attack against Western Europe would be partly dictated by geography. The three main strategic invasion routes include the northern plain, the Fulda gap, and the Hof corridor from East Germany, where the largest concentration of forces remain stationed at the end of 1990. The five USSR divisions in Czechoslovakia since the August 1968 occupation of that country, along with other Soviet divisions deployed in Hungary and Poland, would have added considerable military power to those assault formations if they had ever moved West.[20] It is probable that a violation of Austria's neutrality would have occurred. At the same time, the USSR must have assumed that southern Europe and the Balkans might become NATO targets, if Warsaw Pact troops supported the main drive toward the English Channel.

A successful occupation of Western Europe by the East would have destroyed the main forces of NATO, denied the United States a beachhead for counterattack, acquired resources to substitute for those lost in the event of a retaliatory strike with nuclear weapons against the Soviet homeland, and provided a possible safe haven for Warsaw Pact troops. All this was based on the Soviet assumption that the administration in Washington, D.C., would have been reluctant to attack NATO territory with nuclear missiles—an attack that would have destroyed Western Europe in order to save it.

Nonetheless, the foregoing scenario required USSR reinforcements to cross East-Central Europe, the northern tier of which the Soviet military high command could no longer consider loyal to its directives. Whether the Czechs and Slovaks would have fought willingly on behalf of their occupation power remained doubtful. Events during 1989 and 1990 suggested that Polish troops also would have been unreliable, and the East Germans most probably never were trusted by the Soviets. The southern tier[21] posed even more complicated problems. The political status of Germany after the 2 December 1990 elections clearly involved the most important national defense issue for the USSR.

Consequently, earlier efforts by Moscow concentrated on making the Federal Republic of Germany less confident in its security policy and on emphasizing the emergence of "new thinking" in Moscow that should be accommodated if not supported. The goal has been to buy time by persuading the United States not to apply high technology to its military and to encourage the exchange of scientific information. Gorbachev appeals to the public in NATO member countries over the heads of their own governments, attempting to convince them that the Soviet problem is also the world's problem[22]—a novel approach to public diplomacy.

Other Conflicts

The USSR looks on wars of "national liberation" as low-risk opportunities for expanding its influence while avoiding the danger of direct confrontation with the West. Over a period of six years, Ethiopia (1974), South Vietnam (1975), Angola and Mozambique (1975), Afghanistan (1979), and Nicaragua (1980) fell successively into the hands of totalitarian ruling groups closely aligned with the USSR. The East had hopes of scoring a similar victory in El Salvador. According to a former USSR defense minister, "In its foreign policy initiatives, the Soviet state actively . . . supports the national liberation struggle . . . in whatever distant region of our planet it may appear"[23] (see table 6.1 for arms delivered to Third World countries by the USSR).

One hundred and fifty instances of low-intensity or geographically limited conflicts occurred during the first four decades after World War II, yet only one escalated into a major confrontation between the superpowers:[24] in October 1973, during a United States worldwide alert, USSR armed forces threatened to intervene if Israel refused to halt its offensive against Egypt. Moscow did not dispatch any troops, although paratroop divisions reportedly had been placed on a ready basis.

According to Soviet military writers, even war in East-Central Europe may have remained limited as long as NATO did not use *tactical* nuclear weapons. In practice, however, nuclear escalation would almost certainly have taken place. Warsaw Pact maneuvers—going as far back as 1965, code-named "October Storm"—included scenarios with simulated battlefield nuclear explosions triggered by both sides.[25]

In USSR strategy, a police action represents the lowest level of conflict, where Moscow expects little or no resistance. Such was the case when, fulfilling their "international duty," Soviet armed forces suppressed East Germany (1953), Hungary (1956), and Czechoslovakia (1968); most recently they were unsuccessful in Afghanistan (1979–1989). See table 6.2 for USSR combat operations in nine additional countries. Formal ideas of sovereignty and national independence did not prevent the USSR from intervening where communist party rule had been threatened by so-called

TABLE 6.1

MAJOR SOVIET EQUIPMENT DELIVERED TO THE THIRD WORLD, 1982–1989

	Total	Near East and South Asia	Sub-Saharan Africa	Latin American	East Asia and Pacific
Tanks and self-propelled guns	7,265	5,255	1,080	735	195
Artillery	13,730	8,760	2,990	1,235	745
Armored personnel carriers	13,060	10,595	1,405	600	460
Major surface combatants	41	31	3	4	3
Minor surface combatants	150	29	28	50	43
Submarines	17	16	0	1	0
Supersonic combat aircraft	1,955	1,225	365	90	275
Subsonic combat aircraft	205	145	25	0	35
Other aircraft	570	380	75	65	50
Helicopters	1,490	965	280	185	60
Guided missile boats	21	11	6	4	0
Surface-to-air-missiles	26,380	18,190	4,415	2,415	1,360

SOURCE: Richard F. Grimmett, "Trends in Conventional Arms Transfers to the Third World by Major Supplier, 1982–1989," CRS Report for Congress (Washington, D.C.: Congressional Research Service, 19 June 1990), tables 4, 5, 6, and 7, pp. CRS–67 to CRS–70.

TABLE 6.2
SOVIET COMBAT OPERATIONS ABROAD, 1950–1989

Country	Period of Time
North Korea	June 1950–July 1953
Algeria	1962–1964
United Arab Republic (Egypt)	18 October 1962–1 April 1963; 1 October 1969–16 July 1972; 5 October 1973–1 April 1974
People's Democratic Republic of (South) Yemen	18 October 1962–1 April 1963
Vietnam	1 July 1965–31 December 1974
Syria	5–13 June 1967; 6–24 October 1972
Angola	November 1975–November 1979
Mozambique	November 1975–November 1979
Ethiopia	9 December 1977–30 November 1979
Afghanistan	22 April 1978–30 November 1979; 25 December 1979–15 February 1989

SOURCES: Lt. Gen. A. D. Sidorov (chief of cadres in the USSR Ministry of Defense), "Dlia tekh, kto voeval," *Krasnaia zvezda*, 12 October 1989, p. 2; Col. V. Izgarshev, "Ne utikhaet bol' afganskaia," *Pravda*, 15 November 1989, p. 4.

counterrevolutionaries (thus, the Soviets invaded Hungary but held back from Poland in 1956). The concept of the inviolability of communist party rule had been at the heart of the so-called Brezhnev Doctrine, discussed in chapter 1. The foregoing examples also illustrate that to date the USSR has never launched an attack, unless it perceived an overwhelming chance for success.

The one exception was Afghanistan, where the "Limited Contingent of Soviet Troops" (OKSV) involved a total of one million men who had tours of duty there during the more than nine years of combat. Official figures claim that only 13,833 soldiers and officers died, with the heaviest losses (2,343) occurring in calendar year 1984. The late Nobel laureate Andrei D. Sakharov, a member of the USSR Congress of People's Deputies, denounced that war as "a criminal adventure." He said that one million Afghans had been killed during the Soviet occupation, which included "the bombing of schools, hospitals, entire regions." Foreign Minister Shevardnadze admitted before the USSR Supreme Soviet that the war in Afghanistan had been "immoral" and "illegal."[26] Unofficial sources estimate that 50,000 Soviets were killed and 150,000 wounded in those hostilities.

SOVIET MILITARY CAPABILITIES

The five military services—strategic missile, ground, air, navy, and air defense forces—would participate in a coordinated arms offensive during an all-out war. According to authoritative information, the USSR has more than five million citizens in uniform, including border guards and internal security, railroad, and construction troops. Between 1.7 and 2 million young men are called up for two or three years of active duty annually (depending on the branch), and the same number is subsequently discharged into the reserve forces.[27] As a consequence, Soviet reserves total more than twenty-five million trained men.

Strategic Missile Forces

The strategic missile forces (SMF) are composed of 260,000 men, plus some 50,000 civilians. Commanded since July 1985 by General of the Army Iu. P. Maksimov, in late 1990 they were servicing 1,406 on-line ICBM launchers in eight different modifications, from the SS-11 through the SS-24. The yearly average of new ICBMs produced remained constant—116 between 1982 and the end of 1988, increasing to 140 during 1989. In tests conducted during September 1987, one of these missiles carrying a dummy warhead exploded only one hundred miles off the northwest coast of the island of Hawaii. Another such ICBM, launched on 11 August 1989 from the Tyuratum space center in Kazakhstan, hit the Pacific Ocean 1,250 miles south of Honolulu.[28]

The Soviets have sought to limit damage to the USSR homeland by deploying superior strategic *offensive* forces capable of preemptively destroying or neutralizing the power of all principal adversaries. In addition, Moscow has developed extensive air and missile defense systems designed to defeat those enemy nuclear forces not eliminated by preemptive Soviet offensive nuclear strikes. Before acquiring a comprehensive antiballistic missile system, the USSR already maintained a civil defense program, including shelters, to protect the top political leadership as well as other key population segments (10 to 20 percent of the total). Preference would be given to those workers essential for continuing economic activity during the war and for the post-attack recovery period.[29]

During the early 1990s, Soviet ICBM accuracy can be expected to improve (although it appears precise enough for military purposes already), as will target flexibility and discrimination. By then, multiple independently targeted reentry vehicles (MIRVs) on strategic missiles should be able to destroy any undefended fixed target in the United States with a single warhead. A second missile would also probably be used to increase the certainty of success. This means that the USSR could destroy more than 90 percent of all American ICBM forces in their prelaunch configuration.[30] The United States continues to lack any comparable counterforce capability against Soviet ICBMs.

Even if one were to set aside the disparity between USSR and U.S. counterforce capabilities, the Soviet Union still possessed superiority in all indexes of strategic power at the beginning of the 1990s. In recent years it has become apparent that Strategic Arms Limitation Treaty (SALT) I and II agreements, the latter unratified by the U.S. Senate, succeeded in providing an institutional justification for the USSR drive toward superiority rather than in controlling or reversing it. If deterrence were to fail and war break out, it would be to Soviet advantage to attack U.S. forces directly and without any warning.[31] Trends in the strategic buildup have been the product of deliberate decisions by the USSR leadership over the past two decades.

For many years, the Soviet Union has been depicted by a large number of Western commentators and strategists as technologically unsophisticated regarding the nuances of war in the nuclear age, a preconception without any basis in fact. During the mid-1960s, decision makers in the United States formulated a nuclear posture designed above all to avoid conflict. The hope was that their Moscow counterparts would reciprocate. Instead, the Kremlin deliberately chose to develop weapons commensurate with a war-fighting posture.[32] Many U.S. leaders believed that by engaging the USSR in arms control forums such as SALT, Western negotiators could help reverse the Soviet war-fighting and war-survival orientation. This expectation had not materialized through the end of 1990.

Ground Forces

The ground forces, the largest service in the Soviet military establishment, have been commanded since February 1989 by General of the Army V. I. Varennikov and are composed of about 1.5 million men organized into 7 airborne, 46 tank, 142 motorized rifle, and 3 static defense divisions. Only 40 percent of these 198 major units are in a ready status, yet they may call into use approximately 61,500 main battle tanks; 50,000 armored personnel carriers, fighting vehicles, and scout cars; 66,880 artillery pieces; 1,723 nuclear-capable surface-to-surface missile launchers; and 12,000 antiaircraft and 4,960 mobile surface-to-air missile (SAM) systems. The ground divisions fall into three categories of combat readiness: (1) three-fourths to full strength, completely equipped; (2) between half and three-quarters manned, with all fighting vehicles; and (3) below half-strength, with some obsolescent equipment.[33]

FIGURE 6.1
STRUCTURE OF THE USSR ARMED FORCES, 1990

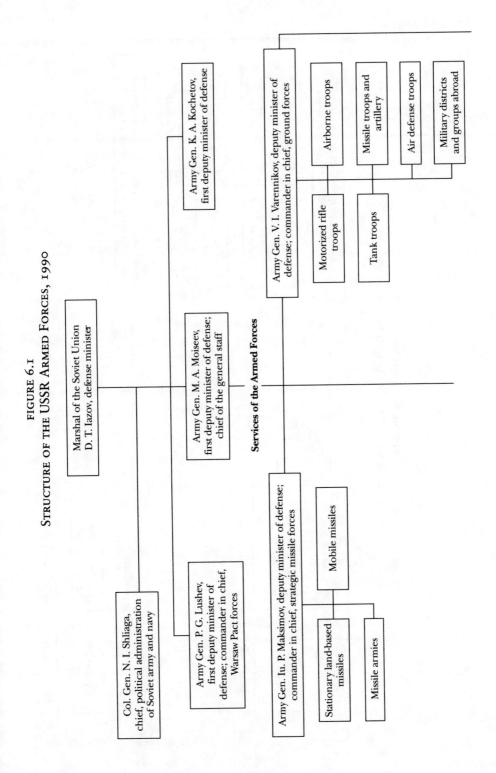

FIGURE 6.1 (*continued*)
STRUCTURE OF THE USSR ARMED FORCES, 1990

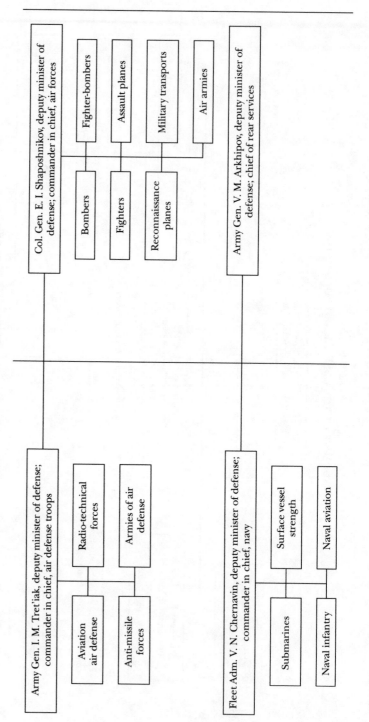

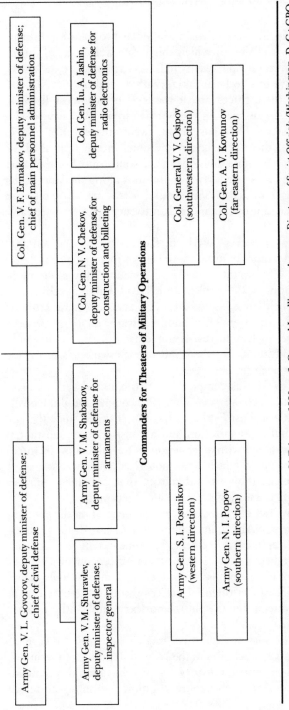

Army Gen. V. L. Govorov, deputy minister of defense; chief of civil defense

Col. Gen. V. F. Ermakov, deputy minister of defense; chief of main personnel administration

Army Gen. V. M. Shuravlev, deputy minister of defense; inspector general

Army Gen. V. M. Shabanov, deputy minister of defense for armaments

Col. Gen. N. V. Chekov, deputy minister of defense for construction and billeting

Col. Gen. Iu. A. Iashin, deputy minister of defense for radio electronics

Commanders for Theaters of Military Operations

Army Gen. S. I. Postnikov (western direction)

Col. General V. V. Osipov (southwestern direction)

Army Gen. N. I. Popov (southern direction)

Col. Gen. A. V. Kovtunov (far eastern direction)

SOURCES: V. Litovkin, "Sekrety bez seketov," *Izvestiia*, 21 February 1990, p. 6; Central Intelligence Agency, *Directory of Soviet Officials* (Washington, D. C.: GPO, 1990), pp. 82–105; "Colonel General Viktor Fedorovich Ermakov," *Krasnaia zvezda*, 17 July 1990, p. 1; "Glavkom VVS," *Izvestiia*, 10 August 1990, p. 7; *Krasnaia zvezda*, 20 September 1990, p. 3.

Deployments include fifty-seven divisions allocated to the western theater of military operations (TVD) of which thirty-one were located during 1989–1990 in East-Central Europe (twenty in East Germany, two in Poland, four in Hungary, and five in Czechoslovakia), with a total of 16,500 tanks and 565,000 men. All these forces are at the level of readiness listed in category 1 above. Military districts in the northwestern TVD have twelve divisions; the southwestern TVD has about twenty-three, only half in category 1. In addition, there are sixteen divisions in the central USSR strategic reserve area, twenty-nine divisions in the south (most of the latter probably in category 3), and some forty-five divisions along the Sino-Soviet border (all in categories 1 or 2).[34] USSR ground forces are also stationed abroad, outside of Eastern Europe, in more than twenty countries (see table 6.3).

The Western Group of Forces (WGF) in East Germany had 380,000 troops with 10,500 tanks (not counting those held in reserve), about 2,400 fighting vehicles, and 1,200 aircraft. The Third Assault Army alone numbered 55,000 men, about 1,200 tanks, and 1,100 fighting vehicles in addition to new battlefield missiles (SS-21, -23, and -22) and artillery. Gorbachev announced a unilateral five hundred warhead, or 5 percent, reduction in short-range nuclear forces. If implemented, the result would still be a twelve to one advantage for the USSR in such warheads versus the United States in the European theater.[35]

The central core of WGF was composed of two hundred battalion-size combat groups that could achieve several breakthroughs simultaneously. The Soviet order of battle in East Germany has not changed since the late 1960s, except for internal reorganization and a consistent yet substantial increase in firepower combined with a reduction in the allocation of forces qualifying as support elements. Each new motorized rifle division as of August 1990 had eighteen battalions and sixteen thousand men—smaller than a NATO division yet possessing much greater firepower.

A successful Warsaw Pact offensive had been predicated on the assumption that forward-deployed NATO units would be unable to stop an attack without large-scale and rapid reinforcement. To some extent Western alliance deployments still reflect zones of occupation agreed on in 1945, as devised by the Allied Control Commission, rather than current logistic and tactical requirements. The Soviet offensive strategy would, then, be one of envelopment, probably attempting to split the northern and southern zones of the West with the Third Assault Army.

The first objective of such an offensive might have been to seize or destroy U.S. nuclear weapon stockpiles in the Federal Republic of Germany. Physical occupation of as much territory as possible would follow to preclude rapid reinforcement and encourage political disintegration. In

TABLE 6.3
SOVIET ARMED FORCES ABROAD, 1990

Country	Number
Afghanistan	10,000[a]
Mongolia	37,000
Algeria	700
Angola	1,000
Cambodia	500
Congo	75
Cuba	8,100
Ethiopia	600
India	500
Iraq	200
Laos	500
Libya	1,500
Mali	75
Mozambique	700
Nicaragua	100[b]
Peru	50
South Yemen	1,000
Syria	2,000
Vietnam	2,800
Africa (remainder)	600
Total	68,000[b]

[a]MVD and KGB personnel remaining after official withdrawal.
[b]Does not include the 565,000 Soviet troops in East Germany, Czechoslovakia, Hungary, and Poland.
SOURCE: International Institute for Strategic Studies, The Military Balance, 1990–1991 (London: IISS, Autumn, 1990), p. 43.

contrast to NATO thinking, there exists no short war versus long war controversy in Soviet military thought. A briefer conflict is preferred,[36] although capabilities for a protracted struggle are in place. If attained, strategists in Moscow reason that a quick victory might preclude expansion of the conflict to other theaters, such as northeast Asia or in the area between eastern Turkey and the Soviet republic of Armenia. However, the emphasis on modernizing USSR ground forces is evidence of the determination to prosecute a long war, if necessary.

Soviet ground forces require a minimum of maneuver time before attack. Hence, the West may have relied on questionable assumptions about the warning that would be available before an offensive from the East. Would NATO have had enough time to mobilize? Soviet leaders might also have assumed that the Americans would not be the first to use nuclear weapons, unless faced with imminent defeat at the conventional level. The East's use of such weapons, meanwhile, would necessitate rapid dispersal of Western anti-tank forces, putting NATO at a serious disadvantage. This in turn could have influenced the main directions of a Warsaw Pact attack, leading to a new allocation of tactical resources, more use of artillery and chemical weapons,[37] and prosecution of the general ground offensive at the highest possible rates of speed.

The Air Forces

The 520,000-man Soviet air forces, under Col. Gen. E. I. Shaposhnikov since August 1990, are divided into three components: strategic, frontal, and transport aviation. Frontal aviation, the most important component, has sixteen air force groups: four are deployed throughout East-Central Europe and the other twelve allocated to the most important military districts. About 4,335 tactical combat aircraft plus 2,510 interceptors and 530 reconnaissance planes belong to these units. Military transport includes approximately 669 aircraft and is augmented, both in peace and war, by the civilian airline Aeroflot, which currently maintains more than fourteen hundred passenger planes.[38]

Not content with an output of about 625 new fighters and fighter-bombers during 1989 or maintaining the production of Sukhoi-24 Fencers, the USSR is turning out the Sukhoi-25 Frogfoot and the MIG-29 Fulcrum as well as new fighters like the MIG-31 Foxhound equipped with look-down shoot-down radar. Soviet aircraft deployed in East-Central Europe have improved markedly, possessing several times the weapons delivery and range of earlier models. These new developments have given frontal aviation the means to attack targets throughout all of Western Europe. Just as important, the 1989 USSR rate of military aircraft production is 120 more a year than that of the United States. Long-range strategic aviation as of August 1990 included about 160 Bears, 330 Backfires, and 21 new Blackjacks, which became operational in 1988.

General Naval Forces

The Soviet navy, commanded since December 1985 by Admiral of the Fleet V. N. Chernavin, totals 410,000 men and includes a naval air arm of 1,369 planes, some 15,000 marines in five naval infantry brigades, rocket and coastal artillery troops, and four groups of *spetsnaz* (special forces) organized into twenty independent units. The navy numbers 1,469 surface combat ships, 62 intelligence collection vessels, about 372 submarines, and 331 auxiliaries for a total of 2,234 operational and reserve units. In addition, since 1975 the USSR has been deploying new classes of heavy cruisers—the latest being nuclear-powered and the largest noncarrier surface combatants ever built—as well as antisubmarine warfare ships. *Tbilisi*, the first of eight large aircraft carriers, has been commissioned with a length of approximately 1,000 feet, a top speed of 30 knots, and space for sixty to seventy combat planes and helicopters. The latest cruise missile-firing attack submarine, *Oscar*, is about twice the size of any U.S. equivalent and is believed to have a titanium hull. The new Soviet ballistic missile-firing *Typhoon* displaces 27,000 tons or almost 50 percent more than the U.S. *Trident* submarine. Only the attack submarine *Akula*, which became operational in 1988, is matched by the U.S. *Sea Wolf*.[39]

One of the four major USSR fleets is on the Baltic Sea and consists of 26 submarines, about 120 surface ships, and 335 aircraft. Most of the naval schools are located in Leningrad, along with a major shipbuilding facility. The Black Sea fleet has 35 submarines, some 124 surface vessels, and 227 planes. A squadron of thirty-one to forty-five additional ships in the Mediterranean is assigned from the Black Sea and the northern fleets. The most rapid expansion during the post-World War II era occurred in the Pacific fleet which, by August 1990, had grown to include 100 submarines, about 126 surface ships (these forces reportedly are to be cut some 27 percent by the end of the century),[40] and 421 aircraft. Between twenty and twenty-five of the ships in the past had been stationed at Cam Ranh Bay in Vietnam.

The northern fleet is somewhat smaller, consisting of approximately 122 surface ships and 386 aircraft. Its primary strength are the 159 submarines. In the event of a global conflict with the United States, all these Soviet fleets would have breakout difficulties in reaching the open oceans. The northern fleet, however, has less of a problem owing to its access to the Barents Sea. An explosion in mid-1984 at Severomorsk on the Kola Peninsula reportedly killed several hundred persons and destroyed two-thirds of that fleet's surface-to-air and surface-to-surface missiles.[41] *Typhoon* submarines as well as squadrons of SU-27 Flanker interceptors and MIG-27 fighter bombers are also based here.

Air Defense Troops

The fifth Soviet military service is air defense, with about 500,000 men and, since February 1987, commanded by General of the Army I. M. Tret'iak. In the early 1980s approximately one-half of the aircraft under *PVO Strany*

(National Air Defense) were transferred to the air forces, where they were placed under the operational command of the military districts or groups of forces in East-Central Europe. PVO *Strany* was redesignated simply VPVO, or troops of air defense (*Voiska Protivo-Vozdushnoi Oborony*). In the mid-1980s, the aircraft previously lost to the air forces were transferred back, suggesting a return to the same organization and autonomy as a separate service that had existed in the late 1970s. (The reorganization in the early 1980s appears to have been a result of Marshal N. V. Ogarkov's plans for establishing theaters of military operations [TVDs]. Soon after Ogarkov's replacement as chief of the general staff, the troops of air defense began to recover the aircraft previously lost to the air forces.)[42]

Apart from the original sixty-four Galosh antiballistic missile (ABM) launchers with nuclear warheads in four complexes and eight sites around Moscow (already upgraded to one hundred ABM launchers), VPVO has 2,315 fighter aircraft, 8,650 surface-to-air missile launchers (with fourteen thousand launcher rails) in about twelve hundred fixed sites, and approximately seven thousand warning systems, including satellites and early warning/ground control intercept radars. A new ABM system had been completed, although not made operational, at Krasnoiarsk in Central Asia.[43] This treaty violation, discussed in chapter 12, was admitted by Foreign Minister Shevardnadze in his report of 23 October 1989 to the USSR Supreme Soviet.

Civil Defense

The USSR maintains two widespread shelter programs down to the city/rural/industrial level, including fifteen hundred hardened command post facilities within 120 kilometers of Moscow with accommodations for at least 175,000 high-ranking officials. The system has been assigned four basic missions: preparing for a possible nuclear attack, protecting the population, safeguarding national economic resources, and providing post-attack recovery and rescue operations. Since 1961, civil defense has been under Ministry of Defense control and now encompasses both military as well as civilian components. An estimated 150,000 permanent staff in the various republics have been working in civil defense activities under a deputy defense minister, General of the Army V. L. Govorov, appointed in July 1986. The number of civilians engaged in similar duties probably totals several hundred thousand, both full-time and part-time. Sixteen million individuals could be mobilized for these tasks during war-time.[44]

In the Soviet view, post-attack recovery is essential to war planning and will play a key role in determining the winner of a nuclear war. To prepare for such a possible conflict, the USSR has dispersed and hardened many industrial sites, revised urban planning, made preparations to decontaminate agricultural areas, and stockpiled essential resources. Many deep bunkers and blast shelters can be found in USSR cities. The Soviet approach to nuclear conflict, therefore, definitely emphasizes "assured survival" as opposed to "assured destruction." Civil defense represents an integral component of overall USSR strategic preparedness. Combined with superior strategic offensive forces and a more dynamic strategy, it demonstrates a commitment to war preparation and war survival unmatched by any country in the world.

Other Forces

To the foregoing must be added the other military units, including about 300,000 KGB border troops and another 340,000 Ministry of Internal Affairs, or MVD, domestic security personnel and uniformed police. Neither is subordinate to the defense ministry, but both are considered parts of the Soviet armed forces in time of war.[45] The best units from the Red Army historically were assigned to the border guards. As a result, they were the first to be attacked on 22 June 1941 by German troops. Currently, they are equipped with a full panoply of modern weapons.

Until March 1989, both the KGB border guards and the MVD internal troops were part of the USSR armed forces, although not subordinated to the Ministry of Defense. At that time an edict of the Supreme Soviet stated that the border guards of the KGB, the internal troops of the Interior Ministry (MVD), and the railroad troops of the Defense Ministry were no longer part of the USSR armed forces. This edict made it possible for official spokesmen to claim that the size of the Soviet armed forces had been reduced by more than one million men. More important, if internal troops were used to maintain law and order, the USSR government could state that they were not part of the Soviet armed forces. These military units are being strengthened. They have been commanded since October 1987 by Lt. Gen. Iu. V. Shatalin, who had served as a combat officer in Afghanistan. As before, MVD troops have infantry weapons as well as light tanks and armored personnel carriers.

A civilian military training organization called DOSAAF (Voluntary Society for Promotion of the Army, Aviation, and Navy) instructs youth fifteen years of age and older at schools and workers' centers. Claiming a membership in 1988 of more than 107 million, at least 5 million of whom were instructors and activists, DOSAAF is organized into 330,000 units that prepare young people in thirty-six military specialties. In 1986–1988, nearly thirty million adolescent boys and girls in the Young Pioneers were given a taste of war using blank ammunition in a two-year long cycle of war games. DOSAAF is headed by Col. Gen. N. N. Kotlovtsev, who was appointed on 20 October 1988, suggesting that it plays an important role in the military-educational system.[46] Its name was changed to Union of Societies and Organizations Promoting Defense of the State (SOOSO) on 2 December 1989.

FUTURE PROSPECTS

The *Saliut*-7 space station continues to orbit the earth, with the goal of deploying structures housing up to twelve persons in the early 1990s. The *Cosmos 1267* satellite had been identified by experts as a prototype that could serve as a building block for space stations larger than the current one, which weighs 660,000 pounds. At least seven out of every ten Soviet space launches are military in nature, and the space stations represent huge orbiting military workshops. *Saliut*-7 has been joined since February 1986 by the *Mir* space station, which is 56 feet long and has five docking ports.[47] Although designed for a permanent crew, *Mir* remained empty during four months of 1989 to cut expenditures. Each launch costs 1.4 billion rubles.

Some observers are convinced that the USSR began working on a charged particle beam weapon in 1965 and built an experimental facility, at Semipalatinsk in southern central Asia, where Soviet scientists reportedly invented a nuclear device to generate a giant electrical pulse that could totally neutralize the U.S. strategic deterrent if perfected. The chief of U.S. Air Force research and development, Lt. Gen. Kelly Burke, predicted that the USSR would be capable of building an operational laser weapon that could disable U.S. space satellites. Reports indicate that a Soviet hunter-killer space vehicle caught up with a target satellite over East-Central Europe and damaged it. The USSR has been conducting such experiments since 1977, according to unclassified U.S. Department of Defense publications. As a result of these Soviet advances, the same sources report that "most [U.S.] military systems are vulnerable to damage and require survivability enhancement." USSR navy ships are suspected of having fired a beam weapon at four U.S. air force planes over the Pacific, possibly injuring the eyesight of a U.S. crew member.[48] The Soviet laser research program is estimated to cost one billion rubles per year.

Although trends are difficult to project with any degree of accuracy, it is now apparent that Kremlin decision makers have at least the capability to implement offensive options, depending on where they place their priorities. During the period from 1971 through 1980, Soviet outlays for defense were at least 40 percent higher than those of the United States. During calendar year 1985, the USSR spent the equivalent of almost $400 billion (up from

$155 billion for 1970) on its military—about 25 percent higher than the U.S. figure of $290 billion for 1986–1987, as voted by Congress. As mentioned earlier, in his speech to the twenty-eighth CPSU congress in July 1990, Shevardnadze stated that defense still takes one-fourth of net material product. All of the above, then, could be accomplished with a gross national product that is less than half that of the United States. What the future holds, of course, is a preponderance of USSR military capability during the early 1990s and potentially beyond.[49]

Whether the Soviets decide to pursue a more openly aggressive policy against the West, specifically NATO, will depend on future decision makers in the Kremlin. In October 1962, during the Cuban missile crisis, the USSR found itself close to a nuclear war with the United States, even though it suffered gross inferiorities both in strategic and in conventional forces. One thing is clear: Soviet participation in the arms control process in particular and détente in general has done little to change the USSR's strategic doctrine, which continues to emphasize counterforce, war fighting, and war survival rather than simple deterrence. Despite official statements to the contrary, the Soviets have continued to modernize their offensive nuclear forces with

- Two new classes of ballistic missile submarines
- Two new submarine-launched ballistic missiles
- One new sea-launched cruise missile
- One new air-launched cruise missile
- Two new strategic bombers[50]

The USSR is also upgrading its strategic defense network by deploying

- Modern look-down shoot-down fighters
- A new airborne warning and control system aircraft
- A new generation of surface-to-air missiles
- A modernized antiballistic missile system around Moscow
- Extensive research facilities on land-, air-, and space-based defenses against ballistic missiles

Similar improvements are being undertaken with conventional forces by fielding

- Four new fighter interceptors and ground attack aircraft

- A new class of aircraft carriers
- A new class of extremely quiet attack submarines
- New tactical surface-to-air missiles
- New short-range ballistic missiles

All military production decisions in the Soviet Union, with regard to both strategic and general-purpose forces, are directed at rendering inconceivable a nuclear retaliatory strike by the United States. With its preponderance of military power, the USSR political leadership wants to ensure that the West will never risk a direct attack on its own initiative. Certainty of this condition will enhance Moscow's international political status and opportunities along its extensive frontiers for future expansion that commenced toward the end of World War II in East-Central Europe. The military procurement level of $55 to $60 billion a year from 1976 through 1982 has increased by 5 to 10 percent annually since then. Gorbachev revealed that the national income during the eleventh (1981–1985) and twelfth (1986–1990) five-year plans was to grow by 21–22 percent, while military expenditures increased by 45 percent.[51]

Figures released by the USSR State Committee for Statistics claimed that the budget for maintaining the armed forces totaled 19.1 billion rubles a year for 1985 and 1986, rising to 20.2 billion rubles for 1987 and 1988. The last entry is marked by two asterisks, with the following explanatory note: "Not counting expenditures for purchasing weapons and equipment, for scientific research work, for military construction, for servicemen's pensions, and other; in 1989, it is envisioned that R 77.3 billion will be spent for these purposes, counting expenditures for maintaining the armed forces."[52]

The last figure was officially announced by Gorbachev when he addressed the USSR Congress of People's Deputies. Prime Minister Ryzhkov later presented a breakdown (in billions of rubles) as follows: procurement (32.6), R&D (15.3), operations and maintenance (20.2), pensions (2.3), military construction (4.6), and other expenditures (2.3). He also mentioned that space programs for the military cost 3.9 billion rubles, making a grand total of 81.2 billion rubles. If the Soviet net material product during 1989 reached one trillion rubles, the 8 percent represents only half or perhaps even one-third of the true military expenditures.[53] With the unabating production of new weapons systems, a large surplus of older equipment remains available for shipment abroad. This plays an important role in Soviet foreign trade, the subject of the next chapter.

NOTES

1. Marshal of the Soviet Union A. A. Grechko, "Voennoe prevoskhodstvo," in A. A. Grechko, chief ed., *Sovetskaia voennaia entsiklopedia*, vol. 2 (Moscow: Voenizdat, 1976), p. 258; cited in William T. Lee and Richard F. Staar, *Soviet Military Policy since World War II* (Stanford: Hoover Institution Press, 1986), p. 30. A new military encyclopedia will appear in the mid-1990s, according to Chief of Staff M. A. Moiseev (TASS, 24 July 1990).

   See also speech by M. S. Gorbachev before the Supreme Soviet that confirmed the old doctrine over Moscow radio, 3 July 1989; *Foreign Broadcast Information Service (FBIS)-Soviet Union* 89–127 (5 July 1989): 48–49. The same formulation appeared in the twenty-eighth CPSU congress resolution, "Ob osnovnykh napravleniiakh voennoi politiki partii na sovremennom etape," *Pravda*, 11 July 1990, p. 2.

2. Interview with L. N. Zaikov, at that time CPSU secretary in charge of defense matters, by V. Izgarshev, "Na sovete oborony," *Pravda*, 27 November 1989, p. 2. Gorbachev stated in a speech at Odessa that the "Defense Council will interact with the appropriate committees of the USSR Supreme Soviet." See M. S. Gorbachev, "Dostoino proiti pereval v istorii strany," *Pravda*, 19 August 1990, pp. 1–2.

3. Harriet Fast Scott and William F. Scott, *Soviet Military Doctrine: Continuity, Formulation and Dissemination* (Boulder, Colo.: Westview Press, 1988), p. 256.

4. Army Gen. D. T. Iazov, "Voennaia doktrina Varshavskogo Dogovora," *Pravda*, 27 July 1987, p. 5; promoted since to the rank of marshal.

5. KPSS, *XXVII S"ezd Kommunisticheskoi Partii Sovetskogo Soiuza* (Moscow: Politizdat, 1986), p. 544. See also Col. V. A. Chirvin, "Oboronnaia dostatochnost' i problemy predotvrashcheniia voiny," *Voennaia mysl'*, no. 7 (July 1990): 5–12.

6. Frank C. Carlucci, "Prospects for the U.S.-Soviet Dialogue," *DoD Press Release*, no. 381–88 (1 August 1988): 3.

7. U.S. Department of Defense, *Soviet Military Power: 1990* (Washington, D.C.: GPO, September 1990), p. 28; TASS, "Zasedanie Voennogo Soveta," *Krasnaia zvezda*, 19 October 1989, p. 1, suggested that this body also included Generals of the Army Iu. P. Maksimov, V. I. Varennikov, I. M. Tret'iak, as well as Fleet Adm. V. N. Chernavin, all of whom were service chiefs.

8. V. S. Golubovich, *Marshal R. Ia. Malinovsky* (Moscow: Voenizdat, 1984), p. 207, states that the original Military Council became known as the Main Military Council in November 1957.

9. *Vedomosti Verkhovnogo Soveta*, no. 12 (March 1989): 136; cited by Viktor Yasmann, "Internal Security Situation and the Defense Council," *Report on the USSR* 1, no. 35 (1 September 1989): 11.

10. Marshal of the Soviet Union S. F. Akhromeev, "Nasha voennaia doktrina," *Agitator armii i flota*, no. 24 (1990): 2–4, gives the whole article.

11. U.S. Congress, House, Committee on Armed Services, 101st Cong., 1st. sess., *Gorbachev's Force Reductions and the Restructuring of Soviet Forces* (Washington, D.C.: GPO, 1989), pp. 49–50.

12. Alexander R. Alexiev and Robert C. Nurick, *The Soviet Military under Gorbachev*, R-3907-RC (Santa Monica, Calif.: RAND Corporation, February 1990), especially chapter 2, pp. 3–12.

13. A. A. Grechko, *Vooruzhennye sily sovetskogo gosudarstva* (Moscow: Voenizdat, 1974), p. 319. See also John J. Dziak, *Soviet Perceptions of Military Power* (New York: National Strategy Information Center, 1981), especially pp. 39–58; Peter Vigor, "Western Perceptions of Soviet Strategic Thought and Doctrine," in Gregory Flynn, ed., *Soviet Military Doctrine and Western Policy* (London: Routledge, 1989), pp. 29–105.

14. A first deputy defense minister and Warsaw Pact commander has written that permanent military readiness is an "objective necessity, a sacred law, and principal guideline of all our military policy." Army Gen. P. G. Lushev, "Na strazhe zavoevanii revoliutsii," *Mezhdunarodnaia zhizn'*, no. 8 (August 1987): 68. The military threat has not disappeared, according to Army Gen. M. A. Moiseev (chief of the general staff), "V rusle obnovleniia," *Krasnaia zvezda*, 22 July 1990, p. 2.

15. Army Gen. D. T. Iazov, "Zashchita otechestva," *Pravda*, 13 November 1989, p. 3. See also Marshal of the Soviet Union S. F. Akhromeev, "Nasha voennaia doktrina," *Za rubezhom*, no. 46 (10–16 November 1989): 1–3.

16. Finance Minister V. S. Pavlov, "O gosudarstvennom biudzhete SSSR na 1990 g.," in *Pravda*, 26 September 1989, p. 4; M. S. Gorbachev, "O gosudarstvennom plane," *Pravda*, 11 November 1989, p. 2; E. A. Shevardnadze, "Otchety chlenov Politbiuro," *Pravda*, 5 July 1990, p. 2.

17. Leon Gouré, "Soviet Doctrine and Nuclear Forces," in William C. Green and Theodore Karasik, eds., *Gorbachev and His Generals* (Boulder, Colo.: Westview Press, 1989), pp. 97–101, for the three schools of thought.

18. U.S. Department of Defense, *Soviet Military Power 1990* (Washington, D.C.: GPO, September 1990), map insert. See V. Chebakov, "Grom nad poluboi," *Pravda*, 22 November 1989, p. 3, for sea trials of the heavy aircraft carrier *Tbilisi*.

19. Kirsten Amundsen, "*Spetsnaz* and Soviet Far North Strategy," *Armed Forces Journal International*, no. 12 (December 1989): 70.

20. North Atlantic Treaty Organization, *Conventional Forces in Europe* (Brussels: NATO Information Service, November 1988); "Zaiavlenie o sootnoshenii vooruzhennykh sil," *Pravda*, 30 January 1989, p. 5, gave other figures. See also U.S. Department of Defense, *Soviet Military Power* (1990), p. 94, for the status of Warsaw Pact forces in East-Central Europe.

21. Teresa Rakowska-Harmstone et al., *Warsaw Pact: The Question of Cohesion*, vol. 3 (Ottawa, Canada: Department of National Defence, March 1986), especially pp. 291–340 and 404–68 on Bulgaria and Hungary.

22. M. S. Gorbachev, *Perestroika i novoe myshlenie* (Moscow: Politizdat, 1987), p. 143; E. A. Shevardnadze, "Sudby mira neotdelimy ot sudeb nashei perestroiki,"

Pravda, 27 September 1989, pp. 4–5, repeated these themes in his speech before the U.N. General Assembly.

23. A. A. Grechko, "Rukovodiashchaia rol' KPSS v stroitel'stve armii," *Voprosy istorii KPSS* 16, no. 5 (May 1974): 39. See also Stephen T. Hosmer and Thomas W. Wolfe, *Soviet Policy and Practice toward Third World Conflicts* (Lexington, Mass.: D.C. Heath, 1983), pp. 129–33; I. F. Chernikov, chief ed., *Osvobodivshiesia strany* (Kiev: Naukova dymka, 1988); Steven R. David, "Why the Third World Matters," *International Security* 14, no. 1 (Summer 1989): 50–85.

24. The figures on limited wars (150) are from United Nations, *Disarmament Fact Sheet*, no. 38 (May 1985): 4, which gives a total of 71 involved countries.

25. Richard F. Staar, *Communist Regimes in Eastern Europe*, 5th rev. ed. (Stanford: Hoover Institution Press, 1988), pp. 267–68.

26. Lt. Col. A. Oleinik, "S voinoi pokonchili my schety?" *Krasnaia zvezda*, 15 February 1990, p. 4; Michael Dobbs, "Parliamentary Jeers Rain down on Sakharov," *Washington Post*, 3 June 1989, p. A-11, quoting Sakharov. E. A. Shevardnadze, "Vneshniaia politika i perestroika," *Pravda*, 24 October 1989, pp. 2–4.

27. International Institute for Strategic Studies (IISS), *The Military Balance, 1990–1991* (London, IISS, Autumn 1990), p. 33. The 329,000 construction troops are to be disbanded during 1991. Because of draft evasion, the armed forces experienced a shortfall of 400,000 men, according to Interfaks, "Uklonenie ot prizyva v armiiu," *Izvestiia*, 4 October 1990, p. 3.

28. U.S. Department of Defense, *Soviet Military Power 1990*, pp. 38–39, for production numbers; Michael R. Gordon, "U.S. Protests Test of Soviet Missiles North of Hawaii," *New York Times*, 2 October 1987, p. 1; and Maj. Gen. Henry Mohr, AUS (ret.), *High Frontier Newswatch*, October 1989, p. 2, for the two test flights.

29. H. F. Scott and W. F. Scott, *The Soviet Control Structure: Capabilities for Wartime Survival* (New York: Crane, Russak, 1983), pp. 121–28; Lee and Staar, *Soviet Military Policy*, pp. 51–53; U.S. Department of Defense, *1989 Joint Military Net Assessment* (Washington, D.C.: GPO, June 1989), p. 3–2, for civil defense.

30. "The Soviets nevertheless now probably possess the necessary combination of ICBM numbers, reliability, accuracy and warhead yield to destroy *almost all* of the 1,047 U.S. ICBM silos, using only a portion of their own ICBM force" (emphasis added). *Report of the President's Commission on Strategic Forces* (Washington, D.C.: GPO, 1983), p. 4. See also Lee and Staar, *Soviet Military Policy*, pp. 183–84, for accuracy of Soviet ICBMs. Deployment of the rail-mobile SS-24 commenced during 1987, and some eighty had been deployed within three years. U.S. Department of Defense, *Soviet Military Power 1990*, p. 52.

31. U.S. Department of Defense, *1989 Joint Military Net Assessment*, pp. 3–1 through 3–6, for USSR offensive nuclear capabilities; *Statement of the Secretary*

of Defense before the Senate Armed Services Committee (Washington, D.C.: GPO, 1 February 1990), pp. 1–2.

32. Lee and Staar, *Soviet Military Policy*, pp. 61–78.

33. U.S. Department of Defense, *Soviet Military Power 1990*, map insert; IISS, *The Military Balance 1990–1991*, pp. 34–35.

34. Ibid. See also L. Litovkin, "Sekrety bez sekretov," *Izvestiia*, 21 February 1990, p. 6, for names of TVD commanders, listed also in figure 6.1.

35. Thomas L. Friedman, "Gorbachev Hands a Surprised Baker an Arms Proposal," *New York Times*, 12 May 1989, pp. A-10, A-11.

36. Scott and Scott, *Soviet Military Doctrine*, pp. 81–85.

37. The USSR had four types of chemical agents in its stockpile, which totaled 300,000 tons at seven centers. Michael R. Gordon, "Soviets to Start Trimming Arsenal," *New York Times*, 9 January 1989, pp. A-1 and A-8. See also the interview with Col. Gen. S. V. Petrov, chief of chemical troops, who claims that the USSR stockpile contains only 40,000 tons. V. Nikanorov, "Khimicheskii drakon," *Pravda*, 2 August 1990, p. 5.

38. U.S. Department of Defense, *Soviet Military Power 1990*, pp. 78–82; IISS, *Military Balance*, p. 36. A. Pavlov, "Nebesnyi marafonets," *Sotsialisticheskaia industriia*, 1 November 1989, p. 2, discusses Aeroflot's new wide-bodied IL 96–300 that reportedly can fly 10,000 kilometers without refueling.

39. U.S. Department of Defense, *Soviet Military Power 1990*, pp. 82–92; IISS, *Military Balance*, pp. 36–38. On sea trials of *Tbilisi*, see TASS report over Moscow radio, 22 November 1989; *FBIS-Soviet Union 89–224* (22 Novemer 1989): 121–22.

40. Japanese Defense Agency, *Annual Report* (Tokyo: 18 September 1990); *Radio Free Europe/Radio Liberty, Daily Report*, no. 179 (19 September 1990): 7.

41. IISS, *Military Balance*, p. 39. U.S. Department of Defense, *Soviet Military Power 1990*, map insert; explosion reported in *Jane's Defence Weekly* and discussed by Drew Middleton, "Soviet Naval Blast Called Crippling," *New York Times*, 11 July 1984, p. A-6. For more on the Kola Peninsula base complex, see editorial on "Defense Credibility," in *Aftenposten* (Oslo), 6 January 1990, p. 2.

42. Information from the Honorable Harriet F. Scott and Col. William F. Scott, USAF (Ret.)

43. U.S. Department of Defense, *Soviet Military Power 1990*, pp. 56–59 and map insert; *Military Balance 1990–1991*, pp. 35–36.

44. U.S. Department of Defense, *1989 Joint Military Net Assessment*, p. 6–2, and *Soviet Military Power 1990*, pp. 58–59; Central Intelligence Agency (CIA), *Directory of Soviet Officials* (Washington, D.C.: GPO, 1990), p. 83.

45. H. F. Scott and W. F. Scott, *Armed Forces of USSR*, 3d rev. ed. (Boulder, Colo.: Westview Press, 1984), pp. 236–39; U.S. Department of Defense, *Soviet Military Power 1990*, p. 75; V. Yasmann, "Internal Security Forces," *Report on the USSR* 2, no. 43 (26 October 1990): 12–15.

46. F. Semianovskii, "Plenum DOSAAF," *Krasnaia zvezda*, 22 November 1985, p. 3; D. Volkogonov, "Zashchita sotsializma i voenno-patrioticheskoe vospitanie,"

Pravda, 15 August 1986, pp. 2–3; CIA, *Directory of Soviet Officials*, 1990, p. 179.

On 1 September 1990, a new system of "predraft training" replaced the old "introductory military training" in schools. It concentrates on physical education. See N. Burbyga, "Otmena nachal'naia voennaia podgotovka," *Izvestiia*, 18 August 1990, p. 3.

47. Thomas Y. Canby, "Are the Soviets ahead in Space?" *National Geographic* 170, no. 4 (October 1986): 420–58; U.S. Congress, Senate Committee on Commerce, Science, and Transportation, *Soviet Space Programs: 1981–87* (Washington, D.C.: GPO, May 1988), pp. 280; Nicholas L. Johnson, *The Soviet Year in Space: 1989* (Colorado Springs, Colo.: Teledyne Brown Engineering, 1990).

48. Stephen Engelberg, "U.S. Says Lasers Strike Its Planes," *New York Times*, 10 November 1989, p. A-11.

49. See Defense Minister D. T. Iazov, "Na osnove novogo myshleniia," *Krasnaia zvezda*, 13 April 1989, pp. 1–2, for official USSR troop strength; U.S. Department of Defense, *Soviet Military Power 1990*, map insert, for U.S. estimates.

50. Lt. Gen. E. G. Shuler (USAF), "Despite Glasnost, Soviet Military Is Unchanged," *ROA National Security Record* 7, no. 10 (October 1989): 10–11. See also John Lenczowski, "Military Glasnost' and Strategic Deception," *International Freedom Review*, Winter 1990, pp. 3–43; Secretary of Defense Dick Cheney, "Preface," *Soviet Military Power 1990*, pp. 3–5.

51. M. S. Gorbachev, "Na ural'tsev mozhno polozhit'sia," *Pravda*, 29 April 1990, p. 2.

52. R. Iur'ev, "Raskryvaem tainy biudzheta," *Pravitelstvennyi vestnik*, no. 18 (September 1989): 6. See also William T. Lee, *Trends in Soviet Military Outlays and Economic Priorities* (Washington, D.C.: Senate Committee on Foreign Relations, 30 July 1990), testimony.

53. Colonel V. Deinega, "Oboronnyi biudzhet i ego realizatsiia," *Kommunist vooruzhennykh sil*, no. 3 (February 1990): 30–36, provides justification for spending increases on procurement, military construction, research, and development. Soviet economists V. Belkin, O. Bogomolev, and V. Tikhonov estimated that Soviet gross national product is only about 28 percent of the U.S. at a conference in Washington, D.C., on 23 April 1990. Cited by W. T. Lee, *Trends in Soviet Military Outlays*, p. 9. V. Petrovskii, "Voennyi biudzhet v svete glasnosti," *Pravitel'stvennyi vestnik*, no. 45 (November 1990): 9, provides figures on defense expenditures and foreign military assistance that were submitted to the United Nations.

See, however, M. S. Gorbachev, "Dostoino proiti pereval," *Krasnaia zvezda*, 19 August 1990, p. 2, where he delineates a five-part program of military reform. He reversed himself on several points when addressing about one thousand military men who were elected legislators in "Sud'ba naroda—sud'ba armii," *Pravda*, 16 November 1990, pp. 1 and 3. See also the two concepts of military reform (Defense Ministry and working group of Supreme Soviet) in *Pravitel'stvennyi vestnik*, no. 48 (November 1990): 5–12.

7

FOREIGN TRADE

Commercial relations with other countries are an important instrument of Soviet foreign policy. The objective of trade is not just to make money but to promote the USSR's economic power and influence throughout the world. Within the East-Central European bloc, the USSR aimed to totally integrate the individual country economies—a goal met with increasing resistance from those countries. Trade with developed capitalist states chiefly involved purchases of food and technology, either on credit or in return for hard currency from the sale of natural resources. This relationship was tempered in the late 1980s by the Soviet Union's relative lack of monetary reserves, absence of high-quality manufactured goods for export, and domestic economic problems. In the Third World, the USSR has used trade, even encouraging indebtedness, to promote its foreign policy objectives, although at times this involved dealing with governments it condemned politically.

For almost seventy-two years, the Soviet government did not reveal much information about its commercial transactions. Organizations in the West were forced to estimate terms of trade and other indexes. The first official disclosure regarding the USSR hard currency debt came in mid-1989, when Prime Minister N. I. Ryzhkov told the Congress of People's Deputies that the government owed the West 34 billion rubles ($57 billion), which was costing 12 billion rubles ($19 billion) to service each year.[1] The government could pay off the principal in about two years from increased hard currency sales of oil, natural gas, gold, diamonds, and weapons.

The Soviets have, on several occasions, curtailed or cut off trade with certain foreign countries to penalize them. This happened with imports of fish from Iceland in 1948, when that state's government showed an inclination to become a charter member of NATO. There was also a total embargo against Yugoslavia in 1949, following its expulsion from the Cominform (Communist Information Bureau). Wool imports from Australia were eliminated for a time after 1954, when that country granted political asylum to a defecting Soviet intelligence officer and his wife. Exports to the People's Republic of China (PRC) were cut back drastically in 1965 after the withdrawal of Soviet technicians during the previous year. The PRC retaliated by demanding that trade be conducted on a cash basis, which subsequently developed into a barter system.

In 1980, the Soviet Union temporarily stopped deliveries of petroleum to Romania because of statements by the late President Nicolae Ceauşescu equating USSR missile deployments in East-Central Europe with those of NATO in Western Europe.[2] In June 1990 the USSR threatened to terminate bilateral trade with Finland, even though an extension (to 1995) had been signed the previous October. This may have been done in response to a report that the Finns were considering a halt in the delivery of newsprint due to Soviet nonpayment of bills.[3] The commercial exchange agreement had obligated both signatories to specific terms of reference, elimination of which would have hurt Finland more than it would the USSR.

FOREIGN TRADE DECISIONS

The Ministry of Foreign Trade was abruptly abolished in 1988 as preparation for the joint venture drive. Although several other Soviet governmental agencies are involved in making decisions, apart from the Ministry of Foreign Economic Relations (under K. F. Katushev since early 1988), only the following ones will be mentioned here: Gosplan (the State Planning Committee), the State Committee for Science and Technology, the Ministry of Finance, Gosbank (the USSR state bank), and the State Foreign Economic Commission attached to the Council of Ministers.

Gosplan prepares targets for the five-year planning cycle. Its chairman since February 1988, Iu. D. Masliukov, directs about five thousand employees[4] and also serves as a first deputy prime minister. His organization is responsible for monitoring the implementation of national economic plans. The foreign trade department, one of sixty-seven such units at Gosplan, compiles trade and payment components.

The State Committee for Science and Technology, under N. P. Laverov since mid-1989, is responsible for negotiating technical cooperation agreements with foreign governments and business firms. These usually include exchanging information and specialists who are assigned the additional task of obtaining Western technology. Machinery, equipment, patents, and licenses are the purview of this state committee.[5]

The Ministry of Finance and the USSR State Bank have joint responsibilities, with the bank providing the funds. The bank board chairman since August 1989, V. V. Gerashchenko, reportedly is subordinate to the finance minister (V. S. Pavlov since mid-1989), even though both officials are members of the Council of Ministers. The government's budget is presented to the USSR Supreme Soviet by the finance minister once a year. *Gosbank* monitors plan fulfillment, especially monetary transactions between domestic firms, through the specialized Bank for Foreign Economic Activity (*Vneshekonombank*). *Gosbank* had authority over all credit operations, fixed loan rates for borrowers, and remained the sole source of cash. This central bank, however, was criticized for sitting on 300 billion rubles in savings, without using these funds effectively. By early 1989, some sixty commercial and cooperative banks had registered with the government or had applications pending.[6]

However, proposed reforms drafted in December 1989 would transform *Gosbank* into a Western-style financial institution operating through market methods as well as developing commercial banks with the authority to engage in direct foreign operations. This new law on the USSR state bank and other banks reportedly will come into force during 1992, according to TASS. A possible complication may be an alleged agreement to establish a largely autonomous banking system for the Russian Soviet Federated Socialist Republic.[7]

Last, the State Foreign Economic Commission, under Deputy Premier S. A. Sitarian since October 1989, administers the Soviet overseas aid program, which coordinates the export of complete industrial plants, including nuclear-powered ones, as well as of petroleum and natural gas. Pipelines for the latter do not extend beyond the borders of the Council for Mutual Economic Assistance (CMEA) member-states in East-Central Europe, although they are linked with West European networks. Ia. P. Riabov, commission chairman during 1983–1984, may have received orders to eliminate corruption from the foreign trade bureaucracy. During this period, the chief as well as the imports director of *Technopromexport*, which administers technical assistance for Soviet power plants built abroad, reportedly were executed because of "systematically taking large bribes."[8]

Twenty-one government ministries and seventy major industries received permission as of 1 January 1987 to establish direct contractual ties with foreign countries, even those outside the CMEA area, including joint ventures. At midyear, a state enterprise law introduced self-management and freedom from centrally directed quotas (except for macroeconomic guidance). As of October 1989, some eight thousand enterprises had the right to engage in foreign trade operations. By year's end, about 60 percent of the forty-eight thousand industrial enterprises were to have adopted self-financing (*khozrazchet*); theoretically, at least, that could mean bankruptcy in a case where receipts do not equal costs. One problem is that the USSR maintains some three thousand different exchange rates for products and trading partners, which complicates foreign trade to an almost impossible degree.[9]

For example, the *Soiuzkhimexport* organization used government funds to purchase all chemicals and plastics imported by the USSR. These expenditures were not covered by revenues from exports, although orders continued to be made despite debts totaling some $700 million to U.S. Dupont, West Germany's Hoechst, and Holland's AKZO. Many companies stopped deliveries pending receipt of payment. Prime Minister Ryzhkov himself reportedly told the USSR Supreme Soviet that steps must be taken "to bring back the confidence of our overseas partners." By autumn 1990, these delayed payments totaled several billion dollars.[10]

EAST–CENTRAL EUROPE AND THE BLOC

Trade with the ten members of CMEA as well as other "socialist" countries more than doubled during the last two five-year planning cycles. For calendar year 1989, that trade made up almost two-thirds (61.6 percent) of the Soviet total. Seven of the ten CMEA members showed a positive balance of trade with the USSR. The disparities for Poland and Bulgaria were especially large.[11] (See table 8.4.) Soviet trade figures do not include statistics on the export of weapons or other military supplies.

In response to a request from deputies to the USSR Supreme Soviet, the Finance Ministry produced a "unique document" providing details on the extent of foreign indebtedness to the Soviet Union. More than half of the total (43.8 billion rubles, or some 51 percent of 85.8 billion rubles) is owed by other "socialist" countries, of which only 1 percent has been written off. The remainder represents debts owed by Third World governments (see table 7.1), most of which will never be repaid.

CMEA was established in January 1949 on Stalin's orders as a response to the Marshall Plan and, most probably, to attain economic self-sufficiency for the bloc. Original signatories included those in East-Central Europe, with East Germany becoming a member the next year, followed by Mongolia (1962), Cuba (1972), and finally Vietnam (1978). Yugoslavia remains an associate member; Albania dropped out in December 1961; and China

TABLE 7.1

DEBTS OWED TO THE USSR, 1989
(IN MILLIONS OF RUBLES)

Country	Sum	Original Amount	Written Off 1 January 1989 (including interest)	Deferred 1986–1989 (including interest)
			DEBT AS OF 11 JANUARY 1989	
Socialist countries				
Albania	127.8	80.3	19.6	—
Bulgaria	433.6	433.6	—	—
Hungary	622.5	622.5	—	—
North Vietnam	9,131.2	8,856.1	406.4	1,568.7
East Germany	110.0	110.0	—	—
North Korea	2,234.1	2,234.1	—	417.6
China	6.2	6.2	—	—
Cuba	15,490.6	15,092.0	—	2,360.4
Laos	758.2	758.2	—	49.8
Mongolia	9,542.7	8,981.3	57.2	2,031.5
Poland	4,955.0	4,952.1	—	3,157.7
Yugoslavia	394.0	375.6	—	—
Subtotals	43,805.9	42,502.0	483.2	9,585.7
Developing countries				
Algeria	2,519.3	2,447.7	—	560.0
Angola	2,028.9	1,930.2	—	768.0
Afghanistan	3,055.0	2,898.6	—	624.0
Bangladesh	6.6	6.6	—	—
Benin	31.6	30.4	—	12.1
Burundi	14.8	14.8	—	—
Burkina Faso	4.3	3.9	—	—
Ghana	9.6	8.7	—	—
Guinea	258.3	256.8	—	—
Guinea-Bissau	66.0	63.2	—	12.7
Grenada	0.2	0.2	—	—
Egypt	1,711.3	1,711.3	—	8.2
Zambia	206.0	151.4	—	23.3
India	8,907.5	8,907.4	—	—
Indonesia	404.5	330.9	—	—
Jordan	369.0	355.8	—	99.5
Iraq	3,795.6	3,514.5	—	1,414.8
Iran	1.0	1.0	—	—
North Yemen	979.6	955.6	—	285.1

Cameroon	0.6	0.6	—	—
Cambodia	714.8	714.5	—	29.8
Congo	199.5	174.0	—	83.7
Libya	1,707.3	1,584.6	—	360.1
Madagascar	100.6	92.9	—	36.0
Mali	285.0	271.6	1.2	88.4
Morocco	2.2	2.0	—	—
Mozambique	808.6	722.6	—	363.0
South Yemen	1,847.6	1,835.7	0.8	581.2
Nepal	2.0	2.0	—	—
Nigeria	26.7	21.8	—	—
Nicaragua	917.3	837.6	—	473.0
Cape Verde	7.2	7.2	—	—
Pakistan	173.8	169.0	—	—
Peru	541.1	541.1	—	50.5
São Tomé and Príncipe	4.8	4.7	—	1.8
Seychelles	0.2	0.2	—	—
Senegal	1.6	1.6	—	0.1
Syria	6,742.6	6,514.6	1.7	992.7
Somalia	260.8	228.2	3.5	—
Sudan	3.8	3.2	—	—
Tanzania	310.3	269.6	—	88.6
Tunisia	17.7	17.7	—	—
Turkey	91.8	91.7	—	—
Uganda	36.4	35.5	3.0	0.8
Central African Republic	1.0	0.8	—	—
Chad	2.2	1.7	—	—
Sri Lanka	1.1	1.1	—	—
Equitorial Guinea	1.5	1.4	—	0.2
Ethiopia	2,860.5	2,849.7	51.7	854.9
Subtotals	42,039.7	40,587.9	61.9	7,812.5
Grand totals	85,845.6	83,089.9	545.1	17,398.2

SOURCE: Originally published by the Leningrad branch of the Union of USSR Journalists in its newspaper, *Chas pik*, no. 1 (26 February 1990); reprinted as "Unikalnyi dokument," *Izvestiia*, 1 March 1990, p. 3.

as well as North Korea never joined. A comprehensive plan for economic integration was adopted in 1971, although implementation has fallen well short of the announced goals.[12] The CMEA summit conference, held at Sofia during 9–10 January 1990, reportedly did not solve any of the key problems (see chapter 8) and only served to demonstrate the organization's moribund state, with Czechoslovakia and Hungary suggesting they may withdraw from membership.

Not only is the Soviet Union's economy overwhelmingly larger than that of all the other CMEA members combined, but the East-Central European governments depend on USSR raw materials and energy. For example, during 1989 the Soviet versus the East-Central European share of the bloc's output was as follows: 33.3 million versus 6.8 million barrels of crude oil equivalent; 160.0 versus 60.9 million metric tons of unfinished steel; 1,722 versus 506 billion kilowatt-hours of electricity; and 140 versus 62.2 million metric tons of cement.[13] Through the year 1984, the East-Central European regimes were receiving Soviet economic assistance on a net basis as well as price subsidies. Traditional colonialism involved deliveries of raw materials to the metropole, which sent its dependencies manufactured products in return. The Soviet Union reversed these procedures: its client states provided Moscow with semifinished goods or even complete factories in exchange for raw materials and energy.

Two CMEA banks finance these exchanges as well as the various cooperative investments that have been launched over the years. The International Bank for Economic Cooperation (headed by V. S. Khoklov since the end of 1988) issues short-term trade credits and is responsible for clearing accounts among members. The International Investment Bank (chaired by A. N. Belichenko since early 1976) provides funds for construction, reconstruction, and extension of joint projects. Both banks have borrowed large amounts of hard currency from Western financial institutions.[14]

Reflecting the world market, prices for Soviet raw materials delivered to East-Central Europe increased by 200 percent during calendar year 1977 alone. The rise primarily affected oil, deliveries of which remained at the same level during 1981–1985 as earlier or may have declined somewhat. The former USSR prime minister, A. N. Kosygin, had promised East-Central Europe 20 percent more energy in the course of the above-mentioned five-year period. Most of the increase, however, came in the form of natural gas and electricity rather than petroleum. After the price of oil dropped in 1986, the East-Central European regimes were still forced to pay more than the world level to the USSR based on the preceding five-year average formula. In return the Soviets demanded the highest-quality goods, which otherwise could have been sold in the West for hard currency.

Joint CMEA ventures have resulted in the *Druzhba* (friendship) oil pipeline, the *Bratstvo* (brotherhood) natural gas pipeline, and the *Mir* (peace) electric power grid connecting East-Central Europe with the Soviet Union. Other projects under way involve nuclear energy plants as well as extracting Soviet raw materials, with labor and construction costs being shared among CMEA members. Several East-Central European governments have imported grain from the USSR, although of a lower quality than that which the Soviets purchase from the West.

In general, some 44.6 billion rubles in exports (70 percent raw materials) went to "socialist" countries from the USSR during 1989 and almost 42.2 billion rubles worth of goods came back. CMEA has had to reduce imports from Western industrialized states because foreign exchange loans have become difficult to obtain. In addition, beginning in 1991, the USSR is forcing its former client regimes in East-Central Europe to convert transactions into foreign currency, which will mean considerable losses for the latter. It has been estimated that the Soviet Union will gain the equivalent of $16 billion annually from such an arrangement.[15]

EAST–WEST TRADE

From 1976 through 1980, Soviet trade with industrially developed countries amounted to 30.1 percent of its total, declining to just 23.4 percent during 1988 with a trade gap of about $2.4 billion. For 1989, the figures were 26.2 percent and a 4.1 billion-ruble adverse balance of payments. The United States was in seventh place; in 1978, it had been third (after the Federal Republic of Germany and Japan). The USSR's largest trade deficits were with the United States, West Germany, Japan, and India, in that order (see table 7.2). Western countries, especially Argentina, Australia, Canada, France, Great Britain, and the United States, continue to export large amounts of grain and soybeans to the Soviet Union. The total USSR foreign trade deficit for 1989 amounted to almost 3.4 billion rubles, much of which was spent for imported consumer goods,[16] and represented the first acknowledged adverse balance of payments in fourteen years.

During the decade of the 1970s, the USSR spent about $40 billion for agricultural imports, or $4 billion a year. More than one-fifth of all grain traded on the world market during the twelve months in 1985 (about 44.2 million metric tons) was purchased by the Soviet Union at a cost of more than $7 billion. Soviet agricultural output, which grew at an annual rate of 2.2 percent during the 1950s and at a rate of only 1 percent during the 1960s, has been declining from the late 1970s and into the early 1990s. No official figures on grain harvests were released until Chernenko finally announced that 190 million metric tons were brought in during 1983, despite "bad weather." The U.S. Department of Agriculture estimated that U.S. corn and wheat sales to the USSR during fiscal year (FY) 1990, October 1989–September 1990, would be at their second-highest level ever and could exceed FY 1989's record of $3.3 billion. The Soviet harvest for

TABLE 7.2
LARGEST NONCOMMUNIST TRADE PARTNERS BY RANK, 1989
(IN MILLIONS OF RUBLES)

Country	Exports	Imports	Balance
1. West Germany	2,478.3	4,076.4	− 1,598.1
2. Finland	1,758.8	2,126.8	− 368.0
3. Italy	1,920.1	1,606.3	+ 313.8
4. Japan	1,343.0	2,138.0	− 795.0
5. United States	529.9	2,865.2	− 2,335.3
6. Great Britain*	2,208.7	1,009.1	+ 1,199.6
7. India	1,147.2	1,770.6	− 623.4
8. France	1,348.6	1,218.4	+ 130.2
9. Austria	429.6	1,004.5	− 574.9
10. Switzerland	559.9	434.8	+ 125.1

*Despite this rather substantial trade, the USSR had given the British coal miners' trade union during 1985 some $1.4 million in strike assistance. See the TASS interview with M. Srebrnyi, chief of research at the All-Union Council of Trade Unions in Moscow, "I vnov' o pomoshchi britanskim gorniakam," *Trud,* 25 September 1990, p. 3. See also A. Liutyi, "Sovetsko-britanskaia," *Pravda,* 22 October 1990, p. 4.

NOTE: In 1985, Canada was the USSR's eighth-largest Western trading partner; by 1987, it had dropped to thirteenth. In 1985, Australia ranked ninth; by 1987, it had dropped to fourteenth place.

SOURCE: USSR, *Vneshnie ekonomicheskie sviazi SSSR v 1989 g.* (Moscow: Finansy i statistika, 1989), pp. 27–30.

calendar year 1990 is estimated at 260 million metric tons,[17] although how much of that will be brought in remains problematical.

Inefficiency is also evident in other aspects of agriculture: during 1989 farm animals produced only 108.1 million metric tons of milk compared with the same amount from half that number of livestock in the (West) European Community. The peak USSR beef production in 1989 reached just 20 million metric tons from 120 million head of cattle compared with 23 million tons from only 78 million head in Western Europe. Meat output per million hogs (total, 78.1 million head) in the USSR is only about two-thirds of that in West Germany or the United States.[18]

To obtain the foreign exchange needed to purchase food from the West, the former East-Central European regimes and the Soviet Union at times engaged in dumping low-priced items and services that disrupted foreign markets. The Federal Republic of Germany accused Hungary, Poland, and Yugoslavia of offering certain pharmaceuticals at prices 39 to 47 percent less than their domestic cost of production. In addition, visitors to the USSR had been forced to pay the artificial and arbitrary exchange rate of $1.60 for one ruble (on the black market, one dollar brought up to 20 rubles) until 1 November 1989, when it went up to 5.6 rubles for one tourist dollar. Foreign businessmen one year later began receiving 1.8 rubles for the dollar.[19]

Whether the rate of exchange that devalued the ruble from $1.60 down to 16 cents for tourists in the USSR has had any impact on Soviet foreign trade remains unknown. This special rate, however, does not apply to imports or exports. It may be the first step toward convertibility of the ruble, perhaps linking it to raw material reserves. Back in the early 1920s, the Soviet Union had a special currency called *chervonets*, which it used exclusively in foreign trade during the New Economic Policy period.[20]

Combined with the new rates of exchange are the pricing practices of the Soviet merchant fleet, which according to Lloyd's Register of Shipping is the sixth largest in the world, with 23.5 million gross tons and 2,800 ships. It earns foreign currency as a third-flag carrier and has undercut Liner Conference rates by up to 40 percent. At a 1982 meeting in Moscow, representatives of five West European governments (West Germany, Britain, France, the Netherlands, and Belgium) heard Soviet officials agree to restrict such shipping activities on certain routes. Meanwhile, three U.S. shipping lines (Pacific, Far East, and United States) were driven out of business. However, following the twelfth five-year plan (1986–1990), after 185 diesel-powered ships had been written off, just 300 remained; according to a USSR maritime fleet spokesman, only 60 new ones were expected.[21]

The USSR was nonetheless able to obtain more than $50 billion worth of high technology from the West during the decade of the 1970s. According to testimony by Dr. Jack Vorona, assistant director for science and technology at the Defense Intelligence Agency, the 1973–1974 sale of 164 U.S.-made miniature precision ball bearing machines enabled the USSR to develop heavy multiwarhead intercontinental ballistic missiles at a more rapid rate than would otherwise have been possible. From 1979 to 1989, military trucks in Afghanistan were produced by the supposedly civilian Kama River plant, built with $1.5 billion worth of Western technology.[22] The automated foundry, engines, production line, and computers all came from the United States.

Legal technology transfer has primarily taken the form of agreements for scientific cooperation, licensing arrangements, turnkey projects, coproduction ventures, and three-party or even multilateral schemes.[23] J. Fred Bucy, president of Texas Instruments and chairman of the U.S. Defense Science Board task force on the export to the USSR of American technology, testified before a Senate panel that transfer of militarily significant technology has been of major proportions. During 1986, however, the United States ranked only ninth among Western countries contributing to this outflow, the largest suppliers being West Germany and Japan (see table 7.3).[24]

Legal shipments to the Soviet Union during the 1980s included semiconductors, computer hardware and software, and chemical processes in all fields not only from the United States but also from Western Europe and Japan. NATO members (except Iceland), Japan, and Australia belong to a Coordinating Committee on Multilateral Export Controls (CoCom), which had policed trade in 125 categories of industrial items. Militarily significant ones required unanimous approval before export, but less-important technology could be shipped to the USSR and East-Central Europe after the other CoCom members had been notified. Trade between members of the two blocs during 1986 totaled about $59 billion, only some $2 billion of which was in the high-technology field, with credits continuing to flow from West to East.[25] (See table 7.3.)

CoCom representatives met in Paris during 6–7 June 1990 on relaxing embargo restrictions. The United States took the lead, proposing a distinction between those countries in East-Central Europe that had freely elected governments and the USSR, where dual use of high technology is of great concern. Even after accepting this principle, CoCom members eliminated

TABLE 7.3
LEADING SUPPLIERS OF SOVIET HIGH TECHNOLOGY, 1986

Country	Millions of dollars	Percentage to USSR of countries' high-tech imports
West Germany	$654.3	32.4%
Japan	262.3	13.0
Finland	238.4	11.8
Italy	218.0	10.8
France	167.3	8.3
Switzerland	127.6	6.3
United Kingdom	124.9	6.2
Austria	63.5	3.1
United States	38.6	1.9
Netherlands	37.7	1.9
Total	$1,932.6	Average 9.57%

SOURCE: Communications with U.S. Department of Commerce experts, 1987–1990.

about one-fourth of the banned categories. Six midsized mainframe Cyber 960 computers, which Gorbachev had seen demonstrated in Minnesota earlier that same month, were approved for sale by the U.S. Department of Commerce.[26]

According to U.S. defense officials, there has been a "large-scale leakage of this technology to the East" as a result of USSR espionage or theft and "gaping holes in the CoCom structure." Indeed, these sources reported that the USSR has adapted Western technology for "in excess of 150 Soviet weapons systems." The same U.S. officials, who attended the CoCom meeting in Paris, spoke of about twenty thousand USSR personnel stationed abroad who were involved in the acquisition, both legal and illegal, of high technology from the West. Some $1.4 billion was spent each year during the mid-1980s by Soviet and bloc intelligence agencies to obtain such information.[27]

Moscow, focusing its efforts to secure Western technology—especially computers, microelectronics, fiber optics, and lasers—can divert these items with relative ease after they have left the United States through one of approximately three hundred air, sea, and highway exit points. During 1981, about forty-five of these diversion cases were discussed by a federal interagency committee in Washington, D.C., but just thirty-six were brought to the attention of foreign governments. Administrative penalties could be imposed in twelve instances, and criminal proceedings were instituted against only four individuals. Two computer systems plus parts, valued at approximately 180,000 British pounds sterling, were seized before being shipped from England to the Soviet Union. The boxes had been labeled "pipe setting equipment."[28]

Another, more recent case (1985–1986) involved two Digital Equipment Corporation VAX 11–782 computers, powerful enough to guide long-range missiles. In the midst of being transshipped to the USSR both were seized, one in the Federal Republic of Germany and the other (weighing 30 tons) in Sweden. They were returned to the United States by the respective customs authorities. The equipment had been purchased legally and sent first under license to the Republic of South Africa by a German citizen who reportedly operated seventy-seven such fronts. A federal judge in the United States subsequently fined a Swedish firm $3.1 million for illegally exporting U.S. strategic materials to the Soviet Union over a three-year period.[29]

Soviet acquisition programs are directed by the Military Industrial Commission (*Voenno-promyshlennaia Kommissiia*, VPK) attached to the presidium of the USSR Council of Ministers and since early 1988 headed by I. S. Belousov, as discussed in chapter 5. A parallel program is operated by the Foreign Economic Relations Ministry, headed since January 1988 by K. F. Katushev.[30]

Interestingly, a considerable amount of advanced technology has been obtained by the East on credit from the West. Soviet and East-Central European debts in 1990 totaled more than $163 billion (see table 8.5). With only $42 billion in annual hard currency earnings, some 31 percent of which came from the sale of petroleum or natural gas (and the remainder from weapons' exports), the USSR received almost $15 billion in lines of credit during the last three months of 1988 from the United Kingdom, France, West Germany, Italy, Japan, and Canada. Gold brought in $3.5 billion, and other hard currency was borrowed from the interbank market through Soviet-owned financial institutions in New York (*Vneshekonombank*), Paris (*Banque Commerciale pour l'Europe du Nord*), London (*Narodnyi Bank*), Frankfurt (*Ost-West Handelsbank*), Vienna (*Donau Bank*), and Luxembourg (East-West United Bank), with others in Zurich and Singapore. Roughly $5 billion in Western deposits are held by these banks, some of whose managers are foreign nationals to obscure Soviet ownership. Eduard P. Gostev, deputy chairman of *Vneshekonombank*, stated in July 1990 that the USSR gross hard currency debt stood at 34 billion rubles or $54.5 billion.[31]

THE NATURAL GAS PIPELINE

Ignoring previous experience and its own embargo on high-technology items, the Carter administration, only two weeks after having lost the 1980 election, approved sales to the USSR of two hundred bulldozers especially configured for laying a new natural gas pipeline. When completed in 1990, at an estimated cost of $14 billion, this pipeline—extending some 4,000 kilometers across the USSR, through Czechoslovakia to the border with the Federal Republic of Germany—could carry 40 billion cubic meters of natural gas each year from Siberia to both East-Central and Western Europe. Consequently, the Federal Republic increased its dependence on Soviet natural gas to a projected 30 percent; France's imports also climbed to that same percentage of total consumption. Between 1980 and 1988, natural gas exports to Western Europe grew from 913 billion to 1.35 trillion cubic feet, or by almost 50 percent.[32]

When a second pipeline was completed, the USSR could threaten to stop deliveries as a means of exercising political pressure. Such a reduction in deliveries to Western Europe occurred in January 1981, when major Soviet natural gas supply cutbacks took place because of alleged "technical difficulties" with the existing pipeline. Moreover, the USSR used the oil weapon on at least two previous occasions against its own allies: Cuba in 1967 and Romania in 1980. In both cases, the communist leaders of those countries were proving recalcitrant. Moscow television announced on 29 October 1984 that Soviet ships would stop supplying Britain with any kind of fuel during the coal miners' strike (subsidized with $1.4 million by Moscow during 1985) in that country. Five days later, TASS disavowed such "Western fabrications."[33]

Crude oil—some of which has been imported from Saudi Arabia, Iraq, and Libya as payment for arms—and indigenous natural gas provided the Soviet Union with more than $20 billion a year in hard currency earnings until the 1987 drop in world prices resulted in only $13 billion of such income. Prices shot up three years later, after Iraq occupied Kuwait. Apart from such resources, the USSR has a stockpile totaling 2,500 tons of gold. Exports of platinum, palladium, chrome, and other metals are also sources of foreign exchange. The five-year agreement signed at the end of July 1990 to sell uncut diamonds through the De Beers cartel of South Africa should bring in $5 billion, although Foreign Economic Relations Minister K. F. Katushev complained that the Soviet Union had been "reduced to the role of exporting fossil fuels and raw materials." During 1989, USSR production of oil dropped by one-tenth, reflected in a 10 percent export decline. It went down another 3.35 million barrels during the first nine months of 1990.[34]

To construct the natural gas pipeline, the Soviets relied heavily on Western technology; for instance, only the U.S. General Electric (GE) Company could produce the special rotor for the turbine engines. An engineering group in France, Alsthom-Atlantique, purchased the license from GE and then made the device. The Reagan administration attempted to prevent delivery of the turbines to the USSR by invoking trade sanctions under U.S. law against the French firm, but even before the sanctions had been lifted, other West European companies were delivering key components to the Soviet Union. Nuovo Pignone of Italy supplied nineteen compressor stations and fifty-seven turbines. West Germany's AEG-Kanis benefited from a $1 billion credit line extended to Moscow by a consortium of West European banks, which later offered an additional $500 million equivalent. The John Brown Company in the United Kingdom also shipped turbines to the USSR. Gaz de France and Ruhrgas in the Federal Republic of Germany even contracted to pay $5 above the Organization of Petroleum Exporting Countries' (OPEC) established level at that time (linked to the basic oil price of $34 a barrel) for Soviet natural gas.[35]

THE THIRD WORLD

USSR trade with the less-developed countries, although it doubled in the course of an earlier five-year plan (1975–1980), still represented only 12.2

percent of total turnover in 1985 and dropped slightly, to 12.1 percent, during 1989. The largest amount of trade is with India (623-million-ruble deficit), followed by China and Iraq (720-million-ruble deficit) in 1989 (see table 7.4). Other substantial deficits occurred in commercial transactions with Argentina, Syria, and Brazil. However, total commerce, involving 102 Afro-Asian and Latin American countries, remained just above 17 billion rubles.[36]

Some favorable trade balances are misleading because certain partners lack the means to pay. This is the case with Afghanistan, the former South Yemen, Ethiopia, Angola, and Cuba, all of which have become tied economically to the USSR through credits and military assistance. Dramatic increases have taken place in trade with Afghanistan, up 100 percent since the occupation of that country during 1979–1989 by the Soviet army. The former People's Democratic Republic of (South) Yemen, which merged in 1990 with the Arab Republic of (North) Yemen, ships almost nothing to Moscow although it did provide the USSR with valuable military bases at Aden and on the island of Socotra.

TABLE 7.4
SOVIET TRADE WITH SELECTED LESS-DEVELOPED COUNTRIES, 1989
(IN MILLIONS OF RUBLES)

Country	Exports	Imports	Balance
India	1,147.2	1,770.6	− 623.4
China	1,328.5	1,083.5	+ 245.0
Iraq	255.4	975.9	− 720.5
Afghanistan	504.5	79.3	+ 425.2
Egypt	306.0	329.3	− 23.3
Argentina	69.3	626.6	− 557.3
Libya	33.6	93.5	− 59.9
Syria	207.9	704.6	− 496.7
Algeria	188.6	98.9	+ 89.7
Iran	125.4	61.2	+ 64.2
Brazil	22.3	245.9	− 223.6
South Yemen	12.2	0.0	+ 12.2
Ethiopia	122.3	28.5	+ 93.8
Angola	47.0	3.3	+ 43.7
Nigeria	31.9	0.8	+ 31.1

SOURCE: USSR, *Vneshnie ekonomicheskie sviazi SSSR v 1989 g.* (Moscow: Finansy i statistika, March 1990), pp. 11–15.

On most occasions, Soviet trade with the Third World is designed to parallel political objectives and extend USSR influence. When it requires a given product, however, Moscow will deal with any type of government. Examples include rubber imports from Malaysia as well as agricultural commodities from countries like Argentina, Brazil, and the United States. The current sale of diamonds to a company in South Africa, mentioned above, is the latest case in point.

In the past the USSR may have hoped to gain control over certain strategic raw materials throughout the Third World[37] and then proceed to establish a cartel similar to OPEC. Of the ninety-three minerals the U.S. government lists as critical, the USSR imports only six. Over time, the Soviet Union has sold chromite, manganese, and platinum to the West. During the early 1980s, however, these exports dropped by 50 percent or more, and the USSR began to purchase these minerals as well as titanium, vanadium, lead, beryllium, tantalum, and lithium from the Third World.[38] The USSR has negotiated, alone or through CMEA, several dozen technical/economic aid agreements with less-developed countries that have stores of strategic minerals (see table 7.5).

In addition, over the years the Soviet Union has offered to participate in joint development projects that would give it access to alumina from Greece, Guyana, Indonesia, Jamaica, and Turkey; bauxite from Guinea and India; natural gas from Afghanistan and Iran; oil from Syria and Iraq; and phosphates from Morocco.[39] In certain instances, the USSR has purchased raw materials it maintains in surplus, apparently to deny the West access to a given resource and to build up its own strategic reserve stockpile.

The former Eastern bloc was not self-sufficient in cobalt, and the USSR bought up large quantities from Zaire just before the 1978 invasion of that country by Cuban-trained mercenaries. This action represented the second attempt by Cuba, in its role as a Soviet proxy, to seize the ore-rich province of Katanga. In 1980, the USSR agreed to deliver $85 million worth of arms to Zambia in return for cobalt. Zimbabwe is the world's main supplier of chrome. Because the Soviets are a major producer of both cobalt and chrome, they may have been attempting to control the world market in cooperation with Zaire or Zimbabwe or both.[40]

The outlook for Western access to strategic minerals would become even more critical should the USSR ever exercise influence over the Republic of South Africa to the extent that it did until the end of 1989 in neighboring Angola and Mozambique. The combination of those three countries would provide the Soviet Union with access to the following percentages of raw materials available in the world: 94 percent of the platinum, 67 percent of the chrome, 62 percent of the manganese, 72 percent of the gold, 70 percent

TABLE 7.5
SOVIET IMPORT DEPENDENCE, 1990

Mineral	Percentage Imported	Source	Reported Production Source
Fluorspar	52%	Kenya (54%), Morocco (36%), Thailand (10%)	all
Molybdenum	16	Mongolia	Mongolia
Bauxite and Alumina	49	Guinea (70%), Yugoslavia (18%), Greece (12%)	
		Hungary (44%), Jamaica (18%), Guyana (13%)	all
Cobalt	45	Cuba	Cuba
Tungsten	43	China and Mongolia (20%); Australia and West (80%)	all
Antimony	19	Turkey (72%), Yugoslavia (26%), China (2%)	all
Tin	34	United Kingdom (67%), Malaysia (22%), Bolivia (10%), Vietnam (1%)	all
Mica	13	India	India

SOURCES: "Import SSSR po tovaram," *Vneshnie ekonomicheskie sviazi SSSR v 1989 g.* (Moscow: Finansy i statistika, 1990), pp. 36–48; Central Intelligence Agency, *Handbook of Economic Statistics* (Washington, D.C.: Directorate of Intelligence, September 1990), table 138, p. 167; Kenneth A. Kessel, *Strategic Minerals: U.S. Alternatives* (Washington, D.C.: National Defense University Press, 1990), figure 5, p. 18.

of the vanadium, 26 percent of the fluorspar, 47 percent of the asbestos, and 43 percent of the uranium.[41] The implications are obvious.

The USSR also has been involved in joint mining operations throughout Mongolia, which provided Soviet industry with fluorspar, copper, and molybdenum concentrates. In addition, during 1989 Mongolia sent more than one billion rubles worth of exports while taking only 397 million rubles as imports from its metropole. Another example is Cambodia, where a Soviet program is developing rubber plantations. Again, the negative trade balance is ten to one.[42]

FOREIGN ASSISTANCE

Within the Third World, six countries—Cuba, Vietnam, Mongolia (all members of CMEA), Afghanistan (a CMEA observer and until mid-February 1989 occupied by Soviet troops), Laos, and Cambodia (both former satellites of Vietnam)—are special friends of the USSR. The first four obtain about 90 percent of all Soviet aid to the Third World. Together the six received approximately $6.5 billion in assistance during calendar year 1989 (see table 7.6). The USSR Supreme Soviet voted to allocate only 9.7 billion rubles during 1990 for purposes of foreign aid and expects to receive 7.2 billion rubles in repayments over that same period.[43]

During the past several years noncommunist aid recipients, which account for the remaining 10 percent of Soviet aid, paid back to the Soviet Union in capital and interest more than they had received over that same period of time. Aid promised to various countries by the USSR sometimes fails to materialize; since 1954, in fact, less than half the offers have been delivered to Third World countries. A British study[44] concluded that the actual amount of Soviet aid to noncommunist governments during the five years from 1976 through 1980 totaled only $8 billion, as opposed to the $45 billion claimed by Moscow.

Cuba's share of Soviet largesse has amounted to one-fourth of that island's gross national product. For 1989, economic aid to Havana from Moscow may have totaled just over $5 billion, more than $11 million a day. On top of that comes free Soviet military assistance, valued at about $700 million a year. Two-thirds of the economic aid involves balance of payments

TABLE 7.6

SOVIET ECONOMIC ASSISTANCE TO SPECIAL FRIENDS, 1954–1989
(IN MILLIONS OF DOLLARS)

Country	1954–1989	1980	1984	1988	1989
Cuba	$61,757	$3,243	$5,153	$4,345	$4,160
Vietnam	14,620	935	1,040	1,366	1,046
Cambodia	1,018	0	87	139	194
Laos	831	57	77	86	110
Mongolia	14,994	835	785	987	995
Afghanistan	4,576	276	na	776	2
Totals	$97,796	$5,346	$7,142	$7,699	$6,507

SOURCES: U.S. Department of State, *Soviet and East European Aid to the Third World, 1981*, Publication No. 9345, February 1983, pp. 17–19; U.K. Foreign and Commonwealth Office, Economic Service (International Division), *Soviet, East European and Western Development Aid, 1976–1982*, Foreign Policy Report No. 85 (London, May 1983), p. 22. Central Intelligence Agency, *Handbook of Economic Statistics, 1990* (Washington, D.C.: Directorate of Intelligence, September 1990), tables 154 and 157, pp. 181 and 184.

support, and the other one-third goes for development projects. The USSR also pays almost three times (38 cents a pound) the world market price (14 cents in December 1989) for Cuban sugar. At the same time, petroleum is delivered to Cuba at less than OPEC charges; that subsidy alone totaled $1.7 billion in 1989, although supplies were cut by 20 percent in 1990. Cuba also received almost $11.5 billion in arms deliveries between 1982 and 1989 from the USSR.[45]

Vietnam received just over $1 billion worth of economic assistance during 1989, plus $775 million free military aid, and $350 million for additional project support (1987). Some eighty thousand Vietnamese were sent to work in the USSR, their labor charged against repayment of debts (only four thousand remained in 1989). Moscow continues to supply Hanoi with about 1.5 million tons of petroleum a year, at a price below former world levels. The USSR raised the cost considerably in 1981, however, forcing Hanoi to reduce imports of other goods. The oil subsidy amounted to about $7 million in 1982; during that same year roughly 200,000 tons of Soviet foodstuffs were delivered to Vietnam. Arms transfers from the Soviet Union totaled $12.7 billion during the period from 1982 through 1989. Moscow's aid to Hanoi for 1990 will be cut by $500 million, even though two-thirds of the latter's foreign trade will still be with the USSR.[46]

In contrast to Cuba and Vietnam, Afghanistan does not receive any free USSR military equipment. During 1982–1989, arms deliveries cost Afghanistan almost $11.6 billion, exclusive of maintenance costs for Soviet troops in that country. Moscow's economic assistance commitments during 1989 totaled only $2 million.[47] Much of the aid includes commodities such as petroleum, foodstuffs, and textiles. The USSR imports 95 percent of Afghanistan's natural gas at below world market prices and is also believed to resell the latter's produce (olives, nuts, raisins, honey) at a profit in East-Central Europe.

During 1989, Soviet project assistance to its oldest satellite, Mongolia, totaled the equivalent of $995 million. That year, Ulaanbaatar's accumulated debt reached 9.5 billion rubles, earmarked for the mining projects mentioned earlier. The USSR share of Mongolia's foreign trade amounts to 85 percent.[48] Ulaanbaatar also received an annual subsidy in the form of low prices for petroleum from the USSR. Bordering on the People's Republic of China, Mongolia provided a huge base for Soviet troops stationed in that country, all of which are scheduled to be withdrawn (see chapter 11).

Aid to Laos, mainly in the form of commodity grants as well as assistance for some projects, reached $110 million in 1989. The country received arms transfers between 1983 and 1988 valued at $767 million.[49] The USSR also delivered some oil at below market prices and paid for part of the petroleum imported by Laos from other countries. Cambodia received about $194 million during 1989. However, the USSR has not contributed to the U.N. humanitarian program for that country; Moscow's aid seems devoted to propping up the Heng Samrin regime.[50]

Although the USSR and the former communist-ruled states in East-Central Europe contributed only about one-tenth of the economic aid received by the Third World, they outperformed the West in military assistance. During 1989 the Soviet Union ranked first in that category, with $11.2 billion (38.4 percent of the world total) in the value of arms transfer agreements, as compared with $7.7 billion, or 26 percent, for the United States.[51] In the future, production of arms for export by the USSR may not decrease because this represents the sole manufactured product that has an overseas market and remains a reliable source of hard currency income.

In the past the Soviet Union was able to exploit the impact of its foreign assistance program by becoming involved with projects of high visibility. Building the Aswan Dam in Egypt and the Bokaro steel plant in India are prime examples of a technique that maximizes foreign policy returns with showplace projects turned down by the United States.[52]

Of greater long-range significance are the 769 (or more) Soviet and East-Central European multinational companies with financial investments in twenty-three countries outside the region during 1989. Examples include a partnership selling Hungarian coal technology to the United States, a company from Poland with equity in thirty West European firms, a Czechoslovak-owned enterprise in Canada with branches in South America, and a forklift truck plant in Bulgaria that attempted to purchase its French competitor.[53] Soviet leaders are only too well aware of both the economic and the strategic value of such multinational companies. Radical changes in relations between the USSR and its former client regimes in East-Central Europe are the topic of the next chapter.

NOTES

1. "Zakliuchitel'noe slovo N. I. Ryzhkova," *Pravda*, 10 June 1989, p. 3.
2. H. Stephen Gardner, *Soviet Foreign Trade: The Decision Process* (Boston, Mass.: Kluwer-Nijhoff, 1983), p. 27. See also Marshall I. Goldman, *Gorbachev's Challenge* (New York: W. W. Norton, 1987).
3. Stephen D. Moore, "Finland Fears Economic Consequences," *Wall Street Journal*, 9 July 1990, p. B-5A; Danielle Pletka, "Soviet Spin on Trade," *Insight*, 23 July 1990, pp. 24–25.
4. Central Intelligence Agency (CIA), *Directory of Soviet Officials* (Washington, D.C.: GPO, 1990), p. 123; Gardner, *Soviet Foreign Trade*, p. 43.
5. Gardner, *Soviet Foreign Trade*, p. 47; CIA, *Directory of Soviet Officials* (1990), pp. 117 and 189.

6. Peter Gumbel, "Soviet Bank Reforms," *Wall Street Journal,* 29 March 1989, p. A-10. See also Nikolai Domanov, "The New Banking with the Old System in Ruins," *Business in the USSR,* July–August 1990, p. 3.

7. Aleksandr Khandruev, *Gosbank* research institute director, TASS statement, reported in *Radio Free Europe/Radio Liberty Daily Report,* 6 February 1990, p. 7; CIA, *The Soviet Banking Industry: Blueprint for Change,* LDA 90–13125 (Washington, D.C.: Directorate of Intelligence, May 1990); Bill Keller, "Gorbachev Is Said to Yield in 'War of Banks,' " *New York Times,* 25 July 1990, p. A-4.

8. "Two High Soviet Officials," *New York Times,* 14 January 1984, p. 4.

9. General Accounting Office, *International Trade: Soviet Export Data,* GAO/NSIAD-90–209 BR (Washington, D.C.: GPO, July 1990), p. 23.

10. "Russia's Latest Queue: For Creditors," *The Economist* (London), 19 May 1990, pp. 101–2; Peter Gumbel, "Soviet Push to Pay Debts Short by $3.5 billion," *Wall Street Journal,* 10 October 1990, p. A-12. Iurii S. Moskovskii, chairman of *Vneshekonombank,* interviewed by O. Mikheev, "Urok na budush-chee," *Pravda,* 29 September 1990, p. 2. See also V. Izgarshev, "Chto u nas s valiutoi?" *Pravda,* 21 November 1990.

11. "Soviet Foreign Trade, January–December 1989," *Foreign Trade* (Moscow), no. 4 (April 1990): 33–36.

12. Richard F. Staar, *Communist Regimes in Eastern Europe,* 5th rev. ed. (Stanford: Hoover Institution Press, 1988), pp. 291–314; Bartlomiej Kaminski, "Council for Mutual Economic Assistance: Disintegrating Tendencies," in Richard F. Staar, ed., *Yearbook on International Communist Affairs, 1990* (Stanford: Hoover Institution Press, 1990), pp. 468–87.

13. CIA, Directorate of Intelligence, *Handbook of Economic Statistics, 1990,* series CPAS 90–10001 (Washington, D.C.: GPO, September 1990), table 3, p. 31.

14. Gardner, *Soviet Foreign Trade,* p. 54. See also Harriet Matejka, "More Joint Enterprises within the CMEA," in John P. Hardt and Carl H. McMillan, eds., *Planned Economies Confronting the Challenges of the 1980s* (Cambridge, Eng.: Cambridge University Press, 1988), pp. 171–89; CIA, *Directory of Soviet Officials* (1990), p. 491; and CIA, *Soviet Banking Industry.*

15. Andrei Sharyi, "SEV: poiski novogo oblika," *Pravda,* 12 May 1990, p. 6. See also E. Lautov, "O perestroike tsenovykh i valiutno-finansovykh instrumentov," *Vneshniaia torgovlia,* no. 4 (April 1990): 6–9.

16. Anders Åslund ("Soviet Foreign Trade: Red Ink Rising," *New York Times,* 3 June 1990, p. E-4) also mentions that $6 billion was spent on grain imports during 1989.

17. "Rech tovarishcha K. U. Chernenko," *Pravda,* 3 March 1984, p. 1, on the harvest; CIA and Defense Intelligence Agency, *The Soviet Economy Stumbles Badly in 1989,* submitted to the Joint Economic Committee of Congress, 19 June 1990, table C-9; U.S. Department of Agriculture, *CPE Agriculture Report* 3, no. 2 (May–June 1990): 9, for U.S. sales; John Fialka, "Soviet Union Gets Windfalls," *Wall Street Journal,* 13 August 1990, p. A-6, for 1990 harvest estimate.

18. CIA, *Handbook of Economic Statistics* (1990), tables 47, 48, and 49, pp. 79–80. The Common Market in Western Europe sold the USSR 175,000 tons of frozen beef from its surplus of 800,000 tons at less than one-third the cost of production (*Daily Telegraph* [London], 21 September 1985, p. 36). About 110,000 tons of butter, also at low prices, were delivered the following year (*Bild* [Hamburg], 4 September 1986).

19. Interview with L. I. Abalkin, "Skol'ko v dollare rublei?" *Komsomol'skaia pravda*, 28 October 1989, p. 2. An American businessman paid $180 a night for a Moscow hotel room that looked like the Chico (California) Hyatt Regency, according to T. J. Rogers, "In Kiev: Balking at Competition," *San Francisco Examiner*, 15 July 1990, p. D-5. Reuters dispatch from Moscow, "Gorbachev Decree on Ruble," *New York Times*, 27 October 1990, p. 18.

20. Interview with Gorbachev's economic adviser, N. Ia. Petrakov, "Vernut' rubliu byluiu slavu," *Argumenty i fakty*, no. 39 (30 September–6 October 1989): 5–6.

21. Curtis Cate, ed., *The Challenge of Soviet Shipping* (New York: National Strategy Information Center, 1984), pp. 6–9; *Sea Power* 28, no. 5 (15 April 1985): 185; U.S. Department of Transportation, *A Statistical Analysis of the World's Merchant Ships* (Washington, D.C.: GPO, 1985), p. iv; I. Fedorov, "Passazhirskii flot bez sudov? *Izvestiia*, 20 June 1990, p. 4; IISS, *Military Balance, 1990–1991*, p. 38, for number of ships.

22. CIA, *Soviet Acquisition of Western Technology* (Washington, D.C.: GPO, September 1985), p. 3. See also Roger W. Robinson, Jr., "Soviet Cash and Western Banks," *National Interest*, no. 4 (Summer 1986): 37–44. Robinson served on the National Security Council staff from 1983 to 1986.

23. Eugene Zaleski and Helgard Wienert, *Technology Transfer between East and West* (Paris: OECD, 1980), p. 113. See also Gardner, *Soviet Foreign Trade*, p. 29. By mid-1990, only 124 U.S.-USSR joint ventures had been registered in Moscow, according to *Bloc: The Soviet and East Europe Business Journal* 2, no. 3 (June–July 1990): 28–30, which lists all of them. The average size is capitalized at 2.7 million rubles, or $4.4 million.

24. U.S. Department of Commerce figures, cited in the *Christian Science Monitor*, 22 April 1983, pp. 1 and 12; Richard F. Staar, "High-Tech Transfer Offensive of the Soviet Union," *Strategic Review* 17, no. 2 (Spring 1989): 32–39.

25. U.S. Department of State, "Controlling Transfer of Strategic Technology," *Gist*, April 1986, p. 2. See also table 7.3.

26. AP dispatch from Paris, "CoCom May Ease Curbs," *New York Times*, 6 June 1990, p. C-8; John Markoff, "Control Data Allowed to Sell Six Computers," *New York Times*, 23 August 1990, pp. C-1 and C-2.

27. CIA, *Soviet Acquisition of Western Technology* (September 1985), table 2, pp. 9 and 10; Bundesministerium des Innern, *Das 'Rote Buch' oder wie die UdSSR westliche Technologien beschafft* (Bonn: 1985), mimeographed.

28. Statement by Frank C. Conahan, director, International Division, General Accounting Office, before the U.S. Senate, Committee on Banking, Housing, and Urban Affairs, Subcommittee on International Finance and Monetary

Policy, *Hearings on Functions of the Treasury and the Export Administration Act*, 97th Cong., 1st sess., 1981, pp. 37–39; London BBC radio, 31 May 1983, as cited in *Foreign Broadcast Information Service (FBIS)*, 1 June 1983.

29. Richard N. Perle, "Strategic Impact of Technology Transfer," in Robert L. Pfaltzgraff, Jr., and Uri Ra'anan, eds., *East-West Trade and Technology Transfer* (Cambridge, Mass.: Institute for Foreign Policy Analysis, 1986), p. 22.

30. Staar, "High-Tech Transfer," p. 35.

31. Keith Bush, "Economic Disorder and Trade Problems," *Soviet/East European Report* 7, no. 22 (15 March 1990): 2; The Economist Intelligence Unit, *USSR Country Report*, no. 1 (1990): 3, for external debt; Gabriel Partos, "Moscow Stands by Its Debt," *BBC Caris Talk*, no. 166/90 (19 July 1990): 1, citing Gostev.

32. Milton R. Copulos, "Moscow's New Lever," *The World & I*, no. 12 (December 1989): 187, for aggregate natural gas exports to Western Europe. See also A. Nikolaev, "Sovetskii gaz dlia Gretsii," *Izvestiia*, 20 October 1990, p. 4, for new pipeline to Greece that will be built in 1993 with EC financing.

33. Staar, *Communist Regimes in Eastern Europe*, pp. 212–13; "More on British Miners," *Wall Street Journal*, 20 November 1984, p. 36; TASS, "I vnov' o pomoshchi britanskim gorniakam," *Trud*, 25 September 1990, p. 3.

34. CIA, *Handbook of Economic Statistics* (1990), table 44, p. 76, for gold production; Deborah Stead, "Moscow's Call to De Beers," *New York Times*, 2 August 1990, p. C-2; Peter Gumbel and James Tanner, "Soviet Oil Industry," *Wall Street Journal*, 22 August 1990, pp. A-1 and A-4, for drop in oil production. See also Reuters dispatch from Moscow, "Soviets Expect New Oil Drop," *New York Times*, 23 October 1990, p. C-8; Daniel Yergin, "The Next Oil Surprise," *New York Times Magazine*, 2 December 1990, pp. 8 and 26.

35. Gaz de France subsequently negotiated a price reduction of 5 to 10 percent and a delivery growth slowdown, according to "Soviets Agree to Cut Price," *Wall Street Journal*, 7 June 1985, p. 29.

36. *Soviet Foreign Trade* (Moscow), no. 4 (1990): 33.

37. James Arnold Miller, Daniel I. Fine, and R. Daniel McMichael, eds., *The Resource War in 3-D: Dependency, Diplomacy, Defense* (Pittsburgh, Pa.: World Affairs Council of Pittsburgh, 1982), pp. 37–56. See also John R. Thomas, *Natural Resources in Soviet Foreign Policy* (New York: National Strategy Information Center, 1985), especially pp. 47–49.

38. John P. Hardt, "Soviet Non-Fuel Minerals Policy: The Global Context," *Journal of Resource Management and Technology* 12, no. 1 (January 1983): 57–62, table M-6; "U.S. Net Import Reliance on Metals and Minerals," *Sea Power* 28, no. 5 (15 April 1985); Kenneth A. Kessel, *Strategic Minerals: U.S. Alternatives* (Washington, D.C.: National Defense University Press, 1990), pp. 17–18.

39. Gardner, *Soviet Foreign Trade*, p. 30. See also M. Ryzhkov, "Sodeistvie SSSR s razvivaiushchimsia stranam v osvoenii mineralnykh resursov," *Vneshniaia torgovlia*, no. 7 (July 1986): 21–25.

40. Peter Vanneman and Martin James, "Soviet Coercive Diplomacy," *Air Force Magazine* 64, no. 3 (March 1981): 122. See also Robert England, with Bill

Gertz, "Metals More Precious Than Diamonds," *Insight*, 30 September 1985, pp. 52–55.

41. James A. Miller, *Strategic Minerals and the West* (Washington, D.C.: American African Affairs Association, 1980), p. 58; James E. Sinclair and Robert Parker, *The Strategic Metals War* (New York: Arlington House, 1983), especially pp. 66–77; U.S. Congress, Office of Technology Assessment, *Strategic Materials* (Washington, D.C.: GPO, May 1985), p. 409; "Pondering the Cost of Sanctions," *Insight*, 14 July 1986, pp. 8–12.

42. *Soviet Foreign Trade* (Moscow), no. 4 (April 1990): 35.

43. Reply to questions from USSR Supreme Soviet deputy by V. G. Panskov from the Ministry of Finance in "Unikalnyi dokument: Komu my dali 'v dolg' 85,800,000,000 rublei," *Izvestiia*, 1 March 1990, p. 3. See also V. Gankovskii, "O nashikh kreditakh," *Pravda*, 25 April 1990, p. 2; Elena Aref'eva, "Miloserdie ili vse zhe ideologiia?" *Izvestiia*, 24 July 1990, p. 1; A. Kabannikov, "Bezvozmezdka," *Komsomol'skaia pravda*, 17 October 1990, p. 3, about Vietnam's debts.

44. United Kingdom, Foreign and Commonwealth Office, Economic Service (International Division), *Soviet, East European and Western Development Aid, 1976–1982*, Foreign Policy Report no. 85 (London, Her Majesty's Printing Office, May 1983), p. 3.

45. Some 80 percent of Cuban sugar goes to the Soviet bloc and China. Boris Lesik, "Solenyi pot sladkoi safry," *Sel'skaia zhizn'*, 19 May 1990, p. 3. The USSR sugar subsidy in 1989 totaled $4.5 billion according to CIA, *Handbook of Economic Statistics* (1990), table 158, p. 185, table 157, p. 184; Richard F. Grimmett, "Trends in Conventional Arms Transfers to the Third World," *CRS Report for Congress* (Washington, D.C.: Congressional Research Service, 19 June 1990), table 21, p. 59. Yelena Gorovaya, "The Twilight of Ideology," *Moscow News*, no. 36 (16–23 September 1990): 12, questions whether the official figure of 15.5 billion rubles is accurate and states that certain items have been "deliberately omitted."

46. Interview with V. M. Buinovskii, "Zagranitsa nam pomozhet?" *Argumenty i fakty*, no. 12 (24–30 March 1990): 6–7; Grimmett, "Trends in Conventional Arms Transfer," table 2-J, p. 60; Murray Hiebert, "Straitened Superpowers," *Far Eastern Economic Review*, 4 January 1990, p. 6; CIA, *Handbook of Economic Statistics* (1990), tables 154 and 157, pp. 181 and 184.

47. CIA, *Handbook of Economic Statistics* (1990), table 154, p. 181; Grimmett, "Trends in Conventional Arms Transfers," p. 59.

48. B. Sergeev, "Shchedra ruka daiushchego," *Ekonomika i zhizn*, no. 12 (March 1990): 6; CIA, *Handbook of Economic Statistics* (1990), table 157, p. 184.

49. Arms Control and Disarmament Agency, ACDA, *World Military Expenditures and Arms Transfers, 1989* (Washington, D.C.: GPO, October 1990), table 11, p. 96; CIA, *Handbook of Economic Statistics* (1990), table 157, p. 184.

50. CIA, *Handbook of Economic Statistics* (1990), table 157, p. 184; Hiebert, "Straitened Superpowers," p. 7.

51. Grimmett, "Trends in Conventional Arms Transfers," pp. 3 and 4. See also

interview with Adm. Iurii Grishin, deputy minister of foreign economic relations, by Vladimir Yanelis, "The Mystery Surrounding Arms Sales," *Business in the USSR*, no. 3 (July–August 1990): 60–61.

52. Gardner, *Soviet Foreign Trade*, pp. 27–28.
53. Carl H. McMillan, "Soviet and East European Participation in Business Firms and Banks Established in the West: Policy Issues," *External Economic Relations of CMEA Countries* (Brussels: Economics and Information Directorates of NATO, 1984), pp. 287–300.

   Carl H. McMillan, chief ed., the *East-West Business Directory* (Kettering, Northants, Eng.: Duncan Publishing, 1989), pp. 383–401, lists 501 Soviet and East-Central European companies established in Organization for Economic Cooperation and Development (OECD) countries. The East-West Project at Carleton University in Ottawa, Canada, identified 268 additional ones in Africa (98), Asia (51), Latin America (59), and the Middle East (60).

PART III

REGIONAL POLICIES

8

POLICIES TOWARD EAST–CENTRAL EUROPE

During 1990, the outside world witnessed the spectacular collapse of the last colonial empire as East–Central Europeans began to regain their independence from a bankrupt and weakened Soviet Union.[1] Until almost the end of 1989 a façade of political unity had existed, with alliance war games taking place on schedule and the most recent multiyear economic plans being implemented. The winds of permanent change soon became evident, however, once the coercive nature of the "fraternal" alliance in East-Central Europe had begun to fade away. By the middle of 1990, the region was virtually unrecognizable to anyone who had been there a year earlier. Almost every country had found its own way to end communist party rule, electing new parliaments and moving toward free market economies. This transition seemed to be taking place with the approval of the USSR and especially of Gorbachev.[2]

In the past, to turn back efforts at political liberalization, Soviet leaders had ordered armed forces to invade several countries within their sphere of influence. Such interventions occurred, directly or indirectly, about once a decade since the end of World War II: Hungary (October-November 1956), Czechoslovakia (August 1968), and Poland (December 1981). In this last country, establishing an indigenous military dictatorship and proclaiming martial law functioned as a surrogate for military occupation by the USSR.[3] With the decline in the Soviet military threat, the imposed political and economic systems were undergoing transformation.

In contrast to Brezhnev, who had summoned East-Central European leaders individually to Oreanda in the Crimea every summer for audiences with him as head of the "socialist commonwealth of nations," Gorbachev began receiving these viceroys at his office in the Kremlin. The funerals of Andropov and Chernenko in February 1984 and March 1985 provided all sides with an opportunity to become acquainted, and the periods before and during regular economic summits offered time for more extended talks. In addition, Gorbachev made a point of attending fraternal party congresses and anniversaries, including the German Democratic Republic's fortieth "sovereignty" celebration held during early October 1989 in East Berlin.[4] (Less than two weeks later, momentous changes would begin in that country.)

The evolution of Soviet policy toward East-Central Europe is a study in making a virtue out of necessity. The "new thinking" in this relationship was revealed when the general secretary of the Hungarian Socialist (communist) Workers' Party, Károly Grósz, interpreted a private conversation with Gorbachev as meaning that the Brezhnev Doctrine would never again be invoked. Addressing the Council of Europe at Strasbourg, the USSR president specifically renounced the use of force against bloc countries in East-Central Europe. One of his aides in the Ideological Department of the CPSU Central Committee apparatus responsible for that region's affairs, Nikolai V. Shishlin, reiterated the policy during an interview for a French publication: "Our present position is that we are opposed to any use of troops in the socialist [communist-ruled] countries' internal affairs."[5]

Hence, the new Gorbachev Doctrine initially appeared to have the following parameters:

1. Member countries may not withdraw from the Warsaw Pact.

2. Communist parties must retain ultimate decision-making power through control over key ministries, such as defense and interior, in future coalition governments.

3. Opposition parties would be acceptable only if they supported the basic "socialist" character of the regime and publicly assumed the responsibility to do so.

Moscow decisionmakers seemed to believe that, under such conditions, the Soviet sphere of influence could be maintained. Gorbachev, however, as later developments showed, modified the above guidelines. His statement at the end of October 1989 in Helsinki[6] seemed to offer the USSR-Finland relationship as a model to be emulated for future relations with individual East-Central European states.

THE ROMANIAN EXCEPTION

The communist will to remain in power seemed to crumble in the face of massive yet peaceful public demonstrations that escalated (for example, some 500,000 people in Prague's Wenceslas Square), as the population lost its fear of the local authorities and of Soviet military intervention. The singular exception took place in Romania, where Nicolae Ceauşescu and Elena Ceauşescu were executed on 25 December 1989 and where a violent struggle against the local secret police (*securitade*) resulted in thousands of casualties. About 3.8 million members of the former ruling party destroyed their membership cards.

A small group of former Romanian communist functionaries, calling itself the National Salvation Front (NSF), seized power and won 66 percent of the vote in the 20 May 1990 parliamentary elections. Its presidential candidate, Ion Iliescu, took 83 percent, even though he had been the Ceauşescus' chief ideologist. Before the election opposition members were beaten with iron pipes by coal miners who had been called into Bucharest for that purpose by NSF leaders.[7] Thus, although former apparatus workers appear to have "hijacked" the Romanian revolution, the Soviets apparently played only a minor role, if any, in these developments.

On his seventieth birthday in January 1988 Nicolae Ceauşescu had received an Order of Lenin from the USSR. Two other bloc regimes followed this example with their own decorations: East Germany with the Order of Karl Marx and Czechoslovakia with the Order of the White Lion First Class. Reports from Bucharest about congratulatory messages from the queen of England, the king of Spain, and the king of Sweden were all exposed as fakes by the press in those three countries. Later in the year, Ceauşescu outlined his objectives for Romania in an interview with a journalist from *Pravda*. The following month, a Soviet writer called those objectives "a negative experiment" from the USSR point of view. After Ceauşescu's overthrow, Foreign Minister Shevardnadze sent the new provisional government a message expressing congratulations.[8]

POLAND IN THE LEAD

Because of its geographic location within the staging area for the second echelon of Warsaw Pact troops facing North Atlantic Treaty Organization countries, the western region of Poland had been of significant military importance to the USSR. In case of war, it was anticipated that Soviet naval infantry would move out from the Baltic coast for assaults against the

Danish islands and the West German port city of Kiel. According to U.S. military analysts,[9] Warsaw Pact commander in chief Marshal Viktor G. Kulikov reportedly attempted to convince Brezhnev that Soviet armed forces should invade and occupy Poland in 1981 because activities by the Solidarity free trade union represented a threat to local communist authority.

Rather than risk the use of military force, Kremlin decision makers at first applied psychological pressure to contain the dissident movement in Poland. During early July 1981, Western intelligence indicated that USSR troop readiness along Polish borders was reduced to the point where as many as three days would be required before an invasion could be launched, compared with a few hours during the previous "high-alert" period.[10] In view of what followed, this may have been a simple case of deception.

The local communist regime's indigenous armed forces, then, became the surrogate occupation authority for the USSR. Invoking martial law on 13 December 1981, the government of Poland implemented a plan drawn up under the supervision of Army Gen. A. F. Shcheglov, who headed the eight-hundred-member Soviet military mission in Warsaw. By that time, the ruling Polish United Workers' (communist) Party had lost all credibility and much of its membership.[11] Economic power, and hence political authority, appeared to have gravitated toward the twelve-million-strong urban and rural Solidarność labor unions.

Nineteen months of military rule under Gen. Wojciech Jaruzelski (first party secretary, premier, defense minister, commander in chief of the armed forces, and junta chairman) officially ended on 21 July 1983. After the ban on Solidarity as a legal organization, however, many martial law controls had become permanently institutionalized through additions to the penal code. Regime spokesmen admitted to holding one hundred and ninety political prisoners (non-government estimates placed the total at between four thousand and five thousand). The last two hundred and twenty-five individuals were released under the September 1986 amnesty. At the same time, police visited about three thousand others who were known to be in contact with the political underground and warned them to cease their support.[12]

Three years later, in the course of his speech to the tenth congress of the Polish United Workers' Party in Warsaw on 30 June 1986, Gorbachev declared that the crisis of the late 1970s and early 1980s in Poland had involved a protest against "distortions of socialism," adding, however, "that to attack the socialist system, attempt to subvert it from the outside, to tear away this or that country from the socialist community—means to encroach not only on the will of the people but also on the entire postwar settlement and, in the last analysis, on peace."[13] Earlier in the address, Gorbachev stated that "socialist conquests are irreversible," which at that time sounded as if the USSR would fight to protect them.

Two years later, Gorbachev returned to Poland and made twenty-one public appearances. He attempted to convince Polish television viewers how fortunate they were that "at this stage of history there has appeared a man like General Jaruzelski."[14] Economic conditions, however, continued to deteriorate. Faced with widespread civil disobedience, the Warsaw regime legalized both Solidarity (in April 1989) and the Roman Catholic church the following month. Successfully concluded roundtable discussions between regime and opposition set the stage for national elections on 5 June 1989.

The Polish communists, attempting to control the ballot box, allowed Solidarity only 35 percent of the seats in the lower house (*Sejm*) of parliament; in the newly established upper chamber, or senate, where no such restriction prevailed, Solidarity won ninety-nine of the one hundred mandates. When the two subordinate peasant and democratic parties refused to support the communist candidate for prime minister, Jaruzelski was forced to ask Solidarity to form a government. Among the twenty-three cabinet-level appointments that were approved by the new *Sejm*, only four (defense, foreign economic cooperation, internal affairs, and transportation) were allocated to communists. Two days before that vote, Gorbachev reportedly convinced Polish communist party leader Mieczysław Rakowski over the telephone that he should cooperate with Solidarity.[15]

The 27 May 1990 local elections were also dominated by Citizens' Committees founded by Lech Wałęsa, even though economic conditions had deteriorated. Five months earlier, a two-year "shock therapy" transition to a market economy had begun, and Soviet advisers to Gorbachev watched these developments carefully. As the USSR economy continues to deteriorate, the Polish model may yet be emulated. The Solidarity prime minister accepted "resignations" from communist heads of Defense, Interior, and Transportation ministries.[16] On 19 September 1990 General Jaruzelski announced that he would step down before elections for a new president took place on 9 December. These resulted in a landslide victory for Wałęsa.

HUNGARY FOLLOWS

Another country where the drive for pluralism has been accepted by the USSR is Hungary. The twelve-day uprising by freedom fighters in October–November 1956 had been crushed by Soviet tanks to maintain local communists in power. One-third of a century later, that same Hungarian ruling party negotiated a transition in government at an opposition roundtable with eight other political movements. After three months of talks, an agreement was reached on 18 September 1989 that would allow free, multiparty elections for a new parliament. The communist party congress dropped the word *Workers'* from the organization's name, making it the Hungarian Socialist Party. The new movement, which has neither a political bureau nor a central committee, will be patterned after West European socialist or labor parties.[17] Membership in the party dropped from 700,000 to 50,000 after the name change was announced.

During 17–20 October 1989, the old parliament adopted nearly a hundred changes to the 1949 Stalinist constitution and deleted the first word from the designation, *People's* Republic of Hungary. The modified basic law provided the framework for a multiparty election that took place in March, with runoffs in April 1990, and outlined a set of guarantees for human and civil rights as well as a tripartite separation of powers. A new executive president was to replace the former presidential council. Other adopted laws dealt with political parties, elections, and a new constitutional court. Parliament also disbanded the paramilitary workers' guard, the communist party's private army. About 100,000 Hungarians assembled in front of parliament on the thirty-third anniversary of their uprising[18] carrying national flags from which the hammer and sickle had been torn out, just as in 1956.

Free elections on 8 April 1990 brought the Hungarian Democratic Forum to power and its leader, József Antall, to the prime ministership. The new parliament elected writer Árpád Göncz as president of the country four months later, with the support of deputies from all six political parties.[19] It appears that Hungary had been able to achieve the foregoing ahead of Poland, where elections to parliament would take place in early 1991.

EAST GERMANY MERGES

Until the end of 1989, the German Democratic Republic (GDR) had been envied throughout the Soviet bloc because of its relative prosperity and seeming political stability. Under communist party leader Erich Honecker, law and order prevailed. The slogan "fewer people produce more" did not seem to have the desired effect during 1988, however, when the gross national product growth rate declined to its lowest point (2.7 percent) in six years and the grain harvest registered a 1.4-million-metric-ton shortfall. Neither centralized planning nor other economic controls were relaxed, however.[20] A top East German functionary openly rejected USSR-style *glasnost'* with the remark that, "just because your neighbor changes his wallpaper, you do not have to redecorate."

A purge in the GDR communist party leadership took place soon after Gorbachev's visit to East Berlin on the fortieth anniversary of the regime.[21] His conversations with other East German leaders may have precipitated the ouster of Honecker, who was replaced by fifty-two-year-old Egon Krenz only eleven days later. Selected communist party head, chief of state, and chairman of the Defense Council, Krenz had held the security portfolio in the Politburo. Within less than a week several hundred thousand East German citizens marched peacefully in Leipzig, with smaller demonstrations in five other large cities, demanding legalization of opposition parties, independent labor unions, and separation of powers between the ruling communist movement and the government.[22] Dismantling the wall between East and West Berlin commenced on 9 November 1989.

Although he visited Moscow in early November, Krenz lasted only forty-four days. An extraordinary congress replaced the entire Politburo,[23] and the government resigned. Multiparty national elections announced for 18 March 1990 resulted in victory by the Alliance for Germany coalition, which wanted unification with the Federal Republic. By year's end, the "friendly takeover" had been consummated. After being assured of German financial support for Soviet economic reforms, Gorbachev even agreed that the unified country could join NATO (see chapter 9).

LAGGING REFORMERS: BULGARIA

A year older than Honecker, Todor Zhivkov (born 1911) had held power in Bulgaria since 1954 and showed no signs of retiring. During 1988 two successive purges seemingly eliminated all potential contenders for his mantle. Zhivkov's general approach involved paying lip service to *perestroika* and postponing implementation. In local elections that same year, for example, some 80 percent of the districts offered uncontested seats or disqualified second candidates. Leasing of land, approved in theory, was not to be put into practice until a nationwide discussion could take place. A decision on basic reforms was postponed until the next scheduled communist party congress in 1991. However, even in this small country of nine million, there were about a dozen illegal "discussion clubs" and human rights organizations. Total membership was estimated at no more than three thousand individuals.[24]

Without any advance notice and apparently as the result of a carefully orchestrated coup, Zhivkov resigned on 10 November 1989 and was succeeded by Petur Mladenov, who had served as foreign minister.[25] The latter flew to meet with Gorbachev in Moscow after purging six Zhivkov loyalists from the politburo. Mladenov was elected president of Bulgaria in April 1990 by the old national legislature.

Elections for a new parliament, held two months later, were won by the BSP, or Bulgarian Socialist (formerly, communist) Party. The opposition Union of Democratic Forces received one hundred and forty-five seats to the BSP's two hundred and eleven out of a total of four hundred in the Grand National Assembly. Complaints of government harassment and intimidation were heard, especially during the runoff elections. A new constitution will be drafted in parliament by 1992. Meanwhile, Mladenov resigned from the presidency and was succeeded on 1 August 1990 by Zhelyu Zhelev, a former dissident and professor. The following month, a Soviet journalist wrote an article from Sofia about the day of victory over fascism being commemorated by the Bulgarian "socialists."[26] Dimitur Popov, a judge who does not belong to any party, became the new prime minister on 7 December 1990 after street demonstrations brought down the "socialist" government.

CZECHS AND SLOVAKS

The communist regime in Czechoslovakia also moved carefully, despite the leadership change in December 1987 when Miloš Jakeš, the same man who had supervised the purge of about 500,000 supporters of reformist Alexander Dubček from the ruling party some nineteen years earlier, became general secretary. Having praised the Soviet invasion and Dubček's ouster, Jakeš depended on suppressing all political dissent to remain in power. For this reason, perestroika-style reforms were postponed until 1991. One concession to regime opponents was the promise of a new constitution that would supersede the 1960 one and emphasize human rights. In the streets, peaceful demonstrators were being clubbed and then jailed.[27]

After ten days of successive demonstrations that grew in size to half a million participants, the ruling communist politburo resigned on 24 November 1989. Dubček, making his first public speech in more than two decades, addressed the crowd in Wenceslas Square calling for ouster of the regime. Three days later, a general strike brought all activities to a halt at noon and forced the government to negotiate with the opposition Civic Forum.[28] Noncommunists were admitted into the government. Before year's end, Vaclav Havel, a well-known playwright, had become president of the country. A high-level message, reportedly sent through USSR ambassador Viktor P. Lomakin, warned the local communists that delay in political change would mean trouble.

Elections during 8–9 June 1990 gave Civic Forum and its Slovak sister party, Public Against Violence, 46 percent of the seats in the parliament.[29] The communists won only 13.6 percent of the vote, compared with 38 percent in the last free election at the end of World War II. A new constitution has been promised for 1992 that should provide a division of power between the two major ethnic groups in the new Czechoslovakia. In the meanwhile, transition to a market economy is proceeding slowly.[30]

WARSAW TREATY ORGANIZATION

For almost thirty-five years the Warsaw Pact, or Warsaw Treaty Organization (WTO), had been the basis of Soviet military control over East bloc countries, providing the USSR with the means to intervene if local communist authority appeared threatened. The pact's members included all East-Central European states, except Yugoslavia and Albania. The USSR dominated militarily and politically: it supplied two-thirds of the pact's conventional and all of its nuclear capabilities. In addition, most advanced weapons systems and equipment came from Moscow. The highest alliance military commanders, chiefs of staff, and WTO representatives in member-country defense ministries were career Soviet officers. The USSR's distrust of its allies also manifested itself in the weakness of pact organizational integration; during peacetime, the unified command supervised only combat readiness and participation in joint maneuvers.

The treaty that created the alliance had been signed in Warsaw on 14 May 1955, although East German armed forces did not become part of WTO until the following January. Albania left the organization de facto in 1961, announcing its formal withdrawal after the Soviet invasion of Czechoslovakia seven years later.[31] The Chinese stopped sending observers to maneuvers in 1962. The northern tier states (Czechoslovakia, East Germany, and Poland) received better equipment than other pact members. Of these three countries, only East Germany spent almost as much per capita on defense as the USSR (see table 8.1).

One study of the northern tier during the mid-1980s concluded that because of the radically different institutional histories of the Czechoslovak, East German, and Polish military forces, the Soviets could face serious constraints in attempting to deploy these pact armies in combination against the West. With even the individual national interests of the different countries at odds, coalition warfare might have proven difficult. Only a surprise pact offensive against NATO, then, would have created the necessary momentum to pull the northern tier armed forces along.[32] Indeed, those troops were not considered completely reliable even at the height of WTO power. Under martial law in Poland, therefore, when the indigenous military ruled as a Soviet proxy, motorized ZOMO citizens' militia (uniformed riot police) units, not regular army troops, were brought in to quell demonstrations.

TABLE 8.1
WARSAW PACT ARMED FORCES, 1990

Country	MANPOWER			EQUIPMENT			EXPENDITURES	
	Army	Air	Navy	Tanks	Combat aircraft (including helicopters)	Vessels (including submarines)	Defense budget 1989 (billion $)	Estimated gross national product, 1989 (billion $)
Bulgaria	97,000	22,000	10,000	2,880	380	117	2.33	1.2
Czechoslovakia	125,700 (80,000)*	44,800	—	3,995	465	—	2.94	123.2
East Germany	96,300 (380,000)*	27,400	14,000	2,800 (1,600 storage)	285	126	11.86	159.5
Hungary	72,000 (65,000)*	22,000	—	1,516	151	—	0.77	64.6
Poland	206,600 (40,000)*	86,200	20,000	2,960	616	120	0.68	172.4
Romania	126,000	28,000	9,000	2,817	370	258	0.79	79.0
USSR	1,473,000** (excluding long-range air force)	420,000	437,000	61,500	8,794 (tactical only)	1,991	119.44	2,663.7

*USSR troops located in East-Central Europe.

**This number includes Soviet forces in the western military districts of the USSR proper that would reinforce those deployed against NATO.

SOURCES: International Institute for Strategic Studies, *The Military Balance 1990–1991* (London: IISS, Autumn 1990), pp. 33–43, 46–53; Central Intelligence Agency, *Handbook of Economic Statistics, 1990* (Washington, D.C.: GPO, September 1990), table 3, p. 31 for gross national product.

The East-Central European members of WTO were intended to secure lines of communication and provide logistic support between the USSR proper and its NATO-facing forward military deployments. Thus status-of-forces agreements[33] existed with Czechoslovakia (which had 80,000 Soviet troops), East Germany (380,000), Hungary (65,000), and Poland (40,000). Only the Bulgarians and Romanians had no such arrangements. After the 7 December 1988 speech by Gorbachev to the U.N. General Assembly, in which he announced unilateral cuts in Soviet troops deployed in these countries, all, except Romania, indicated that they would also reduce their armed forces in the course of 1989 and 1990 (see table 8.2 for details). Following the return of control over the military to parliament from local communist parties, Czechoslovakia and Hungary signed agreements with the USSR for complete withdrawal of its troops by mid-1991.

WTO maneuvers traditionally took place in several segments during the spring, summer, and fall of each year. For 1988, WTO members forecast twenty-two notifiable military activities that included fourteen national and eight combined exercises. These began with "Friendship 88" war games at the end of January/early February north of Lake Balaton in Hungary wherein indigenous troops were joined by Soviet and Czechoslovak units to prepare for a defensive engagement. (Since 1964 the Romanians had refused to allow any foreign armed forces on their national territory and, instead, sent staff officers to observe maneuvers in other pact countries.) A joint

TABLE 8.2

UNILATERAL REDUCTIONS ANNOUNCED BY THE WARSAW PACT, 1990

	Tanks	Divisions	Troops	Aircraft
Soviet forces in				
East Germany	3,300	4.00	n.a.	n.a.
Czechoslovakia	300	1.00	73,500	n.a.
Poland	100	0.33	n.a.	n.a.
All of Europe*	10,000	6.00	240,000	800
East German forces	600	2.00	10,000	50
Czechoslovak forces	850	3.00	12,000	51
Polish forces	850	2.66	33,000	80

*Includes all reductions in Soviet ground forces west of the Ural Mountains, including those in East Germany, Czechoslovakia, Poland, Hungary, and the European part of the Soviet Union.

NOTE: n.a. = not available

SOURCE: U.S. Congressional Budget Office, *Budgetary and Military Effects of a Treaty Limiting Conventional Forces in Europe* (Washington, D.C.: GPO, September 1990), p. 13.

USSR-Czechoslovak exercise took place toward the end of March in northern Bohemia, its objective being improved field-training standards. The second phase of "Friendship 88" took place the following month in East Germany, with host troops joined by Polish and Soviet units. Both war games were attended by NATO and neutral observers. Code named "Shield 88," maneuvers in northwestern Poland during June included GDR, Czechoslovak, Polish, and USSR armed forces. Bilateral Soviet and East German exercises were held in the GDR at the end of July and again in mid-August. That same month USSR and Bulgarian units held joint maneuvers as did Soviet/Hungarian and Soviet/GDR forces during October. In mid-April 1989, this last pair repeated their combination.[34] The following year, USSR troops held war games alone in East Germany with the Hungarians also refusing to participate.

As arrangements stood by virtue of the pact agreement, the armed forces of WTO member states would have been under direct Soviet military command in the event of a war with NATO. Elite units from several East-Central European armies had been selected and integrated with the second echelon, behind forward-deployed USSR troops. None of the client states, however, was ever allowed to produce enough weapons for its own national army. Furthermore, those of their officers who aspired to the rank of general or admiral had to be graduates of Soviet military colleges and speak fluent Russian.

Despite thirty years of Moscow-supplied training and indoctrination, however, the East-Central European armed forces never became efficient or loyal to the USSR.[35] As of 1990, none of the subordinate pact members would consider taking arms against the West European countries or the United States, both of whom they all rely on for major economic assistance. In fact, most of these WTO members are attempting to adopt the political and economic system of their former "enemies."

Although the Warsaw Pact was extended for another two decades in March 1988, two years later the military alliance seemed to be transforming itself into a political instrument. First came the statement by the WTO Political Consultative Committee (PCC) on 4 December 1989 apologizing for the 1968 invasion of Czechoslovakia. Next, in mid-1990, the Czechoslovak foreign minister announced that the Soviet Union had agreed to convert the Warsaw Pact from a military to a political alliance, respecting the sovereignty of all member states. The PCC is to become a genuine decision-making forum, no longer attended by local communist satraps and military officers who accepted Soviet-prepared WTO statements or declarations without discussion. After the June 1990 meeting in Moscow, the PCC began to encourage East-West relations between the two alliances, and it was reported that pact military functions would be eliminated within a year.[36]

THE COUNCIL FOR MUTUAL
ECONOMIC ASSISTANCE

For most of the last four decades, the Soviet Union has maintained substantial economic leverage throughout the bloc. The Council for Mutual Economic Assistance (CMEA) was established by the USSR in East-Central Europe supposedly as a response to the Marshall Plan.[37] Membership expanded subsequently to include Mongolia, Cuba, and Vietnam. Other "fraternal" governments, such as those in Afghanistan, Angola, Cambodia, Ethiopia, North Korea, Laos, Mozambique, and South Yemen, have sent observers to meetings; cooperation agreements were signed by CMEA with Finland, Mexico, Iraq, and Nicaragua.

Some 98 percent of the iron ore, about 70 percent of the hard coal, 98 percent of the petroleum, and 96 percent of the natural gas on which East-Central Europe depended were produced by the USSR.[38] However, the substantial problems within CMEA—low efficiency, inadequate assimilation of new technology and equipment, rising prices of raw materials and energy from outside the bloc, shortages of skilled manpower, and misuse of assets through waste—have brought it to the point of disintegration. See table 8.3. The most pressing problem for the organization is how to restructure in order to satisfy the immediate needs of its members. Eventu-

TABLE 8.3

REAL GROSS NATIONAL PRODUCT GROWTH IN USSR AND EAST–CENTRAL
EUROPE, 1981–1989
(PERCENTAGE OF AVERAGE GROWTH/DECLINE)

	1981–1985	1987	1989
Bulgaria	0.30	− 1.00	− 0.10
Czechoslovakia	1.30	1.10	1.00
East Germany	1.50	1.70	1.20
Hungary	0.50	0.70	− 1.30
Poland	1.80	− 2.00	− 1.60
Romania	1.00	− 0.80	− 1.50
USSR	1.80	1.30	1.40
Average	1.17	1.00	− 0.90

SOURCE: Central Intelligence Agency, *Handbook of Economic Statistics* (1990), CPAS 90-10001 (Washington, D.C.: GPO, September 1990), table 9, p. 39. The same source gives an average growth of 3.6 percent for the European Community during 1988–1989.

ally, however, CMEA (at least in its present form) will be dissolved because most of the countries in East-Central Europe are changing over to market economies more rapidly than is the USSR.

Soviet spokesman Oleg T. Bogomolev, director of the Institute on the Economics of the World Socialist System, had warned the East-Central Europeans that by 1990 they would be forced to import half their energy needs from outside the bloc.[39] During the first seven months of 1990, Soviet ethnic unrest and the increasing cost of production led to a 20 percent decline in exported oil. Czechoslovakia and Hungary, most vocal in their discontent with WTO and CMEA, reportedly have suffered most from this shortfall. The drop in world petroleum prices from $29 a barrel in 1984 to $16 a barrel in July 1990 did not help East-Central Europe because it has no surplus foreign exchange. A doubling of prices only two months later, owing to the Iraqi occupation of Kuwait and the U.N.-sponsored blockade, made the situation even worse.[40]

Some of the loss in oil supplies from the USSR may be made up for by electricity generated from nuclear power plants now under construction and by increased deliveries of natural gas from the Soviet Union. The USSR is already supplying gas from Orenburg to East-Central Europe via a 2,677-kilometer-long pipeline at its planned annual capacity of 15.5 billion cubic meters (bcm), almost half of what the region receives from the USSR. During 1990, the total gas for East-Central Europe was expected to increase by 6.4 bcm through the new *Progress* pipeline between Tiumen in western Siberia and Czechoslovakia. Before the current problems, some 40 percent of all Soviet petroleum exports went to East-Central Europe, 50 percent to the West for $13 billion in hard currency, and the remaining 10 percent to soft currency recipients such as Cuba.[41]

At their thirty-third council session, all East-Central European CMEA members, including associate member Yugoslavia, agreed to produce equipment for the construction of nuclear power stations on Soviet territory. The first of these plants had a 4,000-megawatt capacity. Each major contributor to the project (Czechoslovakia, East Germany, Poland, Romania, and Yugoslavia) is scheduled to receive electricity in proportion to individual investment through the year 2003. A second plant with the same capacity was to have been completed by 1990, but it was delayed by the disaster at Chernobyl four years earlier.

Nuclear experts from three East-Central European countries reported that the USSR had withheld data required for safe operation of their nuclear plants. During the 1970s and 1980s, the Soviet Union built twenty-three such installations for the bloc, half of them below Western safety standards. The GDR had closed down its five reactors, claiming that the "Russians just lied to us." These nuclear power stations are said to be comparable, in poor workmanship and mismanagement, to the one at Chernobyl. Four countries, however, depend on their nuclear plants for the following percentages of electricity: Hungary (33 percent), Bulgaria (30 percent), Czechoslovakia (27 percent), and East Germany (22 percent).[42]

An aroused public, which has become vocal under *glasnost'*, is obstructing work on nuclear power stations in the USSR. Triggered by reports that radioactive fallout from Chernobyl is spreading throughout Zhitomir province in the Ukraine, the project to expand the Khmelnitskii power station is running into difficulties, the fifth reactor at Zaporozhe is being held up subject to foreign inspections, and plans to construct a new atomic energy station for Cheliabinsk province in the southern Urals has provoked intense controversy, which may even result in a referendum. The USSR government, nonetheless, decided to begin building a nuclear power plant outside of Kharkhov late in 1990 after moving the site farther away from the city.[43]

Financial problems throughout East-Central Europe are a result of the worldwide recession during the late 1970s and early 1980s, the slowdown in the Soviet economy, and the disastrous effects of central planning and barter trade. The USSR had been supplying energy and raw materials to other CMEA member states, but not enough to even accounts for the machinery and agricultural products from the region. Only Romania during calendar year 1989 imported less than it exported to the USSR. (See table 8.4.)

After being postponed twice, the forty-fifth CMEA council meeting, which demonstrated the USSR hold on East-Central Europe, took place during 9–10 January 1990 at Sofia. Prime Minister Nikolai Ryzhkov stated the Soviet position as follows: "Simply to leave CMEA would be ruinous. . . . To think today of withdrawing . . . would be the equivalent of suicide." Ryzhkov then proposed that oil deliveries after 1 January 1991 be paid for in hard currency at prevailing world prices, transforming the $4 billion equivalent Soviet trade deficit from past years with CMEA into a $16 billion surplus.[44]

Although Ryzhkov agreed to wait until 1995, the transition to world price levels will begin on a gradual basis in January 1991. A special committee has been appointed to draw up specific proposals for reform, including a two-tiered organization that would exempt the least-developed members (Mongolia and Vietnam) from market prices, a successor organization to CMEA, a focus on contacts with international bodies in the West (diplomatic relations with the European Community were established on 25 June 1988), and the introduction of market economies as rapidly as possible to reverse the stagnation of the 1980s.

Apart from the incipient problems of satisfying future energy requirements, all CMEA countries in the bloc are in debt to Western financial

TABLE 8.4

SOVIET TRADE WITHIN THE COUNCIL FOR MUTUAL ECONOMIC ASSISTANCE,

1989

(IN MILLIONS OF RUBLES)

Country	Exports	Imports	Balance
East Germany	6,662.5	7,175.4	− 512.9
Czechoslovakia	6,255.4	6,609.8	− 354.4
Bulgaria	6,170.5	7,307.1	− 1,136.6
Poland	5,770.6	7,409.8	− 1,639.2
Hungary	4,187.7	4,813.3	− 625.6
Cuba	3,833.5	3,867.0	− 33.5
Romania	2,681.3	2,488.7	+ 192.6
Yugoslavia	1,926.4	2,405.5	− 479.1
Vietnam	1,390.9	519.7	+ 871.2
Mongolia	1,005.2	397.3	+ 607.9
Total/average	39,884.0	42,993.6	− 3,108.6

SOURCES: *Vneshniaia torgovlia SSSR v 1989 g.* (Moscow: Finansy i statistika, 1990), pp. 27–30; "Soviet Foreign Trade, January–December 1989," *Foreign Trade* (Moscow), no. 4 (April 1990): 33–37. The same issue in Russian, *Vneshniaia torgovlia*, does not carry any figures for calendar year 1989.

institutions. The total amounted to more than $163 billion in 1990, most of which had been used to purchase modern industrial plants and equipment from capitalist countries (see table 8.5). In addition, at different times Bulgaria, Hungary, Poland, Romania, and Yugoslavia have received most-favored-nation treatment from the United States—despite the U.S. semi-embargo against the Soviet Union.

By early 1990 Bulgaria's gross debt to Western banks had increased to about $10 billion. Austerity is required for stabilization, although gradual-ism best describes the approach being pursued. By the summer of that year, some 40 percent of commodity prices were to become market determined. Staples, however, are still receiving government subsidies. Double-digit inflation, accompanied by a 2.4 percent drop in real wages, aggravated living conditions. In addition, the exodus of 300,000 ethnic Turks created a labor shortage.[45]

Czechoslovakia's relatively low gross foreign currency debt (although up 30 percent to $7.8 billion) has been seen as the reason not to introduce "shock therapy" economic reforms. Furthermore, some four-fifths of its trade had been conducted within CMEA, five-eighths of that with the USSR.

TABLE 8.5
BASIC DATA FOR THE USSR AND EAST–CENTRAL EUROPE, 1990

	Population	Per Capita Income (dollars)	Gross Debt (billions of dollars)
Bulgaria	8,933,544	5,710	10.0
Czechoslovakia	15,683,234	7,878	7.8
East Germany	16,307,170	9,679	21.2
Hungary	10,568,686	6,108	20.7
Poland	37,776,725	4,565	39.7
Romania	23,273,285	3,447	0.4
Yugoslavia	23,841,608	5,464	16.2
USSR	290,938,469	9,230	47.8
	427,322,721 (Total)	6,510 (average)	163.8 (total)

SOURCES: Central Intelligence Agency, *Eastern Europe: Long Road ahead to Economic Well-Being* (Washington, D.C.: GPO, 16 May 1990), figure 2 and table C-1; Central Intelligence Agency, *Handbook of Economic Statistics, 1990* (Washington, D.C.: GPO, September 1990), tables 3, 19 and 43, pp. 31, 48 and 76; Central Intelligence Agency, *The World Factbook 1990* (Washington, D.C.: GPO, August 1990), pp. 43, 79, 111, 139, 253, 261, 344, and 287.

Estimates are that modernization of Czechoslovak industry would cost between $20 and $30 billion. Total output grew by only 1 percent in 1989, with industrial productivity registering no gain owing to the excessive use of raw materials and energy without applying new technologies. Consumers were affected by shortages and a lag in housing construction.[46]

East Germany was, after Bulgaria, the country most loyal to Moscow and its largest trading partner (more than 13.8 billion rubles in turnover during 1989) despite the disparity in populations: 16.3 million in the GDR compared with 290.9 million in the Soviet Union. Some 172,000 indigenous troops, together with 380,000 "guests" from the USSR, provided the so-called German Democratic Republic at one time with the world's highest concentration of military manpower and hardware per square mile.[47] Just prior to unification with the Federal Republic of Germany (FRG) on 3 October 1990, East Germany withdrew from CMEA.

Between 50 and 60 percent of East Germany's foreign trade involved the FRG, and about 20 percent of its produced income derived from subsidies provided by West Germany. The GDR had an estimated per capita income of $9,679, or almost three times that of Romania. However, political turmoil and the flight of 340,000 young skilled workers in 1989 led to one of the slowest growth rates ever. Foreign debt payments on $21.2 billion took nearly half the income from hard currency exports, and the budget deficit almost reached six billion East German marks.[48]

Hungary's industrial production fell 3.4 percent during 1989, accompanied by a 17 percent inflation rate. The International Monetary Fund suspended the last part of a loan after Budapest's budget deficit went out of control and ended up five times higher than planned. A hard currency foreign trade deficit of $1.4 billion pushed the gross debt up to $20.7 billion, the third highest in East–Central Europe.[49]

Poland's gross debt rivals that of the USSR, and living standards are close to those of the late 1970s. The "shock therapy," however, seems to have curbed inflation, and a program of privatization was adopted on 13 July 1990. Although state-run industrial production dropped some 30 percent due to the elimination of subsidies, a trade account surplus of $2 billion and $3.2 billion in reserves had been attained by midyear. Even the official unemployment of 700,000 (5.2 percent) of the labor force as of August 1990 included some 200,000 who had not worked during the previous six to twelve months and hence would not qualify for benefits.[50]

Romania, which has the lowest per capita income of the East-Central European countries, inherited an economy that had been grossly mismanaged by the Ceauşescu clique. Repayment of almost $10 billion in foreign debts between 1981 and the end of 1989 left the country on the verge of collapse. Despite a 1.5 percent drop in gross national product during 1989, the Ceauşescu regime achieved a $2.5 billion foreign trade surplus by restricting consumption and increasing exports.[51] Except for staples, subsidies on prices ended 1 November 1990.

FUTURE TRENDS

A transition away from command economies and political power monopolized by local communist parties has begun throughout the region. Only Romania and Bulgaria have yet to attain any political pluralism in their governments. The Soviet Union is not in a position to frustrate these developments, however, and could hardly have anticipated the results.

Each country of East–Central Europe is at a different stage in the transition process. As suggested earlier, the former East Germany will make the most rapid transition since becoming an integral part of the Federal Republic. The USSR will withdraw all of its military forces from the former GDR by 1994. Moscow already has received an advance payment in the form of $3 billion in credits from Bonn, as well as a commitment of 12 billion deutsche marks through the above period of time.

Poland, Czechoslovakia, and Hungary belong to the West and should be the first to integrate with the European Community. All have applied or indicated their intent to do so when conditions are favorable. In the case of Bulgaria and Romania, it will take much longer for their applications to be considered because of some of the factors discussed in the next chapter. However, a report from East Berlin indicated that CMEA will discontinue all activities after the 46th and last council meeting in December 1990 at Budapest.[52] Poland announced on the twelfth of that month withdrawal from *Interatomenergo* (nuclear energy), *Interelektro* (power engineering), *Interrobot* (automation), as well as the Computer and Electronic Center of CMEA.

NOTES

1. For a comprehensive survey of the preceding four decades published in December 1988, see Richard F. Staar, *Communist Regimes in Eastern Europe*, 5th rev. ed (Stanford: Hoover Institution Press, 1988).
2. See M. Antiasov, "Vremia peremen," *Izvestiia*, 30 July 1990, p. 5; E. Spekhov and A. Sharyi, "Vostochnaia Evropa," *Pravda*, 31 August 1990, p. 5.
3. Andrew A. Michta, *Red Eagle: The Army in Polish Politics* (Stanford: Hoover Institution Press, 1989), pp. 131–48.
4. "Prazdnik sozidaniia na nemetskoi zemle," *Pravda*, 7 October 1989, pp. 1, 4, and 5.
5. James M. Markham, "Gorbachev Spurns the Use of Force in E. Europe," *New York Times*, 7 July 1989, pp. 1 and 6; interview with Nikolai V. Shishlin, "Nous pouvons comprendre la décision hongroise," *Liberation* (Paris), 22 September 1989, p. 4.
6. "Vystuplenie M. S. Gorbacheva," *Pravda*, 27 October 1989, pp. 1–2, for Gorbachev's speech in Finland. Former member of the CPSU Politburo, E. K. Ligachev, claims that the Kremlin leaders decided in late 1985 and 1986 not to intervene. See David Remnick, "A Soviet Conservative," *Washington Post*, 15 December 1990, p. A-22.
7. V. Vedrashko and A. Sharyi, "Logichnyi itog," *Pravda*, 26 May 1990, p. 6; Richard Wagner, "Rumänien nach Ceauşescu," *Kontinent* 16, no. 55 (December 1990): 27–32.
8. "Put' izbrannyi narodom," *Pravda*, 23 August 1989, p. 4; Shishlin, "Nous pouvons comprendr la décision hongroise," p. 4; Robert R. King, "Romania," in Richard F. Staar, ed., *Yearbook on International Communist Affairs 1990*, (Stanford: Hoover Institution Press, 1990), pp. 384–406, hereafter cited as *YICA*.
9. Quoted in an article by Drew Middleton, "Poland's Geography: Russia's Gateway to West," *New York Times*, 6 April 1981, p. A-11. Former Gen. S. Prochazka states that 45,000 of his Czech troops had been poised to invade

Polish Silesia, coordinated with Soviet movements from the USSR and a token East German presence from the west. The attack was called off on 5 December 1981. Leszek Mazan's interview, "Już siedzieliśmy w czołgach," *Polityka* (Warsaw), no. 37 (15 September 1990): 13.

10. Quadripartite military maneuvers on Polish territory, code-named "Soiuz-81," lasted twenty-two days, ending on 7 April, the longest in Warsaw Pact history. The USSR itself conducted combined arms exercises during 4–12 September 1981 in Belorussia and along the Baltic seacoast. They were described by Maj. Gen. A. I. Skryl'nik, chief ed., *Zapad-81* (Moscow: Voenizdat, 1982).

11. For a discussion of the martial law decision by an insider, see R. J. Kukliński, "Wojna przeciw narodowi," *Kultura* (Paris), May 1987, pp. 3–57. Some 800,000 members officially left the communist party during 1980–1982, according to Józef Barecki et al., eds., *Rocznik polityczny i gospodarczy, 1981–1983* (Warsaw: PWE, 1984), p. 151.

12. Amnesty International, *Report* (London: Amnesty International, 1984), pp. 293–97; editorial, "Freedom as Seen from Poland," *New York Times*, 23 August 1986, p. 22.

13. "Vystuplenie tovarishcha Gorbacheva, M. S.," *Pravda*, 1 July 1986, p. 1.

14. Quoted in an article by Jackson Diehl, "Gorbachev Plays It Safe—and Makes No Gains—in Polish Visit," *Washington Post*, 15 July 1988, p. A-15. See also Arthur R. Rachwald, *In Search of Poland: The Superpowers' Response to Solidarity, 1980–1989* (Stanford: Hoover Institution Press, 1990).

15. Richard F. Staar, "Poland: Renewal or Stagnation?" *Current History* 88, no. 541 (November 1989): 373–76; Arthur R. Rachwald, "Poland," in *YICA 1990*, pp. 358–84.

16. Speech by Tadeusz Mazowiecki to parliament, "Premier apeluje," *Gazeta wyborcza*, 7–8 July 1990, p. 1. See also Richard F. Staar, "Transition in Poland," *Current History* 89, no. 551 (December 1990): 401–404 and 426–27.

17. V. Gerasimov and S. Ivanov, "Kursom reform," *Pravda*, 9 October 1989, p. 5; "Struktura VSP," *Pravda*, 13 October 1989, p. 5; Miklos K. Radvanyi, "Hungary," *YICA 1990*, pp. 345–58.

18. "Hungary Purges Stalinism from Constitution," *New York Times*, 19 October 1989, p. A-8; Serge Schmemann, "New Hungary Marks '56 Uprising," *New York Times*, 24 October 1989, pp. 1 and 17.

19. See the congratulatory telegram from M. Gorbachev in *Pravda*, 4 August 1990, p. 1. See also V. Gerasimov, "V buduschee, pomnia o proshlom," *Pravda*, 6 November 1990, p. 5.

20. John M. Starrels, "Germany: German Democratic Republic," in *YICA 1989*, pp. 326–27. See also Davis W. Daycock in *YICA 1990*, pp. 331–45.

21. The speech in East Berlin appeared as "Rech' M. S. Gorbacheva," *Pravda*, 7 October 1989, pp. 4–5.

22. Serge Schmemann, "East Germany Removes Honecker and His Protégé Takes His Place," *New York Times*, 19 October 1989, pp. 1 and 8; Henry Kamm, "300,000 Reported to March in Largest East German Protest," *New York Times*, 24 October 1989, p. 14.

23. Craig R. Whitney, "East Germans Pick New Party Leader," *New York Times*, 10 December 1989, pp. A-1 and 31. For the unification timetable through 1 January 1991, see "One Germany: Next Steps," *New York Times*, 18 July 1990, p. A-4. See also E. Bovkun, "Proshchanie s 'prusskim' sotsializmom," *Izvestiia*, 29 August 1990, p. 5.

24. John D. Bell, "Bulgaria," *YICA 1989*, pp. 299–302; Clyde Haberman, "Bulgarian Change Barely Plods Along," *New York Times*, 7 October 1989, p. 5.

25. His biography appeared in "Petr Mladenov," *Pravda*, 11 November 1989, p. 6. See also Bell, *YICA 1990*, pp. 308–18.

26. L. Zhmyrev, "Zarubka na serdtse," *Pravda*, 8 September 1990, p. 5. V. Brovkin and L. Zhmyrev, "Vstan' i skazhi," *Pravda*, 24 September 1990, p. 5; "Ot storiat'moloduiu demokratiiu," *Pravda*, 11 November, 1990, p. 6.

27. John Tagliabue, "Police Force Used a 3rd Day in Prague," *New York Times*, 20 November 1989, pp. 1 and 10.

28. Editorial, "Prague Autumn," *Wall Street Journal*, 27 November 1989, p. A-10.

29. See Jiri Pehe, "The New Federal Assembly," *Report on Eastern Europe*, 17 August 1990, pp. 7–11.

30. A. Krushinskii, "Razdel'no ili vmeste?" *Pravda*, 10 September 1990, p. 5; D. Valovoi and A. Krushinskii, "Ot plana k rynku," *Pravda*, 28 September 1990, p. 4; A. Krushinskii, "I vnov'na perelome, *Pravda*, 9 November 1990, p. 5.

31. Staar, *Communist Regimes in Eastern Europe*, pp. 261–90.

32. Teresa Rakowska-Harmstone et al., *Warsaw Pact: The Question of Cohesion*, 4 vols. (Ottawa: Department of National Defense, 1984–86). See also Daniel N. Nelson, *Alliance Behavior in the Warsaw Pact* (Boulder, Colo.: Westview Press, 1986), pp. 27–70.

33. International Institute for Strategic Studies (IISS), *The Military Balance, 1990–1991* (London, Autumn 1990), pp. 48–52.

34. John J. Karch, "Warsaw Treaty Organization," *YICA 1989*, pp. 438–40; Christopher D. Jones in *YICA 1990*, pp. 488–99.

35. Jeffrey Simon, ed., *NATO-Warsaw Pact Force Mobilization* (Washington, D.C.: National Defense University Press, 1988), pp. 31–178. For the new Polish defensive military doctrine, see "Doktryna obronna Rzeczypospolitej Polskiej," *Trybuna* (Warsaw), 26 February 1990, p. 3.

36. Linda Feldmann, "Gorbachev Debriefs Warsaw Pact," *Christian Science Monitor*, 6 December 1989, p. 3. Henry Kamm, "Prague Says Moscow Has Agreed," *New York Times*, 13 June 1990, p. A-8. For the East German departure ceremony from WTO, see the photograph in the *New York Times*, 25 September 1990, p. A-8.

37. V. A. Menzhinskii, chief ed., *Mezhdunarodnye organizatsii sotsialisticheskikh gosudarstv* (Moscow: Mezhdunarodnye otnosheniia, 1980), p. 57; Bartlomiej Kaminski, "Council for Mutual Economic Assistance," in *YICA 1990*, pp. 468–87.

38. Central Intelligence Agency (CIA), *Handbook of Economic Statistics* (1990) (Washington, D.C.: GPO, 1990), tables 86, 92, 93, 107 on pp. 102, 107, 108, and 126.

39. Gábor Miklós and István Zalai, "Interjú Oleg Bogomolev," *Népszabadság* (Budapest), 13 September 1986, p. 5.
40. A. Iakushin and V. Voloshin, "Neft' i dollary," *Komsomol'skaia pravda*, 29 August 1990, p. 3. See also Matthew L. Wald, "Effect of Fall in Soviet Oil Output," *New York Times*, 6 September 1990, pp. C-1 and 7.
41. CIA, *Soviet Energy Data Resource Book*, SOV-90–10021 (Washington, D.C.: Directorate of Intelligence, May 1990), pp. 1 and 19.
42. Paul Lewis, "Anxiety Rises in Eastern Europe," *New York Times*, 7 April 1990, p. 5; Marlise Simons, "At East Europe Nuclear Plants," *New York Times*, 24 June 1990, p. 6. Quotation comes from the first source in this note.
43. David Marples, "Nuclear Energy Debate," *Report on the USSR* 1, no. 40 (6 October 1989): 11–12; D. J. Peterson, "Nuclear Plant to Be Built," Radio Free Europe/Radio Liberty (RFE/RL) *Daily Report*, no. 82 (27 April 1990): 3.
44. Ryzhkov quotation from Iu. Popov, "SEV-vtoroi dykhanie," *Pravitel'stvennyi vestnik*, no. 3 (January 1990): 2; The bloc deficit projection is from Andrei Sharyi, "SEV: poiski novogo oblika," *Pravda*, 12 May 1990, p. 6. See Yuri Sinyakov, "Comecon: Time to Write an Obit?" *Business in the USSR*, no. 3 (July-August 1990): 42–43; V. Sharov, "Proschai perevodnyi rubl'," *Pravda*, 18 September 1990, p. 5.
45. John D. Bell, "Bulgaria," in *YICA 1990*, pp. 308–18; CIA, *Eastern Europe: Long Road ahead to Economic Well-Being* (Washington, D.C.: Joint Economic Committee, U.S. Congress, 16 May 1990), table C-1 and p. 5; "Bolgariia," *Pravda*, 1 November 1990, p. 4.
46. Zdenek Suda, "Czechoslovakia," in *YICA 1990*, pp. 319–30; CIA, *Eastern Europe*, table C-1 and p. 5, for statistics; A. Krushinskii, "Na poroge konfiskatsii?" *Pravda*, 19 October 1990, p. 5.
47. CIA, *The World Factbook 1990* (Washington, D.C.: GPO, August 1990), pp. 111 and 287; International Institute of Strategic Studies, *Military Balance, 1990–1991* (London: IISS, Autumn 1990), p. 39.
48. CIA, *Eastern Europe*, table C-1 and p. 7.
49. Ibid., table C-1 and pp. 5–6. See also Reuters dispatch, "Hungary Rift on Asset Sale," *New York Times*, 8 November 1990, p. C-7.
50. Therese Raphael, "Trail-blazing Poles," *Wall Street Journal*, 30 July 1990, p. A-11; *Rzeczpospolita*, 1 August 1990, p. 3; Jacek Kuroń, labor minister, quoted by RFE/RL *Daily Report*, no. 161 (24 August 1990): 3. See also A. Drabkin, "Bukhgalteriia po-pol'ski," *Sovetskaia Rossiia*, 2 September 1990, p. 5; A. Starukhin, "Gazetnaia rasprodazha," *Pravda*, 11 November 1990, p. 6.
51. CIA, *Eastern Europe*, p. 6. Dan Ionescu, "Romania toward Post-Communism?" *Soviet/East European Report*, no. 8 (15 November 1990): 1 and 4.
52. The Council of Europe's parliamentary assembly in Strasbourg unanimously approved Hungary's request for full membership and did the same for Poland, subject to the spring 1991 parliamentary election. However, it denied guest status to Romania because of "fundamental doubts" concerning progress toward democracy since December 1989. RFE/RL *Daily Report*, no. 189 (4 October 1990): 1. See also the item on CMEA's demise in *Neues Deutschland* (East Berlin), 2 October 1990, p. 1.

9

EAST–WEST RELATIONS IN EUROPE

As seen from Moscow, the small peninsula of Western Europe occupies the mere edge of a vast Eurasian landmass that is almost completely dominated by the USSR. Western Europe's population, however, is not only larger than that of adjacent East–Central Europe but is also more versed in applying advanced technology and pursuing basic research and development. Because of their enormous capacity to produce wealth and thus the potential to rescue the USSR from economic collapse, the West Europeans represent the most important immediate target of Soviet foreign policy.

Although long-range goals of the USSR remain essentially unchanged, the tactics for achieving them are new. One observer suggests that Gorbachev seeks

> to enlist Western aid to *perestroika* and to the unsettled [East-Central European] satellite empire. Beyond that, through the deceptive construction of a "common European house," the Soviets would take a long stride toward the dismantling of NATO's defenses, Western Europe's progressive separation from the United States, and its ultimate transformation into an economic tributary of the Soviet Union.[1]

In contrast to his predecessors, Gorbachev supports West European economic unification in 1992. On the basis of the "new political thinking," the USSR now presents itself as a large market eager to exchange natural resources for consumers' goods. According to the Soviets, both the North Atlantic Treaty Organization (NATO) and the Warsaw Treaty Organization (WTO) can be expected to dissolve themselves because the new collective security system in Europe will render them obsolete, although the ultimate fate of "restructuring" and the "common European house" will depend on the West's willingness to invest in current Soviet reforms. In the words of Foreign Minister Shevardnadze, "economic help—or, we say it differently, economic cooperation, the supply of credit—of course this will help *perestroika*, democratization, and the humanization of our society."[2]

President George Bush, Chancellor Helmut Kohl, former Prime Minister Margaret Thatcher, and President François Mitterrand have said that they want *perestroika* to succeed. Mrs. Thatcher seemed especially captivated by Gorbachev when she spoke with him in the summer of 1990 at the Kremlin; two years earlier, she had declared that he was "a man I can do business with." More recently, however, the British prime minister blocked the European Community (EC) immediate aid package of $5 billion for the USSR, explaining at the end of June 1990 that Gorbachev had not taken enough steps to introduce democracy and a market economy in the Soviet Union. Chancellor Kohl, in contrast, has urged massive monetary aid to bolster the Soviet economy,[3] even pledging to honor USSR contracts with former East Germany until 1992 because half of the GDR's eight thousand industrial enterprises produced equipment for the Soviet armed forces.

LONG-RANGE OBJECTIVES

USSR objectives have overlapping military, economic, and political ramifications. The basic prerequisite for achieving long-range Soviet goals is the withdrawal of U.S. troops from Western Europe, especially from a united Germany. Moscow has already proposed dissolving both military alliances and replacing them with a new, all-European security system, although details were not offered.[4] Whether U.S. forces unilaterally leave as part of the new concept for stabilization in Europe or withdraw as a result of an agreement at the Conventional Armed Forces in Europe (CFE) negotiations at Vienna, the Soviets hope for the collapse of the North Atlantic alliance. If WTO were to be dissolved unilaterally as a symbolic part of a bargain, still in place would be the web of twenty-year bilateral treaties that bind all of the WTO states in East-Central Europe to the USSR. These treaties would take on less significance as Soviet troops withdraw completely from eastern Germany by 1994 and as WTO disintegrates.

Were NATO to break up, the Soviet Union might next attempt to frustrate the development of an independent West European nuclear force. In particular, Moscow would probably try to block any U.K.-French cooperation, such as a joint command, that could enhance their individual deterrent forces. Indicative of such an approach are previous Soviet demands that the nuclear delivery systems of these two countries be counted in the intermediate-range nuclear forces (INF) and strategic arms reduction treaty (START) negotiations during 1981–1983 as well as at the beginning of the resumed talks with the United States at Geneva after 12 March 1985. Gorbachev seemingly had agreed with Mrs. Thatcher's contention that a limited number of nuclear weapons in Western Europe under NATO control may indeed prove stabilizing, especially because such a phenomenon would require at least some WTO unity as a counterweight.

Despite their reported fascination with Gorbachev, the French appear committed to preserving military strength under President Mitterrand, whose second seven-year term expires in 1995. This French attitude is manifested by a four-hundred-warhead nuclear arsenal, a *Force d'Action Rapide* to be dispatched to Germany in time of crisis, the development of French troops as a strategic reserve, and the Franco-German brigade. Gorbachev also "disappointed many people who wanted their admiration confirmed . . . by his [July 1989] visit to Paris." Mitterrand, however, has become the second strongest supporter (after Kohl) of major aid to the Soviet Union. During the next visit at Paris, the two leaders signed a French-Soviet *entente* on 29 October 1990 which calls for consultations in case of a threat to national security.[5]

Gorbachev has made it clear that "the Germans have a right to unity" and that "only peace must come from German land."[6] After permitting self-determination to proceed throughout East-Central Europe, the Soviet president also decided to apply this principle to both Germanys. The NATO summit in London during 5–9 July 1990 suggested that the defensive military alliance be transformed into a political structure for peaceful, friendly international relations. Gorbachev accepted an invitation to Brussels by Western leaders, and Warsaw Pact member states have been encouraged to establish "regular diplomatic liaison" with NATO. Manfred Woerner, NATO secretary general, told the Soviet leader in Moscow that "we trust you and you can trust us."[7] Supreme allied commander in Europe, U.S. Gen. John Galvin, is quoted in the CPSU daily newspaper as follows:

In our new [NATO] strategy, there will no longer be an image of the enemy. At the London session of the NATO Council, we extended the hand of friendship to the East. Neither the Soviet Union nor the Warsaw Pact appear to be our enemies.[8]

The economic "weapon" may assume increasing importance in future Soviet-West European relations. For example, during 1989 France had a deficit in its trade with the USSR, largely because some 83 percent of French imports from the Soviet Union consist of oil and natural gas. Natural gas delivery accelerated after the pipeline between Urengoi and the border of West Germany was completed;[9] that pipeline now operates at full capacity. During 1989 gas deliveries for the Federal Republic of Germany amounted to 710 million rubles, followed by Italy (415 million rubles), France (323 million rubles), and Austria (179 million rubles). Development of offshore gas reserves at Troll, Norway, suggests that Oslo, not Moscow, may become the swing supplier of energy to other NATO countries. In the short term, however, the Soviet Union remains an immediately available source.[10]

Depending on fuel from the USSR may be dangerous (see chapter 7), especially if Moscow decides to suspend deliveries at various points because of what the Soviets call "technical difficulties." Even though the chairman of Ruhrgas, A.G., the privately owned utility in Germany, is quoted as stating that the USSR has been a reliable supplier, Moscow did cut petroleum supplies by between 15 and 28 percent to Czechoslovakia, Hungary, and Poland through the first half of 1990 without any assurance that these shortfalls would be made up by year's end. Prime Minister N. I. Ryzhkov explained to the twenty-eighth CPSU congress that the Soviet Union had been forced to reduce oil exports in order to supply its own agriculture with fuel.[11]

The growth of other kinds of East-West trade continues, however. Addressing the Congress of People's Deputies in mid-1989, an economist at the USA and Canada Institute, N. P. Shmelev, advised members of parliament that $15 billion worth of consumer goods should be imported immediately and that at least the same amount spread over the next three years would be needed to maintain domestic peace. Prime Minister Ryzhkov revealed to the same gathering the following day that the foreign currency debt of 34 billion rubles (more than $50 billion) was costing 12 billion rubles each year in service charges.[12] This figure suggests that it would be impossible to implement Shmelev's plan completely, unless huge credits become available from the West.

Four weeks later, Gorbachev addressed the Council of Europe at Strasbourg and attempted to convince the audience that the Soviets should be accepted as equal partners in international business. In his words, "We are convinced that [the people of Europe] need one Europe. We see our own future in such a Europe." Gorbachev then offered the following:

> Let us not forget either that the metastases of colonial slavery spread throughout the world from Europe. It was here that fascism was born. It

was here that the most destructive wars began. And the Europe which can legitimately be proud of its accomplishments, at the same time, has far from paid its debts to mankind yet. This still remains to be done, to be done by striving to achieve a transformation of international relations in the spirit of humanism, equality, and justice, by providing an example of democracy and social achievements in its own countries.[13]

At one time, Soviet decision makers hoped that local leftist parties as well as agents of influence might play a part in their long-range objectives. The communist movements in Western Europe have become fragmented, however, with pro-Moscow groups standing little chance of participating in coalition governments or even of influencing them if they do gain access and share power. Only in Finland could the USSR still prevent a noncooperative candidate from running for the presidency or a local politician from standing for parliament.[14] By contrast, the three communist cabinet members (they resigned in 1984) in the socialist government of France exercised little if any influence on the foreign policies of President Mitterrand.

What the Soviets have lost in terms of political power they may regain through economic interdependence. Credits totaling five billion deutsche marks (ca. $3 billion)—almost twice the $1.6 billion credit line offered in October 1988 by the West Germans—were extended to the USSR in June 1990.[15] Official statements claimed that these loans had nothing to do with a future Soviet withdrawal of troops from the eastern part of a united Germany. A few months later, however, Bonn signed an agreement with Moscow that specifies 12 billion deutsche marks (ca. $7.5 billion) to be allocated as follows:

Purpose	(Billions of) deutsche marks
1. Construction of new housing in the USSR for returning troops	7.8
2. Soviet costs inside eastern Germany over next four years	3.0
3. Transporting troops back to USSR	1.0
4. Retraining those troops that are demobilized	0.2
	12.0

plus interest of 1 billion deutsche marks on item 2 above, in conjunction with a treaty on "good neighborliness, partnership, and cooperation."[16]

Banks and industry in the Federal Republic of Germany (FRG) were anxious to invest capital and technological know-how outside their borders.

Locomotives produced by the GDR had been shipped to Greece under contract with an FRG company, small engines for Volkswagen cars were being made in East Germany. An energy conglomerate in Düsseldorf purchased chemicals from the GDR and in January 1991 began supplying electricity to East German cities. The ban on direct Western investments, which restricted establishment of joint ventures, was finally lifted in mid-1990. About 3,600 state-owned manufacturing *kombinats*, which represented the foundation of the GDR economy, were broken up into smaller units and then privatized, commencing even before the 2 December 1990 all-German elections that resulted in a new national parliament.

SHORT-TERM OBJECTIVES

Almost all the proposals offered by the USSR and its then East-Central European client regimes (as well as the nonruling communist parties from Western Europe) at the 24–26 April 1967 conference in Karlovy Vary, Czechoslovakia, although initially resisted by the West, were accepted by the latter within the ensuing eight years. These demands included the following:

1. Recognition of de facto existing borders in Europe
2. Acceptance of two sovereign and equal German states
3. A ban on nuclear weapons for the Federal Republic of Germany
4. Acknowledgment that the 1938 Munich agreement had been invalid ab initio
5. A treaty renouncing the use or threat of force by all European states
6. Diplomatic recognition of East Germany and of West Berlin as separate independent political entities
7. Abrogation of the ban on the communist party in the Federal Republic of Germany
8. Conclusion of a nonproliferation treaty as a step toward halting the arms race[17]

The Soviet invasion of Czechoslovakia in August 1968, only sixteen months after the Karlovy Vary conference, interrupted the beginning of a thaw in East-West relations. Yet by the end of the following year, the U.S. government had decided to ignore the Soviet military occupation of this supposedly independent country and initiate strategic arms limitation talks with the USSR.

THE HELSINKI FINAL ACT

In 1973 the West began preparing for a Conference on Security and Cooperation in Europe (CSCE) after the East agreed that both the United States and Canada would participate, that access to the USSR and East-Central Europe would be liberalized (the four-power protocol on Berlin had been signed in 1972), and that talks on mutual and balanced conventional force reductions would begin in Vienna. Preliminary proceedings at the foreign ministers' level opened the CSCE discussions. The working phase lasted almost two years, and the Final Act[18] was approved by thirty-five heads of government on 1 August 1975 at Helsinki.

In retrospect, the outcome appears to have been one-sided. The West had hoped to create the necessary conditions for arms control, cooperation, and the promotion of human rights throughout the East. Few of these goals were achieved over the next decade. Eastern objectives included recognizing *de jure* postwar borders in Europe, acquiring advanced technology through trade, strengthening the appearance of détente, and encouraging unilateral Western disarmament. All except the last were attained, although Washington later issued an official statement to the effect that the USSR annexation of the Baltic States had not been recognized by the U.S. government.

The East violated the Helsinki accords from the beginning. The most blatant transgression occurred in December 1979 when Soviet troops invaded Afghanistan. Six of the agreed-on basic principles (sovereign equality, nonuse of force, inviolability of frontiers, territorial integrity, nonintervention in internal affairs, and self-determination) were completely ignored by Moscow and continued to be violated until the withdrawal of Soviet combat forces by the negotiated 15 February 1989 deadline.

Less than a year after the USSR had occupied Afghanistan, the second CSCE review conference (the first was held in Belgrade during 1977–1978) convened in November 1980 at Madrid and continued well into 1983 because of disagreements over the wording of the final communiqué. The process revealed, from the U.S. viewpoint, a "serious decline in the necessary good faith compliance with the provisions of the Final Act on the part of a number of important signatories, including the Soviet Union."[19]

The third CSCE review conference opened at Vienna in early November 1986 and lasted until mid-January 1989. The resulting long document laid down elaborate principles for security in Europe, scheduling follow-up activities, arms control negotiations, and confidence-building measures. The United States' objectives centered on improving human rights in the Soviet Union and East-Central Europe. The document also included new commitments to respect CSCE monitors, cease jamming foreign radio stations, maintain privacy of mail and telecommunications, expedite family reunification and emergency travel, as well as expand freedom of religion. Signatories agreed to open the fourth review conference on 24 March 1992 at Helsinki.[20]

Although earlier USSR behavior appeared to have been unmodified by the Helsinki agreement, talks on confidence-building measures between East and West were undertaken again at Stockholm. This so-called Conference on Confidence- and Security-Building Measures and Disarmament in Europe (CDE) included delegations from the same thirty-five governments that had participated in the original 1975 meeting at Helsinki and at the three review conferences. In the week after the CDE convened, the NATO alliance proposed to discuss the following in detail: (1) exchanging information on the organization and location of all armed forces in Europe, (2) exchanging annual plans for military activities, (3) requiring at least forty-five days' notice before significant maneuvers, (4) the presence of observers at such maneuvers, (5) monitoring and verifying compliance with agreements reached by the CDE, and (6) improved communications.[21]

In contrast to these specific proposals, then USSR foreign minister Andrei A. Gromyko indicated at the CDE opening session that the East wanted a broad agreement on no first use of nuclear weapons, nonaggression, limitation of defense budgets, a ban on chemical weapons, and nuclear-free zones in Europe.[22] In exchange, the Soviet representative promised to elaborate on limits and prenotification of military maneuvers at some point in the future. The USSR proposal in essence was a general statement of intent rather than a specific basis for negotiations. In an attempt to break the stalemate, the U.S. delegation head spent two days in Moscow at the end of April 1984 meeting with his Soviet counterpart. President Reagan, addressing the parliament of Ireland, offered to accept the USSR proposal for a renunciation of force agreement if the latter would make concessions on confidence-building measures. TASS immediately rejected the proposed compromise.[23]

Almost four months after the CDE talks began, a formal proposal was put forward by the Soviet Union, acting on its own and not in the name of other Warsaw Pact members, perhaps because Romania submitted an outline on 25 January 1984, the day after NATO had made its offer. The USSR representative suggested, without any further details, the following confidence-building measures:

1. Limitation on military exercises to a *certain* numerical level
2. Prior notification of *major* military maneuvers
3. Prior notification of *major* movements and troop transfers

4. Development of the *existing* practice for inviting observers to major military maneuvers

5. *Adequate* forms of verification [all italics added]

After thirty-one months, the negotiations at Stockholm ended on 19 September 1986 with a compromise agreement that led to some "confidence-building measures."[24]

CONVENTIONAL FORCE REDUCTIONS

Objectives also differed at the Mutual and Balanced Force Reduction (MBFR) talks in Vienna, which opened 30 October 1973 with twelve Western and seven Eastern delegations. (France refused to join.) The reluctance with which the Soviets agreed to participate gave them an advantage from the beginning. In the course of the talks, the USSR sought to solidify the favorable correlation of conventional armed forces in East–Central Europe, to take advantage of Western concessions, and to exploit as well as create differences among the NATO allies.

In December 1975 the West offered to withdraw one thousand theater nuclear warheads, fifty-four aircraft (F-4s), and thirty-six Pershing I missile launchers, as well as twenty-nine-thousand U.S. troops if the East removed an entire sixty-eight-thousand-man Soviet tank army with its full complement of seventeen hundred tanks. No satisfactory response ever came from the East, which continued to propose that each side reduce troops by the same percentage, thus increasing ratios in favor of the already overwhelming Warsaw Pact preponderance.

Reductions will not work unless agreement can be reached on figures for existing manpower. To obtain such data from the East, NATO negotiators offered not to consider the four Soviet divisions stationed in Hungary. The Eastern count of Warsaw Pact ground forces issued in mid-1976 contained 120,000 fewer men than the lowest Western estimate. Less than seven years later, that discrepancy had risen to approximately 180,000 for ground troops;[25] if air force manpower were added, the total would be 210,000 (see table 9.1). Despite both sides eventually submitting proposals in treaty form, the deadlock could not be broken.

The NATO draft agreement of mid-July 1982 included a major concession: individual reductions would be specified when a single comprehensive treaty was signed, something the East had insisted on from the start of the talks. Thus it was left to the Soviets to clear up the data problem and agree on a set of Western-proposed confidence-building and associated measures including verification.[26] The USSR and its allies did not appear to want an

TABLE 9.1
DISPARITIES BETWEEN EASTERN AND WESTERN DIRECT PARTICIPANTS IN
THE MUTUAL AND BALANCED FORCE REDUCTION (MBFR) AREA,
1 JANUARY 1981

	NATO Estimate for WTO Forces	Western Figures for NATO Forces	Disparity
Ground	960,000	790,000	− 170,000*
Air	230,00	200,000	− 30,000
Total	1,190,000	990,000	− 200,000*
	Eastern Figures for WTO Forces	Western Figures for NATO Forces	Disparity
Ground	800,000	790,000	+ 10,000
Air	180,000	200,000	− 20,000
Total	980,000	990,000	− 10,000

*A more recent source (see note 27 in this chapter) raised this figure by ten thousand men.
SOURCE: U.S. Delegation to MBFR, *Mutual and Balanced Force Reductions* (June 1983), appendix to a mimeographed and unclassified report from Vienna, Austria.

agreement at this time, however, because they would have had to reduce their ground forces by 270,000 men, compared with approximately 90,000 for NATO, to bring both sides to genuine parity.

One approach to solving this data discrepancy—namely, concentrating on residual troop levels after reductions had taken place—implied that the East might be willing to take out more than a quarter of a million men, if unwatched by Western observers, and then allow inspection of the remaining 700,000-man ground force in the reduction area (East Germany, Poland, Czechoslovakia).[27] Such a resolution would require subsequent intrusive verification measures, including mandatory on-site inspection, at that time resisted by the Soviet Union.

After criticizing the comprehensive Western proposal for almost a year, in June 1983 the East submitted a new draft treaty of its own. This document concentrated on monitoring final ceilings, not on the reductions themselves, as the West had suggested. Among the associated measures proposed by the Warsaw Pact was the "opportunity to carry out on-the-spot checks, provided certain conditions are observed."[28] This deliberately vague formulation did not imply mandatory inspection.

The long recess between mid-December 1983 and mid-March 1984, after the East reversed its decision and agreed on a date for resumption of the talks, was used by the Western delegations to prepare a compromise proposal. This document cleared the NATO council and was ready to be submitted to the East on 19 April 1984 along the following lines:

1. Data to be exchanged only on ground combat and combat support forces.

2. This information should fall within an acceptable range of Western estimates (that is, no precise agreement necessary).

3. Initial token Soviet and U.S. reductions.

4. Satisfactory verification of remaining forces and only then a full agreement on data.[29]

In return, the Warsaw Pact was asked to accept the associated measures proposed by the West as far back as December 1979. The East had raised the possibility of a trade-off between data and verification on many occasions in the past. On 7 June 1984, however, the East rejected the NATO attempt at breaking the deadlock in MBFR.

Other proposals were presented during 1985. In February the USSR offered to remove 20,000 troops if the United States would take out 13,000 troops from the respective reduction areas, with a freeze on the remaining force levels. Only "three or four" observation points would be allowed on each side. The West responded in December, proposing a withdrawal of 11,500 Soviet and 5,000 U.S. soldiers, a collective no-increase commitment for three years, and verification measures, including thirty annual on-site inspections. Gorbachev complicated matters at the eleventh East German communist party congress on 18 April 1986 by offering an extended reduction area "from the Atlantic to the Urals" that would involve withdrawing 500,000 men from each side. In December 1986, NATO accepted the extended area,[30] which had previously included only West Germany and Benelux (Belgium, Netherlands, Luxembourg) as well as East Germany, Poland, and Czechoslovakia.

The MBFR talks were discontinued on 2 February 1989, after 472 plenary meetings. They had lasted fifteen years and three months and were superseded by the Conventional Armed Forces in Europe (CFE) negotiations covering an expanded area between the Atlantic and the Urals. The day these new NATO/WTO talks opened on 9 March 1989, the East offered a general proposal for reductions in three phases that would transform both alliances by the year 2000 into defensive ones. The West's position paper specified the exact number of tanks, artillery pieces, and armored troop carriers that would remain on each side.[31] France, Portugal, and Spain fully participated in CFE on the NATO side.

Unfortunately, just as at the MBFR talks, substantial differences existed in troops levels and offensive weapons systems throughout the expanded reduction area (see table 9.2). Three months before the CFE talks opened, Gorbachev announced at the U.N. General Assembly that the USSR would unilaterally reduce its ground forces by 500,000 men (from a total of 5.2 million) and withdraw 10,000 tanks (59,470 total) from active service by the end of 1990. He did not specify whether the latter would be the old T-55 models, about 20,000 of which were in storage, or the latest T-80s.[32]

Apparently the Soviets are implementing these announced measures by replacing one tank regiment from each division with a motorized rifle regiment. Although the number of tanks will be reduced, units will be larger and more balanced, with a higher sustained offensive capability. Beginning in May 1989, a "public" supervisory group was to verify USSR withdrawals from East Germany and Czechoslovakia. The group consists of twenty

TABLE 9.2
EQUIPMENT AND TROOPS BETWEEN THE ATLANTIC AND THE URALS, 1990

	NATO			WARSAW PACT			
	Total	U.S.	U.S. share (percent)	Total	Soviet	Soviet share (percent)	Pact/NATO (ratio)
Tanks	23,000	6,000	26	59,800	38,100	64	2.6
Armored Combat Vehicles[a]	34,025	7,400	22	74,000	51,200	69	2.2
Artillery	17,700	2,232	13	46,270	33,000	71	2.6
Aircraft	5,700	700	12	10,400	7,600	73	1.8
Helicopters	2,235	700	31	3,500	2,850	81	1.6
Ground Troops (thousands)	2,214	216	10	3,090	2,200	71	1.4
Divisions[b]	103	5⅔	6	224⅓	161⅔	72	2.2

[a]National totals may not be consistent with alliance totals because of definitional differences between sources.

[b]Includes separate brigades and regiments. Assumes three brigades or regiments are equivalent to one division.

SOURCE: U.S. Congressional Budget Office, *Budgetary and Military Effects of a Treaty Limiting Conventional Forces in Europe* (Washington, D.C.: September 1990), p. 8, which is based primarily on NATO and U.S. assessments of alliance totals.

experts from the Soviet Committee on Security and Cooperation in Europe, the Soviet Peace Fund, the Soviet Peace Committee, the Soviet Women's Committee, and other unspecified "social" organizations under the chairmanship of Andrei A. Kokoshin,[33] who is one of the deputy directors at the USA and Canada Institute (see chapter 4). Nothing has been heard from this group.

This same Kokoshin, together with two other colleagues from the same institute, presented statements on conventional arms control before the defense policy panel of the U.S. House of Representatives on 9 May 1989 in Washington, D.C. The hearing was chaired by Congressman Les Aspin of the Committee on the Armed Services.[34] Such an opportunity to influence important legislators in the United States has not been reciprocated by the USSR Supreme Soviet.

The negotiators in Vienna had a deadline to meet, namely, 19–21 November 1990, when the CSCE summit was scheduled to meet in Paris and approve a CFE treaty. U.S. secretary of state James A. Baker and Foreign Minister Shevardnadze agreed on troop and aircraft limits in early October so as to expedite the Vienna talks. Almost simultaneously, the United States ordered forty-thousand troops withdrawn from Europe and their units disbanded within the next twelve months. The CFE treaty was signed on 19 November 1990, covering only equipment, not manpower. The Soviet Union reportedly moved thousands of tanks beyond the Urals so they could not be counted.[35]

INTERMEDIATE-RANGE NUCLEAR FORCES

Despite the USSR's announcement on 6 May 1978 that it accepted military parity as a principle, there followed a steady and constant buildup of Soviet intermediate-range nuclear forces (INF). As of December 1987, when the INF treaty was signed, these included 484 launchers plus about 470 deployed mobile triple warhead SS-20s. Some 270 of the latter were targeted against Western Europe. The first INF salvo could have delivered three times that number of nuclear warheads. Every launcher reportedly stocked at least one but probably more refire missiles, each with three SS-20 warheads.[36]

Perhaps anticipating these developments, NATO agreed on a "dual track" decision in December 1979, that is, modernizing its weapons' systems through deployment of 572 Pershing IIs and ground-launched cruise missiles (GLCMs), both with one warhead each, while supporting U.S. bilateral negotiations for an INF arms control agreement with the Soviet Union. Deployment was scheduled to begin in December 1983 and continue through 1988, unless a treaty between the United States and the USSR were attained before the latter year.

In February 1982, the U.S. delegation submitted a draft agreement embodying a "zero option" that envisaged nondeployment of any new Pershings or GLCMs if the Soviets eliminated all their intermediate-range missiles, of which they had a monopoly. In response, the USSR claimed that a balance between East and West already existed and proposed that the sides reduce their totals to three hundred each. It later modified this by suggesting a level equal to the combined total of British and French ballistic missiles (these are not assigned to NATO and, in any event, represent strategic rather than intermediate-range systems). At the time, then Defense Minister Dmitrii F. Ustinov warned[37] that the USSR would retaliate directly against the United States and those NATO countries that accepted INF deployments.

This blackmail approach registered only limited success. The Federal Republic of Germany, after the March 1983 national elections, reaffirmed that it would accept 110 Pershing II and 96 Tomahawk GLCMs. Another 160 of the Tomahawks would be deployed by the United Kingdom; Italy would take 110; and 48 each would be accepted by Belgium and the Netherlands. The first nine Pershing IIs arrived in West Germany at the end of December 1983, more than a month *after* the Soviets had walked out of the Geneva talks. During that time, England and Italy installed 16 GLCMs each. Because no agreement had been reached at Geneva, almost all of the NATO allies accepted the new U.S. weapons systems. Although these would not redress the balance completely, they probably convinced the USSR to resume negotiations in March 1985 (see table 9.3).

Attendant on the missile controversy were peace demonstrations in the Federal Republic of Germany and throughout Western Europe. These protests were largely spearheaded by the generation of 1968, members of which had begun to occupy positions of influence in government, education, and the churches during the mid-1970s. One conspicuous group in this movement is the anti-industry, apolitical, and ecological Greens. The West German parliament, or *Bundestag*, as of mid-1990, out of 497 total, included 42 Greens,[38] whose underlying aim is destruction of the political system. The Soviets have proven themselves extremely efficient at exploiting such indigenous movements for their own purposes. The demonstrations, however, seem to have lost momentum after December 1987, when the INF treaty was signed.

The protocol on procedures, which is appended to that treaty, permits both the United States and the USSR to retain all warheads from the intermediate- and short-range nuclear weapons scheduled for destruction. In the Soviet case, this means that fissionable material from 1,846 missiles

TABLE 9.3
INF DEPLOYMENTS: USSR AND U.S. PERSPECTIVES IN 1983

USSR Assessment

WESTERN SYSTEMS		SOVIET SYSTEMS	
System	*Number*	*System*	*Number*
United States		Land-based missiles	
Fighter-bombers		(SS-20s, SS-5s, SS-4s)	496
F-111s	172	Submarine missiles	18
FB-111s	65	Medium-range bombers	
F-4s	246	(Backfire/Badger/Blinder)	461
A-6s & A-7s	240		
United Kingdom			
Polaris missiles	64		
Vulcan bombers	55		
France			
Land-based missiles	18		
Submarine missiles	80		
Mirage-4 bombers	46		
Total	986	Total	975

United States Assessment

AMERICAN SYSTEMS		SOVIET SYSTEMS	
F-111 fighter-bombers	164	SS-20s	378
F-4s	265	SS-4s and SS-5s	350
A-6s and A-7s	68	SS-12s and 22s	100
FB-111s (U.S.-based for		TU-26 Backfire bombers	45
use in Europe)	63	TU-16 Badgers and	
Pershing I	9	TU-22 Blinders	350
Ground-launched		SU-17, SU-24, and MiG-27	
cruise missiles	32	fighter-bombers	2,700
		SS-N-5s	30
Total	601	Total	3,953

NOTE: The USSR included third-country missile and bomber systems in its overall count. However, placing French and British strategic systems in the NATO balance is incorrect and therefore misleading. French forces are totally independent of the NATO nuclear deterrent, and France does not participate in NATO's integrated military command. Although the United Kingdom participates in the integrated command, its submarine-launched ballistic missiles are clearly strategic deterrent forces.

SOURCE: U.S. Department of Defense, "Soviet Claims on the Nuclear Balance in Europe," *Background Paper* (Washington, D.C.: GPO, 1983), pp. 6–9.

has been extracted and is being stored as a reserve for the future. Hence, when Gorbachev announced in London on 7 April 1989 that the USSR would close down production of weapons-grade uranium (the United States did this in 1964) as well as two reactors that make plutonium by the end of that year, he mentioned neither the retention of warheads nor the eleven other Soviet plutonium-producing plants remaining operational.

Another example of adroit public diplomacy came at the end of a three-hour meeting in the Kremlin between U.S. secretary of state Baker and Gorbachev when the Soviet leader announced[39] a unilateral withdrawal of five hundred battlefield nuclear warheads mounted on air-launched bombs, short-range missiles, and artillery shells by the end of 1989. This represents only 5 percent of approximately ten thousand such warheads in the USSR arsenal and, in any event, cannot be verified. By contrast, NATO maintains about four thousand such weapons after a unilateral reduction of twenty-four hundred warheads over the past decade.[40] For the continuing production of military equipment by the USSR, see table 9.4.

Finally, after three new East–Central European governments had revealed this information several months earlier, USSR representative M. N. Strel'tsov at the Soviet-U.S. Special Verification Commission admitted the existence of SS-23 launchers with conventional warhead missiles on the territories of East Germany, Czechoslovakia, and Bulgaria. He claimed that they had been transferred before the INF treaty was signed and, in any event, now belonged to third countries that were not covered by the agreement to destroy them.[41]

WEST-EAST TECHNOLOGY TRANSFER

The huge quantities of conventional weaponry at the disposal of the USSR and its allies in East-Central Europe have been offset to a certain extent by NATO technological superiority. In some areas, the development gap between West and East has widened. The introduction of "smart" weapons, especially those that use microelectronics and computers, has begun to revolutionize the battlefield. The NATO Defense Planning Council had adopted new guidelines, the so-called follow-on forces attack, to hit enemy reinforcements up to hundreds of miles beyond the East-West border.

That the Soviet Union is deeply interested in obtaining such high technology data can be seen by the activities of KGB Directorate T, which sends approximately three hundred specialist intelligence officers abroad to direct this effort. As described in chapter 5, these men operate out of USSR embassies, trade missions, and export-import companies designed to acquire advanced technology as well as to conduct industrial espionage and theft.

TABLE 9.4
SOVIET MILITARY PRODUCTION, 1982–1989[a]

Equipment Type	Pre-Gorbachev (Yearly Averages) (1982–1984)	Gorbachev Era (Yearly Averages) (1986–1988)	(1989)
Tanks	2,800	3,400	1,700
Other armored vehicles	5,400	4,600	5,700
Towed field artillery	1,300	1,000	800
Self-propelled field artillery	900	900	750
Multiple rocket launchers[a]	600	480	300
Self-propelled antiaircraft artillery	200	100	250
Submarines	9	9	9
Surface warships	9	9	12
Minor surface combatants	57	55	54
Bombers	40	47	40
Fighters	950	700	625
Military helicopters	580	450	400
Intercontinental ballistic missiles (ICBMs)	116	116	140
Short-range ballistic missiles (SRBMs)[a]	580	700	700
Long-range submarine-launched cruise missiles (SLCMs)	35	200	200
Short-range SLCMs	980	1,100	1,100
Surface-to-air missiles (SAMs)[a][b]	15,000	16,000	14,000

[a]totals include exports
[b]excludes man-portable SAMs

SOURCE: U.S. Department of Defense, *Soviet Military Power, 1990* (Washington, D.C.: GPO, September 1990), p. 38.

More than half the expulsions of Soviet "diplomats" from various Western countries during recent years were the result of such activities (see table 5.1).

As discussed in chapter 7, during 1949 NATO (minus Iceland and later joined by Australia) and Japan established the Coordinating Committee for Multilateral Export Controls, or CoCom, to curtail such illegal shipments and thefts. CoCom drew up three lists of military, atomic energy, and dual-use items and commercial goods with military applications from which it reviewed license requests from companies throughout its seventeen member states in an attempt to harmonize enforcement.

During the late 1970s and into the mid-1980s, the Soviet military-industrial complex benefited from the acquisition of Western technological equipment and information each year (in order of priority) to:

1. Redirect technical approaches in about one hundred projects for weapons systems and key military equipment

2. Initiate several hundred new short- and long-term projects in technical areas hitherto not considered

3. Raise the technical levels of several thousand developmental projects for military equipment, manufacturing, and design procedures

4. Eliminate the need for or shorten more than a thousand military research projects, thereby reducing—up to three years—the lead time required to produce advanced weapons and equipment[42]

Abundant evidence shows that technology and equipment from Western Europe and North America directly contribute to improving USSR military programs, which in turn saves research and development costs and reveals the directions of NATO planning, and thus assists in the development of countermeasures. When reverse engineering is achieved—that is, reproduction and modification of systems on the basis of stolen technology—series production from copies can be initiated. Items with dual civilian and military application also benefit the Soviet economy. Even personal computers can be put to use by the military in battlefield communications and management. For these reasons CoCom maintained its export controls on computers until mid-1990, after a U.S. National Academy of Sciences study (1989) had recommended that the United States restrict its exports of hardware and software to certain advanced technologies.[43]

Under pressure from other CoCom members, the United States finally agreed at the 6–7 June 1990 meeting in Paris to end controls on 38 of the 116 categories under embargo. Henceforth, U.S.-made mainframe computers (IBM 3031, 4331, 4341) could be sold to the USSR. Poland, Czechoslovakia, and Hungary will receive preferential access to modern telecommunications equipment; East Germany would also be treated as a special case. Finally, the dual-use control list will be completely overhauled by the end of the year, when a core list will be created.[44]

Starting on 1 July 1990, West Germany began making payments, which would continue for the next six months, toward $780 million for the USSR to station its troops in East Germany. These payments will continue over several years at reduced levels. Meanwhile, all-German elections on 2 December 1990 completed the unification process. The thirty-five-member Conference on Security and Cooperation in Europe, meeting two weeks earlier in Paris, received details about Germany's future. The new all-European structure, according to Foreign Minister Hans-Dietrich Genscher, will include regular meetings by heads of state, a center for conflict prevention, and a secretariat.[45] Soviet foreign policy has not been as successful in the Third World, which is discussed in the next chapter.

NOTES

1. Sol W. Sanders, "A 'Common European House'—or a New Design for Soviet Hegemony?" *Strategic Review* 17, no. 2 (Spring 1989): 27.
2. Quoted by Bill Keller, "Western Aid Issue," *New York Times*, 10 July 1990, p. A-1.
3. "Rabochii vizit M. Tetcher v SSSR, 7–10 iiunia," *Vestnik MID SSSR*, no. 13 (15 July 1990): 24–26. Gorbachev had suggested about $15 billion in aid from the West, according to Craig Whitney, "European Leaders Back Kohl's Plea," *New York Times*, 27 June 1990, p. A-4.
4. E. Grigor'ev, "Realizm i doverie," *Pravda*, 19 July 1990, p. 6; Serge Schmemann, "Gorbachev Rings the Doorbell," *New York Times*, 22 July 1990, section 4, pp. 1–2.
5. Jacques Amalric, "Route Glissante," *Le Monde*, 7 July 1989, pp. 1 and 4; V. Bolshakov, "V pol'zu zdravogo smysla," *Pravda*, 30 October 1989, p. 6, about Mitterrand; "Dogovor o soglasii i sotrudnichestva mezhdu SSSR i Frantsuskoi Respublikoi," *Pravda*, 30 October 1990, pp. 1 and 4.
6. "Otvety M. S. Gorbacheva na voprosy," *Vestnik MID SSSR*, no. 5 (15 March 1990): 3 and 4.
7. Craig R. Whitney, "NATO Leaders Proclaim End of Cold War," *New York Times*, 7 July 1990, pp. 1 and 4, and "NATO Declaration" on p. 5; see also Gary Lee, "Gorbachev Accepts Call," *Washington Post*, 15 July 1990, p. 24.
8. TASS dispatch from Bonn, "Elementy novoi strategii," *Pravda*, 23 July 1990, p. 4. See also Vladislav Drobkov, "Skazhi mne, kto tvoi vrag?" *Pravda*, 6 November 1990, p. 4.
9. *Soviet Foreign Trade* (Moscow), no. 4 (April 1990): 34; *Vneshnie ekonomicheskie sviazi SSSR v 1989 g.* (Moscow: Finansy i statistika, 1990), pp. 112, 182, 156, 192.
10. U.S. Congress, House, Committee on Foreign Affairs, Subcommittee on International Economic Policy and Trade, "Commercial Lending to the Soviet Bloc," *Hearing* (Washington, D.C.: GPO, 1989), p. 30.
11. "Otvety na voprosy uchastnikov s"ezda," *Pravda*, 11 July 1990, p. 4.
12. "S"ezd narodnykh deputatov SSSR, N. P. Shmelev," *Pravda*, 9 June 1989, p. 2; "Zakliuchitel'noe slovo N. I. Ryzhkova," *Pravda*, 10 June 1989, p. 3.
13. "Obshcheevropeiskii protsess idet vpered—rech' M. S. Gorbacheva," *Pravda*, 7 July 1989, pp. 1–2.
14. USSR trade with Finland ranked high during 1989, with a turnover of almost 3.9 billion rubles (*Soviet Foreign Trade* [Moscow], no. 4 [April 1990]: 34). See

also the report on Gorbachev's visit to Helsinki in "Ukrepliaia fundament obshcheevropeiskogo doma," *Pravda,* 26 October 1989, pp. 1–2.

15. Ferdinand Protzman, "Bonn to Prop up Kremlin," *New York Times,* 23 June 1990, p. 1. Credits and subsidies from Germany reached 20 billion deutsch marks for the year, according to Frederick Kempe, "Gorbachev with Little to Offer," *Wall Street Journal,* 9 November 1990, p. A-6.

16. Timothy Reppel, "Bonn and Moscow Agree," *Wall Street Journal,* 14 September 1990, p. A-8. See "Dogovor o dobrososedstve, partnerstve i sotrudnichestve mezhdu SSSR i FRG," *Pravda,* 10 November 1990, pp. 1 and 4.

17. *Information Bulletin* (Prague: Peace and Socialism Publishers), no. 8(96), pp. 5–77 and no. 10(98) pp. 5–109; both in the 1967 volume.

18. U.S. Department of State, *Conference on Security and Cooperation in Europe: Final Act* (Washington., D.C.: GPO, 1975), pp. 75–135, gives the full text.

19. U.S. Congress, Commission on Security and Cooperation in Europe, *Implementation of the Final Act to the Conference on Security and Cooperation in Europe: Findings and Recommendations Seven Years after Helsinki,* 97th Cong., 2d sess. (Washington, D.C.: GPO, 1982), Committee Print. Quotation is from the letter of transmittal.

20. U.S. Congress, Commission on Security and Cooperation in Europe, *The Vienna CSCE Follow-Up Meeting,* 101st Cong., 2d sess. (Washington, D.C.: GPO, January 1990), p. 150. See also Iurii Deriabin, "Khel'sinkskii ekspress mchitsia k Parizhu," *Novoe vremia,* no. 35 (24 August 1990): 10–11.

21. Conference on Confidence- and Security-Building Measures and Disarmament in Europe (CDE), *Confidence- and Security-Building Measures (CSBMs) Proposed by the Delegations of Belgium, Canada, Denmark, France, Federal Republic of Germany, Greece, Iceland, Italy, Luxembourg, Netherlands, Norway, Portugal, Spain, Turkey, United Kingdom, United States of America,* series CSCE/SC.1 (Stockholm: U.S. Delegation to CDE, 24 January 1984), pp. 2–4.

22. See, for example, O. N. Bykov, *Mery doveriia* (Moscow: Nauka, 1983), pp. 71–72, who listed these same measures one year before the conference opened in Stockholm.

23. Moscow radio, 27 April 1984; *Foreign Broadcast Information Service-Soviet Union* 84–084 (30 April 1984): AA-1, on the Moscow meetings; Rich Jaroslovsky, "Reagan Bids Again in Dublin Address for Soviet Talks," *Wall Street Journal,* 5 June 1984, p. 39, for the speech and its rejection by TASS.

24. Conference on Confidence- and Security-Building Measures and Disarmament in Europe, *Confidence- and Security-Building Measures in Europe: Proposals of the Soviet Union,* series CSCE/SC.4 (Stockholm: U.S. Delegation to CDE, 8 May 1984), pp. 4–5.

Part 5 of "Key Sections of Document at Stockholm Meeting," *New York Times,* 22 September 1986, mentions only three inspections a year in the agreement. On implementation, see U.S. Department of State, *Strengthening Stability through Openness* (Washington, D.C., GPO, April 1989), pp. 13–21.

25. U.S. Department of State, "Arms Control: MBFR Talks," *Gist,* March 1983, p. 2.

26. Richard F. Staar, "The MBFR Process and Its Prospects," in Staar, ed., *Arms Control: Myth Versus Reality* (Stanford: Hoover Institution Press, 1988), pp. 47–58.
27. U.S. Congress, House Committee on Foreign Affairs, Subcommittee on International Security and Scientific Affairs, *East-West Troop Reductions in Europe: Is Agreement Possible?* 98th Cong., 1st sess. (Washington, D.C.: GPO, 1983), pp. 14–16.
28. Interview with head of the Soviet delegation, as reported in the Austrian communist party newspaper: "Walerian Michailow: Jetzt ist der Westen am Zug," *Volksstimme* (Vienna), 2 July 1983, p. 3. See also Michael Alexander, "MBFR—Verification Is the Key," *NATO Review* 34, no. 3 (June 1986): 6–11.
29. Wilfried Aichinger, "Die Wiener Truppenabbauverhandlungen: Eine Bestandsaufnahme," *Österreichische Militärische Zeitschrift* 22, no. 3 (May-June 1984): 189–95. See also Carnes Lord, "The MBFR Mystery," *American Spectator* 19, no. 6 (June 1986): 14–15.
30. Heinz König, "Signale konstruktiv aufgreifen," *Horizont* (East Berlin), no. 6 (June 1986): 9. See also Elizabeth Pond, "NATO Proposes Talking within a Pan-European Framework," *Christian Science Monitor*, 12 December 1986, p. 14.
31. Richard F. Staar, "Military Balance between the Atlantic and the Urals," *Mediterranean Quarterly*, Fall 1989, pp. 36–37.
32. Ibid., pp. 35–36. See also U.S. Department of State, *CFE Negotiation on Conventional Armed Forces in Europe* (Washington, D.C.: GPO, March 1989).
33. Vladimir Markov, "Public Control over Troop Withdrawal," *Moscow News*, no. 18 (7–14 May 1989): 2. See also Harry Gelman, *The Soviet Turn toward Force Reduction: The Internal Struggle and the Variables at Play*, R-3876-AF (Santa Monica, Calif.: RAND, December 1989).
34. U.S. Congress, House of Representatives, "Prospects of U.S./Soviet Relations with Emphasis on Conventional Arms Control," *Hearing* (Washington, D.C.: GPO, 1989).
35. Colonel V. Nazarenko, "Bez kanikul rabotaiut delegatsii v Vene," *Krasnaia zvezda*, 28 August 1990, p. 3; "U.S. Ordering 40,000 Troops From Europe," *New York Times*, 27 September 1990, p. A-7. "Dogovor ob obychnykh vooruzhennykh silakh v Evrope," *Pravda*, 21 November 1990, pp. 3–4; ACDA, *Treaty on Conventional Armed Forces in Europe* (Paris: 19 November 1990). See also Michael R. Gordon, "Soviets Shift Many Tanks to Siberia," *New York Times*, 15 November 1990, p. A-3. Admitted by the TASS military correspondent over Moscow radio, 22 November 1990; "V. Chernyshev on CFE Treaty," *FBIS-Soviet Union* 90–228, 27 November 1990, pp. 1–2.
36. U.S. Department of State, "Memorandum of Understanding," in *Treaty Between USA and USSR on Elimination of Intermediate-Range and Shorter-Range Missiles* (Washington, D.C.: GPO, December 1987), p. 3.
37. "Otvety ministra oborony, D. F. Ustinova na voprosy korrespondenta TASS," *Pravda*, 31 July 1983, p. 4.
38. *Europa World Yearbook 1990* (London: Europa Publishers, 1990), p. 1131.

39. "Vstrecha M. S. Gorbacheva s Dzh. Beikerom," *Pravda*, 12 May 1989, p. 2.
40. U.S. Congress, Senate Committee on Armed Services, *Intermediate-Range Nuclear Forces Treaty and the Conventional Balance in Europe*, 100th Cong., 2d sess. (Washington, D.C.: GPO, 3 February 1988).
41. TASS, "Na brifinge v MID SSSR," *Izvestiia*, 15 May 1990, p. 4.
42. U.S. Department of Defense, *Soviet Acquisition of Militarily Significant Western Technology: An Update* (Washington, D.C.: GPO, September 1985), p. 8.
43. National Research Council, *Global Trends in Computer Technology and Their Impact on Export Control* (Washington, D.C.: National Academy Press, 1988).
44. U.S. Department of State, "U.S. Exports: Strategic Technology Controls," *Gist*, June 1990. See also U.S. Department of State, "COCOM High Level Meeting," *Fact Sheet*, July 1990; Peter Passell, "The Cold War on U.S. Exports," *New York Times*, 19 September 1990, p. C-2; John Markoff, "U.S. Proposes Easing Curbs," *New York Times*, 26 October 1990, p. C-3.
45. Craig R. Whitney, "Promise of Yalta: Redeemed at Last?" *New York Times*, 17 July 1990, pp. A-1 and A-7. Paul Lewis, "Hopes of a New European Security Structure," *New York Times*, 27 September 1990, p. A-7. See also the article from Bonn by E. Grigor'ev, "Real'naia neveroiatnost' " *Pravda*, 1 October 1990, p. 5, and the interview with the German foreign minister in "Geheimnis des Genscherismus," *Der Spiegel*, no. 40 (1 October 1990): 30–35.

10

THE THIRD WORLD

Less-developed countries (LDCs) make up approximately 66 percent of the world's 159 self-governing political units, occupy some 40 percent of the global land area, and account for almost 50 percent of the total population. These states' vast holdings of raw materials, their ability to exercise economic leverage through an oil embargo, their influence in the United Nations and other international organizations such as the Group of 77, and their proximity to twenty-three of thirty-one maritime choke points (trade channels essential to the United States and the free world) all critically figure in the Soviet approach to LDCs. Although the USSR does not openly emphasize this point, in his book on *perestroika* Gorbachev saw the Third World as a place where "regional conflicts are spawned by the colonial past, new social processes, or recurrences of predatory policies, or by all three."[1]

The influence of new political thinking, in the words of a Soviet political analyst, has produced "less impressive changes" in the Third World than in "relations with our former 'enemy'—the West." However, he goes on to say,

A detailed assessment of the previous policy is still at the development stage, and the tenet on repudiation of confrontation has not yet been brought to the logical conclusion that the system of priorities and the nature of the ties that have taken shape in the epoch of support for the anti-imperialist struggle in the Third World should be reassessed.[2]

Two years earlier a prominent member of the Institute of Economics of the World Socialist System in Moscow explained the central problem in pre-Gorbachev foreign policy vis-à-vis the Third World as follows:

> Though we were politically, militarily (via weapons, supplies, advisors), and diplomatically involved in regional conflicts, we disregarded their influence on the relaxation of tension between the USSR and the West and on their entire system of relationships. There were no clear ideas of the Soviet Union's true national state interests. These interests by no means consisted in chasing petty and essentially formal gains associated with leadership coups in certain developing countries.[3]

Certainly a vague notion of national interest appeared to be operative when Libyan dictator Mu'ammar Qaddafi was told by Brezhnev himself that the USSR adheres to a code of conduct including the following:

1. Recognition of the right of each people to decide its domestic affairs without outside interference
2. Strict respect for territorial integrity and inviolability of frontiers
3. Unconditional recognition of the right of each African, Asian, and Latin American state to equal participation in international life
4. Complete and unconditional recognition of sovereignty of these states over their natural resources
5. Respect for the status of nonalignment chosen by the majority of African, Asian, and Latin American states[4]

None of the foregoing corresponded to Soviet activities in the Third World, however. In fact, all five points have been violated overtly and covertly by every USSR leader from Lenin to Gorbachev.

The continuing appeal of these would be principles can be seen in a message from Gorbachev, hand-carried by K. N. Brutents in 1988 to Lt. Col. Haile Mariam Mengistu of Ethiopia, that is summarized as follows:

> A common conviction was expressed that the way to the elimination of tension in the area in the Horn of Africa lies through solution of existing problems by political means on the basis of the principles of territorial integrity of states, non-interference in their internal affairs on the part of external forces, and the development of good neighborly relations.[5]

Nevertheless, the correctness of this course is not obvious to everyone. Some apparently view it as a betrayal of principles in which elements of Marxism-Leninism in the Stalinist understanding of it, imperial monarchism, and blind patriotism are grouped under the common denominator of reluctance for change.[6]

CATEGORIES OF LDCs

In 1981, at the twenty-sixth CPSU congress, Brezhnev spoke of certain governments in the Third World—Angola, Ethiopia, Mozambique, Afghanistan, and the People's Democratic Republic of [South] Yemen[7]—that had taken the "revolutionary-democratic path" toward socialist development. The late CPSU general secretary then listed the similar developments within these countries: the gradual liquidation of imperialist monopolies, the upper middle class, and feudal lords; the curbing of foreign capital; the transition to economic planning; the creation of cooperatives (collective farms) in rural areas; an anti-imperialist foreign policy; and the growth of a strong revolutionary party.

Brezhnev cited a second group of states—as "genuinely independent" countries that have strong "anti-imperialist" governments or "revolutionary parties," including Syria, India, Iran, and Iraq. In the Iranian case, he mentioned that under the banner of Islam, the progressive struggle could be swept away by "counterrevolutionary mutinies," making the ultimate outcome dependent on "the real content of a particular movement."[8]

The Nonaligned Movement

The so-called nonaligned organization, which claims to reject dependence on or alliance with either of the superpowers, includes states in both categories. When it met for its sixth summit conference at Havana in September 1979, the movement had ninety-five members and twenty-one observers. Romanian and Yugoslav delegates blocked a Cuban resolution proclaiming the USSR as "patron" of the organization. Several months later, in January 1980, when the U.N. General Assembly considered a resolution calling for withdrawal of foreign (Soviet) troops from Afghanistan, fifty-seven nonaligned states voted in favor, twenty-four abstained, and only nine opposed it.

At the seventh meeting, held from 7 to 12 March 1983 in New Delhi, participating delegations had increased to 101 full members, 19 observer countries, and 26 guests. Cambodia's seat remained vacant. A final declaration, emphasizing the movement's independence from all blocs, attacked the Republic of South Africa's "destabilization attempts" in the region and also condemned Israel as well as the United States regarding the Middle

East. Strong anti-American language appeared in the section on Nicaragua and El Salvador.

The eighth conference, which took place from 1 to 7 September 1986 at Harare, Zimbabwe, attracted heads of state from twenty-eight Asian, fifty African, eighteen Latin American, and three European countries as well as one from Oceania plus leaders from the Palestine Liberation Organization (PLO) and the South-West African People's Organization. Observers represented several other governments as well as national and international organizations. The nonaligned group is hardly united, however. Mu'ammar Qaddafi has called it "useless," although he continues to attend its summits, and the Iran-Iraq war led to heated disagreements among members, who have little in common except that most of them voted to condemn South Africa as well as the United States.[9]

The ninth summit convened between 3 and 8 September 1989 at Belgrade in Yugoslavia, where at least thirty-two members openly aligned with Moscow (see table 10.1). The ninety-eight participants voted in favor of PLO membership in the United Nations, the withdrawal of Israel from occupied Arab territories, the reunification of Korea, U.N. Resolution 435 on independence for Namibia, the sovereignty of Panama over the canal, and better terms of international trade (during calendar year 1988 the nonaligned countries had only a 20 percent share of international trade). The need to acknowledge the "new political thinking" by de-emphasizing the "enemy image" was demonstrated when no blanket condemnation of the United States appeared in the Final Declaration.[10] The Group of 77 states also belongs to this movement.

Theory

The developing countries in Africa, Asia, Latin America, and the Middle East have received considerable attention from USSR foreign policymakers since the early 1960s. A theoretical framework within which so-called national liberation movements operate has also been elaborated on by Soviet ideologists. The economic basis for revolutions in the Third World is the alleged conflict between independence and "imperialist monopoly." This and other contradictions can only be resolved in alliance with the "world socialist system" (that is, the communist-ruled states), which, it was claimed as far back as 1980, represented a natural ally of the Third World.[11]

Specifically, the USSR claims that both the 1917 revolution as well as the Soviet policy of peace coincide with the "aspirations of peoples in Asia, Africa, Latin America, and Oceania." The Soviet Union further asserts that it was "the first ever non-aligned country, the main anti-imperialist force, an ally of the liberation movement" on the above continents. Thus,

TABLE 10.1
MEMBERS OF THE NONALIGNED MOVEMENT, EARLY 1990

Afghanistan	Egypt	*Madagascar*	*Seychelles*
Algeria	*Equatorial*	*Malawi*	Sierra Leone
Angola	*Guinea*	Malaysia	Singapore
Argentina	*Ethiopia*	Maldives	Somalia
Bahamas	Gabon	*Mali*	*South-West Africa*
Bahrain	Gambia	Malta	*People's Organization*
Bangladesh	*Ghana*	Mauritania	Sri Lanka
Barbados	Grenada	Mauritius	Sudan
Benin	*Guinea*	Morocco	Suriname
Bhutan	*Guinea-Bissau*	*Mozambique*	Swaziland
Bolivia	Guyana	Nepal	*Syria*
Botswana	India	*Nicaragua*	*Tanzania*
Burkina Faso	Indonesia	Niger	Togo
Burundi	Iraq	Nigeria	Trinidad and
Cambodia	Ivory Coast	Oman	Tobago
Cape Verde	Jamaica	Pakistan	Tunisia
Central	Jordan	*Palestine*	Uganda
African Republic	Kenya	*Liberation*	United Arab
Chad	*Korea (DPR)*	*Organization*	Emirates
Colombia	Kuwait	Panama	Vanuatu
Cameroon	*Laos (PDR)*	Peru	*Vietnam*
Comoros	Lebanon	Qatar	Republic of
Congo	Lesotho	Rwanda	Yemen
Cuba	Liberia	Saint Lucia	*Yugoslavia*
Cyprus	Libya	*São Tomé* and	Zaire
Djibouti		*Príncipe*	*Zambia*
		Saudi Arabia	*Zimbabwe*
		Senegal	

Italics designates Soviet alignment.
SOURCES: *New York Times*, 4 September 1989, p. A-5; Central Intelligence Agency, *World Factbook 1990* (Washington, D.C.: GPO, 1990), pp. 356–62. *Post*, 14 May 1978).

> In contrast to the Western powers, the Soviet Union and the other countries of the Socialist Community support the non-aligned movement, its goals and principles and its anti-imperialist and anti-colonialist positions. Soviet leaders . . . have always regarded the non-aligned movement as a major positive factor of international affairs.[12]

At the same time, the United States and a number of other Western powers were said to be confirming their destabilizing interference in "hot spots" throughout the Third World.[13] In this way, the U.S.-USSR cold war had been transformed into a phenomenon of global proportions.

To achieve convergence with the so-called world socialist system, however, a national liberation movement must overcome the following obstacles:

1. Resistance by local bourgeois and petit-bourgeois elements
2. Anticommunist prejudices among certain groups in the liberation movement itself
3. Narrow-minded nationalist leaders who maneuver between the two camps
4. Subversive activities of the "imperialists," who are aided by Beijing

In brief, Soviet experts believed that the above difficulties could be resolved and that the national liberation movement could "gain victory only in alliance with the other major revolutionary force—the world socialist system."[14]

The revolution, then, could not succeed on a global basis without eliminating the basic contradiction or conflict between the two worldwide systems—"socialism" versus "imperialism" as defined by Soviet ideologues. In the USSR view, the capitalist economy would be undermined by the proliferation of national liberation movements that, in turn, will accelerate the revolutionary process. This, however, is only one factor, allegedly neither decisive nor predominant, among those that will operate during the world transition from capitalism to socialism.[15]

It was not until 1985, however, that a Soviet scholar was permitted to express reservations toward his government's official policies in the Third World. In an article for *Literaturnaia gazeta*, Viacheslav Dashichev wrote the following:

> Could such a severe exacerbation of tension in Soviet-Western relations in the late 'seventies and early 'eighties have been avoided? Unquestionably so. It is our conviction that the crisis was caused chiefly by the miscalculations and incompetent approach of the Brezhnev leadership toward the resolution of foreign policy tasks.[16]

According to traditional Soviet theory, a small number of developing countries have already chosen the "noncapitalist path," and their leaders are moving toward "scientific socialism," that is, communism, after the temporary national front alliance with "anti-imperialist" elements runs its course. In 1978, only nine countries were definitely in this category; by 1990, the number had increased to twenty-eight (see table 1.4). One source placed the number of "revolutionary-democratic" parties at forty, albeit without listing them.[17] Of course, the policies or leaderships or both may change in such countries and thus move the process either forward or back.

For example, the abortive coup in Indonesia (1965) and subsequent developments there resulted in its loss of the revolutionary-democratic designation. Cuba was promoted to socialist status on the basis of personal remarks by Fidel Castro in 1962, only two years after its revolution. Ghana left the progressive path following the ouster of Kwame Nkrumah (1966). The formerly noncapitalist Iraq remains in an uncertain status, with, since 1975, the Ba'th Party ruling and communists in and out of the government. The most dramatic reversal occurred during 1972 in Egypt, while Mali (1968) and Somalia (1977) also have regressed in Soviet eyes. In all three countries, the USSR lost influence.

National or revolutionary democracies have been said to possess similar characteristics. According to a professional apparatus worker in the CPSU Central Committee, they include the following:

1. Rapid growth of the state sector and limitation on private enterprise
2. Nationalization of foreign capital investments
3. Undermining the influence of landlords and the middle class
4. Introduction of one-party, "anti-imperialist" dictatorships
5. Reforms in labor, agriculture, and industry
6. "Friendly relations" with the Soviet Union and other socialist states[18]

This last condition is actively fostered by the USSR and its dependencies throughout the world. The Soviet Union claims that in 1986 it allocated 1.4 percent of its gross national product, or 12 billion rubles, toward construction of thirty-eight hundred industrial and other economic projects commissioned on the basis of agreements signed with seventy governments in Africa, Asia, and Latin America. An estimated 98,775 Soviet and East–Central European economic and military technicians served in underdeveloped countries during 1989 for periods of one month or more. Although economic aid to the LDCs totaled some $7.25 billion in 1988, the troubled state of the Soviet economy necessitated a drastic cut in such assistance, to $1.86 billion for 1989. Of that amount, $1.4 billion went to India, making it the largest recipient of USSR aid.[19]

SUB-SAHARAN AFRICA

Gorbachev revealed that more than half of all foreign students in the USSR come from Asia, Africa, and Latin America. One of the more spectacular

Moscow schools and training establishments is the Peoples' Friendship University named after Patrice Lumumba who had been a leader in the Congo. Founded in the 1960s, by 1975 approximately 5,600 individuals from eighty-nine countries had received diplomas and 450 others had completed postgraduate courses, according to the official Soviet press agency.[20] The Soviet interest in Africa is long-standing; in 1959, the Association for Friendship with the Peoples of Africa was launched in Moscow. Nonetheless, although the USSR maintains trade relations with thirty-one countries south of the Sahara, as of 1968 the friendship association had counterparts in only seven:[21] Congo (Brazzaville), Ethiopia, Mali, Nigeria, Senegal, Somalia, and Uganda.

One problem facing the Kremlin is the high proportion of rural inhabitants among the working populations in many Third World countries, estimated to be some 80 percent. Hence, in the absence of a large industrial proletariat, an alliance is needed to mobilize the rural majority throughout these underdeveloped regions.[22] In discussing past relations with these newly emerging states, a leading Soviet scholar, Evgenii Tarabrin, said the following:

> The slogan was, "do as I do!" Advice in those days took into account very little regarding specific local conditions of African countries. As a result, our recommendations had no appropriate effect. The slogan, "those who are not with us are against us" was also present in our policies toward Africa.[23]

Only after fifteen years of experience did the Soviet Union finally seem to grasp some of the realities concerning Africa. An article in the leading Moscow journal devoted to the Third World recognized that "nationalism, religious superstition and attachment to private property and also patriarchal and peasant ideas of social justice—these are what distinguish many radical non-proletarian revolutionaries . . . from Marxists."[24] Another study, edited by the then director of the Africa Institute at the USSR Academy of Sciences, indicated that the Soviets had become aware of the errors made between 1960 and 1970. This volume divides African political parties into three types: Marxist-Leninist, revolutionary-democratic, and bourgeois or pro-bourgeois.[25]

As of 1970 Marxist-Leninists were said to be active in Algeria, Lesotho, Morocco, Nigeria (Socialist Workers' and Farmers' party), Réunion, Senegal, South Africa, the Sudan, and Tunisia. According to this source, virtually all had been banned and forced to operate underground, but the revolutionary-democratic ruling parties in Algeria, Congo (Brazzaville),[26] Egypt, Guinea, and Tanzania were cited as "reliable detachments" of the world revolutionary process. The national liberation movements in Angola (independent as of 11 November 1975), Guinea-Bissau (independent as of 12 September 1974), and Mozambique (independent as of 25 June 1975) were viewed at the time as having short-term prospects for attaining power.

How nationalist movements were to be transformed into avowedly communist ones has never been explained. Presumably, dedicated agents[27] would infiltrate and revolutionize the population. Applying a Marxist analysis, unafraid of contradictions, Solodovnikov's book on the political parties of Africa defined the single-party system as one that was progressive in revolutionary-democratic states, but one that "suppresses democratic freedoms" in pro-Western countries.[28]

One lesson learned by Moscow even before the 1970s (presumably due to the many expulsions of its diplomats) was that Africans resent heavy-handed interference in domestic affairs, which for the Soviets had been the order of the day. For example, in Guinea, USSR ambassador Daniil S. Solod became persona non grata after he attempted to organize local schoolteachers and overthrow the government of Ahmed Sekou Touré. In 1982, however, Guinea, under the same leader, was marching in the vanguard of progressive forces on the African continent. The rift between Moscow and Conakry (Guinea's capital) apparently healed for a time at least although Touré finally became disenchanted with Moscow. During 1983, Guinea's repayments on loans reportedly exceeded its earnings from bauxite delivered to the Soviets. The death of Touré in March 1984 and the subsequent coup by the military altered relations with the USSR.

In 1989, however, Guinea still was considered to have a "socialist" orientation. Many of the army officers who took over the government were graduates of Soviet military academies, despite the fact that a free market revolution had commenced four years earlier. The World Bank and International Monetary Fund insisted on radical economic reforms as a prerequisite for financial assistance. In early 1990, E. A. Shevardnadze, the first USSR foreign minister to visit sub-Saharan Africa avoided Guinea and stopped instead in Namibia, Zambia, Mozambique, Zimbabwe, Tanzania, and Nigeria.[29]

Moscow seemingly made its greatest gains in Ethiopia. The sole political movement, the Commission for Organizing the Party of the Working People of Ethiopia, transformed itself into the Ethiopian Workers' Party (EWP) at a founding congress in September 1984. According to the leader, Lt. Col. Mengistu Haile Mariam, the EWP was to become "the sole instrument to effect the realization of communism." During 1989, some 2,465 technicians from the USSR and East Central Europe plus about 2,800 from Cuba were guiding the new Ethiopian economic, political, and military structures. (The Cubans had withdrawn by March 1990.) In the spring of 1990, a decision was made to postpone "socialism" and encourage private enterprise as well as joint-stock companies.[30]

At the same time, the Soviet Union cut its economic aid to Ethiopia from $158 million in 1987 to $6 million in 1988 and to zero in 1989. It also reportedly refused to sign a new arms delivery agreement or to reschedule debt payments. More than half (perhaps even 65 percent) of the Ethiopian annual budget was being allocated for the military effort against Eritrean and Tigrean insurgents. Mengistu visited North Korea, Zimbabwe, and South Yemen, possibly in search of arms. An abortive attempt to seize power on 16 May 1989 ended with the execution of nine generals and the arrest of three to four hundred officers. With insurgent victories apparently demoralizing the Ethiopian army, in July 1990, Mengistu visited Israel and requested more military assistance to stave off defeat. His situation appeared desperate in the fall of that year.[31]

Although the $11 billion plus given by the USSR in military aid to Mengistu since 1977 is not mentioned, a Soviet scholar at the Africa Institute in Moscow condemns the Ethiopians for applying oversimplified Marxism, for not understanding their own peasantry, and for using military force against separatists. Her article includes a general condemnation of Moscow's policies in Africa, which, she says, should have been applied with great caution. Collectivization led to "millions of people dying from hunger, and our [Soviet] country being transformed from exporter to heavy importer of food." The Stalinist model of forced industrialization, applied to Ghana under Kwame Nkrumah and other African countries, was not opposed by any politicians or scholars in the USSR.[32]

As suggested in the foregoing, Kwame Nkrumah was a dedicated "socialist" whose efforts to make Ghana an industrial giant with USSR and East-Central European assistance began in the 1960s, when many neighboring countries also adopted central planning. After 1982, when Libya as well as the Soviet bloc refused more financial support, the Ghanaian government discarded "copybook socialism" and adopted a free market economy. As many as twenty-five countries in Africa have been moving in this same direction; however, only five (Namibia, Botswana, Mauritius, Senegal, Zambia) of the forty-six sub-Saharan states technically qualify as multiparty democracies.[33]

BETWEEN THE MAGHREB AND INDIA

Among the countries that occupy the area from North Africa through India, the two states that the Soviets claim led the Arab anti-imperialist movement during the mid-1970s were Algeria and Syria because they "officially adhered to a socialist orientation." Iraq, Libya, and South Yemen at that time strove only "to place their natural riches at the service of the people,"[34] although they still represent, in Moscow's eyes, an important part of the Arab national liberation movement.

The USSR's strategy in the Middle East has been more complicated than the one in Africa, owing primarily to the Arab conflict with Israel. Moscow's attitude toward Tel Aviv appears to have changed for the better in recent times, although it continues to support the Palestine Liberation Organization (PLO), which has an embassy in the Soviet Union.

In November 1988, the USSR recognized the proclamation of a Palestinian state.[35] Within a year, however, there had been an exchange of consular representatives with Israel. During February 1990, Foreign Minister Shevardnadze held separate meetings in Cairo with PLO Executive Committee chairman Yasser Arafat and Israeli acting foreign minister Moshe Arens. These were followed in September by conversations between Gorbachev and two Israeli cabinet members at the Kremlin.

Originally Moscow's attention had centered around Cairo, even though then Foreign Minister Gromyko pledged USSR support for a separate Palestinian state at the November 1974 Arab summit meeting in Morocco. The high point in Soviet-Egyptian relations came toward the end of May 1971, when Presidents Nikolai V. Podgorny and Muhammad Anwar Sadat signed a fifteen-year treaty, the first of its kind in the Arab world (see table 10.2). The twelve articles included provisions for economic and military assistance; Article 7 stipulated that both sides "will contact each other without delay in order to concert their positions with a view to removing a threat that has arisen or re-establishing peace."[36]

Earlier that same month, however, a purge eliminated six ministers (housing, information, interior, electric power, presidential affairs, and war) from the Egyptian cabinet. Their arrests followed soon after Vice-President Ali Sabry, leader of a radical pro-Soviet faction in Cairo, was expelled from office. Reportedly, Sabry and Interior Minister Shaarawi Gomaa had established a secret organization within Sadat's ruling Arab Socialist Union that, if successful, would have transformed it into a "vanguard party" and led to a "dictatorship of the proletariat."[37]

Despite this setback for the USSR, the treaty was ratified in just over a month, and President Sadat subsequently visited Moscow. Estimates were that, before the agreement, the Soviet Union had already delivered to Cairo about $2.5 billion in weapons since its 1967 defeat in the war against Israel. Less than nine months later, however, some twenty thousand USSR military advisers were ordered out of Egypt. Despite the inconclusiveness of the fourth Arab-Israeli war in October 1973 and Cairo's dissatisfaction with Moscow, relations between the two capitals improved to the extent of

TABLE 10.2
TREATIES OF FRIENDSHIP AND COOPERATION IN THE THIRD WORLD,
1971–1989

Country	Date	Place Signed	Duration (years)	Abrogated
Egypt	27 May 1971	Cairo	15	15 March 1976
India*	9 August 1971	New Delhi	20	
Iraq	9 April 1972	Baghdad	15	
Somalia	11 July 1974	Mogadishu	20	13 November 1977
Angola	8 October 1976	Moscow	20	
Mozambique	31 March 1977	Maputo	20	
Vietnam*	3 November 1978	Moscow	25	
Ethiopia*	20 November 1978	Moscow	20	
Afghanistan*	5 December 1978	Moscow	20	
South Yemen*	25 October 1979	Moscow	20	
Syria	8 October 1980	Moscow	20	
Congo	13 May 1981	Moscow	20	
North Yemen	9 October 1984	Moscow	20	
Mali	18 July 1986	Moscow	**	
Burkina Faso	12 October 1986	Moscow	**	
Benin	25 November 1986	Moscow	**	
Cuba	4 April 1989	Havana	25	
Indonesia*	11 September 1989	Moscow	**	

*These countries had the lowest ($265 or less) annual per capita income of all the less-developed countries, according to the World Bank.
**Called declarations on further development of friendship and cooperation, these may represent preliminary steps toward formal treaties.
SOURCES: *Pravda*, 28 May 1971, 10 August 1971, 10 April 1972, 13 July 1974, 9 October 1976, 2 April 1977, 4 November 1978, 21 November 1978, 6 December 1978, 26 October 1979, 9 October 1980, 14 May 1981, 11 October 1984, 20 July 1986, 13 October 1986, 28 November 1986, 6 April 1989, 12 September 1989; "Egypt Breaks off Soviet Pact," *Facts on File*, 1976, p. 193; "Somalia Expels Soviets, Cubans," *Facts on File*, 1977, p. 874.

rescheduling debts in 1975 and USSR deliveries of military equipment after Sadat publicly criticized the USSR for not having replaced the arms destroyed in the most recent round of fighting.[38]

Sadat's successor, Hosni Mubarak, after a three-year break in diplomatic relations, during late September 1984 exchanged ambassadors with Moscow. The USSR subsequently rescheduled repayments for $70 million in economic aid, canceled the interest on the old $3 billion debt for weapons, and resumed delivery of military spare parts. Foreign Minister Shevardnadze visited Cairo on 20 February 1989, the highest official to do so since the friendship treaty was abrogated in 1976 by the Egyptians.[39] Mubarak came to Moscow during May 1990 to demonstrate that the "ice age" in relations had ended, the first visit by an Egyptian president in eighteen years.

The USSR had more success in maintaining a foothold at the southern end of the Red Sea. Ali Nasir Muhammad, the premier and defense minister of the People's Democratic Republic of Yemen (PDRY), spent ten days during August 1984 in the Soviet Union. Subsequently, all PDRY debts to the USSR were canceled. Fleet Adm. Sergei G. Gorshkov visited Yemen, presumably to survey base facilities at Aden and anchorages off the island of Socotra. By the mid-1980s, the PDRY had moved solidly into the Soviet orbit, making possible regular political and military consultations. A coup d'état in January 1986 overthrew President Ali Nasir, whose successor, Haidar Abu Bakr al Attas, had been in Moscow during most of the fighting. Approximately ten thousand persons were killed and USSR influence re-established. To accomplish this, Soviet pilots flew combat missions and airlifted a battalion of Cubans into South Yemen; USSR navy ships were also deployed. During 1988 and 1989, the PDRY began approaching other Arab countries and Western Europe to save the deteriorating Yemeni economy from collapse. In 1989 some 1,950 Soviet and East European advisers remained in South Yemen.[40]

Five years after the PDRY had done so, North Yemen also signed a treaty of friendship and cooperation with the USSR (see table 10.2). Ruler Ali 'Abdallah Salih may be able to maintain his independence from Moscow thanks to the discovery of 500 million barrels of oil reserves and 4 trillion cubic feet of gas by the Hunt Oil Company of Texas. Salih owes the USSR some $1 billion for military equipment; in October 1988, he received the Soviet first deputy defense minister, Army Gen. Petr G. Lushev. During 1989 there were 670 economic and military advisers from the USSR and Eastern Europe in North Yemen, which merged on 22 May 1990 with South Yemen (PDRY), and Salih became president of the new Yemen republic.[41]

More than a communiqué was involved when the Soviet Union signed a fifteen-year treaty of friendship and cooperation with Iraq. Article 4 attacks colonialism, imperialism, and Zionism; Article 9 mentions strengthening defense capability, which Moscow had already been helping Baghdad to do for more than a decade. An economic agreement followed the treaty, with provisions for the USSR to refine and market Iraq's nationalized petroleum. It was subsequently disclosed that the Soviets would construct an oil refinery at Mosul as well as a pipeline from Baghdad to Basra. Agreements under which the USSR would build a nuclear reactor and supply about $2.5 billion in arms on credit appeared to signal support for Iraq in its war against Iran.[42]

There is evidence that the USSR delivered advanced weapons to Iran, including SAM-7 launchers and antiaircraft missiles. The shipments were flown via Poland and Cyprus, and the North Korean embassy issued deceptive "end-user certificates." Paradoxically, rioters damaged the USSR embassy in Teheran and its consulate at Isfahan for allegedly providing missiles to Iraq, which Moscow denied. Soviet freighters were attacked in the Persian Gulf by the Iranians.[43] In the words of a RAND scholar who has been a member of the U.S. Department of State's policy planning staff, "Playing a complicated double game of trying to improve relations with both sides of the conflict, the Soviets sought to weaken American efforts to build a consensus against Iran, while positioning themselves to pose as mediators at the end of the war."[44]

The 2 August 1990 occupation of Kuwait by Iraq changed the above equation, and the USSR announced that same night that it was suspending arms deliveries to Iraq. With the Soviet Union and the United States in agreement, the U.N. Security Council voted fourteen to zero (Cuba and Yemen abstaining) to condemn the invasion and demand an Iraqi withdrawal. At that time, there were 1,350 members of the USSR and East-Central European armed forces training the Iraqis to use the $26 billion worth of Soviet weapons delivered since 1982. It is highly improbable that USSR military intelligence (GRU) or KGB officers in Baghdad did not have advance information about the attack on Kuwait.[45]

Syria has also been receiving assistance and, in contrast to Egypt, did not expel its bloc economic (2,845) and military (2,300) advisers. (See table 10.3.) The first arms deal concluded with Moscow in 1972 gave Damascus surface-to-air missiles. Ten years later, after Israel had destroyed Syrian air defenses, the USSR quickly supplied more-advanced SS-21 weapons systems. CPSU Politburo member G. A. Aliev spent four days in Damascus during the spring of 1984 and returned with a communiqué that reaffirmed close cooperation between the two countries. In mid-1986, Gorbachev promised to continue sending arms. Moscow rescheduled payments on the $15 billion debt, probably half of which had been accrued by such purchases as MIG-21 and SU-22 fighter aircraft as well as three Romeo-class submarines during 1988 alone. There are indications that Moscow is reevaluating its support of Syria. The USSR ambassador, Aleksander Zotov, is quoted as follows: "The strain of military expenditures is quite obvious in all Arab countries and in Syria too."[46]

USSR relations with a non-Arab country in the Middle East clearly show its adaptability to changing circumstances. Shah Mohammad Reza Pahlavi personally experienced Soviet efforts to detach Iran's northern provinces after World War II, and yet he later entered into many economic agreements with Moscow. In 1969, the USSR extended credits to Teheran

TABLE 10.3

NUMBERS OF COMMUNIST ECONOMIC AND MILITARY TECHNICIANS IN
THE THIRD WORLD, 1989*

	USSR AND EASTERN EUROPE		CHINA	
	Economic	Military	Economic	Military
Total	81,240	17,535	39,905	n/a
Africa	47,495	8,015	6,985	110
North Africa	38,260	2,950	1,085	0
Algeria	7,170	650	500	0
Libya	29,000	2,300	200	0
Mauritania	30	0	260	0
Morocco	1,425	0	75	0
Tunisia	635	0	50	0
Sub-Saharan Africa	9,235	5,065	5,900	110
Angola	1,820	1,500	150	0
Congo	395	45	75	0
Ethiopia	565	1,900	25	0
Gabon	10	0	25	0
Ghana	50	0	15	0
Guinea	515	75	70	0
Guinea-Bissau	55	95	70	0
Kenya	65	0	100	0
Madagascar	225	130	130	0
Mali	555	70	300	5
Mozambique	1,180	900	120	0
Niger	15	0	50	0
Nigeria	3,025	30	100	0
Rwanda	15	0	800	0
São Tomé and Príncipe	20	10	15	0
Senegal	50	0	65	0
Sierra Leone	10	0	200	0
Somalia	10	0	600	20
Sudan	130	5	400	5
Tanzania	70	95	400	0
Zambia	110	60	150	0
Other	345	150	2,040	80
East Asia	50	3,300	310	n/a
Europe	160	0	0	0
Latin America	545	110	80	0
Bolivia	10	0	0	0
Brazil	70	0	0	0
Colombia	0	0	0	0
Nicaragua	235	50	0	0
Peru	30	60	10	0

TABLE 10.3 *(continued)*

Uruguay	0	0	0	0
Other	200	0	70	0
Middle East	29,035	5,010	30,380	n/a
Iran	950	100	0	n/a
Iraq	16,660	1,350	10,000	n/a
North Yemen	365	305	2,000	0
South Yemen	1,075	875	20	0
Syria	2,845	2,300	100	0
Other	7,140	80	18,260	65
South Asia	3,955	1,100	2,150	n/a
Afghanistan	500	400	0	0
Bangladesh	80	0	200	40
India	2,700	700	0	0
Nepal	10	0	750	0
Pakistan	555	0	1,000	25
Sri Lanka	110	0	200	0
Other	0	0	0	0

*Minimum estimates of those present for one month or more. Data are rounded to nearest five persons.

SOURCE: Central Intelligence Agency, *Handbook of Economic Statistics* (1990), series CPAS 90-10001 (Washington, D.C.: GPO, September 1990), table 163, pp. 196–97.

for the purchase of trucks, armored personnel carriers, and light antiaircraft guns. A steel mill at Isfahan and a natural gas pipeline were soon under construction; another agreement included a Soviet polyisoprene factory, prefabricated housing plants, and additions to the steel mill. After the fall of the shah, the USSR ordered the local communist party (Tudeh) to support the Ayatollah Khomeini, warned the new regime of the coming attack by Iraq, and began supplying Iran with weapons during the ensuing war, as mentioned above.

Despite arrests of Tudeh leaders in February 1983 and the dissolution of their movement three months later, the USSR and East-Central European regimes in 1989 maintained about 1,050 economic and military advisers in the country. In June 1989, five months before he died, Khomeini wrote Gorbachev that communism was dead and told him to study Islam. Before the forty-day mourning period had ended, Ali Akbar Hashenii Rafsanjani was received in Moscow as if he were already chief of state. Gorbachev announced that his visit represented "fulfillment of the late Imam's will." Some $6 billion in agreements may have resulted from this meeting for mutual cooperation through the year 2000. Iran will pay the USSR mostly in natural gas[47] through a pipeline into the Transcaucasus.

A different kind of adaptability was evident in Afghanistan, where the Soviets first assisted Muhammad Zahir Shah's development plan. That monarch, while on a visit to Europe, lost his throne in a July 1973 coup that placed in power Mohammed Daoud, whose revolutionary program received support from the indigenous communist rank and file. During the next five years, however, as the new government turned away from the USSR and began diversifying its sources of foreign aid, Soviet leaders most probably saw their influence declining. Another coup in April 1978 led to the murder of Daoud as well as his family and the beginning of communist rule in Afghanistan. The end of the following year, about 120,000 Soviet troops (plus others across the border in the USSR) occupied the country and engaged in military activities against a strong guerrilla movement.[48] Armed forces loyal to the puppet regime dropped from eighty thousand to thirty thousand men, and some 4.5 million refugees fled to neighboring countries.

After nine years and fifty days, at least fifteen thousand men in the Soviet army had been killed or wounded by the time the last troops withdrew on 15 February 1989. The insurgent *mujahedeen* (holy warriors) apparently controlled some 90 percent of the country, although no major cities. To cover the evacuation, USSR pilots flew MIG-27 and TU-26 Backfire bomber missions against guerrilla strongholds; the communist regime in Kabul also received ground-to-ground missiles that could hit targets even in neighboring Pakistan. Soviet transport aircraft continued to deliver military equipment and ammunition in an attempt to keep the puppet government in power. In mid-July 1990 these deliveries still totaled some $300 million a month ($3.7 billion a year). Nevertheless, at the end of June 1990, the Afghan Communist Party convened to renounce its monopoly on power, which it did not surrender.[49]

At the other side of the Middle East lies India, where the USSR has scored impressive gains by removing that state from the objectively non-aligned countries of the world. In 1965, the Soviet Union successfully mediated to bring about the Tashkent agreement between Pakistan and India. No noncommunist head of government visited Moscow more frequently than Prime Minister Indira Gandhi. Economic assistance to India from the USSR between 1954 and the end of 1989 totaled the equivalent of more than $13 billion.[50]

It may have been President Richard M. Nixon's announcement that he would visit Beijing (although more probably it was the approaching showdown with Pakistan over Bangladesh) that prompted Indian leaders to sign a twenty-year friendship treaty with the USSR. Initialed at New Delhi by the respective foreign ministers, the pact received mutual ratification within a record nine days. Subsequent developments indicate that the Soviet Union gave India both essential military equipment and diplomatic support in the war against Pakistan and subsequent proclamation of independence by Bangladesh.

Article 9 of the treaty,[51] which was directed against Pakistan as well as China at that time, calls for "immediate consultations with a view to taking appropriate effective measures" in the event of a threat or an actual attack. Ambiguous language makes it difficult to establish whether the agreement is a military alliance. India considers itself nonaligned, with more justification than countries such as Cuba, Ethiopia, or Vietnam. Apparently, however, this does not prevent the Soviet Union from being its most important benefactor. An arms deal between India and the USSR in 1981 totaled $2.5 billion. Two years later, an agreement allowed New Delhi to begin producing fighter aircraft, including the advanced MIG-29 and MIG-31, during the late 1980s. In early 1984, then Defense Minister D. F. Ustinov visited India and agreed that the USSR would sell it more jets, warships, missiles, army equipment, and electronic surveillance systems.

The new prime minister, Rajiv Gandhi, who succeeded his assassinated mother, visited Moscow in May 1985 and received $1.5 billion equivalent in credits. His foreign trade minister signed an agreement at the end of 1985 that envisaged a two-and-one-half-times greater commercial volume during 1986–1990 than in the previous five years. In mid-July 1989, Gandhi again visited Moscow and conferred with Gorbachev. Between 1983 and 1987, the USSR delivered $7.6 billion worth of weapons to India. Even after Gandhi lost the election, a new minister for external affairs, Inder Kumar, in early 1990 stated the following: "India's cooperation with the USSR now encompasses broad areas and has a wonderful future." At midyear, Prime Minister V. P. Singh and President Gorbachev signed a joint declaration in Moscow on a "nuclear-free and non-violent world."[52]

LATIN AMERICA

Mesmerized by the orthodox requirement for an industrial proletariat, only the vanguard (that is, the communist party) of which can exercise a dictatorship in theory, Soviet writers welcome the growth of the working class in any part of the world. The Latin American countries had an increase of more than 50 percent in this population category from 1960 through the end of 1975, with their working class reportedly totaling 18.7 million people (or almost one-fifth of the labor force). Cuba, singled out as the first example in the Western Hemisphere of a successful revolution, is presented by the Soviets as a model for the liberation struggle.[53] Yet for many years the upsurge in revolutionary activity throughout Latin America predicted by USSR commentators encompassed only the short-lived Popular Unity (socialist plus communist) rule in Chile and the continuing anti-imperialist developments under the current regime in Peru.[54] Nicaragua, however, left the category of Marxist-Leninist regimes after the elections in early 1990.

Fidel Castro, with an almost obsessive hatred of the United States, has pledged support for all "genuine" revolutions in Latin America, promising that the Cubans would consistently and decisively aid any such process carried out in a Latin American country. During 1989, Soviet economic and military aid to that Caribbean island totaled $4.2 billion, or just under 30 percent of the country's gross national product. Millions more came from the six East-Central European regimes. Havana's debt to Moscow was rescheduled, with payments to begin in 1986 extending over a twenty-five-year period. A request that $8 billion of it be waived reportedly brought a negative response. Havana owes between $35 and $40 billion to the USSR and other member-states of the Council for Mutual Economic Assistance.[55]

Soviet specialists had planned the development of the Cuban sugar industry through 1990. The USSR, one of the world's largest sugar producers, did not need all the 3.3 million metric tons of sugar (even though half could be re-exported) that it bought from Havana in 1988 and for which it paid almost three times the market rate. That subsidy alone totaled $4.5 billion. In fact, the Soviet Union resold the surplus for hard currency at less than the world price. In return, the Soviets have access to naval and air base facilities on the island, and twenty-one hundred of their signals intelligence military personnel are stationed at Lourdes, outside Havana. In addition, Cuban mercenaries have acted as surrogates for the USSR in many countries of sub-Saharan Africa.[56]

In Chile, a major breakthrough for Soviet influence on the continent of Latin America seemingly occurred after the election of Salvador Allende Gossens as president of that country in 1970, with the support of indigenous communists. Moscow moved cautiously, nonetheless, at first offering only $50 million in hard currency credit for imports from the USSR. Another equivalent sum in rubles was set aside to finance industrial and construction projects. Total credits soon amounted to $385 million from both the USSR and East-Central Europe.[57]

Following the military coup that overthrew the Allende regime in September 1973, the World Marxist Review published an analysis citing what had gone wrong: (1) the press had not been curtailed soon enough, (2) Allende moved too slowly within both political and economic arenas, (3) the communists should have forced rapid confiscation of private enterprise, (4) soviets or councils of workers and peasants were unavailable to function as pressure groups, (5) occupation of farms and factories by the radical left undermined potential support, and (6) penetration of the armed forces did not extend deeply enough to prevent the coup.[58]

Less than six years later, on 19 July 1979, the Sandinistas came to power in Nicaragua and established the first Marxist-Leninist regime in Central America. Eliminating all opposition, by 1984 they were hosting between seven and nine thousand Cubans, Russians, East Germans, Bulgarians, Libyans, PLO members, and other terrorists (including 3,000 to 3,500 military or security advisers). An additional five to six thousand Cubans were present as teachers and construction or health workers. Castro's modus operandi for consolidating Latin American communist forces was followed in Nicaragua:[59] unification of the extreme left, establishment of a broad coalition including sympathetic noncommunist elements, use of the latter to isolate the target regime on the right, and Soviet bloc aid.

The five top Sandinista leaders received their training after 1960 in Havana. One of them, Henry Ruiz, who became minister for economic planning, spent two full years in Moscow at Lumumba University and was the only cabinet member who spoke Russian. Approximately a thousand young men were being indoctrinated in the USSR. Soviet AK-47 assault rifles were seen throughout Nicaragua. Indeed, from 1980 through mid-July 1989, the Soviet Union delivered more than $3 billion in aid. Freighters arriving from the USSR and its communist allies between August 1987 and August 1989 unloaded more than $1 billion worth of arms, a record amount. Foreign Minister Shevardnadze's announcement toward the end of September 1989 that the Soviet Union would refrain from shipping arms to Nicaragua did not prevent Cuba from acting as a surrogate.[60]

The 75,000-man Nicaraguan army, trained by Cubans, had the following heavy equipment: tanks, armored personnel carriers and reconnaissance vehicles, howitzers, antitank guns, mortars and rocket-propelled grenade launchers, transport aircraft, helicopters, antiaircraft guns, surface-to-air missiles, and machine guns. Foreign economic aid, however, dropped from almost $1.2 billion in 1985 to only $385 million in 1987. Some 81 percent of the credits and 51 percent of the aid, which made up the $385 million, came from the communist bloc. All these deliveries stopped on 25 February 1990 when Violeta Barrios de Chamorro won the national election and became president, displacing the Sandinista regime.[61]

The enormous quantity of weapons shipped to Nicaragua suggests that the USSR had used the country for stockpiling military equipment in anticipation of a protracted struggle throughout Central America and the Caribbean. A similar operation had been envisaged for the island of Grenada, where the New Jewel Movement seized power on 13 March 1979. Within six months, the regime received recognition from the USSR. Four years later, the dictatorship could boast the following:

1. A Marxist-Leninist ruling party, headed by a Soviet-style politburo
2. An army and militia larger than the combined total of its noncommunist neighbors

3. Complete control of the media
4. Mass organizations to compel support for the regime
5. A tight and growing internal security apparatus[62]

The foregoing had been accomplished with guidance from the large Soviet and Cuban embassies on the island and with additional help from other communist bloc representatives.

By 1985 the indigenous military buildup should have resulted in eighteen battalions (up to ten thousand men), giving Grenada the largest ratio of armed forces per head of population (111,000) in the world. Secret agreements with the Soviet Union, Cuba, and North Korea specified delivery of exactly ten thousand rifles and twenty thousand uniforms plus enough heavy weapons to equip the projected eighteen battalions. Czechoslovakia also supplied ammunition, although the Cubans served as intermediaries for all shipments.[63]

Before these agreements could be fully implemented, a struggle for power developed within the New Jewel Movement. A Stalinist-type leader, Bernard Coard, seized control of the party from Maurice Bishop, who was placed under house arrest. After Bishop's execution (together with more than a hundred of his supporters) on 19 October 1983, a Revolutionary Military Council under army commander Hudson Austin announced a shoot-on-sight curfew. Six days later a combined U.S.-Caribbean force landed on Grenada. All Cubans, Libyans, North Koreans, Soviets, East Germans, and Bulgarians were expelled. By 15 December most of the U.S. combat troops had been withdrawn, leaving only 270 U.S. Marines and several hundred soldiers from six Caribbean countries on the island.[64]

The situation in El Salvador has developed along more complicated lines, mainly because of that country's proximity to Nicaragua. Soon after seizing power, the Sandinistas began training guerrillas from other Central American states. During November 1980, encouraged by Castro, five insurgent factions in El Salvador united to form the Farabundo Martí Front for National Liberation (FMLN). Honduras, without the knowledge of its government, was to be used for transit of both guerrillas and arms. In 1980 alone, an estimated 800 tons of weapons were committed to the struggle by the Cuban/Soviet bloc.[65] However, the Salvadoran guerrillas' final offensive in early 1981 did not succeed.

Despite the surge in arms deliveries to the insurgents by air, sea, and land, more than 80 percent of eligible Salvadorans voted on 28 March 1982 for a constituent assembly that repudiated the extreme left. The murder and reported suicide a year later in Managua, Nicaragua, of leaders from the largest Salvadoran insurgent group made clear the guerrillas' immediate source of support. According to the U.S. under secretary of defense for policy, "nearly 80 percent of the ammunition and other 'consummable' material used by the guerrillas in El Salvador [was] provided by Nicaragua." Direct presidential elections on 25 March 1984 were among the most carefully overseen in history—some twenty foreign countries sending observers—and by mid-1986, the guerrillas had lost half their members (down to about five thousand), facing some fifty-two thousand government troops. This imbalance did not prevent the FMLN from attempting to seize power by force in November 1989 and to continue fighting into December. Sporadic talks with the El Salvador administration have taken place since then, only to have a new guerrilla offensive a year later that was supported with Soviet-made SA-14 surface-to-air missiles.[66]

TABLE 10.4
LATIN AMERICAN GROUPS AIDED BY CUBA, 1989–1990

Chile	Movement of the Revolutionary Left (MIR)
	Manuel Rodriguez Patriotic Front (FPMR)
Colombia	Revolutionary Armed Forces of Colombia (FARC), guerrilla group
	of Colombian Communist Party
	National Liberation Army (ELN)
	Simón Bolívar National Guerrilla Coordinating Board (CNG)
Ecuador	Alfaro Vive, Carajo! (AVC)
El Salvador	Farabundo Martí Front of National Liberation (FMLN)
	Armed Forces of National Resistance (FARN)
	Communist Party of El Salvador (PCES)
	Popular Liberation Forces (FPL)
	Popular Revolutionary Army (ERP)
	Central American Revolutionary Workers' Party (PRTC)
Guatemala	Guatemalan National Revolutionary Unity (URNG)
	Guatemalan Party of Labor (PGT)
	Guerrilla Army of the Poor (EGP)
	Armed People's Organization (ORPA)
	Rebel Armed Forces (FAR)
Honduras	Popular Liberation Movement (MLP) (Cinchoneros)
	Lorenzo Zelaya-Popular Revolutionary Forces (FPR-LZ)
Nicaragua	Sandinista Front of National Liberation (FSLN)
Panama	Dignity Battalions
Peru	Tupac Amaru Revolutionary Movement (MRTA)

SOURCES: U.S. Department of Defense, *Terrorist Group Profiles* (Washington, D.C.: GPO, 1989), p. 78; U.S. Department of State, *Patterns of Global Terrorism: 1989,* publication 9743 (Washington, D.C.: GPO, April 1990), pp. 66–75; Richard F. Staar, ed., *Yearbook on International Communist Affairs 1990* (Stanford: Hoover Institution Press, 1990), pp. 43–151.

The remaining three governments on the Central American isthmus have not been immune to Cuban and Soviet revolutionary efforts. In early 1982, a Guatemalan guerrilla leader held a press conference at Havana to announce the unification of four main leftist groups in his country. Terrorists trained by the Sandinistas were sent into Honduras. Nicaragua provided weapons until the end of February 1990 for similar organizations operating in Costa Rica, which then began to be supported by Cuba. Moscow had been delivering more than 65,000 tons of military equipment per year to Havana[67] for destabilization activities throughout the Central American region. (See table 10.4.) Foreign Minister Shevardnadze spent late September and early October 1987 in Cuba, Nicaragua, Brazil, and Argentina. Gorbachev himself visited Havana during 2–5 April 1989 and signed a twenty-five-year friendship and cooperation treaty with Fidel Castro, who began talking about a decline in Soviet aid less than four months later.[68]

The so-called national liberation movements could not have sustained themselves without Soviet bloc assistance in training, weapons, and logistics. Although they claim to be fighting for social justice or independence or both, their objective remains the establishment of totalitarian regimes, which by definition are hostile toward the United States. The USSR has achieved only mixed results from the pursuit of similar basic policies throughout East Asia, as discussed in the next chapter.

NOTES

1. M. S. Gorbachev, *Perestroika: New Thinking for Our Country and the World* (New York: Harper and Row, 1987), p. 159.
2. A. Kolosov, "Pereosmyslenie politiki v 'tret'em mire'," *Mezhdunarodnaia zhizn'*, no. 4 (April 1990): 40.
3. Viacheslav Dashichev, "Vostok-Zapad: poisk," *Literaturnaia gazeta*, 18 May 1988, p. 14.
4. Moscow radio, TASS in English, 29 April 1981; "Joint Soviet-Libyan Communiqué," *Foreign Broadcast Information Service (FBIS)-Soviet Union* 81–083 (30 April 1981): H-4.
5. Moscow radio, TASS in English, 6 May 1988; "Ethiopian President Receives Gorbachev Envoy," *FBIS-Soviet Union* 88–089 (9 May 1988): 32.
6. Kolosov, "Pereosmyslenie politiki v 'tret'em mire', p. 37.
7. "Otchet Tsentral'nogo Komiteta KPSS na XXVI s"ezde L. I. Brezhneva," *Pravda*, 24 February 1981, p. 2.
8. Ibid., p. 3. See also chapter 11 in A. V. Kiva, *Natsional'no-osvoboditel'noe dvizhenie: teoria i praktika* (Moscow: Nauka, 1989), pp. 260–83.
9. Reports from Harare by V. Ovchinnikov and V. Korochantsev, "Vnimanie-

ostreishim problemam," *Pravda*, 3 September 1986, p. 5; V. Ovchinnikov and I. Tarutin, "Otpor neoglobalizma," *Pravda*, 4 September 1986, p. 5.

10. The Final Declaration was summarized in *Keesing's Record of World Events* 35 (1989): 36907. See also "Ninth Nonaligned Conference," *FBIS-Eastern Europe* 89–173–175 (8–12 September 1989): three supplements; R. S. Listopadova, comp., *Dvizhenie neprisoedineniia v dokumentakh i materialakh* (Moscow: Nauka, 1989).

11. Boris N. Ponomarev, "Velikaia zhiznennaia sila Leninizma," *Pravda*, 22 April 1980, pp. 2–3. See also I. I. Kovalenko and R. A. Tuzmukhamedov, eds., *Mirovoi sotsializm i dvizhenie neprisoedineniia* (Moscow: Mezhdunarodnye otnosheniia, 1988).

12. Yuri Alimov, *The Rise and Growth of the Non-Aligned Movement* (Moscow: Progress Publishers, 1987), pp. 161 and 177; quotation from pp. 135–36.

13. Moscow radio, 22 October 1989; "Conference on Third World Ends," *FBIS-Soviet Union* 89–205 (25 October 1989): 10. See also V. Tiurkin, "Tretii mir: put' v zavtra," *Pravda*, 24 October 1989, p. 4.

14. K. N. Brutents, "Rastushchaia revoliutsionnaia sila," *Pravda*, 23 January 1970, pp. 3–4.

15. Gleb Starushenko, "Chosen Path," *New Times* (Moscow), no. 40 (October 1980): 18–20. The same approach is repeated by V. P. Agafonov and V. F. Khalipov, *Sovremennaia epokha i mirovoi revoliutsionnyi protsess* (Moscow: Vysshaia shkola, 1988), in chapters 6–8.

16. Dashichev, "Vostok-Zapad," p. 14. See also interview with Nikolai Kosukhin over Moscow radio, 17 January 1989; *FBIS-Soviet Union* 89–032 (17 February 1989): 27–29.

17. E. M. Primakov, "Nekotorie problemy," *Kommunist*, no. 11 (July 1978): 81–82; K. N. Brutents, "Osvobodivshiesia strany," *Pravda*, 10 January 1986, p. 3, gave the number forty. He may have been also counting communist-ruled states in total.

18. R. A. Ul'ianovskii, "Na novykh rubezhakh," *Pravda*, 3 January 1968, pp. 4–5. See also G. F. Kim, chief ed., *Natsional'no-demokraticheskaia revoliutsiia: sushchnost' i perspektivy* (Moscow: Nauka, 1990), especially pp. 160–95.

19. Moscow radio, TASS in English, 8 July 1986; "Katushev Cited on Aid to Developing Countries," *FBIS-Soviet Union* 86–133 (11 July 1986): R-13, quoting K. F. Katushev on first gross national product percentage; Central Intelligence Agency, *Handbook of Economic Statistics* (Washington, D.C.: GPO, August 1990), tables 163 and 154, pp. 196 and 181, respectively, for 1989 economic assistance.

20. M. S. Gorbachev, "V interesakh druzhby," *Izvestiia*, 23 June 1984, p. 2; TASS report, "Vernost' Leninskomu zavetu," *Pravda*, 18 February 1975, p. 2; "Ryzhkov Greets Friendship University," Moscow radio, 5 February 1990; "Ryzhkov Greets Friendship University," *FBIS-Soviet Union* 90–025 (12 February 1990): 109, for the thirtieth anniversary.

21. V. G. Solodovnikov, "The Soviet Union and Africa," *New Times* (Moscow), no. 21 (28 May 1969): 9; economic and technical cooperation agreements had been

signed with thirty-seven less-developed countries in Africa, according to Moscow radio, TASS in English, 24 June 1986; *FBIS-Soviet Union* 86–121 (24 June 1986): J-2.

22. M. I. Braginskii et al., eds., *Afrika: Problemy zaniatosti* (Moscow: Nauka, 1988), especially pp. 17–36. See also L. V. Goncharov, chief ed., *Sovremennaia Afrika: Ekonomika* (Moscow: Vostochnaia literatura, 1989), pp. 20–41.

23. Moscow radio in English to Africa, 15 December 1989; *FBIS-Soviet Union* 89–244 (21 December 1989): 8.

24. P. N. Andreasian, "Protivorechie i kriterii," *Narody Azii i Afriki* 20, no. 2 (March–April 1974): 41.

25. V. G. Solodovnikov et al., eds., *Politicheskie partii Afriki* (Moscow: Nauka, 1970). See also Iu. A. Iudin, ed., *Partii v politicheskoi sisteme* (Moscow: Nauka, 1983), especially chapter 1 by V. E. Chirkin, pp. 5–35.

26. See, for example, A. A. Spichek, ed., *Deiateli natsional'no-osvoboditel'noe dvizheniia: politicheskoe portrety* (Moscow: Izdatel'stvo Universiteta Druzhby Narodov, 1989), pp. 79–96, for a biography of Congo (Brazzaville) leader Marien Ngouabi, who was killed in 1977 by a group of terrorists.

27. A current illustration is Joe Slovo, chairman of the South African Communist party, who is identified as commanding *Umkhonto we Sizwe* (Spear of the Nation), the African National Congress military organization. Mike Hall and Patti Waldmeir, "ANC Elects Mandela," *Financial Times* (London), 3–4 March 1990, p. 2. See also Peter Vanneman, *Soviet Strategy in Southern Africa: Gorbachev's Pragmatic Approach* (Stanford: Hoover Institution Press, 1990), pp. 21–22.

28. Solodovnikov et al., *Politicheskie partii Afriki*. See also E. I. Dolgopolov, *Sotsial'no-politicheskaia rol' armii osvobodivshikhsia stran* (Moscow: Voenizdat, 1986).

29. The centerpiece of the trip occurred on 21 March 1990, independence day in Namibia. *Facts on File* 50, no. 2547 (23 March 1990): 186–87.

30. International Institute of Strategic Studies, *The Military Balance, 1990–1991* (London: IISS, Autumn 1990), p. 128; CIA, *Handbook of Economic Statistics*, table 163, p. 196; dispatch from Addis Ababa by Sergei Demidov in *Pravda*, 23 March 1990, p. 6.

31. G. B. Tsypkin and V. S. Iag'ia, *Istoriia Efiopii v novoe i noveishee vremia* (Moscow: Nauka, 1989), pp. 353–67; CIA, *Handbook of Economic Statistics*, table 154, p. 181; S. Demidov, "Do poslednego patrona," *Pravda*, 17 September 1990, p. 4.

32. Galina A. Krylova, "Natsional'no-demokraticheskaia revoliutsiia," *Narody Azii i Afriki*, no. 1 (January–February 1989): 42–53; quotation is from p. 53. See, however, N. Gogol', "Posylka iz Gany," *Pravda*, 25 October 1990, p. 5.

33. Jane Perlez, "East Bloc Admirers in Africa," *New York Times*, 22 April 1990, p. 11.

34. N. Iakubov, "Sovetskii Soiuz i arabskii vostok," *Mezhdunarodnaia zhizn'*, no. 8 (August 1974): 27–37.

35. Foreign and Commonwealth Office, "Palestine Liberation Organization," *Background Brief* (London), September 1989, pp. 7–8.

36. "Dogovor o druzhbe," *Pravda*, 28 May 1971, p. 1.

37. Mohamed Heikal, *The Road to Ramadan* (New York: Quadrangle Press, 1975), pp. 122–39. Heikal, editor of *al-Ahram*, was a confidant of President Sadat at the time.

38. For Sadat's explanation about the ouster of Soviet advisers, see William Beecher, "Egypt Tells Soviet to Withdraw," *New York Times*, 20 July 1972, pp. 1 and 15; see also Drew Middleton, "Soviet Arms to Cairo," *New York Times*, 2 February 1977, p. A-7, on Soviet replacement of aircraft engines and delivery of spare parts.

39. See A. Shumilin (dispatch from Cairo), "Konets 'lednikovogo perioda,' " *Komsomol'skaia pravda*, 3 January 1990, p. 3. "SSSR-Egipet: Prebyvanie I. A. Magida v Moskve," *Vestnik MID SSSR*, no. 18 (30 September 1990): 7–8, describes the Egyptian foreign minister's visit. See also V. Beliakov, "Egiptiane protiv," *Pravda*, 6 November 1990, p. 4.

40. Iu. Glukhov, "Trudnyi ekzamen," *Pravda*, 8 September 1986, p. 6, gives names of killed South Yemeni leaders; U.S. Department of Defense, *Soviet Military Power* (Washington, D.C.: GPO, 1987), pp. 140–41, on USSR military intervention; CIA, *Handbook of Economic Statistics*, table 163, p. 197, on advisers.

41. Moscow radio, 20 October 1988; *FBIS-Soviet Union* 88–206 (25 October 1988): 18, on Lushev; see CIA, *Handbook of Economic Statistics*, table 163, p. 197, on advisers; and Geraldine Brooks, "Desert Roughnecks," *Wall Street Journal*, 29 August 1990, pp. A-1 and 3, about Hunt Oil; TASS from Aden, "Dva Iemena—odna strana," *Pravda*, 24 May 1990, p. 5.

42. "Podpisany vazhnye dokumenty," *Pravda*, 20 March 1984, p. 4; "Vstrecha tov. Gorbacheva s Saddatom Khuseinom," *Pravda*, 17 December 1985, p. 1.

    According to the U.S. Department of State, the East-Central European regimes were selling weapons to Iran during the war with Iraq. See Bernard Gwertzman, "Shultz Says Soviet Fails to Stem Gulf Arms Flow," *New York Times*, 2 October 1986, p. A-7, who stated that the USSR was supplying Iraq during that war. See also E. Zhuravlev, "Nashi liudi iz Iraká," *Trud*, 14 October, p. 3, about the 3,400 Soviet specialists in Iraq.

43. John Tagliabue, "How $18 Million Got Soviet Weapons to Iran," *New York Times*, 27 May 1987, pp. 1 and 14; Bill Keller, "Soviet Reports Riot at Embassy in Iran," *New York Times*, 7 March 1988, p. 3.

44. Francis Fukuyama, *Gorbachev and the New Soviet Agenda in the Third World*, report R-3634A (Santa Monica, Calif: RAND, June 1989), pp. 42–43.

45. Celestine Bohlen, "Arms Flow to Iraq" and chart listing Soviet equipment, *New York Times*, 3 August 1990, p. A-6. On USSR military advisers, see Lt. Gen. V. Nikitiuk's interview, "Chem zaniaty nashi voennye v Irake?" *Izvestiia*, 15 August 1990, p. 1; Petr Gladkov, "Ne veriu!" *Novoe vremia*, no. 36 (31 August 1990), p. 7. Reliable sources about Soviet advance knowledge of the invasion are suggested by Igor' Beliaev, "Irak versiia," *Literaturnaia gazeta*, no. 37 (12 September 1990): 14.

46. "Sovetsko-siriiskoe kommunike," *Pravda*, 14 March 1984, p. 4; "S druzhestven-nym vizitom," *Pravda*, 16 October 1984, p. 1, for Asad's arrival in Moscow; "Gorbachev Promises Syrians Arms Supplies Will Continue," *New York Times*, 29 May 1986, p. A-12; CIA, *Handbook of Economic Statistics*, table 163, p. 197, for bloc advisers; Anthony Hyman, "Soviet Interests in the Persian Gulf," *Report on the USSR*, no. 11 (16 March 1990): 13, for the Zotov quotation.

47. CIA, *Handbook of Economic Statistics*, table 163, p. 197, for advisers; "Study Islam," *New York Times*, 5 January 1989, p. 7, gives Khomeini's letter to Gorbachev; "S ofitsial'nym vizitom," *Pravda*, 21 June 1989, p. 1, for the quote to Rafsanjani; "Sostoialsia obmen mneniami," *Pravda*, 6 November 1989, p. 7; V. Skosyrev, "Ostorozhnye shagi SSSR i Iran," *Izvestiia*, 19 June 1990, p. 5.

48. On military operations, see Joseph J. Collins, *The Soviet Invasion of Afghanistan* (Lexington, Mass.: Lexington Books, 1986), pp. 144–52.

49. See John F. Burns, "Soldiers Missing in Afghan War," *New York Times*, 28 March 1989, p. 2, for the number of casualties; Thomas L. Friedman, "Soviets' Peace Proposal," *New York Times*, 15 July 1990, p. 6, for costs; TASS report from Kabul, "Otkrylsia s"ezd," *Pravda*, 28 June 1990, p. 6, on the second congress of the People's Democratic Party (communist) of Afghanistan, which changed its name to Fatherland Party. See also "Beseda u prezidenta SSSR," *Pravda*, 24 August 1990, pp. 1 and 3, for Najibullah's visit with Gorbachev; V. Plastun, "Kogda idet voina," *Pravda*, 17 September 1990, p. 5, and his "Poiski mira," *Pravda*, 23 October 1990, p. 5, for the continuing war.

50. For earlier individual years, see United Kingdom, Foreign and Commonwealth Office, Economic Service (International Division), *Soviet, East European, and Western Development Aid, 1976–82*, Foreign Policy Report no. 85, May 1983. The total comes from CIA, *Handbook of Economic Statistics*, table 154, p. 181. See also V. Baikov, "Vyshki v more: Sovetskaia pomoshch' indiiskomu narodu," *Pravda*, 3 January 1990, p. 7.

51. "Dogovor o mire," *Pravda*, 10 August 1971, p. 1.

52. "Moscow Agrees to Sell Advanced Arms to India," *New York Times*, 10 March 1984, p. 5, on the military agreement; Philip Taubman, "Gorbachev's Most Favored Nations," *New York Times*, 8 December 1985, p. 2-E. The five-year agreement was announced in "Net!—Iadernym vzryvam," *Pravda*, 24 December 1985, p. 4; declaration signed at Delhi by Gorbachev in "Podpisanie dokumentov," *Pravda*, 28 November 1986, p. 1; for Gandhi visit, see "Gandhi and Gorbachev Talk," *New York Times*, 16 July 1989, p. 17; Kumar's comments were broadcast over Moscow radio, "India's Gujral on Relations," 23 January 1990, in *FBIS-Soviet Union* 90–015 (23 January 1990): 23; "Sovetsko-Indiiskoe zaiavlenie," *Pravda*, 24 July 1990, p. 1, for the joint declaration.

53. A. V. Bobrovnikov and V. M. Davydov, chief eds., *Latinskaia Amerika v tsifrakh* (Moscow: Nauka, 1989); A. D. Bekarevich et al., *Kuba: stroitel'stvo sotsializma* (Moscow: Nauka, 1988), especially pp. 171–78.

54. At the same time, a ship with more than three thousand pieces of military hardware from East Germany destined for the *Sendero Luminoso* ("Shining Path") guerrillas in Peru was stopped by Panamanian authorities. Peru pur-

chased more than $2.9 billion in foreign weapons from 1978 through 1988. Alan Riding, "Arms Ship Leaves," *New York Times*, 31 August 1986, p. 22; *World Military Expenditures and Arms Transfers, 1989* (Washington, D.C.: U.S. Arms Control and Disarmament Agency, October 1990), table 11, p. 99.

55. CIA, *Handbook of Economic Statistics*, table 158, p. 185; *World Military Expenditures* (1990), table 11, p. 85; *The Military Balance, 1990–1991*, pp. 192–93. Howard W. French, "Cuban Defector Talks of Soviet Cuts," *New York Times*, 13 September 1990, p. A-3. On the Cuban debt, see K. Khachaturov, "Poniat' i otdat' dolzhnoe," *Pravda*, 2 October 1990, p. 5; A. Moiseev, "Poezdka byla plodotvornoi," *Pravda*, 2 November, 1990, p. 4.

56. International Sugar Organization, *Sugar Year Book 1988* (London, July 1989), p. 60; USSR, *Vneshnie ekonomicheskie sviazi SSSR v 1989 g.* (Moscow: Finansy i statistika, 1990), p. 280; CIA, *Handbook of Economic Statistics*, table 158, p. 185. See also A. Komorin, "Igra v slova," *Izvestiia*, 14 July 1990, p. 5, on future Soviet-Cuban economic relations. On the Cuban withdrawal from Angola, see TASS (Havana), "Kubintsy ukhodiat iz Angoly," *Izvestiia*, 3 September 1990, p. 5. TASS from Havana, "Ofitsial 'nye soobsheheniia," *Pravda*, 1 November 1990, p. 4.

57. U.S. Department of State, *Soviet and East European Aid*, p. 18. See also A. F. Shul'govskii, chief ed., *Marksizm-Leninizm i Latinskaia Amerika*, I (Moscow: Nauka, 1989), pp. 144–57.

58. René Castillo, "Lessons and Prospects of the Revolution," *World Marxist Review* 17, no. 7 (July 1974): 83–95; part 2 in no. 8 (August 1974): 107–16.

   Twelve years later, ten caches of buried weapons, including 3,383 used American M-16 rifles (from Vietnam), 117 Soviet rocket launchers, two million rounds of ammunition, about two thousand rocket-propelled grenades, and tons of explosives, were discovered by Chilean authorities. Shirley Christian, "Chile Arms Caches," *New York Times*, 19 October 1986, p. 21.

59. U.S. Departments of State and Defense, *Background Paper: Central America* (Washington, D.C.: GPO, 27 May 1983), pp. 3–4; U.S. Departments of State and Defense, *The Challenge to Democracy in Central America* (Washington, D.C.: GPO, June 1986), pp. 17–36; Nina H. Shea, "Uncovering the Awful Truth of Nicaragua's Killing Fields," *Wall Street Journal*, 24 August 1990, p. A-7.

   See also *La Vanguardia* (Barcelona), 31 July 1984, pp. 3, 8–9, for transcript of a speech given by Bayardo Arce Castaño at a closed meeting in Managua; Daniel Ortega Saavedra's tenth anniversary speech over Managua radio, 19 July 1989; *FBIS-Latin America* 89–138 (20 July 1989): 36–42.

60. CIA, *Handbook of Economic Statistics*, table 154, p. 181; ACDA, *World Military Expenditures* (1990), table 11, p. 101; Thomas L. Friedman, "Baker to Shevardnadze," *New York Times*, 5 March 1989, p. 19; "Moscow Announces Suspension of Arms," *Christian Science Monitor*, 27 September 1989, p. 3.

61. Confidential study prepared in Managua and cited by the *New York Times*, 26 May 1989, pp. A-1 and A-4. Note that L. L. Klochkovskii, chief ed., *SSSR-*

Latinskaia Amerika (Moscow: Nauka, 1989), omits any discussion of Nicaragua. See, however, A. D. Bekarevich, ed., *Sandinistskaia revoliutsiia* (Moscow: Nauka, 1989) and V. Neklesov, "Nikaragua: nelegkii put' k soglasiu," *Pravda,* 3 December 1990, p. 5.

62. U.S. Departments of State and Defense, *Grenada: A Preliminary Report* (Washington, D.C.: GPO, 16 December 1983), p. 8.

63. Ibid., pp. 18–26. Copies of the original agreements are reproduced in this source.

64. Ibid., p. 1. For an analysis of the captured documents, see U.S. Department of State, *Lessons of Grenada,* publication 9457 (Washington, D.C.: GPO, February 1986).

    The trial of Bishop's seventeen accused murderers is described by Joseph B. Treaster, "Two Ordeals in Grenada," *New York Times,* 28 July 1986, p. A-2. See also A. Moiseev, "Tragediia Grenady," *Pravda,* 18 August 1986, p. 5, for the Soviet interpretation.

65. U.S. Departments of State and Defense, *Challenge to Democracy in Central America,* pp. 47–56.

66. Fred C. Iklé to U.S. congressman Mickey Edwards, dated 18 April 1984 (copy of letter released to the author); Clifford Krauss, "El Salvador Army Gains," *Wall Street Journal,* 30 July 1986, p. 22; editorial, "The Managua Offensive," *Wall Street Journal,* 16 November 1989, p. A-14; A. Moiseev, "Dialog kotoromu ne vidno kontsa," *Pravda,* 26 September 1990, p. 5; Lindsey Gruson, "Missiles Give Salvador Rebels New Advantage," *New York Times,* 10 December 1990, p. A-4.

67. U.S. Departments of State and Defense, *Background Paper,* pp. 10–16; *Challenge to Democracy in Central America,* pp. 57–64.

    U.S. secretary of state George P. Shultz, in a speech to the Organization of American States' representatives at Guatemala City, accused the USSR, Cuba, and Nicaragua of distributing U.S. weapons left behind in Vietnam to guerrilla groups in Chile, Colombia, El Salvador, Guatemala, Honduras, Jamaica, and other countries of Latin America. Joanne Omang, "Shultz Says Latins Changing," *Washington Post,* 12 November 1986, p. A-25.

68. Marlise Simons, "Soviet Courts South America," *New York Times,* 4 October 1987, section 4, p. 3. "Dogovor o druzhbe i sotrudnichestve mezhdu SSSR i Respublikoi Kuby," *Vestnik MID SSSR* 41, no. 7 (15 April 1989): 21–22; Lindsey Gruson, "Plane in Salvador with Soviet Arms," *New York Times,* 26 November 1989, pp. 1 and 22, for the crash of a Nicaraguan plane loaded with Soviet-made SAM-7 antiaircraft missiles being shipped to guerrillas in El Salvador. For a discussion of USSR economic aid, see Iu. N. Paniev, *Strany Latinskoi Ameriki* (Moscow: Mezhdunarodnye otnosheniia, 1990), pp. 218–49. See also K. Khachaturov, "Poniat' i otdat' dolzhnoe," *Pravda,* 2 October 1990, p. 5, on the Cuban debt.

11

THE USSR IN EAST ASIA

Soviet foreign policy suffered a major failure on the mainland of China, despite USSR military assistance, which played a significant role in helping the Chinese communists defeat their nationalist opponents. All the arms and munitions taken by the Red Army after the 1945 Japanese surrender in Manchuria were given to Mao Zedong's troops. Normal relations between the two largest communist-ruled states should have prevailed but did not until after May of 1989.

In fact, the People's Republic of China (PRC) allowed its thirty-year friendship treaty with the USSR to expire in February 1980, although the agreement included provisions for automatic extension.[1] Mao Zedong had spent eight weeks in Moscow negotiating this agreement during 1949–1950 and subsequently appeared at the Kremlin as an honored guest during the fortieth anniversary of the Bolshevik revolution in 1957. After that, however, ideological, political, and territorial differences led to a tense situation that did not exclude the possibility of war between the two countries, despite both being ruled by communist parties.

A quotation from an interview with the PRC department head at the Oriental Studies Institute, USSR Academy of Sciences, underlines the extent to which relations had deteriorated: "In this instance, ideological differences between the CPSU and the CPC [Chinese Communist Party] ended by bringing our countries to the edge of a complete severance of all relations, including diplomatic, and even to the brink of war."[2]

The resentment began in 1949, when Mao met with Stalin at Moscow and was treated as a vassal waiting in the entryway. Mao Zedong had not expected such a reception from "the father of the peoples" and was stunned as well as angered. Resentment at the injustice and humiliation to which Stalin subjected the Chinese leaders accumulated, although it was carefully hidden.

SINO-SOVIET RELATIONS

The genesis of the disagreement over ideology apparently predated Mao's 1957 visit to the USSR. N. S. Khrushchev's speech at the twentieth CPSU congress on 14 February 1956 included the statement that many kinds of revolutionary transformation were possible, even by means of democratic elections and attainment of a parliamentary majority. This formulation appeared again in the documents adopted by the 1957 and 1960 world conferences of communist parties held in Moscow. The Chinese voiced their disagreement with this notion in an article published by their official daily newspaper, which stated that "Marxism has always openly proclaimed the inevitability of violent revolution."[3]

Dispute Over Nuclear War

Another subject the two countries disagreed about was the concept of war and the use of nuclear weapons. In the speech cited above, Khrushchev stated that "the world is faced with either peaceful coexistence or the most destructive war in history; there is no third way. War is not fatalistically inevitable." Beijing, again replying in its party newspaper, refused to admit that any qualitative change had occurred in the nature of modern warfare owing to these new weapons of mass destruction. The PRC subsequently issued a press release stating, "The atomic bomb is a paper tiger which U.S. reactionaries use to scare people. The outcome of war is decided by the people, not by one or two new types of weapons."[4]

According to Andrei A. Gromyko, then USSR foreign minister, at one point following the Korean War, Mao proposed that U.S. troops be lured deep into China and then annihilated with Soviet nuclear weapons. Gromyko apparently rejected this offer in August 1958 during a secret visit to Beijing.[5] This may have been when Mao argued China would survive even if three hundred million of its citizens were killed in an atomic war; Chinese soldiers could then destroy capitalism with conventional weapons. This apocalyptic vision most probably made the Soviet leadership decide against helping the Chinese to develop a nuclear military capability.

Only two days after Khrushchev's ouster from power, on 16 October 1964, the PRC exploded its first atomic bomb at the Lop Nor test site. A hydrogen warhead test, which was described by the *Liberation Army Daily* as a victory for Maoist thought over its enemies, took place less than three years later. More than thirty nuclear explosions,[6] including two underground ones, had taken place by the end of 1989. (The nonproliferation treaty has always been opposed by Beijing.) A Soviet historian writes that Chinese nuclear strategy evolved "from total disregard to strenuous development for their own hegemonist purposes" in three stages:

> The first (1945–53) was characterized by underestimating the significance of nuclear weapons. During the second stage (from the end of the Korean war to the 1960s), Chinese military theorists admitted that "science has developed further with the emergence of nuclear missile weapons." Mao Zedong stated in 1956 at a closed conference of leading party personnel: "We should not only have more aircraft and guns but also the atomic bomb. We cannot do without it." The third stage in Beijing's nuclear strategy commenced during the early 1960s, when Chinese leaders steered a course toward an accelerated buildup of their own nuclear missile potential.[7]

According to U.S. Department of Defense information, a PRC medium-range ballistic missile became operational in 1966 and an intercontinental ballistic missile (ICBM) underwent its first test about ten years later. Communist China reportedly sold CSS-2 (DF-3)-type IRBMs to Saudi Arabia in 1988, as well as Silkworm (H 4–2) missiles to Iran during that country's war with Iraq. Such aerospace exports rose about 60 percent in 1988, reaching a value of $2.1 billion in 1989, which made the PRC the world's fifth-largest exporter of military hardware.[8]

The nuclear weapons program continues; in 1990 Beijing was believed to have deployed a force capable of reaching all parts of the Soviet Union. About eight land-based ICBMs and sixty intermediate-range launchers plus one missile-firing submarine were reportedly operational at that time. The PRC can target all its weapons systems against the USSR, whereas the latter must aim most of its arsenal against NATO and the continental United States (see table 11.1). Although China is the third-largest nuclear power in the world, with its curtailed military budget it is embarking on its own "conversion," reportedly[9] increasing consumer goods during 1990 by 150 percent over the previous year. Mao is quoted as having said, "We are prepared to go without trousers so long as we have the atomic bomb," which he needed for prestige, although he believed war was inevitable, according to the same Soviet expert cited above.[10]

Thus the People's Liberation Army has conducted military maneuvers

TABLE 11.1
STRATEGIC BALANCE: USSR—CHINA, 1990

	Soviet Union	China
Intercontinental ballistic missiles (ICBMs)	1,398 +	2 CSS-4 (DF-5), 5-MT warhead 6 CSS-3 (DF-4), 3-MT warhead
Submarine-launched ballistic missiles (SLBMs)	930 in 63 submarines	1 XIA with 12 CSS-N-3 (J-1) (3 more submarines ordered, but second XIA still not operational)
Intercontinental range strategic bombers	175	None
Intermediate- and medium-range ballistic missiles (IRBMs and MRBMs)	174 launchers still to be eliminated in accordance with Intermediate-range Nuclear Forces Treaty	IRBMs: 60 DF-3, 2-MT No MRBMs
Medium-range bombers	390	120 H-6 medium bombers; 3,000 km combat radius
Ballistic missile defense	100 antiballistic missiles (ABMs), including: ABM-1B Galosh, SH-11 modified Galosh, SH-08 Gazelle; 9 long-range phased-array systems; 11 *Hen House*-series; 9 satellites with ICBM/SLBM launch detection capability; 1 *Pillbox* phased-array at Pushkino (Moscow); 3 over-the-horizon radars.	Ballistic missile early warning, phased-array radar complex, and 2 tracking stations

SOURCES: International Institute for Strategic Studies, *The Military Balance, 1990–1991* (London: IISS, Autumn 1990), pp. 34–36 and 148–52; U.S. Department of Defense, *Soviet Military Power, 1990* (Washington, D.C.: GPO, September 1990), p. 52.

with simulated nuclear explosions in the north and northwest areas of the mainland. Approximately 200,000 troops took part in one such exercise held in the Xinjiang-Uighur autonomous region,[11] which borders the People's Republic of Mongolia, the oldest Soviet dependency (since 1921).

Despite receiving membership in the International Atomic Energy Agency (IAEA) and allowing a visit by the IAEA director general in August 1983, the PRC's attitude toward any restraint over nuclear weapons development has been negative. Moscow called on Beijing to join in sponsoring an international freeze on the level of such arsenals. The PRC replied that it would reduce its stockpile only after both the USSR and the United States had cut theirs by half.[12]

The regular PRC armed forces number just over 3 million men, and mainland China shows increasing interest in acquiring Western military technology. Britain has delivered aircraft engines, artillery, and fire-control equipment as well as radar; computers, helicopters, transport planes, and air defense radar systems may come from the United States and Western Europe in the near future. Official annual expenditures for Chinese defense totaled the equivalent of $5.2 billion in 1989, about $640 million less than the preceding year; however, absolute military outlays increased from 15 billion yuan in 1977 to 22 billion yuan in 1988. (These figures exclude pay and allowances for troops as well as other items.) In addition, the estimates may well be understated because Chinese pricing methods differ from those in the West and because certain items are hidden in the budgets of other ministries. Notably, not a single new military project was planned for the 1989 calendar year.[13]

Ideological Differences

Another problem in the dispute between Moscow and Beijing centered on the evaluation of Stalin. Khrushchev's condemnation of his predecessor in the February 1956 secret speech before the twentieth CPSU congress apparently came as a surprise to the Chinese, who continued to praise Stalin as the heir to Lenin and the last true Marxist-Leninist leader of the USSR. Even before Khrushchev's ouster in October 1964, the Soviet press compared Mao with Stalin, specifically in both men's purge of loyal communists, their personality cults, and their use of force. After the fall of Khrushchev, perhaps in an attempt to slow Stalin's rehabilitation, certain writers in the USSR slanted their criticism of Mao to suggest that both men were equally evil.

For their part, the Chinese leaders took the initiative early in the quarrel when they issued the 29 October 1958 resolution calling for the establishment of communes and an accelerated transition to communism, thus inviting invidious comparisons with Moscow. Khrushchev replied[14] at the twenty-first extraordinary CPSU congress, claiming first place for the USSR in the building of communism. The new USSR party program set 1980 as the year when "the present generation of Soviet people shall live under communism." This document also stressed that the "state of the whole people" had replaced the dictatorship of the proletariat in the USSR.[15] Such formulations greatly displeased the Chinese.

Some insight regarding this dispute comes from an already cited source in the USSR who writes that

> Both we and the Chinese, unfortunately, used arguments in the dispute [during the 1960s] that were not entirely honest. Among other things, the Chinese accused us of revisionism of Marxism and compromise with international imperialism. In turn, we tried to prove that China was slipping down the path of capitalism. It was a deeply mistaken idea . . . it seemed [that if our Soviet officials] could convince the whole world that the CPC was taking on a new life and becoming a petty bourgeois party, that would bring us some kind of ideological dividends.[16]

In August 1966, almost two years after Khrushchev's fall from power, Beijing elevated the thoughts of Mao from national to worldwide significance with the attendant claim to ideological leadership over the international communist movement. Taking offense at this, L. I. Brezhnev, the new leader of the Communist Party of the Soviet Union (CPSU) went so far as to label the great cultural revolution in China a "counterrevolution." After that, many articles appeared in Moscow criticizing Beijing for deviating from Marxist doctrine. The weekly *Novoe vremia* even linked Maoism with Trotskyism and anarchism as well as defining it as an "antiproletarian," counterrevolutionary ideology "of the infuriated petty bourgeoisie."[17]

Accusing the Chinese of following "a political course aimed at consolidating great power nationalistic aims in the field of foreign policy and strengthening their interconnection with a hegemonistic, anti-Soviet domestic policy," one writer also complained that about twenty-five hundred items derogatory to the USSR had been published during 1981 alone in the communist party daily newspaper *Renmin Ribao*. Moscow radio continued to broadcast a series of programs about friendship for the Chinese people, emphasizing the difference between the people and the regime that ruled the country. Not until the 1988 speeches by M. S. Gorbachev at Vladivostok and Krasnoiarsk were proposals made for improving Sino-Soviet contacts.[18] Only in September 1989 were party-to-party relations actually resumed, as had been agreed on in principle during the preceding mid-May summit in Beijing. The Chinese Communist Party sent greetings to the twenty-eighth CPSU congress in July 1990.

On another topic, Gorbachev's admission that "mistakes were made in managing the USSR economy" has been used by some to imply that China, in contrast, had been successful because it chose economic before political reform. The Chinese have also criticized the Soviet leader for the "demise of communism in the USSR" and for the"subversion of socialism" throughout the East-Central European bloc. In the words of Premier Li Peng, "No matter what may happen in the world, we will advance unswervingly along the socialist road."[19] The execution of Nicolae Ceauşescu and Elena Ceauşescu on 25 December 1989 in Romania must have come as a shock to the Chinese because their regime had maintained close ties with the PRC. Table 11.2 lists pro-Chinese communist parties throughout the world.

Interstate Relations

Government-to-government contacts, which remain separate from inter-party affairs, had as their foundation the already mentioned 1950 treaty of friendship, alliance, and mutual assistance. The agreement envisaged military aid against Japan or an ally of that country (the United States). The Soviet Union, however, maintained occupation troops in both Port Arthur as well as Dairen until 1955 and subsequently continued to station about twenty thousand politico-military advisers in other parts of the PRC. A secret defense technology agreement of 15 October 1957 was repudiated unilaterally when the USSR refused to transfer a sample atomic bomb and related technical data to the Chinese.[20]

For almost five years diplomatic relations between the two countries remained at the chargé d'affaires level following the mutual withdrawal of ambassadors. The Soviet embassy at Beijing withstood a three-week siege in February 1967, during which personnel venturing outside the compound were beaten by demonstrating Chinese. The appointment of V. S. Tolstikov as ambassador to the PRC in September 1970 ostensibly signified a return to normalization; he had been first secretary of the CPSU in the Leningrad region during the preceding eight years. The seating by the United Nations of a mainland Chinese delegation in the fall of 1971, however, gave the PRC a worldwide forum to publicize its differences with the Soviet Union. In July 1978, I. S. Shcherbakov replaced Tolstikov. In April 1980 a new PRC ambassador arrived in Moscow to fill a vacancy that had existed for eleven months; O. A. Troianovskii presented his credentials in April 1986 at Beijing. He was succeeded four years later by N. N. Solov'ev. At that time approximately 600 Chinese were studying in the USSR, compared with only 320 Soviets in the PRC for the same purpose.[21]

The two heads of state finally met at Beijing in mid-May 1989 after the USSR had satisfied the three Chinese preconditions for a summit: (1) withdrawal of Soviet troops from Afghanistan, (2) a substantial reduction

TABLE 11.2

Argentina	Communist Party (Marxist-Leninist) of Argentina
	Communist Vanguard of Argentina
	Revolutionary Communist Party of Argentina
Australia	Communist Party (Marxist-Leninist) of Australia
Austria	Communist League
	Austrian Marxist-Leninist Party
	Austrian Revolutionary Workers' Association
	Communist League of Vienna
Bangladesh	Communist Party (Marxist-Leninist) of Bangladesh
Belgium	Communist Party (Marxist-Leninist) of Belgium
Bolivia	Communist Party (Marxist-Leninist) of Bolivia
Britain	Communist Federation (Marxist-Leninist) of Britain
	Communist Federation of Britain/East London, Marxist-Leninist Association
	Communist Unity Association (Marxist-Leninist)
Burma	Communist Party of Burma
Canada	Canadian Communist League (Marxist-Leninist)
	Canadian Marxist-Leninist Group
Chile	Revolutionary Communist Party of Chile
Colombia	Marxist-Leninist League of Colombia
	Communist Party (Marxist-Leninist) of Colombia
Denmark	Communist League (Marxist-Leninist) of Denmark
Dominican Republic	"June 14" Revolutionary Movement, Political Committee of Red Line of the Dominican Republic
	Red Banner
	Voice of the Proletariat
	Workers' Party of the Dominican Republic
	Bandera Proletaria (possibly Red Banner/Voice of Proletariat combination)
Ecuador	Communist Party (Marxist-Leninist) of Ecuador
Faroe Islands	Marxist-Leninist Organization of Faroe Islands
Finland	Marxist-Leninist Groups of Finland
France	Marxist-Leninist Communist Party of France
	Marxist-Leninist Revolutionary Communist Party of France
	Marxist-Leninist Communists of L'Humanité Rouge
	Marxist-Leninist Communists of France (probably a renaming of L'Humanité group, above)
Germany	Communist Party of Germany
	German Communist Party (Marxist-Leninist)
	Communist League of Germany
	Communist Party, "New Unity" (Marxist-Leninist)
	League of West German Communists
	Workers' Union for Reconstruction of Communist Party
	Communist Workers' Union of Germany
Greece	Communist Party (Marxist-Leninist) of Greece

TABLE 11.2 *(continued)*
PRO–CHINESE COMMUNIST ORGANIZATIONS, 1989–1990

	Organization of Greek Marxist-Leninists
	Organization of Marxist-Leninists of Greece
	Revolutionary Communist Movement of Greece
Guadeloupe	Workers' Party of Guadeloupe
Haiti	Haitian Workers' Party
Honduras	Communist Party (Marxist-Leninist) of Honduras
Iceland	Communist Party (Marxist-Leninist) of Iceland
	Communist League of Union (Marxist-Leninist)
Indonesia	Communist Party of Indonesia
Italy	Communist Party (Marxist-Leninist) of Italy
	Marxist-Leninist Organization of Italy
	Party of Socialist Revolution of Italy
	Organization of Communists (Marxist-Leninist) of Italy
	"Consciousness of Workers"
	"Proletarian Ideology"
	Italian (Marxist-Leninist) Communist Party
	Red Star Marxist-Leninist Revolutionary Front of Italy
	Coordinating Committee for Unity of Italy (Marxist-Leninist)
	Laborers Movement for Socialism
Japan	Japanese Communist Party (Left)
	Japanese Workers' Party
Korea	South Korean Revolutionary Party for Unification
Luxembourg	Communist League of Luxembourg
Malaya	Communist Party of Malaya
Malaysia	Communist Party of Malaysia
Nepal	Communist Party of Nepal
	Nepal Workers' and Peasants' Organization
Netherlands	Marxist-Leninist Communist Unitarian Movement of Netherlands
	Marxist-Leninist Communist Unity Movement of Netherlands
	Marxist-Leninist League of Netherlands
	Marxist-Leninist Party of Netherlands
	Socialist Party of Netherlands
	League of Dutch Marxist-Leninists
	League of Marxist-Leninists
	Communist Workers' Organization
	Breda Communist Group (Marxist-Leninist)
New Zealand	Communist Party of New Zealand
North Kalimantan	Communist Party of North Kalimantan
Norway	Norwegian Workers' Communist Party (Marxist-Leninist), Working Committee of Norway
Paraguay	Communist Party of Paraguay
Peru	Communist Party of Peru
	Peruvian Communist Party

Philippines	Communist Party of the Philippines
Poland	Communist Party of Poland
Portugal	Communist Party (Marxist-Leninist) of Portugal
	Portuguese Communist Party (reconstituted)
Réunion	Marxist-Leninist Communist Organization
San Marino	Communist Party (Marxist-Leninist) of San Marino
Spain	Labour Party of Spain
	Spanish Workers' Revolutionary Organization
	Spanish Communist Party (Marxist-Leninist)
Sri Lanka	Communist Party (Marxist-Leninist) of Sri Lanka
Suriname	Communist Party of Suriname
	People's Party
Sweden	Communist Party of Sweden
	Marxist-Leninist Union of Struggle
	Swedish Communist Party
	Clarte Federation
	Groups for Communist Unity
Switzerland	Marxist-Leninist Communist Party
Thailand	Communist Party of Thailand
United States	Revolutionary Communist Party
	October League
	Organizing Committee for a Marxist-Leninist Party
Uruguay	Uruguayan Revolutionary Communist Party
	Communist Party of Uruguay
	Revolutionary Communist Party
Venezuela	Party of Venezuelan Revolution
Yugoslavia	Communist Party of Yugoslavia

NOTE: Some of the above may have fused or disbanded.

SOURCE: Richard F. Staar, ed., *Yearbook on International Communist Affairs* (Stanford: Hoover Institution Press), published annually in June; *Beijing Review*, various issues.

in the military buildup along PRC borders, including the People's Republic of Mongolia, and (3) USSR pressure on Vietnam to remove its armed forces from Cambodia. The meetings lasted four days and resulted in a joint communiqué that declared mutual respect for sovereignty and territorial integrity, nonaggression, noninterference in internal affairs, equality and mutual advantage, and peaceful coexistence. As the Soviet ambassador described the situation at year's end, "it goes without saying that we cannot expect to restore the same relations we had in the 'fifties. . . . We can not enter twice into the same river."[22]

Economic Relations

Part of the Sino-Soviet dispute undoubtedly involved economics. Moscow had promised Beijing through 1959 the equivalent of $3.8 billion in financial support for construction of 291 projects, of which only 198 were completed. By 1955, the Chinese already had a trade deficit with the USSR amounting to about $1 billion. Two years later, the debt reached $2.4 billion. Between 1960 and 1970, annual trade turnover declined from almost 1.5 billion rubles to less than 42 million rubles per year. In 1975, it increased to 200 million rubles and in 1980 to 340 million rubles. By 1981, however, the level was down 40 percent from the preceding year, and trade turnover in 1982 did not reach the 1980 level. After that it approximately doubled during each of the following years through 1985 (see table 11.3), and more than ten thousand Chinese came to the USSR for work during 1989.

The following exemplifies early PRC resentment against the Soviet Union in the economic sphere:

It was unreasonable for China to bear all expenses of the Korean War. During World War I and II, the U.S. lent funds to its allies. Afterward,

TABLE 11.3
SOVIET-CHINESE TRADE, 1960–1989
(IN MILLIONS OF RUBLES)

Year	Turnover	Exports	Imports	Balance
1960	1,498.7	735.4	763.3	− 27.9
1965	375.5	172.5	203.0	− 30.5
1970	41.9	22.4	19.5	+ 2.9
1975	200.6	92.8	107.8	− 15.0
1980	340.0	190.8	149.6	+ 41.2
1981	176.8	82.6	94.2	− 11.6
1982	223.5	120.1	103.4	+ 16.7
1983	488.2	255.6	232.6	− 23.0
1984	977.8	467.9	509.9	− 42.0
1985	1,605.0	779.0	826.0	− 47.0
1986	1,822.0	910.3	911.7	− 1.4
1987	1,474.9	724.3	750.6	− 26.3
1988	1,850.1	1,005.2	844.9	+ 160.3
1989	2,412.0	1,328.5	1,083.5	+ 245.0

SOURCES: USSR, *Vneshniaia torgovlia za 1960 god* (Moscow: Statistika, 1961), p. 9, and the same for subsequent years; *Vneshniaia torgovlia*, no. 3 (March 1981, March 1982, March 1983, March 1984); USSR, *Vneshniaia torgovlia v 1987 g.: Statisticheskii sbornik* (Moscow), 1988, pp. 219–20; Economist Intelligence Unit, *USSR Country Profile, 1989–90* (London, 1989), p. 36; *Vneshnie ekonomicheskie sviazi SSSR v 1989 g.: Statisticheskii sbornik* (Moscow: Finansy i statistika, 1990), p. 12.

some countries repudiated their debt, while the U.S. waived some claims. The Soviet loan is repayable in full within ten years. This time is too short and, moreover, interest must be paid. I propose an extension to 20 or 30 years. When the USSR liberated our northeast [Manchuria], it dismantled machinery equipment in our factories. Was there compensation? Will there be repayment?[23]

The appearance of such criticism in the official communist party daily newspaper indicates that these sentiments were shared by the top leadership at Beijing.

During 1985, however, Sino-Soviet trade turnover totaled more than 1.6 billion rubles, reaching its highest level in almost twenty-five years. The Central Asian frontier between the two countries opened at several points for commercial exchange but remained closed for travel by individuals. At the same time, the Mongolian People's Republic began to expel about eight thousand Chinese citizens who had lived there for generations. A deputy foreign minister from the PRC arrived in August 1986 at Ulaanbaatar for talks on improving relations.[24]

Some of the 1,390 Soviet technicians and specialists who had been withdrawn from more than two hundred Chinese projects in July 1960 by Khrushchev returned to the PRC during 1988. They began building or modernizing twenty-four large metallurgical enterprises as well as constructing a railroad from Beijing through Urumchi that will connect with Alma-Ata and Moscow (the Silk Road of the twentieth century), which is scheduled for completion during the second half of 1992. Even before the 1989 summit, the USSR had extended hard currency credits (the first in twenty-eight years) totaling 200 million Swiss francs to China at a low rate of interest. These will be used to modernize one of the main steel mills located at Baotou, Inner Mongolia, which should increase its production by 10 percent. The USSR also will deliver a nuclear reactor for an electric power plant in Liaoning province. Premiers Li Peng and Nikolai Ryzhkov signed a comprehensive agreement in May 1990 for mutual economic, scientific, and technological development through the year 2000. Foreign Ministers Shevardnadze and Qian Qichen agreed on principles for cutting back their respective armed forces along the Sino-Soviet border.[25]

The Border Dispute

Another matter under protracted discussion between the two governments involves a 4,500-mile frontier divided by Mongolia. A seemingly fixed landmark, the Amur River, separates Chinese Manchuria from the Soviet Far East; it was here that pitched battles occurred over which country owned certain islands. Clashes also took place along the Mongolian-Chinese border as late as the end of 1974, in the course of which about thirty casualties were sustained by both sides.[26] One of the most potentially volatile areas is located between Soviet Central Asia and the Xinjiang-Uighur region inside the PRC. The populations on both sides of the frontier are Turkic and distrust Russians as well as Chinese.

Border incidents began in 1962 when some five thousand Uighurs and Kirghiz fled the Ili Valley in the PRC to the USSR. Moscow subsequently charged the Chinese communists with more than five thousand frontier violations during that year.[27] The PRC in turn accused the Soviets of instigating 4,189 incidents during the ensuing five-year period. In an interview given to a Japanese Socialist party delegation, Mao stated, "About 150 years ago, the area east of Lake Baikal became Russian territory; since then, Vladivostok, Khabarovsk, Kamchatka, et alia, have been Soviet territory. We have not yet presented our account for this list."[28] Although negotiations on border problems began in 1969, they were conducted for almost a decade without any apparent progress. Political talks on state-to-state relations suddenly ended in December 1979 when the Chinese announced that it would not be appropriate to continue them because the USSR had invaded Afghanistan.

During the previous year, Beijing accused Soviet border troops of crossing the Ussuri River and assaulting PRC citizens. According to the official news agency, Xinhua, a USSR helicopter and eighteen boats carrying about thirty troops penetrated several miles into Chinese territory and allegedly harassed, beat, and dragged to the river approximately fourteen PRC citizens. The TASS news agency replied that Soviet border guards had been "pursuing a dangerous criminal" and mistakenly crossed the border and that reports of Soviet aggression against Chinese civilians were "pure fabrication."[29]

Another incident began, according to Beijing, when a four-man USSR military patrol forded the Ergun River in a remote region of Heilungkiang province in northeast China and tried to kidnap a local herdsman, killing him in the process. One Soviet soldier was shot in an exchange of fire as the invaders retreated across the river. The PRC claims that as many as fifty-four divisions, or one million hostile USSR troops, were poised along its border. At least that many Chinese soldiers reportedly faced them, according to the Soviets. Premier Zhao Ziyang affirmed that the PRC would stage an active struggle against Moscow's "hegemonism"[30] throughout the world.

Not until October 1982 were government-to-government negotiations resumed at the level of deputy foreign minister, which then took place twice a year. The Chinese held to their three above-mentioned preconditions for resumption of normal relations. Despite the death of Brezhnev within weeks after the resumption of PRC-USSR talks, the new leader, Iu. V. Andropov, indicated that he would follow his predecessor's policy vis-à-vis mainland China. The Soviets apparently were unwilling to meet any of the three PRC demands.

The ninth round of talks, held in Beijing during October 1986, did not result in any progress on the issues of the 171 or more SS-20 intermediate-range nuclear missile launchers in the Far East, the USSR troops along the PRC border, or the Soviet armored divisions totaling 75,000 men in Mongolia. Neither could the other two problems—Vietnamese forces in Cambodia and the USSR occupation of Afghanistan—be resolved. The winds of change were evident, however, when CPSU leader Gorbachev made it clear in his 28 July 1986 speech at Vladivostok that the number of Soviet troops along the Chinese border went far beyond "reasonable sufficiency."[31]

When Gorbachev announced the unilateral demobilization of 500,000 men from the USSR armed forces in his speech on 7 December 1988 before the U.N. General Assembly, he did not provide many details other than to say that 200,000 would be discharged from the eastern part of the Soviet Union. It was subsequently reported that fifty thousand officers and enlisted men, 850 tanks, some 1,100 infantry combat vehicles and armored personnel carriers, about 190 aircraft, and 130 helicopters would be withdrawn by the end of 1990 from Mongolia alone.[32]

VIETNAM AND CAMBODIA

A major issue in the conflict between the two communist giants involves their respective attitudes toward Southeast Asia in general and Vietnam in particular. Before his ouster, Khrushchev may have decided to discontinue USSR support for the Indochinese conflict; his successor, Brezhnev, however, reasserted Soviet interest in the region. Perhaps he thought that North Vietnam would never win its war, although he also probably felt that the USSR could not leave opposition to U.S. "imperialism" to China alone. Prime Minister Aleksei Kosygin spent the first half of February 1965 in Beijing and Hanoi. A secret letter to the PRC on 17 April of that year requested transit rights (by rail) for some four thousand Soviet troops to North Vietnam, the establishment of two airfields with five hundred Soviet ground personnel in southwest China, and an air corridor for unrestricted flights to and from Hanoi. The response from Beijing came three months later and included the following words: "Frankly speaking, we do not trust you. We and other fraternal countries have learned bitter lessons in the past from Khrushchev's evil practice of control under cover of aid. We cannot accept your control. Nor will we help you control others."[33]

A subsequent Chinese statement on 3 May 1966 condemned the USSR for its policy of détente in Europe, which had allegedly enabled the Americans to transfer troops from the Federal Republic of Germany to South Vietnam. It also denied allegations concerning obstruction of Soviet military shipments crossing mainland China by railroad to Hanoi and suggested that the USSR could use sea routes, perhaps in hopes that this would precipitate a confrontation with the United States. Charges that Beijing had stolen two antiaircraft guided missile launchers were denounced as slander, and Moscow was accused of collusion with Washington. This dispute died down in 1975 after U.S. troops had withdrawn from South Vietnam.

Four years later, in 1979, a controlled Chinese invasion of Vietnam was described by Deputy Premier Deng Xiaoping as a punitive action "intended to teach the Vietnamese that their adventurism in Cambodia would not pay, even with assurances of Soviet support." Moscow's restraint was explained when it became clear that the Vietnamese were standing their ground against the Chinese. According to a USSR official, "We did not intervene when the U.S. was bombing Vietnam during the last war, and that was a real provocation. Why should we intervene now?"[34] The Soviet-Vietnamese treaty calls for consultations in the event that either party is threatened. Such meetings have taken place between Hanoi's ambassador to Moscow and a Soviet deputy foreign minister, as well as through other official channels. Both mainland China and Vietnam, however, were criticized by communist parties throughout the world for engaging in war and acting in an "imperialist" manner. According to an unconfirmed USSR tally, fifty-seven of the eighty parties that took a position condemned Beijing, not Hanoi.[35] (See table 11.2 for pro-Chinese communist parties throughout the world.)

Regardless of the impact on these communist parties, the PRC continued to support the ousted Cambodian regime whose guerrillas were fighting Vietnamese occupation troops. An article in the CPSU daily newspaper accused Beijing of assisting those who were committing genocide against the Cambodian people. During the spring and summer of 1984, border skirmishes continued along the Sino-Vietnamese border. Two years later, the Chinese fired mortar and artillery shells into northern Vietnam. The USSR for its part continued to support Hanoi both verbally and financially. The PRC, according to Prince Norodom Sihanouk, offered to help Vietnam rebuild its economy if it withdrew from Cambodia.[36]

The last of the 200,000 Vietnamese troops returned home on 30 September 1989 after almost eleven years of occupation that had cost them 25,300 dead and 55,000 seriously wounded. This had been preceded by a joint USSR-Chinese statement on Cambodia that pledged support of a four-party provisional coalition government under Prince Sihanouk and free elections. The United Nations supported this formula by a vote of 124 to 17, with 12 members abstaining. The four groups would include the Khmer Rouge, a Marxist-Leninist movement formerly led by Pol Pot; the communist regime currently in power under Heng Samrin and Hun Sen, largely not recognized abroad; the Khmer People's National Liberation Front under a previous prime minister, Son Sann; and the National Army of former monarch and chief of state, Sihanouk, who proposed a U.N. trusteeship for Cambodia.[37]

The five permanent members of the U.N. Security Council held five meetings on Cambodia during the first half of 1990. They proposed a peacekeeping force and the establishment of an administrative structure before the elections. The USSR, of course, is partial to the Vietnamese-backed government, whereas the PRC continues to favor the Khmer Rouge. In mid-July 1990, Secretary of State James Baker announced a change in U.S. policy and support for the Heng Samrin regime, that apparently paved the way for an agreement.[38]

RELATIONS WITH NORTH KOREA AND JAPAN

The communist leadership in P'yongyang had avoided taking sides in the Sino-Soviet dispute, supporting neither the puppet regime in Afghanistan nor the Vietnamese occupation of Cambodia. The shooting down of the South Korean civilian airliner by the USSR on 1 September 1983 (for other attacks, see table 11.4), however, appears to have triggered a rapprochement with Moscow. Shortly afterward, in a demonstration of their own cold-bloodedness, three North Korean army officers set off a powerful bomb at Rangoon, killing four Burmese and seventeen high-ranking South Korean officials who were on a government visit in Burma.[39]

North Korean ruler Kim Il Sung traveled by train in May 1984 to Moscow, his first trip since 1967 (he had been to Beijing in 1975), and held three rounds of talks with CPSU general secretary K. U. Chernenko. He reportedly asked for new jet fighters and support against the "Washington-Tokyo-Seoul bloc" as well as against PRC "hegemonism," to which he had referred publicly only a few weeks earlier. Moscow, in addition to delivering between twenty and thirty MIG-23s, also financed North Korea's largest iron and steel works as well as a new port at Najin that provides the USSR with naval facilities. By 1990, P'yongyang's debt to the Soviet Union totaled 2.2 billion rubles.[40]

North Korea was the thirteenth country to withdraw from the summer Olympics in Los Angeles. This must have pleased the Soviet Union, which is

TABLE 11.4

SOVIET ATTACKS ON FOREIGN AIRCRAFT, 1950–1983

Date	Description of Attack	Casualties/Injuries
1. 8 April 1950	U.S. Navy Privateer bomber with ten on board disappears over the Baltic. United States says plane was brought down by Soviets.	*
2. 6 November 1951	U.S. Navy plane lost over international waters off Siberia after Soviet planes fire on it.	Crew of ten missing.
3. 29 April 1952	Soviets attack French commercial airliner.	Two passengers injured.
4. 13 June 1952	U.S. reconnaissance plane missing after interception by Soviet planes over Japan.	*
5. 16 June 1952	Soviet jets down unarmed Swedish military plane over international waters in the Baltic.	Seven crewmen rescued.
6. 7 October 1952	U.S. B-29 bomber with crew of eight disappears over northern Japan after taking Soviet fire.	*
7. 10 March 1953	U.S. Air Force jet fighter shot down by two Soviet MIGs in Germany.	No casualties.
8. 12 March 1953	Soviet MIGs down British bomber above Elbe River valley at the East-West frontier of Germany.	Five crewmen die.
9. 15 March 1953	U.S. reconnaissance plane attacked by MIG about 25 miles from Soviet border.	Shots exchanged, but neither is hit.

	Date	Incident	Casualties
10.	29 July 1953	U.S. B-50 bomber shot down by MIGs over the Sea of Japan.	Sixteen crewmen presumed killed.*
11.	22 January 1954	U.S. reconnaissance plane over Yellow Sea attacked by eight MIGs.	No casualties.
12.	12 March 1954	Two U.S. military planes flying near Czechoslovak border on training flight attacked by MIG.	Both land safely.
13.	3 June 1954	Belgian transport carrying livestock fired on over Yugoslavia by MIG fighter.	One crewman killed, two injured.
14.	4 September 1954	U.S. Navy plane shot down by Soviet jets 30 miles off Siberian coast.	One dead.
15.	7 November 1954	U.S. reconnaissance plane shot down over northern Hokkaido, Japan.	One American killed.
16.	10 May 1955	Eight U.S. fighter planes on patrol over international waters near North Korea attacked by MIGs.	No casualties.
17.	22 May 1955	U.S. Navy patrol bomber attacked by Soviet aircraft near Saint Lawrence Island in Bering Sea.	Seven in crew injured.
18.	27 June 1958	Unarmed U.S. military transport, diverted from its course by storm, shot down over Soviet Armenia.	No casualties.
19.	2 September 1958	C-130 transport aircraft shot down over Armenia near Turkish border.	Seventeen Americans presumed killed.*
20.	7 November 1958	Soviet MIGs fire on U.S. Air Force reconnaissance jets over Baltic and Sea of Japan.	No casualties.
21.	16 June 1959	U.S. Navy patrol plane attacked by Soviet-made MIG over Sea of Japan.	One crewman injured.

TABLE 11.4 (*continued*)

SOVIET ATTACKS ON FOREIGN AIRCRAFT, 1950–1983

22.	1 May 1960	Soviets down U.S. reconnaissance plane piloted by Francis Gary Powers.	U-2 pilot captured, jailed.
23.	1 July 1960	U.S. RB-47 shot down over Barents Sea near Kola Peninsula.	Four of six on board die.
24.	20 November 1963	Soviets down Iranian plane after it strays over Russian border and flies back into Iran.	No information.
25.	28 January 1964	U.S. Air Force jet trainer shot down over East Germany.	Three Americans die.
26.	10 March 1964	U.S. bomber downed by Soviets after it strayed across East German frontier.	No deaths.
27.	20 April 1978	South Korean airliner flying from Paris to Seoul fired at when it crosses over Soviet territory.	Two passengers killed, thirteen injured.
28.	July 1981	Argentine cargo plane crashes after colliding with pursuing Soviet plane in Armenia.	No information.
29.	1 September 1983	South Korean passenger aircraft flying from Anchorage to Seoul shot down as it leaves Soviet territory.	All passengers and crew killed (269).

*In these cases, U.S. airmen may have survived. The Soviet government has denied having any information about the fifty-seven missing crew members, according to Foreign Press International, *FPI International Report* (New York), 26 October 1984, p. 3.

SOURCE: *U.S. News & World Report*, 12 September 1983, p. 25.

in a position to supply more substantial economic and military aid than the Chinese communists. Furthermore, Kim reportedly resented Beijing's "friendly" attitude toward Seoul, for the Chinese communists had accepted, without consulting P'yongyang, a Japanese proposal that Korean residents of the mainland be allowed to visit their relatives in South Korea. Although they do not have diplomatic relations, Beijing and Seoul do conduct trade. However, the North Korean prime minister subsequently spent five days in Beijing discussing economic relations. Kim Il Sung visited Moscow toward the end of October 1986 and met with Gorbachev.[41]

To discourage Asians from participating in the Olympic games in Seoul, North Korean agents placed a bomb on a South Korean passenger jet that exploded over the Indian Ocean on 29 November 1987, killing all 115 persons on board. One of the perpetrators was captured at Abu Dhabi, Bahrain, and confessed to her part in this act of international terrorism.[42] Perhaps the two Kims, father and son, were proving to their patrons that they could emulate what the Soviets had done four years earlier.

The USSR continues to absorb ever-increasing deficits, almost two-fifths of the turnover, in trade with North Korea. Soviet-built plants produce 63 percent of the country's electricity, 50 percent of its coal, and 33 percent of its steel. North Koreans are involved with fifteen joint lumber projects in Siberia, and more than two thousand of their scientists and engineers have been trained in the USSR. Despite all this assistance, the youth of North Korea seems unaware of these developments. The Soviet report on Kim Il Sung's visit to Beijing in late 1989 merely paraphrased the official communiqué. Moscow's rapprochement with Seoul, resulting in diplomatic relations on 30 September 1990, was described by P'yongyang as "a conspiracy to topple" North Korea's socialist system.[43]

The USSR was disturbed by the rapprochement between the PRC and Japan because its own relations with Japan deteriorated after 1980. By that time Tokyo seemed convinced that Moscow would not honor its 1956 promise to return two of the four south Kuril Islands that were occupied at the end of the Second World War. Since 1978, the Soviets have deployed a division of ten thousand ground troops; since 1983, about forty MIG-23 jet fighters. There are also SSC-1 Sepal missiles on Iturup, an island in the chain, and Delta III class submarines in the Sea of Okhotsk.[44]

The USSR, attempting to intimidate Japan, stationed 171 SS-20 intermediate-range nuclear missile launchers and perhaps as many as one hundred Backfire bombers in the Far East. Meetings at the ambassadorial and deputy foreign minister levels could not resolve the problems between the two countries. The Japanese unilaterally renounced the means to project military power in their 1946 constitution, so they pose no armed threat to the Soviets. The invasion of Afghanistan and the 1981–1983 martial law regime in Poland, however, did result in Japanese economic sanctions against Moscow. Export-Import Bank credits stopped, and new enterprises were canceled or delayed by Tokyo. Just a few old projects were still being pursued: coking coal mines in southern Iakutsk, oil and gas development on Sakhalin Island, and a forestry venture. During 1985 commercial exchange increased only moderately. Subsequent negotiations resulted in a 1986–1990 trade agreement.[45]

During his speech at Vladivostok on 28 July 1986, Gorbachev devoted only thirty-nine lines to Japan compared with ninety-six lines to China. His next major address dealing with Asia, at Krasnoiarsk on 16 September 1988, reversed the emphasis: Japan received seventy-two lines, China only thirty-five. The Vladivostok speech proposed a long-term plan that would allocate 200 billion rubles for economic development of the Soviet Far East.[46] It was two years, however, before any serious planning commenced in Moscow. Neither Beijing nor Tokyo seemed enthusiastic about the vague Vladivostok proposals for improving Asian security or about rescuing the Soviet economy from its crisis situation.

The comments about Japan in the Krasnoiarsk address referred to meetings with politicians at the Kremlin, trade and economic relations that need improving, and the 1 percent of gross national product that Tokyo devotes to its military. No mention was made of the four disputed northern islands, which one Soviet historian favors returning to the Japanese. Although the USSR proposes to sign a peace treaty ending the state of war, Japan has refused to negotiate without a settlement of the Kurils dispute. That may be why Gorbachev has postponed his visit to Japan until April 1991, by which time some compromise may have been agreed on. He did send his closest foreign policy adviser, A. N. Iakovlev, to Tokyo. Japan rejected as premature a suggestion in *Pravda* that the northern islands be placed under a United Nations' trusteeship. Foreign Minister Shevardnadze met his counterpart in Japan during 2–3 September 1990 without any reported success. However, by that time, five sessions of a working group on a peace treaty already had been held.[47]

The Japanese public learned about extensive Soviet intelligence activities against its country from KGB defector Stanislav Levchenko, mentioned in chapter 5. He revealed that 40 percent of all TASS correspondents in Japan reported to the KGB and that another 10 to 15 percent were GRU officers. Levchenko claimed to have recruited about two hundred local informants, including a former labor minister and a former chairman of the Japanese Socialist Party.[48] These revelations have negatively affected the image of the USSR and probably influenced the Japanese decision to maintain economic sanctions while the war in Afghanistan continued. Nevertheless, once that war ended, two major findings of rich oil and natural gas fields off the coast of Siberia encouraged Tokyo businessmen to pursue a $4 billion joint development project. Another consortium is studying the feasibility of exporting a complete petroleum complex that will cost $6 billion.[49] All these developments bear on Soviet relations with the United States, which are dealt with in the final chapter.

NOTES

1. The treaty was signed on 14 February 1950 and published in "Sovetsko-kitaiskoe kommiunike o podpisanii dogovora i soglashenii mezhdu Sovetskim Soiuzom i KNR," *Pravda*, 15 February 1950, p. l. The Chinese announced well before the expiration date that the treaty would not be extended.

2. L. Deliusin, "SSSR-KNR: Ostavliaia proshloe v proshlom," *Argumenty i fakty*, no. 5 (3–9 February 1990): 4–5, at p. 5.

3. *Renmin Ribao (People's Daily)*, 31 March 1960. Compare also Lin Biao, "Long Live the Victory of the People's War," *Hongqi (Red Flag)*, 3 September 1965. Translations into English were provided by the U.S. consulate general in Hong Kong.

4. Editorial, "Long Live Leninism!" *Renmin Ribao*, 16 April 1960; quotation from PRC government statement, issued by New China News Agency, 1 September 1963, and cited by the U.S. consulate general in Hong Kong; *Current Background*, no. 712 (4 September 1963).

5. A. A. Gromyko, *Pamiatnoe*, vol. 2 (Moscow: Politizdat, 1988), pp. 132–33.

6. Michael R. Gordon, "Arms Race Shows No Signs," *New York Times*, 23 March 1986, p. E-3, gives a table listing nuclear tests, 1945–1985. The PRC announced that it would no longer test above ground but did set off an underground explosion on 29 September 1988 near Lop Nor, the first since December 1984, registering less than 150 kilotons. Reuters dispatch from Stockholm, "Swedes Report China A-Test," *New York Times*, 8 October 1988, p. 6.

7. B. Gorbachev, "Iadernye ambitsii Pekina," *Krasnaia zvezda*, 25 January 1981, p. 3. Citing unidentified foreign press reports, this article states that the PRC possessed twelve nuclear reactors as well as fourteen accelerators and more than ten processing and enrichment facilities.

   For a PRC source, see Nie Rongzhen, "How China Develops Its Nuclear Weapons," *Beijing Review* 28, no. 17 (29 April 1985): 15–17. These are excerpts from a biography of the man who directed the PRC nuclear weapons program during its first decade and attained the rank of marshal in the armed forces.

8. James R. Schlesinger, secretary of defense, *Annual Defense Department Report for Fiscal Year 1976* (Washington, D.C.: GPO, 1976), pp. II-16 and II-17; Philip Smucker, "China Takes up Slack," *San Francisco Examiner*, 18 March 1990, p. A-8; Michael R. Gordon, "Beijing Avoids Assurances," *New York Times*, 30 March 1990, p. A-4.

9. "China's Nuclear Industry," *Wall Street Journal*, 9 August 1990, p. A-5.

10. Deliusin, "SSSR-KNR," p. 5.

11. David Chen, "Test Highlights Nuclear Build Up," *South China Morning Post* (Hong Kong), 7 July 1982, p. 8. For a description of other maneuvers reportedly in a radioactive and chemical or bacteriological environment, see *Insight*, 13 October 1986, p. 38.

12. Michael Weisskopf, "China Stresses Defensive Aim of Nuclear Force," *Washington Post*, 28 July 1983, p. A-5. Between 1970 and early 1986, the PRC orbited eighteen satellites according to V. Vorontsov, "Pered litsom otvetstvennosti," *Novoe vremia* (Moscow), no. 38 (19 September 1986): 21.

13. "China's Military Budget," *Wall Street Journal*, 24 January 1990, p. A-11; Vladimir Smolko, "Disarmament—The Chinese Version," *Moscow News*, no. 8/9 (11–18 March 1990): 29.

14. Report by N. S. Khrushchev, "Novyi Etap," part IV of "Prodolzhenie doklada Khrushcheva," *Pravda*, 28 January 1959, pp. 8–10.

15. Part VI, "Programma KPSS," in *Pravda*, 2 November 1961, pp. 3–4. The PRC subsequently proclaimed what it called a "people's democratic dictatorship," akin to the "state of the whole people" in the USSR.

16. Deliusin, "SSSR-KNR," p. 5.

17. See, for example, I. Gudoshnikov and G. Sergeeva, "Reviziia Maoistami," *Partiinaia zhizn'*, no. 24 (December 1974): 60–68; editorial, "Pekin meniaet taktiku," *Novoe vremia*, no. 51 (December 1980): 10–12; O. Drugov, "Proletarskii internatsionalizm," *Partiinaia zhizn'*, no. 12 (June 1984): 13–22.

18. Oleg Borisov, "The Situation in the PRC," *Far Eastern Affairs* (Moscow) 36, no. 3 (1982): 13. See "Rech' tovarishcha Gorbacheva na torzhestvennom sobranii," *Izvestiia*, 29 July 1986, pp. 1–3, for the Vladivostok speech and "Vremia deistvii, vremia prakticheskoi raboty," *Pravda*, 18 September 1988, pp. 1–3, for the Krasnoiarsk speech.

19. Adi Ignatius, "China's Soviet Card," *Wall Street Journal*, 19 April 1990, p. A-10; see Stephen Brookes, "Nervous Communist Regimes," *Insight*, 12 March 1990, p. 30, for Li Peng quotation; "Gluboko veriu v Marksizm-Leninizm," *Pravda*, 5 November 1990, p. 4.

20. This is not mentioned by O. Ivanov in "Vopreki interesam kitaiskogo naroda," *Mirovaia ekonomika i mezhdunarodnye otnosheniia*, no. 8 (August 1974): 39–51. However, the PRC announcement in early 1958 that it would develop its own nuclear weapons is significant. See also Nie Rongzhen, "How China Develops Its Nuclear Weapons," p. 17.

21. See B. Borisov, "Reshaia vazhnye zadachi," *Pravda*, 1 October 1986, p. 4, on improvement of Sino-Soviet relations. Iu. Savenkov, "Ispytanie na prochnost'," *Izvestiia*, 16 June 1990, p. 4; A. Zhemchugov, "Nash chelovek v Pekine," *Sel'skaia zhizn'*, 23 September 1990, p. 3, for an interview with Solov'ev.

22. "Sovmestnoe sovetsko-kitaiskoe kommunike," *Pravda*, 19 May 1989, p. 1. This document also provided for resumption of party-to-party relations. Interview with O. A. Troianovskii on Moscow radio in Mandarin, 30 December 1989; *Foreign Broadcast Information Service (FBIS)-Soviet Union* 90–002 (3 January 1990): 70.

23. *Renmin Ribao*, 14 July 1957, as translated in *Current Background*, no. 470 (26 July 1957); Radio Peace and Progress (Moscow), 26 October 1984; *FBIS-Soviet Union* 84–210 (29 October 1984): B-1, broadcast a long commentary in Mandarin about Soviet military aid to the PRC during the Korean War.

See also Aleksandr Makhov, "Stalin odobril prikaz Kim Ir Sena," *Moskovskie novosti*, no. 27 (8 July 1990): 12, who quotes a former North Korean general during that war and later ambassador to Moscow as stating that Stalin had approved the invasion of South Korea.

24. Agenzia Nazionale Stampa Associata (ANSA) dispatch from Frunze, Kirghizia, USSR, in Christopher S. Wren, "Where Iron and Bamboo Curtains Meet," *New York Times*, 26 June 1983, p. 2-E; A. Kir'ianov, "Torgovo-ekonomicheskie otnosheniia mezhdu SSSR i KNR na sovremennom etape," *Vneshniaia torgovlia*, no. 3 (March 1986): 8–11, insert; "Chinese Officials Hold Talks with Mongolia," *New York Times*, 10 August 1986, p. 9.

25. Moscow radio, 7 August 1988; "USSR to Help China in Metallurgical Industry," *FBIS-Soviet Union* 88–155 (11 August 1988): 11–12. Credits were discussed by Belgrade radio, 27 March 1989; "USSR Grants PRC First Credit in 28 Years," *FBIS-Soviet Union* 89–057 (27 March 1989): 15–16. Moscow radio, 16 February 1989; "USSR to Help Build Liaoning Nuclear Plant," *FBIS-Soviet Union* 89–932 (17 February 1989): 6, announced the nuclear reactor. For the latest agreements, see "Dokumenty, podpisannye v khode vizita v SSSR prem'era Gossoveta KNR Li Pena," *Vestnik MID SSSR*, no. 10 (31 May 1990): 16–22. On the railroad, see G. Dil'diaev and T. Esil'baev, "Rel'sy vedut v Urumchi," *Pravda*, 13 September 1990, p. 5. See also dispatch from Beijing by B. Averchenko and B. Barakhta, "Ostrova v okeane rynka," *Pravda*, 25 October 1990, p. 5.

26. David Floyd, "Fighting on China Border," *Daily Telegraph* (London), 17 December 1974, p. 1. During 1989 and 1990, the USSR successively returned the river islands of Heixiazi and Zhenbao to the PRC, according to Radio Free Europe/Radio Liberty (RFE/RL) *Daily Report*, no. 158 (21 August 1990): 8.

27. "Zaiavlenie sovetskogo pravitel'stva," *Pravda*, 21 and 22 September 1963, pp. 1–2 of each issue. The CPSU Politburo reportedly discussed as far back as 1969 a nuclear strike against China, according to Arkady N. Shevchenko, *Breaking with Moscow* (New York: Knopf, 1985), p. 286.

28. Quoted in *Asahi Shimbun* (Tokyo), 1 August 1964. The Chinese claim to 1.5 million square kilometers of territory, annexed under tsarist Russia and retained by the USSR, was rejected in V. Iasenev, "Za chem nuzhny takie 'istoricheskie issledovaniia'?" *Novoe vremia*, no. 15 (April 1984): 23–25.

29. Xinhua (Beijing), 11 May 1978; TASS (Moscow), 12 May 1978.

30. Chen Si, "Behind Moscow's Appeal," *Beijing Review*, 9 March 1981, p. 11–12; see "Soviet, Chinese Troops Clash on Border," *Washington Post*, 7 October 1980, p. A-18, for the quotation. The actual figures were about 600,000 Soviet soldiers, according to "Mr. Gorbachev's China Shuffle," *New York Times*, 1 August 1986, p. A-26.

31. "Ofitsial'nye soobshcheniia," *Izvestiia*, 24 October 1986, p. 4. The source for

Gorbachev's speech at Vladivostok is cited in note 18 above. The first round of arms reduction talks did not take place until 10–28 September 1990, according to TASS over Moscow radio on 4 October 1990; *FBIS-Soviet Union* 90–193 of same date, pp. 16–17.

32. A. Nabatchikov, "SSSR-Mongoliia," *Izvestiia*, 16 May 1989, p. 4. See also K. Vnukov, "Zhivaia tkan," *Pravda*, 31 October 1989, p. 4; Suzanne Crow, "Mongolia: Still the 16th Republic?" *Report on the USSR*, no. 34 (24 August 1990): 3–4; V. Sapov, "Reshaet Malyi khural," *Pravda*, 30 September 1990, p. 7. See also Yu Cheng, "A New Type of Sino-Soviet Relationship," *Foreign Affairs Journal*, no. 17 (September 1990): 47–53, for the view from Beijing.

33. Xinhua (Beijing), 14 July 1965.

34. Cited in Eduardo Lachica, "Russia: The Real Winner in Indochina," *Asian Wall Street Journal* (Hong Kong), 15 March 1979, p. 4.

35. Ibid. See also Paul Quinn-Judge, "A War on Two Fronts," *Far Eastern Economic Review*, 27 September 1984, pp. 56–57, and Pao-min Chang, *The Sino-Vietnamese Territorial Dispute* (New York: Praeger, 1986), pp. 82–94.

36. The current regime in Cambodia claims that its predecessor, headed by Pol Pot, killed 2.7 million individuals between 1975 and 1979 ("Cambodian Day of Hate Marks Pol Pot's Victims," *New York Times*, 21 May 1984, p. A-7). Sihanouk is quoted by Barbara Crossett in "Peking Is Making Offer to Vietnam," *New York Times*, 7 August 1986, p. A-6. See also M. Domogatskikh, "Vzgliad na rynok V'etnama," *Pravda*, 12 November 1990, p. 5.

37. "Zaiavlenie ministrov inostrannikh del SSSR i KNR," *Pravda*, 6 February 1989, p. 5; see Paul Lewis, "U.N. Backs Cambodian Role for Khmer Rouge," *New York Times*, 17 November 1989, p. A-4, on the U.N. vote; see Harriet Culley, "U.S.-Cambodian Relations," *Gist*, October 1989, pp. 1–2, for U.S. Department of State background report; see Sheryl WuDunn, "Sihanouk Backs a U.N. Trusteeship for Cambodia," *New York Times*, 3 December 1989, p. 20, on the Sihanouk plan.

38. Richard H. Solomon and John R. Bolton, "Implementing a Political Settlement in Cambodia," *Current Policy*, no. 129 (August 1990); P. Tsvetov, "Kambodzha na puti k natsional'nomu soglasiiu," *Pravda*, 17 September 1990, p. 4; Youssef M. Ibrahim, "U.S. Praises Cambodia Accord," *New York Times*, 27 November 1990, p. A-4.

39. U.N. General Assembly, Thirty-ninth Session, Agenda Item 128, "The Bomb Attack at the Martyr's Mausoleum in Rangoon," *Report on the Findings by the Enquiry Committee and the Measures Taken by the Burmese Government* A/39/456/Add.1 (27 September 1984).

40. "Zavershenie sovetsko-koreiskikh peregovorov," *Pravda*, 26 May 1984, p. 1; Daryl M. Plunk, "Moscow and Peking Vie for Influence," *Wall Street Journal*, 16 June 1986, p. 13, for details on Soviet military relations with North Korea; A. Mashin, "Severnaia Koreia: legenda i real'nost'," *Argumenty i fakty*, no. 13 (31 March-6 April 1990): 4–5, on the debt.

41. A four-day visit to P'yongyang by USSR foreign minister Shevardnadze resulted in a communiqué that lined up the North Koreans with most Soviet positions.

"Sovmestnoe sovetsko-koreiskoe kommunike," *Pravda*, 24 January 1986, p. 4; "Zavershenie vizita," *Pravda*, 28 October 1986, p. 1, for the Kim meeting with Gorbachev.

42. William M. Carley, "Study in Terror," *Wall Street Journal*, 12 October 1989, pp. A-1 and A-8.

43. S. Tikhomirov, "Vozmozhnosti bol'shie," *Pravda*, 6 July 1989, p. 4; TASS, "Itogi vizita," *Pravda*, 14 November 1989, p. 4; I. Rogachev, "Reshenie problem," *Trud*, 4 September 1990, p. 3. According to the South Korean newspaper *Donga-ilbo* (Seoul), 22 September 1990, the USSR had requested more than two billion dollars in credits and loans before extending official recognition. See also "Seoul Races to USSR," *New York Times*, 11 November 1990, section 3, p. 2.

44. Tetsuya Kataoka, "Japan's Northern Parent," *Problems of Communism* 33, no. 2 (March-April 1984): 1–16. For the buildup on Sakhalin and Kamchatka, see Bruce Rascoe, "Menace from Moscow," *Far Eastern Economic Review*, 21 August 1986, pp. 38–39. See also Japan Defense Agency, *Defense of Japan 1989* (Tokyo: Japan Times, 1990), pp. 45–49.

45. V. Korionov, "Opasny dreif," *Pravda*, 1 August 1984, p. 4, on the sanctions; V. Kel'n, "Novoe soglashenie s Iaponiei," *Vneshniaia torgovlia*, no. 6 (June 1986): 14, on the trade agreement.

46. Both speeches are cited in note 18 above. See also "Podpisan memorandum," *Pravda*, 7 September 1990, p. 4, for the preparation of Gorbachev's visit to Japan in April 1991.

47. The "revisionist" historian is Iurii Afanas'ev, condemned in the article by Igor' Latyshev, "Bezotvetstvennost'," *Pravda*, 20 October 1989, p. 7. See also Nikolai N. Solov'ev, the then Soviet ambassador to Tokyo, "On the Japanese Islands," *International Affairs* (Moscow), September 1989, pp. 111–16; "Press konferentsiia A. N. Iakovleva," *Pravda*, 17 November 1989, p. 5. See also "Vostok—ne Zapad?" *Trud*, 8 September 1990, p. 3, on results of the Shevardnadze visit to Japan; I. Latyshev, "Prozhektora dobrososedstva," *Pravda*, 21 October 1990, p. 6, on the Kuril islands; Steven Weisman, "Tokyo Prepares Soviet Aid," *New York Times*, 5 December 1990, p. 19, on relief package.

48. U.S. Congress, House, Permanent Select Committee on Intelligence, Subcommittee on Oversight, *Hearings on Soviet Active Measures*, 97th Cong., 2d sess., 1982, p. 153; "Former KGB Spy to Name Names," *Japan Times*, 12 December 1982, p. 1, and Kiyoaki Murata, "Levchenko's Legacy," same issue, p. 16.

49. Andrea Adelson, "Japanese in Soviet Chemical Deal," *New York Times*, 12 November 1988, p. 35. See also *International Herald Tribune* (Paris), 14 July 1989, p. 16, on the petroleum complex. It should be noted that the new Soviet ambassador, L. A. Chizov, is a career diplomat who speaks fluent Japanese. Suzanne Crow, "Moscow Appoints Ambassadors," *Report on the USSR* 2, no. 39 (28 September 1990): 9.

12

SOVIET-U.S. RELATIONS

President Richard M. Nixon's visit to Moscow in May 1972—the first ever by a U.S. chief executive—seemingly opened the way to improved relations between the USSR and the United States. Twelve years earlier, the invitation to President Dwight D. Eisenhower had been canceled by Nikita S. Khrushchev, ostensibly because of the shooting down of an American U-2 reconnaissance plane over Soviet territory.

Before March 1953, it would have been inconceivable for a U.S. president to visit the USSR. Stalin believed that the conflict between communism and capitalism remained irreconcilable and would ultimately lead to war. His foreign policy moves reflected this dogma. Soviet attempts to force U.S. troops out of Berlin following World War II took the form of a blockade. An uprising in Greece was staged in an attempt to secure Soviet access to the Mediterranean. The ensuing Greek civil war, however, precipitated the articulation in March 1947 of the Truman Doctrine, which promised U.S. aid to governments faced with external threats or domestic subversion. Shifting his emphasis to the Far East, Stalin successfully brought the Chinese into the Korean War as "volunteers" against the United States during the early 1950s. As mentioned in the preceding chapter, Kim Il Sung received Stalin's permission before launching the invasion of South Korea.

Three years after Stalin's death in February 1956, the twentieth CPSU congress heard Khrushchev denounce the two-camp image and the inevitability of war concept. In their place, he called for "peaceful coexistence," which would give the USSR an opportunity to catch up with and then overtake the United States in all respects. Khrushchev, however, rivaled Stalin in brinksmanship. Under his leadership the Soviet Union acted provocatively in Berlin (1958), the Congo (1960–61), and Cuba (1962). This last gambit almost resulted in a nuclear conflict between the two superpowers and probably contributed to Khrushchev's removal from power two years later.

The collective leadership that succeeded Khrushchev apparently decided to concentrate its resources on a military buildup and an arms race that it had a chance of winning, provided the United States could be convinced that the Soviet Union desired no more than "parity." Interestingly, the new leader, Leonid I. Brezhnev, told the Communist Party of the Soviet Union (CPSU) Central Committee in 1968 that military parity had already been reached. A few months later, he proclaimed the following:[1]

Our party and the Soviet government will use all means and possibilities to push back the aggressive policy of [U.S.] imperialism and to create an international situation favorable in the highest degree to the interest of building socialism and communism, and furthering national and social liberation of all nations.

As the United States withdrew from its various outposts throughout the world, the USSR would attempt to fill each political and military vacuum that emerged.

ARMS CONTROL

The objective of replacing U.S. power and influence on a global basis shaped the Soviet approach to arms negotiations. In 1946, when the United States still enjoyed a monopoly over nuclear weapons, it offered to destroy its stockpile and transfer all fissionable material to international control under a veto-free body.[2] The USSR rejected this approach and instead proposed a general treaty banning nuclear weapons. Two years later, the U.N. General Assembly endorsed the U.S. plan. The Soviets responded by exploding their first atomic bomb, then withdrew from U.N. disarmament commissions. Once again, in 1957, the West proposed a comprehensive disarmament plan that received U.N. endorsement. The USSR refused to negotiate this proposal as well.[3]

A U.S. suggestion to study a test ban in May of the following year, however, was accepted by the Soviet Union. After opening a conference on the subject that fall, both superpowers announced a moratorium on testing nuclear weapons. A ten-member disarmament group resumed negotiations in March 1960 at Geneva. The USSR and four of its East European client states offered vague proposals about "general and complete disarmament," while rejecting Western counterproposals for verification and mandatory compliance. All five communist delegates walked out of these negotiations in June, even after revised proposals had been offered by both sides. The Soviet Union then, without notification, broke the three-year moratorium and began a series of atomic tests during September 1961, which included exploding a 50-megaton device in the Arctic.

A new eighteen-member international disarmament committee convened in March 1962, although once again no agreement could be reached. It took the shock of the Cuban missile crisis in October of that year to achieve a partial nuclear test ban agreement, negotiated within a ten-day period. The resulting Treaty of Moscow, signed on 5 August 1963 by the United States and the USSR, allows only underground explosions, which subsequently were limited to 150 kilotons. Early the following year, the United States again took the initiative and proposed a nuclear nonproliferation treaty. The ouster of Khrushchev in mid-October 1964, the detonation of the first Chinese atomic bomb two days later, and tensions along the Sino-Soviet border may have been factors in the subsequent USSR decision to make limited agreements on arms control.

At the end of 1966 the United Nations endorsed a U.S.-Soviet ban on stationing weapons of mass destruction in space and during mid-1968 approved the concept of a nuclear nonproliferation treaty.[4] It was not until November 1969, however, three years after the United States had offered to discuss a strategic arms limitation treaty (SALT), that such talks finally opened with the USSR. Meanwhile, an agreement was signed in February 1970 that banned nuclear weapons from the seabed, followed a month later by ratification of the treaty on nuclear nonproliferation. Significantly, with the exception of the April 1972 convention outlawing bacteriological warfare (BW),[5] no agreement could be reached to eliminate any kind of weapon from the arsenal of the major powers until December 1987.

Even in the 1972 case, there is no evidence that the USSR had actually disposed of its BW weapons. On the contrary, an accident at a secret biological weapons installation near Sverdlovsk resulted in an anthrax epidemic that killed approximately a thousand inhabitants of the area. The Soviet government has not officially admitted this or that it has also stockpiled other bacteriological weapons.[6] In contrast, the U.S. representative to the forty-nation disarmament conference at Geneva in 1983 invited all delegates to an army base at Tooele, Utah, where U.S. chemical weapons were being destroyed. The USSR representative ridiculed the invitation, suggesting it had been made only because the United States had other things to hide, and did not accompany the foreign diplomats who made the trip to observe the destruction process.[7]

The United States resumed production of binary chemical weapons in 1987, after having unilaterally halted this process over an eighteen-year period. The USSR claimed to have done the same in April 1987, admitting a stockpile of 50,000 tons although not revealing any locations. Experts in the West contend, however, that the Soviets have in fact six times the above amount in storage, in contrast to the United States, which produced only 25,000 tons over the years. As a consequence of the Bush-Gorbachev summit, both sides agreed on 1 June 1990 that their respective stockpiles by the end of 2002 will not exceed 5,000 tons. Two months later, however, the commander of USSR chemical troops admitted that there were no destruction facilities available and that not a single Soviet legislator had volunteered his or her district for construction of such a plant.[8]

SALT I AND II NEGOTIATIONS

The strategic arms limitation talks (SALT) began with preparatory sessions at Helsinki and formally opened in April 1970 at Vienna. Soviet chief ideologist M. A. Suslov reportedly told a group of visiting Japanese socialists in Moscow that the USSR government had rejected a comprehensive agreement, proposed by the United States, on the limitation of intercontinental missile systems. He then voiced hope for a more restricted agreement.[9] A year later, Moscow sent diplomatic notes to the four other nuclear powers suggesting an exchange of views on the whole range of arms control issues. Even the French, who had expressed a readiness to participate, looked on this proposal as merely a propaganda gesture. The United States declined, seeing no reason to divert attention from the SALT negotiations, which resumed in July 1971 at Helsinki.

After twenty-three months of secret talks, two agreements were signed on 30 September 1971 in Washington, D.C., regarding measures to lessen the risk of war due to accidental or unauthorized use of nuclear weapons and to improve direct communications via satellite between the United States and the USSR.[10] Finally, during President Nixon's visit to Moscow in May 1972, a five-year interim agreement was reached that placed *upward* limits on land-based and sea-launched strategic missiles, submarines carrying the latter, as well as antiballistic missile (ABM) systems. The treaties did not reduce the number of these weapons or launchers but instead established ceilings that proved high enough to accommodate strategic programs that the Soviets already had under way.[11] (See the list of summits on table 12.1).

TABLE 12.1
SUMMIT MEETINGS, 1943–1990

No.	Date	Participants	Place
1.	28 November–1 December 1943	Roosevelt, Churchill, Stalin	Teheran
2.	4–11 February 1945	Roosevelt, Churchill, Stalin	Yalta
3.	17 July–2 August 1945	Truman, Churchill, Attlee, Stalin	Potsdam
4.	18–23 July 1955	Eisenhower, Eden, Faure, Bulganin	Geneva
5.	25–27 September 1959	Eisenhower and Khrushchev	Camp David, Md.
6.	3–4 June 1961	Kennedy and Khrushchev	Vienna
7.	23–25 June 1967	Johnson and Kosygin	Glassboro, N.J.
8.	22–29 May 1972	Nixon and Brezhnev	Moscow
9.	18–25 June 1973	Nixon and Brezhnev	Washington, D.C.
10.	27 June–3 July 1974	Nixon and Brezhnev	Moscow and Yalta
11.	23–24 November 1974	Ford and Brezhnev	Vladivostok
12.	30 July–1 August 1975	Ford and Brezhnev	Helsinki
13.	15–18 June 1979	Carter and Brezhnev	Vienna
14.	19–21 November 1985	Reagan and Gorbachev	Geneva
15.	11–12 October 1986	Reagan and Gorbachev	Reykjavik
16.	6–9 December 1987	Reagan and Gorbachev	Washington, D.C.
17.	30 May–3 June 1988	Reagan and Gorbachev	Moscow
18.	2–3 December 1989	Bush and Gorbachev	Malta
19.	30 May–2 June 1990	Bush and Gorbachev	Washington, D.C.
20.	9 September 1990	Bush and Gorbachev	Helsinki

SOURCES: *Facts on File*, vols. 3–39 passim; Gordon R. Weihmiller, *U.S.-Soviet Summits, 1955–1985* (Lanham, Md.: University Press of America, 1986); Richard F. Staar, comp., *The Summit and the Peace Process* (Stanford: Hoover Institution, 1986); for reports by the two principals, see the *New York Times*, 14 October 1986, p. 4, and *Pravda*, 15 October 1986, pp. 1–2; *Facts on File* 47, no. 2455 (11 December 1987): 905–11; *Facts on File*, 48, no. 2480 (3 June 1988): 393–96; *New York Times*, 3 and 4 December 1989; "Press-konferentsiia prezidentov SSSR i SShA," *Pravda*, 11 September 1990, pp. 1 and 4.

At the same time, a statement on "Basic Principles of Relations Between the USSR and the United States" was agreed on and published in the Soviet Union. It pledged both sides to avoid military confrontation and prevent a nuclear war. Efforts to obtain unilateral advantage, directly or indirectly, were recognized as being inconsistent with the objectives of the declaration. Renunciation of the use or threat of force was officially recognized as the prerequisite for peaceful relations between the two countries.[12]

In June of the following year, when Brezhnev came to Washington, D.C., both governments agreed not to use military force or the threat thereof when such action might escalate from conventional to thermonuclear war. A protocol to the ABM treaty, signed on 3 July 1974, reduced the number of ABM sites permitted from two to one for each side. President Gerald R. Ford's trip to Vladivostok resulted in a joint statement on 24 November 1974 enumerating provisions that should appear in a future SALT II agreement.[13]

Again, however, the Soviet Union refused to reduce its growing nuclear arsenal. Under the Vladivostok accord, the number of strategic delivery vehicles (including intercontinental bombers) held by each side could total 2,400, or some 300 more than the United States had proposed. Of these, only 1,320 might be fitted with multiple warheads. Carried over from the 1972 interim agreement were provisions for a limit of 300 (within the 2,400 total) on the largest and heaviest Soviet SS-9 and SS-18 missiles, a ban on new silo construction, and a restriction on increases in the size of existing silos to 15 percent. It was hoped that details could be agreed on by negotiators within a short period of time.

In early 1975 negotiations resumed at Geneva based on the general framework of the Vladivostok accord. Disagreement centered on two major issues: how to classify cruise missiles and whether the new Soviet Backfire bomber would be counted, like the American B-52, in the 2,400 total for strategic delivery systems. In March 1977, at President Jimmy Carter's direction, Secretary of State Cyrus Vance proposed significant reductions in the ceilings that had been agreed on at Vladivostok, with the Backfire and cruise missile issues to be deferred until SALT III. Both proposals were rejected categorically by the USSR at a press conference in Moscow,[14] the first that Foreign Minister Andrei A. Gromyko had ever given.

Negotiations continued through several channels. Carter, Vance, and Gromyko met in Washington during September 1977, and other high-level meetings were held at Moscow over the next two years. SALT delegations from the United States and the Soviet Union continued their sessions in Geneva to work out the language on those issues where agreement in principle had been reached at the ministerial level. The completed SALT II agreement was signed on 18 June 1979 by President Carter and Supreme Soviet chairman Brezhnev in Vienna.[15]

In the fall of 1979, however, the Carter administration found it did not have the necessary influence to obtain U.S. Senate approval for the SALT II treaty. The setback came when the Armed Services Committee voted ten to zero, with several abstentions, that the agreement did not contribute to the national security of the United States. The Soviet invasion of Afghanistan at the end of December 1979 further reduced the prospects for SALT II, and President Carter requested that the treaty be tabled by the Senate majority leader.[16] The new Republican administration of Ronald W. Reagan indicated that it would enter into new strategic arms reduction talks (START) with the Soviet Union before the end of its first year in office.

THE START TALKS

During a commencement address at Eureka College in early May 1982, President Reagan announced that, at the strategic arms negotiations in Geneva, the United States would propose reducing both Soviet and U.S. nuclear arsenals by one-third, so that each side would have approximately five thousand warheads.[17] This represented a new perspective, since neither SALT I nor II had provided for cutting back on stockpiles of weapons. At the same time, in its offer of a new draft treaty, the United States suggested that the number of missile launchers be reduced to 850 for each side.

The authoritative Soviet response from the new leader, Iurii V. Andropov, came toward the end of the year and called for an immediate freeze on all new strategic weapons as well as reduction over an eight-year period of intercontinental ballistic missiles (ICBMs) and submarine-launched ballistic missiles (SLBMs) to 1,800 for each side,[18] a relatively small cut in numbers. The proposed freeze was designed to stop U.S. development of the MX missile, the B-1 bomber, and the Trident II submarine. Soviet weapons systems, already in production, would not have been affected.

To place the START talks in context, during the preceding ten years, the USSR had deployed or developed twenty-one new strategic weapons systems. By contrast, the United States had discontinued the B-1 bomber; closed down its Minuteman production line, thus canceling one hundred ICBMs; deactivated ten Polaris submarines, with a total of 160 missile tubes; and begun disassembling fifty-four Titan I ICBM launchers. This unilateral reduction of strategic forces had been undertaken in good faith, with the hope that the Soviets would eventually reciprocate. No such USSR response was forthcoming. As Secretary of Defense Harold Brown told the

U.S. Congress in 1979, "We build, they build. We stop building, they build."[19]

The U.S. proposal at the START talks, offered on 25 October 1983, was based on the build-down concept. For each new fixed ICBM warhead, two old ones would be destroyed; submarine-launched missiles would be converted on a two-for-three ratio and mobile ICBMs on a one-for-one basis. The United States also indicated a willingness to reduce the number of bombers carrying air-launched cruise missiles and SLBMs on Trident II submarines in return for a reduction in number of the large Soviet SS-18 ICBMs. Moscow, reacting negatively to this approach, insisted that Andropov's offer be accepted and that both sides work from the Soviet rather than the U.S. draft treaty.

On 8 December 1983, after a thirty-five-minute meeting in Geneva, the chief Soviet negotiator, Viktor P. Karpov, told his U.S. counterpart, Ambassador Edward L. Rowny, that he could not set a date for the next round of talks because Moscow wanted to review the issues that had surfaced during the negotiations. The United States delegation expressed its regrets that round 4 would not begin early the following year. In a long interview with the CPSU daily newspaper, the new Soviet leader, Konstantin U. Chernenko, explicitly stated that strategic arms control talks would not be resumed.[20] When, for the first time, a derogatory cartoon of President Reagan appeared in *Pravda* on 15 October 1983, it could well have signaled that the USSR would break off arms control negotiations in Geneva. The Soviets did so in December.

Resumption of the previous START negotiations on 12 March 1985 coincided with the election of a new Soviet leader, Mikhail S. Gorbachev, and with an expanded framework called Nuclear and Space Talks (NST). After the fiasco at the nonsummit in Reykjavik in 1986, the United States presented another draft agreement on 8 May 1987 that codified an earlier proposal. The Soviets responded with their own draft treaty on 31 July. The two could not be reconciled. Attempts to do so at the December summit, as well as the 22–23 May 1988 meeting between Secretary of State George P. Shultz and Foreign Minister Eduard A. Shevardnadze, failed.[21]

A letter from CPSU general secretary Gorbachev to President George H. Bush, delivered by Shevardnadze in late September 1989, offered an apparent concession: It withdrew the USSR demand that both sides adhere to the Soviet interpretation of the ABM treaty, which would have barred Strategic Defense Initiative (SDI) testing and deployment for ten years. However, the letter renewed a call for both sides to agree that any violation of the above treaty would be grounds for withdrawal from future START obligations. It also repeated a suggestion that the types of SDI research and testing in violation of the ABM treaty be clarified. Finally, the two sides did not have to agree on the foregoing issue before signing and implementing a START treaty.[22]

Four weeks before the Bush-Gorbachev summit off the coast of Malta at the beginning of December 1989, the U.S. Arms Control and Disarmament Agency sponsored a seminar in suburban Maryland. One participating government official told a newspaper reporter that nothing was happening at the Geneva negotiations because there were differences over verification, cruise missiles, and SDI testing. This anonymous source suggested that if progress were made at Malta, then a START agreement could be reached by the middle of 1991, that is, after eighteen months of further talks. These reactions contrasted with the reportedly optimistic attitude of President Bush, who expressed the hope that a treaty could be signed during the May–June 1990 summit in Washington, D.C.[23] This did not happen. (See table 12.2 for U.S. and Soviet strategic offensive forces.)

THE INF TALKS

Intermediate-range nuclear force (INF) negotiations between the U.S. and the USSR commenced after the United States had offered a proposal, called the "zero option," in November 1981 to eliminate *all* such land-based missiles.[24] Two years earlier, Chancellor Helmut Schmidt of the Federal Republic of Germany initiated a request through NATO that U.S. ground-launched cruise missiles (GLCM) and Pershing II ballistic missiles be stationed in Western Europe to counter the growing number of SS-20 launchers being deployed by the USSR.

Soviet production of this triple-warhead, reloadable mobile weapons system began in 1977, at the height of détente. About 260 launchers were already operational when the INF talks started in Geneva; another 100 were added during the two years of negotiations. While this buildup continued in the East, not only USSR negotiators but also Kremlin leaders stated repeatedly between 1979 and 1986 that parity or equality existed on both sides. Note that the range of the Soviet SS-20 was three times that of the U.S. single-warhead Pershing II, of which there would only be 108 at the end of 1988 when all were in place.[25]

The U.S. zero option was rejected at Geneva. Instead, the USSR offered to reduce its missiles and bombers to three hundred, if the Americans, British, and French would cut back to the same total for all three countries and make no new deployments. Neither France nor the United Kingdom, however, were participants in the INF negotiations. Both their deterrents remained outside of NATO, and their nuclear weapons were strategic rather than intermediate in range.

TABLE 12.2
U.S.-USSR STRATEGIC OFFENSIVE FORCES, SEPTEMBER 1990

United States		*Soviet Union*	
Intercontinental Ballistic Missiles			
Minuteman II	450	SS-11	350
Minuteman III	500	SS-13	60
Peacekeeper	50	SS-17	75
Midgetman	0	SS-18	308
		SS-19	320
		SS-24 (rail-mobile)	ca. 60
		SS-25 (road-mobile)	ca. 225
Total	1,000		ca. 1,398
Submarine-launched Ballistic Missiles			
Poseidon (C-3)	192	SS-N-6	192
Trident (C-4)	384	SS-N-8	216
Trident (D-5)	48	SS-N-17	12
		SS-N-18	224
		SS-N-20[a]	120
		SS-N-23	96
Total	624		860
Bombers			
B-52G	103	TU-95 (Bear)	160
B-52H	84	TU-160 (Blackjack)	15
FB-111A	24	TU-26 (Backfire)	190
B-1B	90	TU-16 (Badger)	80
		TU-22 (Blinder)	120
Total	301		565
	(+ 37 in storage)		

Approximate Totals

Delivery vehicles	U.S.	USSR
Missiles	1,624	2,258
Bombers	301	565

[a]Includes submarine-launched ballistic missiles potentially carried on Trident and Typhoon-class nuclear-powered ballistic missile submarines (SSBNs).

SOURCES: International Institute for Strategic Studies, *The Military Balance 1990–1991* (London: IISS, Autumn 1990), pp. 17 and 34; U.S. Department of Defense, *Soviet Military Power, 1990* (Washington, D.C.: GPO, September 1990), p. 52.

After fifteen months of talks, the United States presented an interim proposal that envisaged substantial reductions in Pershing II and Ground-launched Cruise Missile (GLCM) deployments if the Soviet Union would reduce its INF missiles to equal numbers on a global basis, including those targeted against East Asian countries. Five days after it had been presented, Gromyko called the offer unacceptable.

When negotiations resumed in May 1983, the United States made a third proposal that would allow any number of missiles between 0 and 450, with parity for the two sides. The USSR refused to discuss this rather flexible approach and rejected the U.S. initiative.

Finally, on 26 October, Soviet leader Andropov proposed a reduction of SS-20 launchers aimed at Western Europe to "about 140," which he claimed would almost equal the number of British and French warheads. This was a simple, although important, misrepresentation. The 300 French and British warheads would have been matched under the Andropov proposal by 420 Soviet warheads (each SS-20 launcher carries three warheads). Moreover, the USSR offer ignored the roughly one hundred SS-20s then targeted against Asia, which—because of their mobile launchers—could be relocated to the European theater on short notice. Simultaneously, *Pravda* announced that new tactical missiles (SS-21, -22, and -23) would be placed in East Germany and Czechoslovakia[26] if the Pershing IIs and GLCMs were deployed in Western Europe.

When the first GLCMs arrived in England on 14 November 1983, the United States offered to cut its INF deployment from 572 to 420 warheads if the USSR would reduce to the same number—that is, 140 launchers multiplied by three warheads each. Senior U.S. government officials indicated that the offer was merely illustrative, that is, negotiable. TASS rejected the proposal even before it had been transmitted to the Soviet delegation at Geneva. A week before, *Pravda* had printed yet a second cartoon of President Reagan, this time showing a caricature of former Nazi propaganda minister Josef Goebbels whispering into his ear.[27]

Following a session that lasted for less than half an hour, U.S. ambassador Paul H. Nitze announced on 23 November 1983 that "the present round of negotiations has been discontinued [by the USSR] and no date has been set for a resumption." At a subsequent press conference, he declared the Soviet action to be "as unjustified as it is unfortunate."[28] Chernenko later stated repeatedly that the INF talks would be resumed only after the Pershing IIs and GLCMs had been withdrawn from Western Europe. In his interview with *Pravda* on 2 September 1984, however, he left the matter open by suggesting that, if the United States were to stop testing an antimissile system and sign an antisatellite (ASAT) treaty on Soviet terms, the USSR might resume other arms control negotiations.

In the early months of 1985, before Chernenko died, there had been an agreement to commence bilateral talks on nuclear and space weapons. These talks began in Geneva the day after Gorbachev's election as the party leader, that is, on 12 March 1985. The Soviets used the new forum to announce a series of old proposals:

1. A moratorium on SS-20 deployments until November 1985, when the Netherlands would decide whether to accept cruise missiles on its territory

2. A ban on Soviet nuclear tests from August through December, if the U.S. government were to do likewise

3. A Star Peace proposal at the United Nations for an international space organization

4. A 50 percent reduction in strategic nuclear weapons by both sides

This public relations campaign, or megaphone diplomacy, continued through the November 1985 summit in Geneva. Although no agreement could be reached on arms control except to accelerate the talks, the two sides decided to resume exchange programs, establish consulates in New York and Kiev, provide for a communications link between Tokyo and Khabarovsk for air safety, and hold another summit before the end of 1986 in the United States. It proved impossible to find common ground on regional issues or human rights.[29]

The INF talks resumed in March 1985 at Geneva. After the Soviet side rather unexpectedly dropped its insistence that the United States make concessions on SDI and that the British and French missiles be included in INF negotiations, it agreed to both on-site as well as challenge inspections. The groundwork had finally been laid for an agreement. Signed on 8 December 1987, it included these documents: (1) a seventeen-article treaty, (2) a protocol on elimination of intermediate-range missiles, (3) a protocol on inspections, and (4) a memorandum of understanding on data, that is, numbers and locations of weapons to be eliminated.[30]

Because the USSR had four times as many missiles in the banned categories as the United States, it was agreed that thirty on each side could be retained as "static display artifacts," that another one hundred were to be launched into the ocean, and that the rest be burned or crushed with inspectors present to verify implementation. By the end of 1991, all inter-mediate-range weapons should be eliminated. (Warheads and electronics, however, are not subject to destruction and can be used for weapons or other purposes.) In addition, inspections at the Votkinsk, USSR, missile plant and at the Magna, Utah, MX/Trident-II factory will continue over a thirteen-year period. Just before the INF treaty was signed, however, the Soviet Union transferred SS-23 launchers and missiles, albeit with conventional warheads, to Bulgaria, Czechoslovakia, and East Germany. As mentioned already, a USSR military spokesman claimed that these transfers had nothing to do with the agreement to destroy such weapons because they were the property of third countries not covered by the INF agreement.[31]

Interestingly enough, no one in the United States had ever seen an SS-20. The Soviets provided a poor-quality telecopy of a photograph on the morning that the treaty was signed. An original photograph did not reach Washington, D.C., until 21 December 1987, or thirteen days later. The picture appearing in U.S. newspapers suggests that the nose cone is not standard for such a missile and that the third stage is not large enough to carry three warheads. Because both launcher and canister of the SS-25 are identical to those of the SS-20, it would be a simple matter to conceal SS-20s among the SS-25s, which have an intercontinental range.[32]

EXCHANGE AGREEMENTS

With the coming of détente during the early 1970s, the exchange programs between the United States and the Soviet Union accelerated. A general understanding on contacts, exchanges, and cooperation signed in 1973 by President Nixon and Chairman Brezhnev extended these agreements to six years from the two envisioned in the original (1958) pact. Other treaties, which went into effect between 1972 and 1974, added the following areas of cooperation:[33]

1. Science and technology
2. Environmental protection
3. Medical science and public health
4. Space
5. Agriculture
6. World oceans
7. Transportation
8. Atomic energy
9. Artificial heart research and development
10. Energy
11. Housing and other construction

During the second half of the 1970s, the pattern of U.S.-USSR exchanges reflected the growing tension between the two countries. President Ford postponed several visits of Soviet delegations concerned with housing and energy (1976) to protest the presence of Cuban mercenaries in Angola. Two years later, President Carter imposed a similar ban on high-level contacts because of legal proceedings in the USSR against "refusenik" Anatolii B. Shcharanskii and other human rights violations. By early 1980, all high-visibility exchanges with the Soviet Union had been suspended in response to the invasion of Afghanistan.

These programs clearly failed to produce an expansion of civil liberties in the USSR or the free flow of ideas hoped for in the early days, especially after the August 1975 Helsinki accord. The academic side continued to be plagued with problems of nonreciprocity and lack of access, even at the height of détente. A Twentieth Century Fund study pointed out that

> Americans are still largely restricted to Moscow, Leningrad and a few other cities, while Soviets travel freely throughout the U.S. Access to archives and laboratories is frequently denied Americans, while Soviets in the U.S. have the same access to resources as Americans. The KGB still harasses Americans and especially their Soviet associates, while legitimate Soviet participants have not reported harassment by an American police agency.[34]

Although only limited progress had been achieved in the SALT II negotiations, the reverse was true for cultural relations. The sixteenth consecutive year (1979–1980) of this exchange included performing groups, graduate students as well as junior faculty, and professors. A new category of environmental problems was added, with delegations from both sides studying oceanography, pollution, management systems, social security, agricultural economics, and treatment of wastewater. Joint projects and information exchanges were envisaged under this agreement. In all, the number of people traveling in both directions expanded from about 1,500 to more than 100,000 over a twenty-year period.[35]

President Carter stopped the one-sided scientific exchanges after the December 1979 invasion of Afghanistan. Even before this White House action, Pan American Air Lines had discontinued as unprofitable its flights to Moscow. Beginning with the Moscow book fair in 1979, certain U.S. publications were regularly confiscated and did not appear on display. That same year, in Tashkent, *U.S. News & World Report's* Robin Knight and his wife were physically mistreated by KGB operatives. During the two preceding years, reporters from *Newsweek*, the *New York Times*, the *Baltimore Sun*, and the *Los Angeles Times* were harassed. Restrictions on travel that dated back to the Second World War remained in force for visitors throughout the Soviet Union.

In 1941, the USSR made it difficult for any foreign diplomat to go beyond a twenty-five-mile radius from the center of Moscow by requiring two days' advance notice for travel to areas not off-limits because of military security. These regulations continued until April 1974, when ambassadors and their families as well as interpreters and drivers no longer needed permission to visit open cities. Lower-ranking diplomats, however, still had to give a day's notice for travel outside the Moscow region, and foreign correspondents, businessmen, and tourists required a stamp on their visas to move outside the twenty-five-mile limit. In 1978, the government reduced the area banned to Americans by 4 percent, making one-fifth of all Soviet territory off-limits. Ten years later, U.S. reporters still had to give forty-eight hours notice and large areas remained closed during times of domestic turmoil.[36]

At the end of 1986 the Soviet Union had 251 diplomats at its embassy in Washington, D.C., and consulate general in San Francisco (compared to the same number of Americans in Moscow and Leningrad). This parity in numbers had been achieved after the United States expelled 25 KGB and GRU officers from the Soviet U.N. delegation in mid-October 1986—one-fourth of those who had to leave over a two-year period. The USSR retaliated by ousting five U.S. diplomats from Moscow. The United States then ordered fifty-five Soviets to leave Washington, D.C., and San Francisco, so that henceforth the numbers would be equal. The USSR next expelled five more Americans and refused to allow 260 Soviet citizens to work for U.S. personnel at either the American embassy in Moscow or its consulate general at Leningrad.[37]

Telephones are tapped and listening devices routinely concealed in the walls of foreign embassies at Moscow. A fire in the U.S. compound in August 1977 led to the discovery of sophisticated electronic bugs. Still unexplained was why the Soviets bombarded the U.S. embassy with low-intensity microwaves beginning in 1960, intensifying to eighteen microwatts after October 1975, stopping six weeks before the June 1979 Vienna summit meeting, and resuming after mid-1983 on an intermittent basis. Despite diplomatic protests by the United States, the radiation bombardment continued.[38] A new U.S. embassy, scheduled for occupation in 1988, was located near the Moscow river. The Soviet compound consists of a ten-acre complex on Mount Alto, the second-highest point in Washington, D.C., and ideal for electronic espionage.

In August 1985, U.S. security experts discovered that the $190 million U.S. embassy structure contained $250 million worth of sophisticated listening devices embedded in steel and concrete columns, beams, precast floor slabs, and even walls. Testimony before the U.S. Senate Foreign Relations Committee revealed the following: on the basis of a 1972 agreement that gave the USSR control over design and construction, the Soviets had manufactured these components away from the building site without any U.S. supervision. Secretary of State James A. Baker III, after several studies, recommended to the White House in mid-October 1989 that the embassy be razed and another one built on a different location. Apart from the costs ($300 million and forty-five months' time), the USSR government has to approve the new site.[39] Until a new U.S. embassy has been completed, however, the Soviets are not permitted to occupy their buildings on Mount Alto.

SOVIET-U.S. TRADE

What USSR leaders desire more than cultural exchanges are advantageous terms of trade with the United States. The purchase of 1.7 million metric tons of U.S. wheat in 1964 for about $100 million and the policy enunciated two years later by President Lyndon B. Johnson of building bridges were hopeful developments from the Soviet point of view. However, U.S.-USSR trade through 1970 remained in the tens of millions of dollars, as opposed to the $5 billion annual U.S. commercial exchange with Western Europe and Japan at that time. Furthermore, the U.S. Congress periodically extended the 1949 Export Control Act, which restricts export licenses and bans transfer of technology to unfriendly countries.

Another obstacle involved the 1934 Johnson Act prohibiting private credits to regimes that had not repaid debts to the United States. The Soviet Union, as successor to the tsarist and Kerensky governments, still owes the United States $837 million plus accrued interest from World War I loans. In addition, lend-lease aid to the USSR—almost $11 billion during the Second World War—had been bargained down to only $722 million. Some $48 million was repaid in 1973; since that time no payments have been remitted. During the mid-1970s, a spokesman in Moscow stated that this debt would not be settled unless the Soviet Union were granted most-favored-nation treatment. In mid-1990, "repayment of the debt depends on how the U.S. fulfills the terms of the new trade agreement," according to USSR deputy minister of foreign economic relations Iu. N. Chumakov.[40]

In 1958 Khrushchev sent a letter to President Eisenhower with a shopping list that included such desiderata as complete factories for the production of petrochemicals, chemical fertilizers, textiles, artificial fibers, food processing, and plastics—all neglected sectors of the Soviet economy. In the past, the USSR would purchase a single piece of U.S. equipment for duplication purposes, as happened in the hydroelectric, steel, automotive, petroleum-refining, and precision tool industries.[41] Once the U.S. prototype had been successfully reproduced, no further machines were imported. This practice figured strongly in the U.S. determination to ban dual-use technology exports from trade with the Soviet Union.

In a speech before the USSR Supreme Soviet, Prime Minister Aleksei N.

Kosygin had called for more trade as well as for its facilitation, that is, the lifting of U.S. restrictions on strategic goods, access to long-term U.S. credits, and most-favored-nation status for the USSR. Kosygin boasted in late 1971 that within four years the Soviet Union would surpass in economic power "the sick man of the capitalist world," that is, the United States.[42] Twelve years earlier Khrushchev predicted that the communist-ruled world would produce half the global output of industrial goods by 1965 and that the USSR would outperform as well as attain a higher living standard than the United States by 1970.

Although commercial exchanges with the United States increased more than sevenfold from 1972 through 1979 (see table 12.3), the USSR refused to accept the Trade Reform Act to which the U.S. Congress had attached certain restrictions. This proposed legislation would have granted renewable, most-favored-nation status for eighteen months instead of three years, as the Soviets wanted. Credits through the Export-Import Bank also were limited to $300 million rather than remaining open-ended. Finally both Senator Henry M. Jackson and Congressman Charles O. Vanik insisted, by way of an amendment to the law,[43] that large numbers of Jewish citizens be permitted to leave the Soviet Union as a condition for passage of the bill and that the USSR must adopt legislation guaranteeing free emigration.

Despite this setback at the government-to-government level, U.S. private enterprise came forward with proposals to help Moscow obtain credits. The Bank of America offered to establish a syndicate that would raise half a billion dollars for financing Soviet imports from the United States. The precedent for this offer was set in September 1973, when ten U.S. banks raised $180 million to build a fertilizer complex in the USSR. During 1985, the Soviets obtained approximately $4.5 billion in new credits from the West. Just three years later the banks of five countries (West Germany, the United Kingdom, Italy, Japan, and France) offered the USSR a total of $9 billion in loans over a ten-day period. For July 1990, cash and credits from the Federal Republic of Germany as well as other countries in the West to the Soviet Union totaled another $9 billion.[44]

Some of this hard currency, it was thought, would be used for the purchase of U.S. grain under a five-year agreement. The USSR fulfilled its obligation during 1983–1984 and bought 9 million tons. Over the next two years, however, it only took the full quota of corn (4 million tons) and 2.8 million tons of wheat. Just 4 percent of the wheat quota was purchased during 1985–1986, even though the U.S. government offered to subsidize a price of $11 to $13 below domestic cost. Instead, the Soviets bought 5 million tons of wheat from Australia, Austria, the West European Common Market, France, and Yugoslavia. At the same time, they signed an agreement

TABLE 12.3
SOVIET–UNITED STATES TRADE, 1968–1989
(IN MILLIONS OF DOLLARS)

Year	Turnover	Soviet Imports	Soviet Exports	Balance
1968	116.2	57.7	58.5	+ 0.8
1969	157.0	105.5	51.5	− 54.0
1970	191.0	118.7	72.3	− 46.4
1971	219.2	162.0	57.2	− 104.8
1972	637.7	542.2	95.5	− 446.7
1973	1,404.0	1,190.0	214.0	− 976.0
1974	987.0	612.0	350.0	− 262.0
1975	2,089.0	1,835.0	254.0	−1,581.0
1976	2,547.0	2,308.0	239.0	−2,581.0
1977	2,528.0	2,240.0	220.0	−2,088.0
1978	2,780.0	2,240.0	540.0	−1,700.0
1979	4,500.0	3,600.0	900.0	−2,700.0
1980	1,960.0	1,500.0	460.0	−1,040.0
1981[a]	2,410.7	2,171.1	239.6	−1,931.6
1982[a]	2,931.4	2,728.2	202.2	−2,526.0
1983[a]	2,482.6	2,050.9	431.7	−1,619.2
1984	3,884.0	3,283.9	600.1	−2,683.8
1985	2,865.4	2,422.8	442.6	−1,980.2
1986[b]	2,072.0	1,628.0	444.0	−1,183.0
1987[c]	1,894.0	1,453.0	441.0	−1,012.0
1988[d]	3,449.3	2,906.0	542.6	−2,363.4
1989[e]	5,397.6	4,555.1	842.4	−3,712.7

[a]One ruble = $0.7655
[b]One ruble = $0.704
[c]One ruble = $0.632
[d]One ruble = $0.61
[e]One ruble = $0.629 (On 1 November 1989, the USSR began using a rate of 6.26 rubles to the dollar for Western tourists buying rubles and for Soviet citizens abroad but retained the official exchange rate for most trade transactions.)

SOURCES: *Statistical Abstract of the United States, 1974* (Washington, D.C.: GPO, 1974), p. 794; *New York Times*, 10 April 1975, citing *Ekonomicheskaia gazeta; Statistical Abstract, 1975*, p. 844; U.S. Bureau of the Census, *Highlights of the U.S. Import-Export Trade*, September 1976; International Monetary Fund, *Direction of Trade: Annual, 1970–1976* (Washington, D.C.: IMF, 1977), p. 291; *New York Times*, 21 October 1977; *Wall Street Journal*, 2 March 1981, p. 20; *Vneshniaia torgovlia*, no. 3 (March 1983): insert; *Vneshniaia torglovia*, March 1984; *Christian Science Monitor*, 7 June 1984, estimate; *Central Intelligence Agency (CIA), Handbook of Economic Statistics, 1988* (Washington, D.C.: GPO, September 1988), tables 45 and 137 on pp. 75 and 163; *Vneshniaia torgovlia SSSR v 1987g.; Statisticheskii sbornik* (Moscow: Finansy i statistika, 1988), p. 14; *USSR, Country Profile 1989–90: Annual Survey of Political & Economic Background* (London), 1989, pp. 2, 37; CIA, *World Fact Book, 1989*, CPAS WF 89–001 (Washington, D.C.: GPO, May 1989), p. 274; Mathew Quinn, "U.S. Traders," *San Francisco Examiner and Chronicle*, 10 December 1989, p. D-3; USSR, *Vneshnie ekonomicheskie sviazi SSSR v 1989g: Statisticheskii sbornik* (Moscow: Finansy i statistika, 1990), p. 15.

with Canada to purchase a minimum of 25 million tons of wheat and seed grain over a five-year period.[45]

During 1987 the USSR bought from the United States 9 million tons of wheat, about 5.5 million tons of corn, and 1.4 million tons of soybeans for a total of $1.6 billion. The agreement had limited purchases to a total of 16 million tons, up from the 12 million allowed previously. American taxpayers were billed $541 million to cover the subsidies from the sale of wheat (1986–1989). A USSR source reported purchases during 1988 of 17.5 million tons of grain from the United States, exactly half of Soviet imports. That figure increased to 21.7 million tons of wheat and corn in 1989, which absorbed 65 percent of total spending for imports. A new five-year agreement (1990–1995) foresees an 11 percent increase in U.S. sales.[46]

Despite the official ban on sales of U.S. products with military potential to communist-ruled states and the January 1980 embargo on high-technology equipment, many useful items have slipped through and ended up in Moscow. Part of the problem is that other Western countries have access to technology that the Soviets cannot obtain directly from the United States. Militarily valuable items were acquired by the USSR in the following ways:

1. American companies sold more than $1.5 billion worth of equipment and technical information to build a truck factory on the Kama River near Kazan. USSR officials promised that the new vehicles would be used in the civilian economy, but they were taken instead by the Soviet army for its invasion of and ten-year war in Afghanistan (see also chapter 7).

2. The USSR purchased navigation and electronic orientation devices from Litton Industries for Aeroflot, the civilian airline. The technology that came with the equipment is now being applied to help Soviet military aircraft and navy ships track U.S. submarines.

3. Japanese and U.S. electronics, acquired purportedly for civilian air-navigation systems, were diverted to missile guidance and filled an important gap in USSR technology.

4. The Gorky auto works, operated with U.S. computers and Japanese business machines, makes not only civilian automobiles and trucks but also amphibious assault vehicles and military transporters.

5. Precision ball bearing machines (see chapter 7), purchased from Bryant Grinder Corporation of Vermont, are said by Pentagon experts to have aided the Soviets in developing their multiple independently targeted reentry vehicle for strategic missiles.[47] (See table 12.2.)

The twelfth annual meeting of the U.S.-USSR Trade and Economic Council (TEC), held in 1989 at McLean, Virginia, with about two hundred U.S. businessmen in attendance, was chaired by V. L. Malkevich from the Soviet Chamber of Commerce and Industry. Earlier, Gorbachev had called for improving commercial ties with the United States, which continued to suffer even after the February 1989 Soviet withdrawal from Afghanistan. He explained the three main obstacles to better relations as follows:

1. Lack of most-favored-nation treatment for the Soviet Union
2. Lack of foreign credits, without which serious trade could not exist
3. The existence of export controls, which had been created under the pretext that certain items, if available, would be used for USSR military production, and which hampered modernization efforts in civilian sectors[48]

A major trade agreement was signed on 3 April 1989 at the Kremlin between six privately owned U.S. companies (Archer Daniels Midland, RJR Nabisco, Chevron, Eastman Kodak, Johnson & Johnson, and Mercator), which combined make up the American Trade Consortium, and about thirty USSR government enterprises belonging to the Soviet Foreign Economic Consortium. The two sides will establish up to twenty-five joint ventures in agriculture, energy, medicine, pharmaceuticals, and oil refining.

The thirteenth TEC session, opened by Prime Minister Nikolai S. Ryzhkov, took place during 21–23 May 1990 at Moscow, where seventeen new joint ventures in the medical industry and health services were agreed on, as well as a contract between *Intourist* and two U.S. companies that will supply equipment and management for the new Slavianskii Hotel, which will be equipped with a business center and eighty-five communications links. The USSR government announced that 160 Soviet-U.S. joint enterprises had been registered, about 100 of these during the previous year. An unattributed Soviet report in mid-August 1990 stated that President Bush had ended "restrictions on entry into and movement within the United States" by businessmen from the USSR.[49]

THE U.S. ASSESSMENT

In his initial press conference, the newly inaugurated President Ronald Reagan replied to a question as follows: "They [the Soviets] reserve unto themselves the right to commit any crime, to lie, to cheat, in order to obtain that [which will further their cause]. . . . I think when you do business with them—even at a détente—you keep that in mind."[50] After less than one year of dealing with Moscow, four aspects of the USSR challenge were enumerated in mid-1983 by then U.S. Secretary of State George Shultz:

> First is the continuing Soviet quest for military superiority even in the face of mounting domestic economic difficulties. . . .
> The second disturbing development is the unconstructive Soviet involvement, direct and indirect, in unstable areas of the Third World. . . .
> Third is the unrelenting effort to impose an alien Soviet model on nominally independent Soviet clients and allies. . . .
> Fourth is Moscow's continuing practice of stretching a series of treaties and agreements to the brink of violation and beyond.[51]

The foregoing Soviet actions broke not only the spirit but the letter of the May 1972 agreement on "Basic Principles of Relations Between the USSR and the United States," mentioned earlier in this chapter.

To what extent did the Soviet Union ever intend to abide by the treaties signed with the United States? A classified report on USSR violations of arms control agreements was presented on 31 January 1984 to a closed session of the U.S. Senate by the national security adviser to President Reagan and by Central Intelligence Agency briefers. The following day, a comprehensive list of other treaties broken by the USSR appeared in the *Congressional Record*.[52] Definite or suspected violations of only five are discussed in the "President's Report to the Congress on Soviet Noncompliance with Arms Control Agreements," as follows:

1. Biological and Toxin Weapons Convention (1972)—yellow rain
2. Helsinki Final Act (1975)—nonnotification of military exercises
3. Anti-Ballistic Missile (ABM) Treaty (1972)—the Krasnoiarsk radar
4. SALT II (1979)
   a. Encryption of missile test telemetry (radio signals), impeding verification
   b. Testing a second new type of ICBM (the SS-X-25), specifically prohibited by treaty
   c. Deployment of the SS-16 type of ICBM, banned by the treaty
5. Threshold Test Ban Treaty (1974)—likely violation of 150-kiloton underground test limit.[53]

In this same report, other examples from the SALT I (1972) and the unratified SALT II (1979) treaties were listed although not immediately revealed to the public.

The nonpartisan U.S. General Advisory Committee (GAC) on Arms Control and Disarmament in 1984 submitted a more detailed, secret study to the White House that traces a pattern of USSR violations extending from 1958 to 1983. The fifteen-page unclassified summary concludes that "aspects of Soviet conduct related to about half their documentary arms control commitments were found to constitute material breaches of contracted duties." In addition to the five mentioned above, the GAC report specified seventeen other violations that covered the test moratorium (1958), the agreement on Cuba (1962), the limited test ban treaty (1963), and the outer space treaty (1967). In August 1986, U.S. Department of Defense testimony before the Foreign Affairs Committee in the House of Representatives revealed that the USSR had been jamming the U.S. surveillance satellites that monitor compliance with nuclear arms agreements.[54]

Despite the foregoing—and contrary to the impression often conveyed by Moscow—dialogue continues between the United States and the USSR in at least eight different forums. These include bilateral talks on the Special Verification Commission (INF treaty), strategic arms (START), defense and space talks (DST), nuclear testing treaty (NTT), and open skies agreement for reconnaissance flights. Multilateral negotiations include the Conventional Armed Forces in Europe (CFE) talks and the parallel Confidence- and Security-Building Measures (CSBM) negotiations, both at Vienna, and the forty-member Committee on Disarmament (CD) meeting under U.N. auspices on chemical weapons in Paris.[55]

The USSR is making a concerted effort to prevent the United States from developing antiballistic missile (ABM) capabilities that would replace the mutual assured destruction (MAD) strategy with one of assured survival. The MAD doctrine, supposedly holding both populations undefended and thus hostage, was accepted by Soviet decision makers. Pretending to disassemble, they built the most powerful military machine in history. Rather than disarming, the USSR has modernized its weapons, making its armed forces even more powerful. Strategic defense alone includes one hundred ABM interceptors around Moscow, some eight thousand surface-to-air missile launchers throughout the country, and about 2,200 air defense fighter planes.[56]

An example of the Soviet quest for power was observed at the Reykjavik summit in mid-October 1986. Gorbachev unexpectedly presented a paper outlining Soviet proposals for tentative agreements on reductions of ballistic missiles and intermediate-range nuclear forces as well as an ultimate test ban. All this depended on the United States' agreeing to confine SDI within the laboratory for a ten-year period. President Reagan refused to compromise basic U.S. national security interests, and the meeting ended.[57]

In fact, an estimated ten thousand scientists have been testing a Soviet version of SDI for many years. Lasers for antimissile weapons were fired as early as 1982 at a manned USSR spacecraft. As discussed in chapter 6, work on particle beam and kinetic energy weapons has gone far beyond the laboratory. Recent activities include expansion of the world's only ABM defense around Moscow, construction of a huge ballistic missile detection and tracking radar at Krasnoiarsk (identified by the U.S. in 1983, halted by the USSR in 1989, though yet to be dismantled), maintenance of the world's only antisatellite system, modernization of strategic air defense, and improvement of passive defenses.[58]

In a report to the USSR Supreme Soviet on 23 October 1989, Foreign Minister Shevardnadze admitted that the Krasnoiarsk radar had been built in violation of the 1972 ABM treaty with the United States:

> It took us four years to get to the bottom of it. We were charged with violation of the ABM Treaty because of the [Krasnoiarsk] station. . . . And all the while, there stood the station, the size of an Egyptian pyramid, representing, to put it bluntly, a violation of the ABM Treaty.[59]

In view of the foregoing admission of violating a major arms control treaty for at least ten years, about which the *Wall Street Journal* has published some twenty editorials since 20 November 1984, perhaps the Soviets will next admit that they have been breaking other treaties and conventions (for example, the one on biological weapons).[60] This would indeed represent a breakthrough for military *glasnost'*.

In conclusion, what can we say about the new pragmatism in USSR foreign policy vis-à-vis the United States? Despite the Soviet economy's stagnation over the past decade, Western intelligence assessed the increase in Soviet military spending during 1986 through 1988 at 3 percent a year.[61] (See table 12.4.) This certainly involved the exploitation of other imperial assets: the sale of raw materials and weapons for hard currency, perhaps a reduction in subsidies to Third World friends, and some concessions regarding human rights of USSR citizens in return for most-favored nation status in trade relations with the United States. It all began at the Malta summit where in a period of three days the Soviet Union "ceased to be regarded as an enemy by the . . . president of the most powerful democracy in the world."[62]

The honeymoon continued in Washington, D.C., and other parts of the United States between 31 May and 4 June 1990. Gorbachev met with journalists, representatives of the U.S. intelligentsia, congressional leaders, business people in the Middle West, and students and faculty of Stanford University. At the White House, he signed a plethora of agreements, protocols, joint declarations, and memoranda.[63]

TABLE 12.4
MILITARY PRODUCTION: USSR AND UNITED STATES, 1988–1989

Equipment Type	USSR		UNITED STATES	
	1988	1989	1988	1989
Missiles				
Intercontinental ballistic	150	140	12	9
Submarine-launched ballistic	100	100	0	21
Short-range ballistic	650	700	0	0
Long-range submarine-launched cruise	200	200	200	420
Short-range submarine-launched cruise	1,100	1,100	380	180
Aircraft				
Bombers	45	40	22	0
Fighters/fighter-bombers	700	625	550	470
Antisubmarine warfare fixed-wing aircraft	5	5	5	10
Airborne warning and control systems	5	5	5	2
Military helicopters	400	400	340	280
Naval ships				
Ballistic missile submarines	1	2	1	1
General-purpose attack submarines	7	7	3	5
Aircraft carriers	0	1	0	0
Cruisers	1	1	3	3
Destroyers	3	3	0	0
Frigates and corvettes	5	7	0	1

SOURCE: U.S. Department of Defense, *Soviet Military Power, 1990* (Washington, D.C.: GPO, September 1990), p. 39.

After the 9 September 1990 summit at Helsinki, the world learned from Gorbachev at the ensuing press conference that President Bush had reversed a long-standing U.S. policy of excluding the USSR from Middle East talks. Gorbachev added that no single country can provide world leadership alone,[64] the implication being that the Soviet Union now claims coequal status with the United States in settling international disputes—a remarkable achievement for a man whose popularity dropped from 36 percent to just 14 percent within the year ending in October 1990, based on public opinion polls published in Moscow.[65] That same month Gorbachev won the Nobel Peace Prize, heralding the "new era" in relations between the U.S. and the USSR. He had reached the pinnacle of success—holding one of the most prestigious awards the world can bestow—only to witness from these heights the disintegration of his own empire.

Neither the declining popular support for Gorbachev nor the disarray in the Soviet domestic economy seemed to deter the United States from voicing complete support for a *perestroika* that has failed. President Bush lifted a fifteen-year ban in mid-December 1990, when he approved one billion dollars in federally guaranteed loans to the USSR. He also announced the dates for the next summit in Moscow, 11–13 February 1991.

NOTES

1. "Rech' tovarishcha L. I. Brezhneva," *Pravda*, 4 July 1968, pp. 1–2. This speech was made at a Kremlin meeting in honor of Soviet-Hungarian friendship.
2. The Baruch plan, after Bernard Baruch, the U.S. representative to the U.N. Atomic Energy Commission, is discussed in U.S. Arms Control and Disarmament Agency (ACDA), *Arms Control and Disarmament Agreements*, 5th ed. (Washington, D.C.: GPO, 1982), pp. 5–6.

   Franklin Lindsay, who accompanied Baruch to a private meeting with his counterpart, Arkady A. Sobolev, recalls that Sobolev listened patiently to a preview of the U.S. proposal and then replied: "The Soviet Union doesn't want equality. The Soviet Union wants complete freedom to pursue its own aims as it sees fit." Quoted by Flora Lewis in "Unthinking Doomsday," *New York Times*, 4 April 1983, p. A-19.
3. For the official USSR view of this period, see G. Trofimenko, "Na sterzhnevom napravlenii," *Mirovaia ekonomika i mezhdunarodnye otnosheniia*, no. 2 (1975): 3–11.
4. It was signed on 1 July 1968, although not ratified by the USSR or the United States until 5 March 1970. Text in ACDA, *Arms Control and Disarmament Agreements*, 6th ed. (Washington, D.C.: GPO, 1990), pp. 89–106.
5. Ibid. pp. 107–17, 89–106, 129–41, contains background information, texts, and signatories to these treaties.
6. U.S. Congress, House Permanent Select Committee on Intelligence, Subcommittee on Oversight, *Hearing on the Sverdlovsk Incident: Soviet Compliance with the Biological Weapons Convention?* 96th Cong., 2d sess. (1980), p. 12.

   The United States has announced it would destroy live smallpox virus stockpiles and urged the USSR, which has the only other repository of such samples, to do the same. Reuters dispatch, 9 May 1990, cited by *Chemical Weapons Convention Bulletin*, no. 8 (June 1990): 17.
7. "U.S. Offers Look at Base for Chemical Weapons," *New York Times*, 24 August 1983, p. A-5. The USSR also refused to send invited experts to observe an underground nuclear test in Nevada, according to Reuters, "U.S. Conducts Test," *New York Times*, 23 March 1986, pp. 1 and 8.
8. The text of this agreement, signed by Presidents Bush and Gorbachev, appeared in *Chemical Weapons Convention Bulletin*, no. 8 (June 1990): 19–22.

The sole USSR destruction facility at Chapaevsk was closed in the summer of 1989 because of complaints by local residents; it has since been converted into a training center for the development of technological processes in inert environments. A. Gorokhov, "Zavod postroen, no," *Pravda* 22 August 1990, p. 2.

9. Broadcast over Vienna radio, 17 July 1970; "Suslov Predicts Recess in Vienna SALT Sessions," *Foreign Broadcast Information Service (FBIS)-Soviet Union* 138, vol. 3 (17 July 1970): F-1.

10. Texts in ACDA, *Arms Control and Disarmament Agreements* (1990), pp. 118–21 and 122–28.

11. Ibid., pp. 157–66 and 169–76, provides complete texts. On the ABM treaty, see Maj. Gen. V. Kuklev, "Vopros postavlen ne sluchaino," *Krasnaia zvezda*, 7 August 1990, p. 3.

12. See "Osnovy vzaimootnoshenii mezhdu SSSR i SShA," *Pravda*, 30 May 1972, p. 1, for the declaration; *U.S. Department of State, Bulletin* 66, no. 1722 (26 June 1972): 898–99, for the English version.

13. See ACDA, *Arms Control and Disarmament Agreements* (1990), pp. 181–83, for the protocol; Leslie H. Gelb, "Vladivostok Pact: How It Was Reached," *New York Times*, 3 December 1974, pp. 1 and 26, for the communiqué.

14. See Christopher S. Wren, "In Moscow Harsh Words," *New York Times*, 1 April 1977, pp. A-1 and A-8, on the press conference.

15. The treaty, protocol, memorandum, and joint statement on subsequent negotiations are in ACDA, *Arms Control and Disarmament Agreements* (1990), pp. 261–300.

16. Ibid., p. 263.

17. U.S. Department of State, *Realism, Strength, Negotiations: Key Foreign Policy Statements of the Reagan Administration* (Washington, D.C.: GPO, May 1984), pp. 27–30, gives the speech.

18. "Shest'desiat let SSSR: Doklad general'nogo sekretaria TsK KPSS tov. Iu. V. Andropova," *Pravda*, 22 December 1982, pp. 1–2.

19. Quoted in Richard F. Staar, ed., *Arms Control: Myth Versus Reality* (Stanford: Hoover Institution Press, 1988), p. 79.

20. "Otvety K. U. Chernenko na voprosy gazety," *Pravda*, 9 April 1984, p. 1. Five months later, he told the same newspaper that "Washington had broken off the negotiations" in obvious disregard of the truth. See *Pravda*, 2 September 1984, p. 1.

21. For a chronology, see ACDA, *Arms Control Update*, no. 6 (May 1988): 4–5. At Reykjavik, the new Soviet leader demanded that the Strategic Defense Initiative in effect be discontinued as the price for a START agreement.

22. R. Jeffrey Smith, "Reassessment of Arms Offer," *International Herald Tribune* (Paris), 2 October 1989, pp. 1 and 4.

23. Michael R. Gordon, "Official Cautious," *New York Times*, 8 November 1989, p. A-13. See also Lt. Gen. M. Vinogradov and Maj. Gen. V. Belous, "Dogovor po SNV i nasha bezopasnost'," *Sovetskaia Rossiia*, 23 August 1990, p. 3.

24. U.S. Department of State, *Realism, Strength, Negotiations*, pp. 23–27, gives the

text of President Reagan's address before the National Press Club in Washington, D.C.

25. Walter Pincus, "Pause Set in Missile Schedule," *Washington Post*, 21 November 1983, pp. A-1 and A-12.

26. A report from NATO in Brussels six weeks earlier revealed that the USSR was deploying SS-21s in East-Central Europe. See the *Baltimore Sun*, 15 September 1983.

27. Cartoon subtitle reads "Opytnyi anti-sovetchik," *Pravda*, 5 November 1983, p. 5.

28. "Soviets Discontinue Talks on Medium-range Missiles," *Washington Post*, 24 November 1983, pp. A-1, A-13, and A-18. Paul H. Nitze, "The Word and the Woods," *Wall Street Journal*, 23 March 1984, discusses Soviet duplicity; see also his article, "The Walk in the Woods," *International Affairs*, no. 12 (December 1989): 109–21, published in Moscow.

29. See "Introduction" by Richard F. Staar, comp., *The Summit and the Peace Process* (Stanford: Hoover Institution Press, 1986), pp. vii-x.

30. U.S. Department of State, *Treaty between the United States of America and the Union of Soviet Socialist Republics on the Elimination of Their Intermediate-range and Shorter-range Missiles* (Washington, D.C.: GPO, December 1987).

31. Col. Vadim Solovev over Moscow radio, 31 March 1990; "INF Treaty Not Violated by SS-23s," *FBIS-Soviet Union* 90–063 (2 April 1990): 7.

32. Michael Gordon, "U.S. Receives Photograph," *New York Times*, 22 December 1987, p. 4; "The INF Treaty," *National Security Record*, no. 109 (January 1988): 4.

   Note also the official justification for the INF treaty at the CPSU congress in "Otvety tov. Zaikova L. N.," *Izvestiia TsK KPSS*, no. 8 (August 1990): 120.

33. U.S. Department of State, Office of the Legal Adviser, *Treaties in Force* (Washington, D.C.: GPO, 1980), pp. 214–17; U.S. Department of State, "U.S.-USSR Exchanges," *Gist*, August 1984, p. 1.

34. Herbert Kupferberg, *The Raised Curtain* (New York: Twentieth Century Fund, 1977), pp. 86–87.

35. From 516 USSR and 950 U.S. citizens in 1958, the numbers grew to nearly 16,600 Soviets and 91,800 Americans, including tourists, in 1977. See V. Voichenko, "Inostrannyi turizm v SSSR—50 let razvitiia," *Vneshniaia torgovlia*, no. 9 (September 1978): 36.

36. Celestine Bohlen, "Newspaper Reporting from Moscow," *Meeting Report* (Washington, D.C.: Kennan Institute at the Wilson Center, 9 May 1988).

37. See "Moscow Expels 5," *New York Times*, 23 October 1986, pp. A-1 and A-12, for a chronology of these retaliatory measures.

38. Serge Schmemann, "Soviet Radiation Is Detected Anew," *New York Times*, 11 November 1983, p. A-9.

39. Note the comments by Victor Sheimov, a former KGB major, and George Carver, a retired deputy for national intelligence at the Central Intelligence Agency, in the article by Jonas Bernstein, "Bugged but Empty Embassy," *Insight*, 9 July 1990, pp. 28–29. A Soviet source denies the charges and accuses

the United States of exactly the same kind of "bugging" on Mount Alto. See I. Belov, "Lomat'—ne stroit'?" *Trud*, 15 June 1990, p. 1.

40. Clyde Farnsworth, "Soviets, in Bid to Borrow, Establish Bank in U.S." *New York Times*, 1 November 1989, p. A-18; F. Ivanov, "Budem platit' po lendlizu," *Izvestiia*, 29 June 1990, p. 4. See also S. V., "Debts Again," *Moscow News*, no. 31 (12–19 August 1990): 13, and Bradford Trebach, "How About Paying Debt to U.S.?" *New York Times*, 15 November 1990, p. A-20.

41. Anthony C. Sutton, *Western Technology and Soviet Economic Development, 1945 to 1965*, vol. 3 (Stanford: Hoover Institution Press, 1973), p. 327.

42. Speech to the USSR Supreme Soviet by A. N. Kosygin, "O gosudarstvennom piatiletnem plane razvitiia," *Pravda*, 25 November 1971, part II, p. 2, and part VI, p. 4.

43. *Congressional Quarterly: Weekly Report* 31, no. 20 (19 May 1973): 1218. The Jackson-Vanik amendment was attached to HR 10710 and appears in *Congressional Quarterly: Weekly Report* 32, no. 49 (7 December 1974): 3266.

   From 51,320 Jewish emigrants in 1979, the number dropped to 1,140 during calendar year 1985 and increased to 132,400 from January through the end of July 1990. Moscow radio, 20 August 1990; *FBIS-Soviet Union* 90–168 (29 August 1990): 40.

44. Roger W. Robinson, Jr., "Financing the Soviet Empire," *National Security Record*, no. 90 (April 1986), pp. 1–3; Michael Farr, "Bonn Sets Credit Line for Soviets," *New York Times*, 12 October 1988, pp. D-1 and D-9; Bill Keller, "Soviet Call to West: Money for Rebuilding," *New York Times*, 29 October 1988, pp. A-1 and A-3; Associated Press dispatch in *New York Times*, 27 July 1990, p. C-13.

45. Oswald Johnson, "Soviets Break Commitment," *Los Angeles Times*, 1 October 1986, part IV, p. 1.

46. Interview with then ambassador to the United States, Iu. V. Dubinin, by Iu. Popov, "SSSR-SShA: problemy i perspektivy," *Pravitel'stvennyi vestnik*, no. 19 (May 1990): 11; "Soglashenie mezhdu SSSR i SShA o postavkakh zerna," *Vestnik MID SSSR*, no. 14 (31 July 1990): 34–36; V. Nefedov, "Valiuta za zerno: svoim ili chuzhim?" *Argumenty i fakty*, no. 26 (30 June–6 July 1990): 1 and 7. See also Scott Kilman, "Soviet Buying U.S. Farm Products Shows Old Unpredictability," *Wall Street Journal*, 8 October 1990, p. A-12.

47. U.S. Department of Defense, *Soviet Acquisition of Militarily Significant Western Technology: An Update* (Washington, D.C.: GPO, September 1985). See also U.S. General Accounting Office, *Export Controls: U.S. Policies and Procedures Regarding the Soviet Union*, NSIAD-90-185FS (Washington, D.C.: GPO, May 1990).

48. Quoted in the *Journal of the U.S.-USSR Trade and Economic Council* 14, no. 2 (1989): 2.

49. A summary appeared in "XIII sobranie Amerikansko-Sovetskogo torgovoekonomicheskogo soveta (ASTES)," *Vestnik MID SSSR*, no. 11 (15 June 1990): 10–14. For the Bush decision, see "Priniato reshenie," *Izvestiia*, 14 August

1990, p. 7. See also V. Sisnev, "Im nuzhny 'mozgi' i 'zolotye ruki,' " *Trud*, 29 September 1990, p. 3.

50. Transcript in Steven R. Weisman, "Reagan Denounces Soviet Intentions," *New York Times*, 30 January 1981, pp. A-1 and A-11.

51. Statement by the U.S. secretary of state before the Foreign Relations Committee of the U.S. Senate, "U.S.-Soviet Relations in the Context of U.S. Foreign Policy," *Current Policy*, no. 492 (15 June 1983): 2.

52. "Soviet Political Treaties and Violations: Chronology," *Congressional Record-Senate* 130, no. 8 (1 February 1984): S 623-S 633, 98th Cong., 2d sess.; "Soviet Violations of Arms Control Agreements," *Congressional Record-Senate* 130, no. 8 (1 February 1984): S 652–54; "The President's Unclassified Report to the Congress on Soviet Noncompliance with Arms Control Agreements," *Press Release* (White House, 1 February 1985).

53. *Congressional Record*, "Soviet Violations," pp. S 648–49. See also U.S. Congress, Senate Committee on Armed Services, *Soviet Treaty Violations*, 99th Congr., 1st sess. (Washington, D.C.: GPO, 1985).

54. U.S. General Advisory Committee on Arms Control and Disarmament, *A Quarter Century of Soviet Compliance Practices under Arms Control Commitments, 1958–1983; Summary* (Washington, D.C.: GPO, 10 October 1984), p. 1; Wayne Biddle, "Study Says Soviets Broke Arms Pacts," *New York Times*, 12 September 1984, p. A-13; Bernard Gwertzman, "U.S. Holds up Study Accusing Soviets on Arms," *New York Times*, 14 September 1984, pp. A-1 and A-4; U.S. Arms Control and Disarmament Agency, *Soviet Noncompliance* (Washington, D.C.: GPO, 1 February 1986); U.S. Department of State, "Interim Restraint: U.S. and Soviet Force Projections," *Special Report*, no. 157 (5 August 1986), for the presidential letter and unclassified report to the U.S. Congress.

55. Central Intelligence Agency, *Soviet Arms Controllers: A Reference Aid*, LDA 89–14404 (Washington, D.C.: Directorate of Intelligence, September 1989), gives short biographical sketches and photographs of thirteen Moscow-based advisers as well as eight key negotiators. See also interview with V. P. Karpov, "Mezhdunarodnaia konferentsiia po 'otkrytomu nebu'," *Vestnik MID SSSR*, no. 6 (31 March 1990): 28–30, on the "open skies" conference that failed to achieve agreement.

56. Edward L. Rowny, "National Power and National Interests," *ROA National Security Report* 8, no. 7 (July 1990): 11.

57. Compare the two men's television speeches after the "nonsummit" (for President Reagan) in "Remarks by Reagan after Reykjavik Talks," *New York Times*, 14 October 1986, p. A-10; for President Gorbachev in "Vystuplenie general-'nogo sekretaria TsK KPSS M.S. Gorbacheva po sovetskomu televideniiu," *Pravda*, 15 October 1986, pp. 1–2. See also text of U.S. counteroffers in Bernard Gwertzman, "Shultz Details Reagan's Arms Bid," *New York Times*, 18 October 1986, pp. 1 and 5.

58. U.S. Department of Defense, *Soviet Military Power, 1990* (Washington, D.C.: GPO, September 1990), pp. 56–63.

59. E. A. Shevardnadze, "Vneshniaia politika i perestroika," *Pravda*, 24 October

1989, p. 6. On Krasnoiarsk, see also Maj. Gen. Boris Surikov (Soviet Air Force, retired), "Will the World Be More Secure?" *Literary Gazette International,* March 1990, p. 14, who admits that the Krasnoiarsk radar was designed in 1979; Moscow radio, 9 October 1990; *FBIS-Soviet Union* 90–196 (10 October 1990): 1, reported that dismantling of the installation had begun. See also N. Paniukov, "Kuvaldoi po sekretnomu ob"ekty," *Rabochaia tribuna,* 9 October 1990, p. 3.

60. See the article by Natalia Zenova, "Voennaia taina," *Literaturnaia gazeta,* 22 August 1990, p. 12, based on interviews with physicians and others concerning the April 1979 deaths from an accident at the nineteenth military installation (bacteriological warfare) near Sverdlovsk.

61. U.S. Congress, Joint Economic Committee, *Hearings* (Washington, D.C.: GPO, 1989), part 13, pp. 111–12.

62. Editorial, "Un pays normal," *Le Monde,* 5 December 1989, p. 1.

63. For a listing of these documents, see "Perechen' sovetsko-amerikanskikh dokumentov," *Vestnik MID SSSR,* no. 14 (31 July 1990): 26–34; no. 15 (15 August 1990), pp. 21–33.

64. "Press-konferentsiia prezidentov SSSR i SShA," *Pravda,* 11 September 1990, p. 4. "Transcript of Bush-Gorbachev News Conference," *New York Times,* 10 September 1990, pp. A-6 and A-7.

65. Tat'iana Zaslavskaia, "Eto kakoe-to nervnoe istoshchenie," *Komsomol'skaia pravda,* 30 October 1990, p. 2.

SELECT BIBLIOGRAPHY

Abarenkov, V. P., and Krasulin, B. P. *Razoruzhenie: spravochnik.* Moscow: Mezhdunarodnye otnosheniia, 1988. 336 pp.

Abrasimov, P. A. *Na diplomaticheskom postu.* Moscow: Mezhdunarodnye otnosheniia, 1987. 256 pp.

Adamishin, A. L., ed. *SSSR i mezhdunarodnoe sotrudnichestvo v oblasti prav cheloveka: Dokumenty i materialy.* Moscow: Mezhdunarodnye otnosheniia, 1989. 709 pp.

Adomeit, Hannes; Höhmann, Hans-Hermann; and Wagenlehner, Günther. *Die Sowjetunion unter Gorbatschow.* Stuttgart: Kohlhammer Verlag, 1990. 412 pp.

Afanas'ev, Iu. N. *Inogo ne dano: Sud'by perestroiki vgliadyvaias' v proshloe; Vozvrashchenie k budushchemu.* Moscow: Progress, 1988. 675 pp.

Agafonov, V. P., and Khalipov, V. F. *Sovremennaia epokha i mirovoi revoliutsionnyi protsess.* Moscow: Vysshaia shkola, 1988. 256 pp.

Agranovskaya, Maria, et al., comps. *USSR Yearbook '90.* Moscow: Novosti, 1990. 352 pp.

Aksiutin, Iu. V., comp. *Nikita Sergeevich Khrushchev: materialy k biografii.* Moscow: Politizdat, 1989. 366 pp.

Albano, Antonio. *Report of State Prosecutor's Office.* Translation from the Italian. Rome: Appeals Court, 28 March 1984. 76 pp.

Aleksandrov, A. M., et al., eds. *Radi mira na zemle: Sovetskaia programma mira dlia 80-kh godov v deistvii.* Moscow: Politizdat, 1983. 496 pp.

Alexander, Yonah, and Sinai, Joshua. *Terrorism: The PLO Connection.* New York: Crane Russak, 1989. 259 pp.

Alimov, Yuri. *The Rise and Growth of the Non-aligned Movement.* Moscow: Progress Publishers, 1987. 230 pp.

Amirov, O. A.; Astaf'ev, A. R.; et al. *Politika sily ili sila razuma?: Gonka vooruzhenii i mezhdunarodnye otnosheniia.* Moscow: Politizdat, 1989. 411 pp.

Anders, Karl. *Mord auf Befehl.* Tübingen/Neckar: Schlichtenmayer, 1963. 111 pp.

Andrew, Christopher, and Gordievsky, Oleg. *K.G.B.: The Inside Story.* London: Harper Collins, 1990. 776 pp.

Andropov, Iu. V. *Izbrannye rechi i stat'i.* 2d ed. Moscow: Politizdat, 1983. 320 pp.

Anufriev, E. A.; Bestuzhev-Lada, I. V.; et al., eds. *Nauchnyi kommunizm: Uchebnoe posobie dlia vuzov.* Moscow: Politizdat, 1988. 463 pp.

Aref'eva, E. B. *Razvivaiushchiesia strany Azii v mirovoi promyshlennosti.* Moscow: Nauka, 1989. 222 pp.

Artsibasov, I. N., and Egorov, S. A. *Vooruzhennyi konflikt: pravo, politika, diplomatiia.* Moscow: Mezhdunarodnye otnosheniia, 1989. 248 pp.

Arzumanov, N. A., ed. *Ofitsery granitsy.* Moscow: Sovetskaia Rossiia, 1988. 288 pp.

Ashby, Timothy. *The Bear in the Back Yard.* Lexington, Mass.: Lexington Books, 1987. 241 pp.

Baranovskii, V. G. *Zapadnaia Evropa: Voenno-politicheskaia integratsiia.* Moscow: Mezhdunarodnye otnosheniia, 1988. 200 pp.

Barecki, Józef, ed. *Rocznik polityczny i gospodarczy, 1981–1983.* Warsaw: PWE, 1983. 464 pp.

Barron, John. *KGB Today: The Hidden Hand.* New York: Reader's Digest Press, 1983. 489 pp.

Beglov, S. I. *Vneshnepoliticheskaia propaganda: Ocherk teorii i praktiki.* 2d rev. ed. Moscow: Vysshaia shkola, 1984. 375 pp.

Bekarevich, A. D., et al. *Sandinistskaia revoliutsiia: Opyt i problemy.* Moscow: Nauka, 1989. 208 pp.

Bektimirova, N. N.; Dement'ev, Iu. P.; and Kobelev, E. V. *Noveishaia istoriia Kampuchii.* Moscow: Nauka, 1989. 228 pp.

Bel'chuk, A. I., and Begma, Iu. S., eds. *Trudiashchiesia i militarizm.* Moscow: Nauka, 1988. 192 pp.

Belousov, S. R. *Kitaiskaia versiia gosudarstvennogo sotsializma.* Moscow: Nauka, 1989. 222 pp.

Berkutov, S. N., ed. *Vooruzhennye sily osnovnykh kapitalisticheskikh gosudarstv.* Moscow: Voennoe izdatel'stvo, 1988. 319 pp.

Bessmertnykh, A. A., et al., eds. *Za mir i bezopasnost': Dokumenty vneshnei politiki SSSR, 1971 g.* 2 vols. Moscow: Politizdat, 1989. 413 pp.

Binnendijk, Hans, ed. *National Negotiating Styles.* Washington, D.C.: Foreign Service Institute, 1987. 147 pp.

Bittman, Ladislav. *The KGB and Soviet Disinformation: An Insider's View.* Washington, D.C.: Pergamon-Brassey's, 1985. 227 pp.

Bobin, A. E., et al., eds. *Razvivaiushchiesia strany v sovremennom mire: Puti revoliutsionnogo protsessa.* Moscow: Nauka, 1986. 406 pp.

Bobrovnikov, A. V., et al. *Latinskaia Amerika v tsifrakh: Spravochnik.* Moscow: Nauka, 1989. 203 pp.

Bogomolov, O. T., chief ed. *Sotsialisticheskoe sodruzhestvo i problemy otnoshenii Vostok-Zapad v 80-e gody.* Moscow: Politizdat, 1987. 296 pp.

Boiko, V. V., and Markin, L. V. *Ustnaia propaganda: Kriterii, pokazateli, usloviia effektivnosti.* Leningrad: Lenizdat, 1983. 198 pp.

Borcke, Astrid von. *Unsichtbare Weltmacht KGB: Steht sie hinter Gorbatschows Perestroika?* Neuhausen-Stuttgart: Hänssler-Verlag, 1989. 388 pp.

Borisov, V. V. *Militarizm i nauka.* Moscow: Voenizdat, 1988. 191 pp.

Bovin, Aleksandr E. *Mirnoe sosushchestvovanie: Istoriia, teoriia, politika.* Moscow: Mezhdunarodnye otnosheniia, 1988. 136 pp.

Brossat, Alain. *Agents de Moscou: le Stalinisme et son Ombre.* Paris: Editions Gallimard, 1988. 313 pp.

Brutents, K. N., et al. *Sotsialisticheskaia orientatsiia osvobodivshikhsia stran.* Moscow: Prosveshchenie, 1984. 310 pp.

Brzezinski, Zbigniew. *The Grand Failure: The Birth and Death of Communism in the Twentieth Century.* New York: Macmillan, 1990. 278 pp.

Bugajski, Janusz, and Pollack, Maxine. *East European Fault Lines: Dissent, Opposition, and Social Activism.* Boulder, Colo: Westview Press, 1989. 333 pp.

Burgess, William H., III, ed. *Inside Spetsnaz: Soviet Special Operations, a Critical Analysis.* Novato, Calif.: Presidio Press, 1990. 308 pp.

Butenko, A. P. *Sotsializm kak mirovaia sistema.* Moscow: Politizdat, 1984. 320 pp.

Bykov, O. N., and Bugrov, E. V., chief eds. *Al'ians mecha i biznesa: Voenno-promyshlennye kompleksy imperialisticheskikh gosudarstv.* Moscow: Mysl', 1988. 300 pp.

Chang, Pao-min. *The Sino-Vietnamese Territorial Dispute.* New York: Praeger, 1986. 119 pp.

Chernenko, K. U. *Izbrannye rechi i stat'i.* 2d rev. ed. Moscow: Politizdat, 1984. 670 pp.

Chernikov, I. F., chief ed. *Osvobodivshiesia strany: osobennosti sotsial'no-ekonomicheskogo i politicheskogo razvitiia.* Kiev: Naukova dymka, 1988. 244 pp.

Chernyshev, I. A. *Sovetsko-frantsuzskie otnosheniia i problemy evropeiskoi bezopasnosti.* Moscow: Nauka, 1990. 336 pp.

Chernysheva, O. V., chief ed. *Severnaia Evropa: problemy noveishei istorii.* Moscow: Nauka, 1988. 232 pp.

Chicherov, A. I., comp. *Problemy mira i bezopasnosti v Azii.* Moscow: Nauka, 1987. 287 pp.

Chkhikvadze, V. M., chief ed. *Human Rights: Yearbook.* Moscow: Nauka, 1989. 192 pp.

Collins, Joseph J. *The Soviet Invasion of Afghanistan: A Study in the Use of Force in Soviet Foreign Policy.* Lexington, Mass.: D.C. Heath and Company, 1986. 197 pp.

Conquest, Robert. *The Last Empire: Nationality and the Soviet Future.* Stanford: Hoover Institution Press, 1986. 406 pp.

————. *The Great Terror: A Reassessment.* New York: Oxford University Press, 1990. 570 pp.

Conte, Francis, and Martres, Jean-Louis, eds. *L'Union Soviétique dans les relations internationales.* Paris: Economica S.A.R.L. Editions, 1982. 548 pp.

Dailey, Brian D., and Parker, Patrick J., eds., *Soviet Strategic Deception.* Lexington, Mass.: Lexington Books, 1987. 539 pp.

Danilov, V. I., chief ed. *Turtsiia: istoriia i sovremennost'.* Moscow: Nauka, 1988. 263 pp.

Dash, Barbara L. *A Defector Reports: The Institute of the USA and Canada.* Falls Church, Va.: Delphic Associates, 1982. 229 pp.

Davydov, V. F. *Bez"iadernye zony i mezhdunarodnaia bezopasnost'.* Moscow: Mezhdunarodnye otnosheniia, 1988. 190 pp.

Denisov, V. I. *Koreiskaia problema: puti uregulirovaniia.* Moscow: Mezhdunarodnye otnosheniia, 1988. 144 pp.

Diligenskii, G. G. *Zapadnaia Evropa 80-kh godov: ideino-politicheskaia bor'ba i rabochee dvizhenie.* Moscow: Nauka, 1988. 440 pp.

Dmitrichev, T. F. *Zhenevskie forumy peregovorov po razoruzheniiu, 1945–1987.* Moscow: Mezhdunarodnye otnosheniia, 1988. 192 pp.

Dneprovskii, A. G. *Pravovye problemy novogo mezhdunarodnogo informatsionnogo poriadka.* Moscow: Nauka, 1989. 142 pp.

Dolgopolov, E. I. *Sotsial'no-politicheskaia rol' armii osvobodivshikhsia stran.* Moscow: Voenizdat, 1986. 140 pp.

Duncan, W. Raymond, and Ekedahl, Carolyn McGiffert. *Moscow and the Third World under Gorbachev.* Boulder, Colo.: Westview Press, 1990. 260 pp.

Dziak, John J. *Chekisty: A History of the KGB.* Lexington, Mass.: D. C. Heath, 1988. 235 pp.

Efanov, V. V., ed. *Soviet Ministrov SSR.* Moscow: Vneshtorgizdat, 1990. 139 pp.

Ehrenfeld, Rachel. *Narco-terrorism.* New York: Basic Books, 1990. 225 pp.

Faramazian, R. A., chief ed. *Gonka vooruzhenii v stranakh NATO: ekonomicheskii aspekt.* Moscow: Nauka, 1988. 190 pp.

Fedorov, V. G. *Sovetskii Soiuz i Finliandiia: Dobrososedstvo i sotrudnichestvo.* Moscow: Mysl', 1988. 296 pp.

Fedoseev, P. N., ed. *Sovremennoe antivoennoe dvizhenie.* Moscow: Nauka, 1987. 128 pp.

Filatova, A. I., ed. *Belaia kniga: Sionizm-orudie imperializma*. Moscow: Iuridicheskaia literatura, 1985. 304 pp.

Finder, Joseph. *Red Carpet*. New York: Holt, Rinehart & Winston, 1983. 372 pp.

Finn, James, ed. *Romania: A Case of "Dynastic" Communism*. New York: Freedom House, 1989. 119 pp.

Firsov, F. I. *Lenin, Komintern i stanovlenie kommunisticheskikh partii*. Moscow: Politizdat, 1985. 357 pp.

Fokeev, G. V., ed. *Istoriia mezhdunarodnykh otnoshenii i vneshnei politiki SSSR, 1970–1987*. Moscow: Mezhdunarodnye otnosheniia, 1987. 512 pp.

Free Trade Union Institute. *Continuity and Change: The World Federation of Trade Unions and International Labor Unity*. Washington, D.C.: AFL-CIO, 1988. 164 pp.

Gafurov, Z. Sh. *Natsional'no-demokraticheskaia revoliutsiia i armiia*. Moscow: Nauka, 1983. 215 pp.

Galiullin, Rustem. *The CIA in Asia: Covert Operations against India and Afghanistan*. Moscow: Progress Publishers, 1988. 144 pp.

Galkin, A. A., ed. *Rabochii klass v mirovom revoliutsionnom protsesse*. Moscow: Nauka, 1988. 279 pp.

Gardner, H. Stephen. *Soviet Foreign Trade: The Decision Process*. Boston: Kluwer-Nijhoff, 1983. 189 pp.

Gavrilov, N. I., ed. *10 let efiopiskoi revoliutsii*. Moscow: Nauka, 1986. 140 pp.

Gelman, Harry. *The Brezhnev Politburo and the Decline of Détente*. Ithaca, N.Y.: Cornell University Press, 1984. 268 pp.

George, James L. *The Nuclear Rules: Strategy and Arms Control after INF and START*. New York: St. Martin's Press, 1990. 194 pp.

German Democratic Republic. *Die DDR stellt sich vor*. East Berlin: Auslandspresseagentur GmbH, 1989. 192 pp.

Germany, Federal Republic of. *Zahlenspiegel: BRD/DDR—Ein Vergleich*. Bonn: Bundesministerium für innerdeutsche Beziehungen, September 1988. 144 pp.

Ghana. Ministry of Information. *Nkrumah's Subversion in Africa: Documentary Evidence*. Accra-Tema: State Publishing Corporation, n.d. 95 pp.

Glagolev, Igor S. *Post-Andropov Kremlin Strategy*. Washington, D.C.: Association for Cooperation of Democratic Countries, 1984. 303 pp.

Glaubitz, Joachim, and Heinzig, Dieter, eds. *Die Sowjetunion und Asien in den 80er Jahren*. Baden-Baden: Nomos, 1988. 370 pp.

Golanskii, M. M., and Goncharov, L. V., eds. *Afrika na puti v XXI vek: Mirokhoziaistvennye i narodnokhoziaistvennye aspekty razvitiia*. Moscow: Nauka, 1989. 192 pp.

Goldman, Marshal I. *Gorbachev's Challenge*. New York: W. W. Norton, 1988. 296 pp.

Golubovich, V. S. *Marshal R. Ia. Malinovskii*. Moscow: Voenizdat, 1984. 213 pp.

Goncharov, L. V., et al., eds. *Agrarnye preobrazovaniia v stranakh Afriki na sovremennom etape.* Moscow: Nauka, 1982. 229 pp.

Gorbachev, M. S. *At the Summit: Speeches and Interviews, February 1987-July 1988.* New York: Richardson, Steirman & Black, 1988. 298 pp.

———. *Perestroika i novoe myshlenie dlia nashei strany i dlia vsego mira.* Moscow: Politizdat, 1988. 271 pp.

———. *Izbrannye rechi i stat'i.* Vol. 6. Moscow: Politizdat, 1989. 606 pp.

Gorbylev, M. I., comp. *Kalendar' voina na 1990 god.* Moscow: Voenizdat, 1989. 480 pp.

Gordienko, N. S. *Osnovy nauchnogo ateizma: Uchebnoe posobie dlia studentov pedagogicheskikh institutov.* Moscow: "Prosveshchenie," 1988. 304 pp.

Goren, Roberta. *The Soviet Union and Terrorism.* London: George Allen & Unwin, 1984. 232 pp.

Goriunov, D. P., and Zubkova, L. Iu., comps. *TASS Soobshchaet.* Moscow: Politizdat, 1988. 287 pp.

Gorizontov, B. B. *Strany SEV: Transport i integratsiia.* Moscow: Mezhdunarodnye otnosheniia, 1989. 232 pp.

Gorshkov, S. G. *Morskaia moshch' gosudarstva.* 2d rev. ed. Moscow: Voenizdat, 1979. 416 pp.

Goshev, V. Iu. *SSSR i strany Persidskogo zaliva.* Moscow: Mezhdunarodnye otnosheniia, 1988. 182 pp.

Grechko, A. A. *Vooruzhennye sily sovetskogo gosudarstva.* Moscow: Voenizdat, 1974. 406 pp.

Green, William C., and Karasik, Theodore, eds. *Gorbachev and His Generals: The Reform of Soviet Military Doctrine.* Boulder, Colo.: Westview Press, 1990. 239 pp.

Grekov, Iu. N.; Kachanov, A. I.; et al. *Ekonomicheskoe i tekhnicheskoe sodeistvie SSSR zarubezhnym stranam.* Moscow: Mezhdunarodnye otnosheniia, 1987. 318 pp.

Grimmett, Richard F. "Trends in Conventional Arms Transfers to the Third World by Major Supplier, 1982–1989." In *CRS Report for Congress.* Washington, D.C.: Congressional Research Service, June 19, 1990. 73 pp.

Gromyko, Anatolii, A. *Afrika: politicheskoe i sotsial'noe razvitie v usloviiakh sotsialisticheskoi orientatsii.* Moscow: Nauka, 1988. 239 pp.

Gromyko, Andrei A. *Pamiatnoe.* 2 vols. Moscow: Politizdat, 1988.

——— et al., eds. *Diplomaticheskii slovar'.* 3 vols. Moscow: Nauka, 1984–1986. Moscow: Mezhdunarodye otnosheniia, 1985–1987.

Gudoshnikov, L. M., chief ed. *Gosudarstvennyi stroi Kitaiskoi Narodnoi Respubliki.* Moscow: Nauka, 1988. 231 pp.

Hamon, Alain, and Marchard, Jean-Charles. *Action directe: Du terrorisme français à l'euroterrorisme.* Paris: Éditions du Seuil, 1986. 256 pp.

Hardt, John P., and McMillan, Carl H., eds. *Planned Economies Confronting the Challenges of the 1980s.* New York: Cambridge University Press, 1988. 191 pp.

Heikal, Mohamed H. *The Road to Ramadan*. New York: Quadrangle, 1975. 285 pp.

Henriksen, Thomas H., ed. *Communist Powers and Sub-Saharan Africa*. Stanford: Hoover Institution Press, 1981. 137 pp.

Henze, Paul B. *The Plot to Kill the Pope*. New York: Scribner's, 1983. 216 pp.

Herrick, Robert Waring. *Soviet Naval Theory and Policy: Gorshkov's Inheritance*. Newport, R.I.: Naval War College Press, 1988. 318 pp.

Iablochkov, L. D., chief ed. *Afrika: problemy zaniatosti*. Moscow: Nauka, 1988. 221 pp.

Iakovlev, Alexander N. *Ot Trumena do Reigana: Doktriny i real'nosti iadernogo veka*. Moscow: Molodaia gvardiia, 1984. 399 pp.

————, et al. *Capitalism at the End of the Century*. Translated by Jane Sayer and Yuri Sdobnikov. Moscow: Progress Publishers, 1988. 371 pp.

Ianovskii, R. G. *Nauka, mirovozzrenie, perestroika: piat' problem*. Moscow: AON pri TsK KPSS, 1990. 192 pp.

Iaz'kov, E. F., chief ed. *Problemy amerikanistiki: Militarizm v SShA*. Moscow: Izdatel'stvo Moskovskogo universiteta, 1989. 320 pp.

Il'ichev, L. F., et al., eds. *SSSR v bor'be za bezopasnost' i sotrudnichestvo v Evrope, 1964–1987: Sbornik dokumentov*. Moscow: Mezhdunarodnye otnosheniia, 1988. 544 pp.

Il'ina, I. V., et al. *Spravochnik propagandista*. Moscow: Politizdat, 1988. 223 pp.

International Institute for Strategic Studies. *The Military Balance, 1990–1991*. London: Pergamon-Brassey's, 1990. 245 pp.

Irkhin, Iu. V. *Revoliutsionnyi protsess v stranakh sotsialisticheskoi orientatsii*. Moscow: Izdatel'stvo Universiteta Druzhby Narodov, 1985. 171 pp.

Ishchenko, E. G. *Ekonomicheskoe sotrudnichestvo SSSR so stranami sotsialisticheskoi orientatsii*. Moscow: Nauka, 1989. 188 pp.

Iskenderov, A. A. *Deiateli natsional'no-osvoboditel'nogo dvizheniia: Politicheskie portrety*. Moscow: Universitet druzhby narodov, 1989. 112 pp.

Israelian, V. L. *Diplomaty litsom k litsu*. Moscow: Mezhdunarodnye otnosheniia, 1990. 352 pp.

Istiagin, L. G. *Obshchestvenno-politicheskaia bor'ba v FRG po voprosam mira i bezopasnosti (1949-1987 gg.)*. Moscow: Nauka, 1988. 168 pp.

Iudin, Iu. A., et al., eds. *Partii v politicheskoi sisteme*. Moscow: Nauka, 1983. 249 pp.

Jackson, Richard L. *The Non-aligned, the U.N., and the Superpowers*. New York: Praeger, 1983. 314 pp.

Japan. Defense Agency. *Defense of Japan 1989*. Japan: Japan Times, 1990. 362 pp.

Jensen, Robert G.; Shabad, Theodore; and Wright, Arthur W. eds. *Soviet Natural Resources in the World Economy*. Chicago: University of Chicago Press, 1983. 700 pp.

Johnson, Nicholas L. *The Soviet Year in Space 1989.* Colorado Springs, Colo.: Teledyne Brown Engineering, 1990. 179 pp.

Kaltakhchian, V. T., comp. *Kratkii slovar' po nauchnomu kommunizmu.* Moscow: Politizdat, 1989. 431 pp.

Kapitsa, M. S., and Kim, G. F., eds. *SSSR i Koreia.* Moscow: Nauka, 1988. 414 pp.

Kaplan, Martin M., ed. *Proceedings of the Thirty-second Pugwash Conference on Science and World Affairs.* Geneva: Pugwash Council, 1984. 424 pp.

Karasova, T. A., chief ed. *Sionizm v sisteme imperializma: Ocherki istorii i sovremennost'.* Moscow: Nauka, 1988. 192 pp.

Kashlev, Iu. B. *Informatsionnyi vzryv: Mezhdunarodnyi aspekt.* Moscow: Mezhdunarodnye otnosheniia, 1988. 208 pp.

Katz, Mark N. *Gorbachev's Military Policy in the Third World.* New York: Praeger Publishers, 1989. 103 pp.

Kelley, Donald R., and Purvis, Hoyt, eds. *Old Myths and New Realities in United States-Soviet Relations.* New York: Praeger, 1990. 181 pp.

Kessel, Kenneth A. *Strategic Minerals: U.S. Alternatives.* Washington, D.C.: National Defense University Press, 1990. 295 pp.

Kessler, Ronald. *Moscow Station: How the KGB Penetrated the American Embassy.* New York: Scribner's, 1989. 305 pp.

Khalipov, V. F. *Voennaia politika KPSS.* Moscow: Voenizdat, 1988. 272 pp.

Khrushchev, Sergei. *Khrushchev on Khrushchev: An Inside Account of the Man and His Era.* Boston, Mass.: Little, Brown and Company, 1990. 423 pp.

Kim, G. F., et al., eds. *Natsional'no-demokraticheskaia revoliutsiia: sushchnost' i perspektivy.* Moscow: Nauka, 1990. 255 pp.

Kim, Seung-Hwan. *The Soviet Union and North Korea.* Seoul: Seoul Computer Press, 1988. 214 pp.

Kirshin, Iu. Ia. *Politicheskoe soderzhanie sovremennykh voin.* Moscow: Nauka, 1987. 336 pp.

Kissinger, Henry. *White House Years.* Boston: Little, Brown and Company, 1979. 1121 pp.

Kiva, A. V. *Natsional'no-osvoboditel'noe dvizhenie: Teoriia i praktika.* Moscow: Nauka, 1989. 331 pp.

Klevanskii, A. Kh.; Mar'ina, V. V.; and Pop, I. I., chief eds. *Kratkaia istoriia Chekhoslovakii.* Moscow: Nauka, 1988. 576 pp.

Klochkovskii, L. L., chief ed. *SSSR—Latinskaia Amerika: puti i perspektivy sotrudnichestva.* Moscow: Nauka, 1989. 216 pp.

Knight, Amy W. *The KGB: Police and Politics in the Soviet Union.* Boston: Allen & Unwin, 1988. 348 pp.

Kofanov, I. T. *Mineral'noe syr'e v ekonomike razvivaiushchikhsiia stran.* Moscow: Nauka, 1988. 165 pp.

Kokoshin, A. A. *V poiskakh vykhoda: Voenno-politicheskie aspekty mezhdunarodnoi bezopasnosti.* Moscow: Politizdat, 1989. 271 pp.

—— and Konovalov, A. A., eds. *Voenno-tekhnicheskaia politika SShA v 80-e goda*. Moscow: Nauka, 1989. 207 pp.

Kolesnikov, S. V., comp. *Knizhka partiinogo aktivista, 1990*. Moscow Politizdat, 1989. 255 pp.

Kommunisticheskaia Partiia Sovetskogo Soiuza. *XX s"ezd, 14–15 fevralia 1956 goda: Stenograficheskii otchet*. 2 vols. Moscow: Politizdat, 1956.

——. *Programma Kommunisticheskoi partii Sovetskogo Soiuza: Novaia redaktsiia. Priniata XXVII s'ezdom KPSS*. Moscow: Politizdat, 1986. 80 pp.

——. *XXVII s'ezd*. Moscow: Politizdat, 1986.

——. TsK. *Semidesiatiletie Velikoi Oktiabr'skoi revoliutsii. (Sovmestnoe torzhestvennoe zasedanie Tsentral'nogo Komiteta KPSS, Verkhovnogo Soveta SSSR i Verkhovnogo Soveta RSFSR, 2–3.XI.1987)*. Moscow: Politizdat, 1988. 512 pp.

——. *Vstrecha predstavitelei partii i dvizhenii, pribyvshikh na prazdnovanie 70-letiia Velikogo Oktiabria, Moskva, 4–5.XI.1987*. Moscow: Politizdat, 1988. 463 pp.

——. *XIX Vsesoiuznaia Konferentsiia Kommunisticheskoi Partii Sovetskogo Soiuza, 28 Iiunia—1 Iiulia 1988 g.: Stenograficheskii otchet*. 2 vols. Moscow: Politizdat, 1988.

——. *Kommunisticheskaia Partiia Sovetskogo Soiuza v rezoliutsiiakh i resheniiakh s"ezdov, konferentsii i plenumov TsK (1985–1988)*. Vol. 15. 1985–1988. Moscow: Politizdat, 1989. 671 pp.

——. *Spravochnik partiinogo rabotnika*. Vol. 29. Moscow: Politizdat, 1989. 607 pp.

Kotliarov, I. I. *"Zvezdnyi mir" protiv "zvezdnykh voin."* Moscow: Mezhdunarodnye otnosheniia, 1988. 224 pp.

Koval', B. I., et al., eds. *Marksizm-leninizm i realii kontsa XX stoletiia*. Moscow: Politizdat, 1988. 399 pp.

Kovalenko, I. I., and Tuzmukhamedov, R. A., chief eds. *Mirovoi sotsializm i dvizhenie neprisoedineniia*. Moscow: Mezhdunarodnye otnosheniia, 1988. 256 pp.

Kovalev, A. N. *Azbuka diplomatii*. 5th rev. ed. Moscow: Mezhdunarodnye otnosheniia, 1988. 288 pp.

Kovalev, E. V., and Sedykh, I. V. *Labirintami provokatsii*. Moscow: Politizdat, 1988. 304 pp.

Kudriavtsev, V. N., chief ed. *The Legal Status of Joint Ventures in the USSR*. Moscow: Nauka, 1989. 183 pp.

Kupferberg, Herbert. *The Raised Curtain*. New York: Twentieth Century Fund, 1977. 101 pp.

Kutakov, L. N. *Moskva—Tokio: ocherki diplomaticheskikh otnoshenii*. Moscow: Mezhdunarodnye otnosheniia, 1988. 272 pp.

Lamphere, Robert J., and Shachtman, Tom. *The FBI-KGB War: A Special Agent's Story*. New York: Random House, 1986. 320 pp.

Lauck, John H. *Katyn Killings: In the Record.* Clifton, N.J.: Kingston Press, 1988. 331 pp.

Lavrin, Aleksandr, comp. *Kto est' kto v perestroike.* Marburg, Germany: Blaue Hörner Verlag, 1990. 203 pp.

Lebedev, N. I., et al., eds. *Nauchnye osnovy sovetskoi vneshnei politiki.* Moscow: Mezhdunarodnye otnosheniia, 1982. 168 pp.

Lee, William T., and Staar, Richard F. *Soviet Military Policy since World War II.* Stanford: Hoover Institution Press, 1986. 263 pp.

Levchenko, Stanislav. *On the Wrong Side.* Washington, D.C.: Pergamon-Brassey's, 1988. 244 pp.

Levitskaia, N. V.; Luganskaia, L. N.; and Lavrova, K. I. *Russkii iazyk: Uchebnoe posobie dlia soldat, ne vladeiushchikh ili slabo vladeiushchikh russkim iazykom.* Moscow: Voenizdat, 1982. 416 pp.

Li, Vladimir F., chief ed. *Klassy, partii i politika v razvivaiushchikhsia stranakh Vostoka.* Moscow: Nauka, 1988. 389 pp.

Lin, Chong-Pin. *China's Nuclear Weapons Strategy: Tradition within Evolution.* Lexington, Mass.: Lexington Books, 1988. 272 pp.

Lindsey, Robert. *The Falcon and the Snowman.* New York: Simon & Schuster, 1979. 359 pp.

Listopadova, R. S., comp. *Dvizhenie neprisoedineniia v dokumentakh i materialakh.* Moscow: Nauka, 1989. 494 pp.

McKinlay, Robert. *Third World Military Expenditure: Determinants and Implications.* London: Pinter Publishers, 1990. 154 pp.

Malakhovskii, K. V. *Strany tikhogo okeana: politika, ekonomika, etnografiia, kul'tura.* Moscow: Nauka, 1988. 220 pp.

Manasov, M. A. *Kuba: dorogami svershenii.* Moscow: Nauka, 1988. 133 pp.

Mann, Dawn; Monyak, Robert; and Teague, Elizabeth. *The Supreme Soviet: A Biographical Directory.* Significant Issues Series, 11, no. 10. Washington, D.C.: Center for Strategic and International Studies, 1989. 168 pp.

Manne, Robert. *The Petrov Affair: Politics and Espionage.* New York: Pergamon Books, 1987. 310 pp.

Maresceau, Marc, ed. *The Political and Legal Framework of Trade Relations between the European Community and Eastern Europe.* Dordrecht, the Netherlands: Martinus Nijhoff, 1989. 351 pp.

Markov, Georgi. *The Truth That Killed.* London: Weidenfeld & Nicolson, 1983. 280 pp.

Matveev, V. M. *Diplomaticheskaia sluzhba SShA.* Moscow: Mezhdunarodnye otnosheniia, 1987. 192 pp.

Meade, Jr., Robert C. *Red Brigades: The Story of Italian Terrorism.* New York: St. Martin's Press, 1990. 301 pp.

Menzhinskii, V. I., et al., eds. *Mezhdunarodnye organizatsii sotsialisticheskikh gosudarstv.* Moscow: Mezhdunarodnye otnosheniia, 1980. 256 pp.

Michta, Andrew A. *Red Eagle: The Army in Polish Politics.* Stanford: Hoover Institution Press, 1989. 371 pp.

Mikhalkin, V. A. F. E. *Dzerzhinski—ekonomist.* Moscow: Ekonomika, 1987. 175 pp.

Mitchell, R. Judson. *Ideology of a Superpower: Contemporary Soviet Doctrine on International Relations.* Stanford: Hoover Institution Press, 1982. 159 pp.

———. *Getting to the Top in the USSR: Cyclical Patterns in the Leadership Succession Process.* Stanford: Hoover Institution Press, 1990. 284 pp.

Mlynar, Zdenek. *Nightfrost in Prague: The End of Humane Socialism.* New York: Karz, 1980. 300 pp.

———. *Can Gorbachev Change the Soviet Union?* Boulder, Colo.: Westview Press, 1990. 184 pp.

Mogilevkin, I. M. *Nevidimye voiny XX veka.* Moscow: Ekonomika, 1989. 207 pp.

Moiseev, M. A., chief ed. *Sovetskaia voennaia entsiklopediia.* 2d ed. Vol. 1. Moscow: Voenizdat, 1990. 543 pp.

Motorin, I. F. *Vneshne-ekonomicheskie sviazi SSSR: kurs na perestroiku.* Moscow: Politizdat, 1989. 95 pp.

Mozhaeva, V. E., and Sergeeva, V. E., chief eds. *Profsoiuzy mira: Spravochnoe izdanie.* Moscow: Profizdat, 1989. 656 pp.

Myagkov, Aleksei. *Inside the KGB: An Exposé of an Officer of the Third Directorate.* Richmond, Eng.: Foreign Affairs Publishing, 1976. 131 pp.

Narochnitskii, A. L., chief ed. *Sotsialisticheskoe sodruzhestvo i khel'sinkskii protsess.* Moscow: Mezhdunarodnye otnoshenii, 1988. 272 pp.

Nelson, Daniel N. *Alliance Behavior in the Warsaw Pact.* Boulder, Colo.: Westview Press, 1986. 134 pp.

Neuberger, Günter, and Opperskalski, Michael. *CIA in Westeuropa.* Bornheim, West Germany: Lamuv Verlag, 1982. 224 pp.

Niiazmatov, Sh. A. *Irano-irakskii konflikt: istoricheskii ocherk.* Moscow: Nauka, 1989. 176 pp.

Nikol'skii, A. V., chief ed. *Za novoe politicheskoe myshlenie v mezhdunarodnykh otnosheniiakh.* Moscow: Politizdat, 1987. 575 pp.

———. *Kto est' kto v mirovoi politike.* Moscow: Politizdat, 1990. 560 pp.

Nikonov, V. A. *Respublikantsy: ot Niksona k Reiganu.* Moscow: Izdatel'stvo Moskovskogo universiteta, 1988. 289 pp.

Nordenstreng, Kaarle; Manet, Enrique G.; and Kleinwächer, Wolfgang. *New International Information and Communication Order: Sourcebook.* 2d rev. ed. Prague: International Organization of Journalists, 1986. 392 pp.

Norten, Augustus R., and Greenberg, Martin, H. *The International Relations of the Palestine Liberation Organization.* Carbondale: Southern Illinois University Press, 1989. 233 pp.

North Atlantic Treaty Organization. *The North Atlantic Treaty Organisation: Facts and Figures.* Brussels: NATO Information Service, 1989. 577 pp.

Oberg, James E. *Uncovering Soviet Disasters: Exploring the Limits of Glasnost.* New York: Random House, 1988. 217 pp.

Oborotova, Marina A. *SShA: Bor'ba s osvoboditel'nym dvizheniem v Tsentral'noi Amerike.* Moscow: Nauka, 1989. 160 pp.

Ogarkov, N. V., chief ed. *Voennyi entsiklopedicheskiy slovar'.* 8 vols. Moscow: Voenizdat, 1983. 863 pp.

Onikov, L. A., and Shishlin, N. V., comps. *Kratkii politicheskii slovar'.* Moscow: Politizdat, 1978. 413 pp.

Page, Stephen. *The Soviet Union and the Yemens: Influence in Asymmetrical Relationships.* New York: Praeger, 1985. 227 pp.

Paniev, Iu. N. *Strany Latinskoi Ameriki: Aktual'nye problemy vneshne-ekonomicheskikh sviazei.* Moscow: Mezhdunarodnye otnosheniia, 1990. 264 pp.

Pavlenko, V. N., comp. *Politbiuro, Orgbiuro, Sekretariat TsK RKP(b)-VK P(b)-KPSS: Spravochnik.* Moscow: Politizdat, 1990. 272 pp.

Penkovskiy, Oleg. *The Penkovskiy Papers.* Garden City, N.Y.: Doubleday, 1965. 411 pp.

Peresypkin, O. G., chief ed. *Diplomaticheskii vestnik: god 1989.* Moscow: Mezhdunarodnye otnosheniia, 1990. 517 pp.

Peters, I. A., and Sushchinskaia, I. Iu. *Mir sotsializma i mirovoi revoliutsionnyi protsess.* Kiev: Naukova Dymka, 1987. 128 pp.

Petrova, N. K. *Internatsional'nye sviazi rabochego klassa SSSR.* Moscow: Mysl', 1987. 254 pp.

Pilevsky, Philip. *Captive Continent: The Stockholm Syndrome in European-Soviet Relations.* New York: Praeger, 1989. 145 pp.

Pipes, Richard. *U.S.-Soviet Relations in the Era of Détente.* Boulder, Colo.: Westview Press, 1981. 227 pp.

Poljanski, Nikolai. *Rote Diplomatie: Gespräche mit Urs Graf.* Zurich: Presdok AG, 1988. 168 pp.

Pollard, Alan P. *USSR Facts & Figures Annual (1990).* Vol. 14. Gulf Breeze, Fla.: Academic International Press, 1990. 437 pp.

Polsky, Yury. *Soviet Research Institutes and the Formulation of Foreign Policy: IMEMO.* Falls Church, Va.: Delphic Associates, 1987. 121 pp.

Popov, G. Kh., chief ed. *Obratnogo khoda net.* Moscow: Politizdat, 1989. 543 pp.

Popov, S. I. *Burzhuaznaia ideologiia na poroge XXI stoletiia.* Moscow: Mysl', 1988. 270 pp.

Poskonina, L. S., chief ed. *Latinskaia Amerika: Kritika levoradikal'nykh kontseptsii.* Moscow: Nauka, 1988. 176 pp.

Powell, S. Steven. *Covert Cadre: Inside the Institute for Policy Studies.* Ottawa, Ill.: Green Hill Publishers, 1987. 469 pp.

Pozdniakov, P. V. *Ustnaia kommunisticheskaia propaganda.* Moscow: Politizdat, 1988. 256 pp.

Prange, Gordon W. *Target Tokyo: The Story of the Sorge Spy Ring*. New York: McGraw-Hill, 1984. 595 pp.

Primakov, E. M., and Martynov, V. A., eds. *Sovremennyi imperializm: tendentsii i protivorechiia*. Moscow: Mysl', 1988. 686 pp.

Proshin, V. N. *Zony prostranstvennogo ogranicheniia vooruzhenii: Mezhdunarodno-pravovye aspekty*. Moscow: Nauka, 1988. 164 pp.

Rachwald, Arthur R. *In Search of Poland: The Superpowers' Response to Solidarity, 1980–1989*. Stanford: Hoover Institution Press, 1990. 146 pp.

Rahr, Alexander G. *A Biographic Directory of 100 Leading Soviet Officials*. 4th rev. ed. Munich: Radio Liberty, January 1989. 241 pp.

Rakowska-Harmstone, Teresa, et al. *Warsaw Pact: The Question of Cohesion*. 4 vols. Ottawa, Canada: Department of National Defense, 1984–1986.

Rashidov, R. T. *Sovetsko-Afganskie otnosheniia i ikh burzhuaznye falsifikatory, 1978–1983*. Tashkent: Izdatel'stvo "Fan," 1986. 116 pp.

Razov, S. S. *Kitaiskaia Narodnaia Respublika: Spravochnik*. Moscow: Politizdat, 1989. 277 pp.

Richelson, Jeffrey. *Sword and Shield: The Soviet Intelligence and Security Apparatus*. Cambridge, Mass.: Ballinger, 1986. 281 pp.

Romanov, D. V. *Sionizm: Pravda i vymysly*. Moscow: Progress, 1987. 200 pp.

Romerstein, Herbert, and Levchenko, Stanislav. *The KGB against the "Main Enemy."* Lexington, Mass: Lexington Books, 1989. 370 pp.

Roth, Paul. *Glasnost und Medienpolitik unter Gorbatschow*. Bonn: Hohwacht, 1990. 365 pp.

Saivetz, Carol R. *The Soviet Union and the Gulf in the 1980s*. Boulder, Colo.: Westview Press, 1989. 139 pp.

Sakharov, Vladimir, and Tosi, Umberto. *High Treason*. New York: G. P. Putnam's Sons, 1980. 318 pp.

Sakovich, E. A., ed. *Za novoe politicheskoe myshlenie v mezhdunarodykh otnosheniiakh*. Moscow: Politizdat, 1987. 676 pp.

Sanakoev, Sh. P. *Voprosy sovetskoi vneshnepoliticheskoi propagandy*. Moscow: Mezhdunarodnye otnosheniia, 1980. 255 pp.

Sayilgar, Aclan. *Education of Foreign Revolutionaries in the USSR: Comintern Schools to Lumumba University*. Ankara: Baylan Press, 1973. 145 pp.

Schecter, Jerrold L., and Luchkov, Vyacheslav V., eds. *Khrushchev Remembers: The Glasnost Tapes*. Boston: Little, Brown & Company, 1990. 219 pp.

Scott, William F., and Scott, Harriet Fast. *The Armed Forces of the USSR*. 3d rev. ed. Boulder, Colo.: Westview Press, 1984. 457 pp.

———. *Soviet Military Doctrine: Continuity, Formulation and Dissemination*. Boulder, Colo.: Westview Press, 1988. 315 pp.

Semenkov, V. I., chief ed. *Deklaratsii i real'nost'*. Minsk: Izdatel'stvo Belarus', 1987. 336 pp.

Sergeev, F. M. *Tainoe orudie agressii: Podryvnaia deiatel'nost' SShA protiv SSSR.* Alma-Ata: Kazakhstan, 1987. 221 pp.

Sergeev, Iu. A. *SShA: Mezhdunarodnyi tekhnologicheskii biznes.* Moscow: Mezhdunarodnye otnosheniia, 1989. 208 pp.

Shabardin, P. M. *Armiia v sovremennoi politicheskoi bor'be.* Moscow: Nauka, 1988. 221 pp.

Shakhnazarov, G. Kh. *Sotsializm i budushchee.* Moscow: Nauka, 1983. 723 pp.

Shakhnazarova, V. S., et al., eds. *Anglo-russkii diplomaticheskii slovar'.* Moscow: Russkii iazyk, 1989. 856 pp.

Shchegolev, B. N., and Nosov, A. B. *Neoglobalizm SShA v Latinskoi Amerike.* Moscow: Mysl', 1988. 174 pp.

Shelepin, Vladimir, and Yastrzhembsky, Sergei, comps. *The Struggle of the Communists and the Policy of Alliances.* Prague: Peace and Socialism, 1987. 212 pp.

Shevchenko, Arkady N. *Breaking with Moscow.* New York: Knopf, 1985. 378 pp.

Shishlin, N. V. *Sovremennaia ideologicheskaia bor'ba: Slovar.* Moscow: Politizdat, 1988. 431 pp.

Sholokhov, A. B., ed. *Voennaia akademiia imeni M. V. Frunze.* Moscow: Voenizdat, 1988. 294 pp.

Shul'govskii, A. F., et al. *Marksizm-Leninizm i Latinskaia Amerika.* 2 vols. Moscow: Nauka, 1989.

Shultz, Richard H., and Godson, Roy. *Dezinformatsia: Active Measures in Soviet Strategy.* New York: Pergamon-Brassey's, 1984. 211 pp.

Shvets, I. A., comp. *Kommunist, 1990.* Moscow: Politizdat, 1989. 365 pp.

Simon, Jeffrey, ed. *NATO-Warsaw Pact Force Mobilization.* Washington, D.C.: National Defense University Press, 1988. 563 pp.

Sinclair, James E., and Parker, Robert. *The Strategic Metals War.* New York: Arlington House, 1983. 185 pp.

Skryl'nik, A. I., chief ed. *Zapad-81.* Moscow: Voenizdat, 1982. 171 pp.

Slavinskii, B. N. *Vneshniaia politika SSSR na Dal'nem Vostoke.* Moscow: Mezhdunarodnye otnosheniia, 1988. 336 pp.

Smith, Raymond F. *Negotiating with the Soviets.* Bloomington: Indiana University Press, 1989. 148 pp.

Smith, Ted J., III. *Moscow Meets Main Street.* Washington, D.C.: Media Institute, 1988. 130 pp.

Socialist International. *Common Security: A Programme for Disarmament.* London: Pan Books, 1982. 202 pp.

Sogrin, V. V., chief ed. *New Political Thinking in the Nuclear Age: USSR and US Policy.* Moscow: Nauka, 1990. 301 pp.

Sokolovskii, V. D. *Voennaia strategiia.* 3d rev. ed. Moscow: Voenizdat, 1968. 464 pp.

Sosna, S. A. *Gosudarstvennyi sektor ekonomiki v razvivaiushchikhsia stranakh: Organizatsiia, upravlenie, pravo.* Moscow: Nauka, 1989. 226 pp.

Sredin, G. V., ed. *Internatsional'nyi kharakter zashchity sotsialisticheskogo ote-chestva*. Moscow: Voenizdat, 1988. 254 pp.

Staar, Richard F. *Communist Regimes in Eastern Europe*. 5th rev. ed. Stanford: Hoover Institution Press, 1988. 369 pp.

———, ed. *Arms Control: Myth Versus Reality*. Stanford: Hoover Institution Press, 1988. 211 pp.

———, ed. *Public Diplomacy: USA Versus USSR*. Stanford: Hoover Institution Press, 1986. 305 pp.

———, ed. *Yearbook on International Communist Affairs*. Stanford: Hoover Institution Press, 1969–1990.

Stavrou, Nikolaos A., ed. *Greece under Socialism: A NATO Ally Adrift*. New Rochelle, N.Y.: Orpheus Publishing, 1988. 428 pp.

Sterling, Claire. *The Time of the Assassins*. New York: Holt, Rinehart & Winston, 1983. 264 pp.

Stookey, Robert W., ed. *The Arabian Peninsula: Zone of Ferment*. Stanford: Hoover Institution Press, 1984. 151 pp.

Sturua, G. M. *Mirovomu okeanu mirnye vody*. Moscow: Nauka, 1988. 103 pp.

Subbotin, Alexander, M., chief ed. *Imperializm 80-kh godov, ekonomicheskii krizis i bor'ba kommunistov*. Prague: Mir i sotsializm, 1987. 296 pp.

———, ed. *First-Hand Information: Communists and Revolutionary Democrats of the World Presenting Their Parties*. Prague: Peace and Socialism International Publishers, 1988. 190 pp.

Sutton, Anthony C. *Western Technology and Soviet Economic Development, 1945 to 1965*. Stanford: Hoover Institution Press, 1974. 482 pp.

Suvorov, Viktor. *Inside the Aquarium: The Making of a Top Soviet Spy*. New York: Macmillan, 1986. 249 pp.

Syzrantsev, V. T., et al. *Kratkii slovar'-spravochnik agitatora i politinformatora*. 6th ed. Moscow: Politizdat, 1988. 318 pp.

Tarle, G. Ia. *Dvizhenie storonnikov mira v SSSR*. Moscow: Nauka, 1988. 240 pp.

Teplinskii, L. B. *Istoriia sovetsko-afganskikh otnoshenii*. Moscow: Mysl', 1988. 381 pp.

Tikhvinskii, S. L., et al., eds. *Kitai i vsemirnaia istoriia*. Moscow: Nauka, 1987. 589 pp.

Titarenko, M. L., chief ed. *40 let KNR*. Moscow: Nauka, 1989. 565 pp.

Tiushkevich, S. A. *Voina i sovremennost'*. Moscow: Nauka, 1986. 214 pp.

Tsukassov, Sergei, chief ed. *The Struggle of the Communists and the Policy of Alliances*. Prague: Peace and Socialism, 1987. 212 pp.

Tsypkin, G. V., and Iag'ia, V. S. *Istoriia Efiopii v novoe i noveishee vremia*. Moscow: Nauka, 1989. 405 pp.

Tsvetkov, G. N. *SSSR i SShA: Otnosheniia, vliiaiushchie na sud'bu mira*. Kiev: Vyshcha shkola, 1988. 272 pp.

Tumanov, V. A., et al., eds. *Sotsialisticheskaia Respublika V'etnam*. Moscow: Progress, 1988. 460 pp.

Ulam, Adam B. *Stalin: The Man and His Era*. Boston: Beacon Press, 1989. 760 pp.

United Nations General Assembly. *Report on the Findings by the Enquiry Committee and the Measures Taken by the Burmese Government*. 39th sess. Agenda item 128, A/39/456/Add. 1. New York: 17 September 1984. 30 pp.

U.S. Congress. Joint Economic Committee. *Pressures for Reform in the East European Economies*. 2 vols. 101st Cong., 1st sess., 20 and 27 October 1989.

————. Office of Technology Assessment. *Strategic Materials: Technologies to Reduce U.S. Import Vulnerability*. May 1985. 409 pp.

————. House. Commission on Security and Cooperation in Europe. *The Vienna CSCE Follow-Up Meeting*. 101st Cong., 2d sess., January 1990. Committee Print. 150 pp.

————. ————. Permanent Select Committee on Intelligence. Subcommittee on Oversight. *Hearings on Soviet Covert Action: The Forgery Offensive*. 96th Cong., 2d sess., 1980. 245 pp.

————. ————. ————. *Hearings on Soviet Active Measures*. 97th Cong., 2d sess., 1982. 337 pp.

————. Senate. Committee on Commerce, Science, and Transportation. *Soviet Space Programs, 1981–87: Piloted Space Activities, Launch Vehicles, Launch Sites, and Tracking Support*. Part I. 100th Cong., 2d sess., 1988. Committee Print. 280 pp.

————. ————. Committee on Foreign Relations and Committee on the Judiciary. *International Terrorism, Insurgency, and Drug Trafficking: Present Trends in Terrorist Activity*. 99th Cong., 1st sess., 13–15 May 1985. 426 pp.

————. ————. Select Committee on Intelligence. *Meeting the Espionage Challenge: A Review of United States Counterintelligence and Security Programs*. 99th Cong., 2d sess., 1986. 156 pp.

U.S. Delegation to CDE. Conference on Confidence- and Security-Building Measures and Disarmament in Europe. *Confidence- and Security-Building Measures (CSBMs) Proposed by the Delegations of Belgium, Canada, Denmark, France, Federal Republic of Germany, Greece, Iceland, Italy, Luxembourg, Netherlands, Norway, Portugal, Spain, Turkey, United Kingdom, United States of America*. Series CSCE/SC.1. Stockholm: 24 January 1984.

————. ————. *Confidence- and Security-Building Measures in Europe: Proposals of the Soviet Union*. Stockholm: 8 May 1984. Series CSCE/SC.4.

U.S. Government. Arms Control and Disarmament Agency. *Arms Control and Disarmament Agreements: Texts and Histories of the Negotiations*. 1990. 459 pp.

————. ————. *Treaty on Conventional Armed Forces in Europe*. Paris: 19 November 1990. 110 pp.

————. ————. *World Military Expenditures and Arms Transfers, 1989*. ACDA Pub. 131. October 1990. 140 pp.

——. Central Intelligence Agency. *Biographic Report: USSR Institute of the United States and Canada.* CR 76–10864. 1976. 144 p.

——. ——. *Measuring Soviet GNP: Problems and Solutions.* SOV 90–10038. September 1990. 195 pp.

——. ——. *Directory of Soviet Officials: National Organizations.* LDA-90–14379. October 1990. 265 pp.

——. ——. *Handbook of Economic Statistics 1990.* CPAS 90–10001. September 1990. 209 pp.

——. ——. *Selected Countries' Trade with the USSR and Eastern Europe.* IR 90–10008/RTT 90–10009. Government Printing Office, July 1990. 136 pp.

——. ——. *Soviet Energy Data Resource Handbook.* SOV 90–10021. Government Printing Office, May 1990. 43 pp.

——. ——. *The World Factbook, 1990.* Government Printing Office, 1990. 382 pp.

——. Department of Defense. *1989 Joint Military Net Assessment.* June 1989.

——. ——. *Soviet Military Power.* 9 vols. Government Printing Office, 1981–1990.

——. Department of State. *Patterns of Global International Terrorism, 1989.* Office of Combating Terrorism, April 1990. 85 pp.

——. ——. *Realism, Strength, Negotiations: Key Foreign Policy Statements of the Reagan Administration.* May 1984. 154 pp.

——. ——. *Report to Congress on Voting Practices in the United Nations.* 1984. 159 pp.

——. ——. *Soviet Influence Activities: A Report on Active Measures and Propaganda, 1987–1988.* August 1989. 64 pp.

——. ——. *Treaty between USA and USSR on Elimination of Intermediate-range and Shorter-range Missiles.* 2 vols. December 1987.

——. ——. *Warsaw Pact Economic Aid to Non-Communist LDCs, 1986.* Publication 9345. August 1988. 17 pp.

——. Foreign Service Institute. Center for the Study of Foreign Affairs. *The International Department of the CC CPSU under Dobrynin.* Publication 9726. Government Printing Office. September 1989. 179 pp.

——. General Accounting Office. *United Nations: Analysis of Selected Media Products Shows Half Oppose Key U.S. Interests.* GAO/NSIAD-86–98. April 1986.

——. General Advisory Committee on Arms Control and Disarmament. *A Quarter Century of Soviet Compliance Practices under Arms Control Commitments, 1958–1983.* October 1984. 15 pp.

——. Office of the Vice-President. Vice-President's Task Force on Combating Terrorism. *Terrorist Group Profiles.* Government Printing Office, February 1986. 131 pp.

——. United States Information Agency. *Documents Pertaining to Relations between Grenada, the USSR, and Cuba.* 3 vols. 1984.

————. ————. *Soviet Active Measures in the Era of Glasnost*. March 1988. 105 pp.

USSR. Academy of Sciences. Institute of State and Law. *Human Rights: Yearbook*. 6th edition. Moscow: Nauka, 1989. 109 pp.

————. Gosudarstvennyi Komitet po Statistike. *Narodnoe khoziaistvo SSSR v 1989 g*. Moscow: Finansy i Statistika, 1990. 767 pp.

————. *SSSR v tsifrakh v 1989 godu: Kratkii statisticheskii sbornik*. Moscow: Finansy i statistika, 1990. 319 pp.

————. Ministerstvo Inostrannykh Del. *Za mir i bezopasnost' narodov: Dokumenty vneshnei politiki SSSR, 1985 god*. 2 vols. Moscow: Politizdat, 1988.

————. ————. *Sbornik mezhdunarodnykh dogovorov SSSR*. Vol. 42. Moscow Mezhdunarodnye otnosheniia, 1988. 454 pp.

————. Ministerstvo Vneshnikh Ekonomicheskikh Sviazei. *Vneshnie ekonomicheskie sviazi SSSR v 1989 g*. Moscow: Finansy i statistika, 1990. 304 pp.

————. Sekretariat, Sovet Ekonomicheskoi Vzaimopomoshchi. *Statisticheskii ezhegodnik stran-chlenov soveta ekonomicheskoi vzaimopomoshchi, 1989*. Moscow: Finansy i statistika, 1989. 495 pp.

Ushakov, Alexander A. *In the Gunsight of the KGB*. New York: Alfred A. Knopf, 1989. 273 pp.

Valeva, E. L.; Volokitina, T. V.; et al. *Stroitel'stvo osnov sotsializma v stranakh tsentral'noi i iugo-vostochnoi Evropy*. Moscow: Nauka, 1989. 440 pp.

Vanneman, Peter. *Soviet Strategy in Southern Africa: Gorbachev's Pragmatic Approach*. Stanford: Hoover Institution Press, 1990. 143 pp.

Vasil'ev, A. M., chief ed. *Nigeriia, vlast' i politika: sbornik statei*. Moscow: Nauka, 1988. 243 pp.

Villemarest, Pierre de. *G.R.U.: Le plus secret des services soviétiques, 1918–1988*. Paris: Editions Stock, 1988. 335 pp.

Vinokurov, Iu. N., chief ed. *Dvizhenie neprisoedineniia v dokumentakh i materialakh*. Moscow: Nauka, 1988. 494 pp.

Vodolazov, G. G., chief ed. *Problemy mirovogo revoliutsionnogo protsessa*. 8th ed. Moscow: Mysl', 1989. 255 pp.

Volkogonov, D. A., ed. *Kontrpropaganda: teoriia i praktika*. Moscow: Voenizdat, 1988. 240 pp.

Vol'skii, V. V., chief ed. *Kuba: stroitel'stvo sotsializma*. Moscow: Nauka, 1988. 256 pp.

Voslensky, Michael S. *Nomenklatura: The Soviet Ruling Class*. Garden City, N.Y.: Doubleday, 1984. 455 pp.

Wagenlehner, Günther, ed. *Feind Bild: Gechichte, Dokumentation, Problematik*. Frankfurt am Main: Report Verlag, 1989. 263 pp.

Wardak, Ghulam Dastagir, comp. *The Voroshilov Lectures: Materials from the Soviet General Staff Academy*, vol. 1, *Issues of Soviet Military Strategy*. Washington, D.C.: National Defense University Press, 1989. 411 pp.

Weber, Wolfgang. *Kriegspläne der NATO für Zentraleuropa*. East Berlin: Militärverlag der DDR, 1989. 88 pp.

Weichhardt, Reiner, ed. *Les réformes économiques en URSS: la mise en oeuvre: colloque, 15–17 mars 1989*. Brussels: NATO, 1989. 289 pp.

Weihmiller, Gordon R. *U.S.-Soviet Summits: An Account of East-West Diplomacy at the Top, 1955–1985*. Lanham, Md.: University Press of America, 1986. 211 pp.

Wells, Samuel F., Jr., ed. *The Helsinki Process and the Future of Europe*. Washington, D.C.: Wilson Center Press, 1990. 207 pp.

West, Nigel. *Mole Hunt: Searching for Soviet Spies in M.I.5*. New York: William Morrow, 1987. 254 pp.

Wettig, Gerhard, ed. *Die sowjetische Militärmacht und die Stabilität in Europa*. Baden-Baden, Germany: Nomos Verlag, 1990. 207 pp.

Wolf, Jr., Charles, et al. *The Costs and Benefits of the Soviet Empire, 1981–1983*. Santa Monica, Calif.: RAND Corporation, August 1986.

Wolton, Thierry. *Le KGB en France*. Paris: Grasset et Fasquelle, 1986. 311 pp.

World Peace Council. *List of Members: 1983–1986*. Helsinki: Information Centre of the World Peace Council, 1986. 175 pp.

Yao, Ming-le. *The Conspiracy and Death of Lin Biao*. New York: Alfred A. Knopf, 1983. 231 pp.

Yeltsin, Boris. *Against the Grain: An Autobiography*. New York: Simon and Schuster, 1990. 263 pp.

Zagladin, N. V., chief ed. *Vneshnepoliticheskaia strategiia KPSS i novoe politicheskoe myshlenie v iadernyi vek: Uchebnoe posobie*. Moscow: Politizdat, 1988. 368 pp.

Zagladin, V. V., ed. *Revoliutsionnyi protsess: Natsional'noe i internatsional'noe*. Moscow: Mysl', 1985. 340 p.

———, and Kiselev, G. A., comps. *Politicheskie partii: Spravochnik*. Moscow: Politizdat, 1986. 382 pp.

———, and Koval', B. I., eds. *Mezhdunarodnoe rabochee dvizhenie: Spravochnik*. Moscow: Politizdat, 1987. 429 pp.

———, and Shishlin, N. V., eds. *Spravochnik propagandista-mezhdunarodnika*. Moscow: Politizdat, 1988. 239 pp.

Zaichuk, O. V. *Politicheskie repressii v SShA*. Kiev: Politizdat Ukrainy, 1989. 198 pp.

Zaleski, Eugene, and Wienert, Helgard. *Technology Transfer between East and West*. Paris: Organization for Economic Cooperation and Development, 1980. 435 pp.

Zaloga, Steven J. *Red Thrust: Attack on the Central Front, Soviet Tactics and Capabilities in the 1990s*. London: Brassey's, 1989. 274 p.

Zarodov, K. I., ed. *One Thousand Days of Revolution: Communist Party of Chile Leaders on Lessons of the Events in Chile*. Prague: Peace and Socialism, 1978. 149 pp.

Zhelitski, B. I., chief ed. *Iz istorii sotsial'no-politicheskogo razvitiia sotsialisticheskikh stran Evropy.* Moscow: Nauka, 1987. 204 pp.

Zmeev, V. M. *Politicheskaia ideologiia v stranakh tropicheskoi Afriki: genezis i sotsial'nye funktsii.* Leningrad: Leningradskii universitet, 1988. 152 pp.

Zorin, V. A. *Osnovy diplomaticheskoi sluzhby.* 2d ed. Moscow: Mezhdunarodnye otnosheniia, 1977. 368 pp.

INDEX

ABOUT THE AUTHOR

RICHARD F. STAAR is a Senior Fellow at the Hoover Institution and served as U.S. ambassador to the Mutual and Balanced Force Reductions talks in Vienna (1981–1983). Dr. Staar received his B.A. from Dickinson College, his M.A. from Yale, and his Ph.D. in political science from the University of Michigan. In addition to this book, he has written *Communist Regimes in Eastern Europe*, has coauthored *USSR Military Policy Since World War II*, and edits the *Yearbook on International Communist Affairs*.